The German Chancellors

The German Chancellors

Edited by Hans Klein

Translated by Edna McCown

edition q, inc.
Chicago, Berlin, Tokyo, and Moscow

Photo Credits

Bundesbildstelle, Bonn (76)
Ullstein–Bilderdienst, Berlin (35)
Archiv Hans Klein (7)
Sven Simon, Munchen (1)
ZDF–Archiv, Mainz (2)
Deutsche Presse-Agentur (2)
Ludwig–Erhard–Stiftung, Bonn (1)

The publisher and editor thank all for their generosity.

DD258.6
.B8513
1996

© 1996 by edition q, inc.

Originally published as *Die Bundeskanzler*, © 1993 edition q, Berlin.

edition q, inc.
551 North Kimberly Drive
Carol Stream, Illinois 60188

Library of Congress Cataloging-in-Publication Data

Bundeskanzler.   English
    The German chancellors / edited by Hans Klein.
        p.   cm.
    Includes bibliographical references and index.
    ISBN 1-883695-05-8
        1. Statesmen—Germany (West)—Biography.   2. Germany (West)—Politics and government.   3. Germany—Politics and government—1990-   4. Statemen—Germany—Biography.   I. Klein, Hans, 1931- .   II. Title.
    DD258.6.B8513   1996
    943.08—dc20   95-26316
                                                                              CIP

Printed in the United States of America

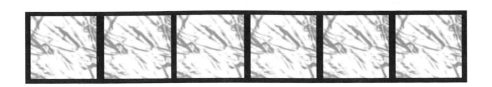

Contents

Acknowledgments

Not convention but conscience prompts me to thank publisher Horst-Wolfgang Haase for the idea and the generous design for this book; editor Dr. Jürgen Schebera for his professionalism and understanding in editing the German-language edition and selecting the photographs; Ute Martensen for her skilled research and relentless stylistic suggestions; and above all Dr. Horst Osterheld, retired undersecretary, Günter Diehl, retired ambassador, Dr. Peter Zudeick, Reinhard Appel, and Dr. Oskar Fehrenbach, for their substantive contributions, for their collegial cooperation on the total concept of this book, and for delivering their contributions so promptly.

Two platitudes pass for German sayings: "History teaches that one can learn nothing from history," and "The wiser head gives in." The first serves to justify repeated destruction, subjugation, and aggression by those who commit political acts of violence, and the second to establish the eternal domination of the faint-hearted. The lives of these six German statesmen refute both.

Introduction

by Hans Klein

In 1995 the world marked the fiftieth anniversary of the end of the Second World War, an occasion for much searching thought about the astonishing changes that have occurred in the past half century. Few can match those that have been experienced by Germany. From total devastation in the war, West Germany, cut off from its eastern part, rose from its ruins to build an economy that became the envy of the world; on the debris of its totalitarian past it established a robust democracy where the free contest of opposing political forces flourished with admirable vigor; starting out as an international pariah, it regained the respect of the world to become a pillar of the free community of nations.

If the Federal Republic of Germany, the entity constituted in the western part of the country, was sequel to World War II, it was also prelude to the new Germany that arose after unification. For the network of laws, governmental institutions, and democratic political organizations as well as the economic system developed there, has now been largely extended to the territory that was the former communist East Germany. For an American reader to begin to understand the reality of the new Germany—its potential for democratic stability, its economic power, and its political influence—an acquaintance with the history of the Federal Republic over the last half century is indispensable.

Instead of telling this history in terms of the dry dates of the most crucial events, this book has chosen another path: to recreate the human drama of the six extraordinary personalities who stood at the helm of the Federal Republic from the fateful moments of its formation after a crushing defeat in war, through the time of its economic

recovery and democratic growth, to its re-emergence as a major political and economic power that played an inestimable role in the contest of the West against its communist foe, which ended in the West's
ultimate triumph and the unification of Germany.

The stories of these six men produce a surprisingly vivid and dramatic account of contemporary history. These biographical essays,
each written by a different author, reflect not only the personalities
and temperaments of the six heads of state of the postwar Federal
Republic, but also the diverse experiences and views of the authors.
Each was, or is, close to "his chancellor" in a particular way, and this
is what gives these essays their underlying sense of sympathy with
their subjects—without, however, sacrificing the truth.

Weaving back and forth in time, these portraits with their conflicting and unabashedly partisan viewpoints complement, illumi-
nate, and correct each other to create a multi-dimensional picture of
postwar German history. Of course, this work does not presume to
compete with other recent histories, by German and non-German
scholars alike, which trace the Federal Republic's course over the
years. Instead, it hopes to engage the interest of the American reader
curious about the shape of the world we are about to enter. As for the
German reader, it wanted to tell the story of what these six chancellors accomplished to a younger, less knowledgeable generation, in the
process disabusing it of the notion that the world of plenty it regards
as its birthright came about by itself. Indeed, what does the younger
generation really know about the road their nation has traveled—the
twenty-year-old just completing an apprenticeship or beginning university, or the fifty-year-old who has spent his active years advancing
his career?

But if you don't know where you come from, you don't know
where you are, let alone where you are going. Those who fail to try to
understand history beyond the events and circumstances of their own
time are destined to have no sense of where they are headed. Because
many parents and teachers, and countless politicians and journalists,
ignore this fact, younger generations have a difficult time finding
their bearings and identifying with their own people, without which
they run the danger of becoming the victims of a special German
attitude, whether as "constitutional patriots" or in pursuit of "Western values."

Germany's neighbors perceive themselves as nations—and so, indeed,
do the peoples of all the countries of the world, with the exception of

regions where the right to self-determination and principles of nationality collide. The refusal to accept a national identity, which many Germans regard as appropriate atonement for Hitler, arouses feelings of distrust abroad and creates a psycho-political vacuum that extremist groups may be quick to fill. To redefine the German national consciousness as something that is neither arrogant nor submissive was an obvious goal of all these chancellors.

More than a decade before German unification, Swiss literary critic Adolf Muschg said that "what worries Germany's neighbors is its lack of inbred political instincts; it is not only imperialism that knows no borders, it is also the lack of patriotism." Muschg felt it likely that "the spirit of nationalism that has been suppressed and repressed will return as a ghost to whom Germans believe they can deny a national identity. Only gratified self-respect can make good neighbors; repressed self-respect wavers between self-denigration and arrogance."

Many of Germany's neighbors near and far found German self-alienation, prompted by the memory of the Nazi horrors, to be quite profitable, something to be encouraged both politically and in the media. And many West Germans, soon economically successful, though in a state of prolonged shock about the crimes Germans had committed in their name, believed this was the way to prevent yet another misuse of their spirit of communal loyalty or their willingness to make sacrifices. Those who felt that way thus cultivated a superior sense of moral purity, while others who no longer believed notions of national dignity had any meaning accommodated themselves to this self-alienation.

The totalitarian regime in communist-ruled East Germany—with the support of "useful idiots" in the West—undertook an equally energetic and futile attempt to create a de-nationalized, socialistic state consciousness. But though communist rulers eliminated the word "German" from official texts whenever possible, by the seventies they began to base a purely Marxist interpretation of history on German-Prussian traditions. Thus they took possession of at least some part of German history in a more clear and conscious fashion than was the case in West Germany.

As unjust in individual cases and as questionable under international law as the Nuremberg trials were, and despite the many untrue statements and denunciations of the denazification process, which relied heavily on questionnaire, the Allies relieved Germans of one of their most difficult postwar tasks. They drew a clear line separating the majority of the German people and those responsible for the deeds and atrocities committed under National Socialism.

Following German unification, when the injustices of the East German system were being addressed, it once again became clear how difficult it is to differentiate between victims and perpetrators in a totalitarian regime, to discover the instigators, organizers, and henchmen of criminal acts, and to evaluate the degree of damage done by the general population, ranging from a fearful or cowardly avoidance of the truth to the expectation of personal advantage. The number of heroes and saints of any nation is small.

For their part the Western Allies created the preconditions for a new and democratic beginning, for the establishment of a pluralistic, constitutional state, and—once the Morgenthau Plan had been relegated to the files and the free West sought to place the Federal Republic's industrial and military potential at its own disposal in the coming Cold War—for economic recovery.

Democracy was soon in full bloom in the Federal Republic of Germany, for it was as deeply rooted there as in most other countries of Europe, and had not totally withered. One of its most important achievements is that the votes of all are counted as being of equal weight. Even if the principle of men's equality before God and the law were to be abolished, there would still be no valid criteria for giving different weight to electoral votes. Education and income, evident economic, cultural, or social accomplishments—none of these offer protection against political fallibility or bias favoring one's own interests. Responsible political leadership must promote actions that lead to the long-term well-being of the general population, though this may require short-term sacrifice and temporary limitations on individual or group interests.

But there are several troublesome factors inherent in democracy. According to Article 21 of the Basic Law, political parties, as the pillars of pluralistic, parliamentary democracy, are supposed to help formulate political objectives. They seek the majority vote both by setting goals and attempting to meet them and by expressing the needs, wishes, and opinions of broad sectors of the population. The danger, of course, is that the former will be neglected in favor of the latter—expedient, opportunistic policies will be pursued against better knowledge and conviction, group interests will be gratified, or governmental regulations will be improperly enacted to please some marginal groups.

Because today's media not only disseminate such individual

demands but also give them greater currency, Western democracies are threatened by a phenomenon resembling feeding time at the zoo. Whoever roars the loudest gets the biggest share.

On the one hand, the freedom of expression guaranteed by the constitution is an unconditional constituent of democracy. For solid historical reasons, it was cultivated with special care in the Federal Republic. During the postwar years of reconstruction the media prevented a great many wrong-headed developments and stimulated a number of sensible innovations. But the all-encompassing medium of television, long before the arrival of the commercial networks in the fifties, signaled a quantum leap that affected the print media as well.

This unrecognized new cultural power, first noted by the famous media critic Otto Groth, has evolved into the universally recognized and effective power of the political media. And just like the absolute rulers of yesteryear, it is beyond criticism. It investigates, condemns, and judges, mostly in the name of democracy, but always without democratic controls. The Federal Republic's highest courts have increasingly extended the jurisdiction of Article 5 of the Basic Law (freedom of expression) at the cost of Article 1 (human dignity)—for which politicians, with their frequently extreme language, are partly to blame. No modern-day politician, whether village mayor who enjoys an in with the local paper, or federal chancellor whose ideas cannot reach the public without the exposure provided by television, can now survive without the media.

But it is not only Allah who is with the brave. The voters as well, whose consensus is often underestimated by politicians, know to honor courage. And of the many qualities that helped Germany's federal chancellors to office, at the top of this list stands the courage to forgo short-term benefits and throw their own political fate in the balance in order to accomplish what was right, even in the face of widespread resistance. Had Konrad Adenauer given in to the "count me out" movement against rearmament, which was fostered not only by pacifists and other such moralists, but also by countless members of the reviled war generation, the Federal Republic would not have become a member of NATO. The consequences, in the face of Stalinist Russia's unconcealed attempts at hegemony, would have been unthinkable. In 1957, at any rate, Adenauer would not have captured the absolute majority of votes.

Horst Osterheld, author of the essay on Konrad Adenauer, headed the foreign policy bureau of the chancellor's office for a decade. Though Adenauer was his boss for the first three years only, Oster-

*Horst Osterheld
congratulates Konrad
Adenauer on the
occasion of his eighty-
fifth birthday, 1961.*

held, a Catholic from the Palatinate, remained a loyal advocate of Adenauer's basic principles under Chancellors Erhard and Kiesinger. He was born in Ludwigshafen, not fifty kilometers from the French border, and this fact, along with the geopolitical fate of the Palatinate and his ideological convictions, obviously made him receptive to the historical opportunity of a lasting reconciliation between France and Germany, as it did Helmut Kohl, his fellow Palatine.

He has already recorded his personal and political thoughts on Adenauer in several notable publications. To compress into eighty manuscript pages the achievements of the federal chancellor who held office longer than any other was a difficult achievement.[1] Adenauer, after all, was chancellor for fourteen years, lived to be ninety-one, and began his prominent career in the era of Kaiser Wilhelm II. I find that Osterheld, now seventy-five himself, his eyesight failing, has succeeded magnificently.

Space limitations clearly were unavoidable were this work not to become one of "Teutonic erudition," a phrase that originated with Hans-Peter Schwarz, the most up-to-date and significant of Adenauer's biographers, who employed it as justification for excluding the use of footnotes in the first volume ("only" 1,022 pages long) of his two-volume work on the founding chancellor.

Like all the authors in this book, Horst Osterheld is not a historian, but writes as a contemporary, whose profession brought him into close proximity to his subject. He writes as an eyewitness, not only to pass on his knowledge of the man and his work, but also—for both himself and others—to record how close the great statesman's thoughts and beliefs were to his own.

For these same reasons I authored a book on Ludwig Erhard twenty-five years ago, in addition to a number of newspaper and magazine articles, contributions to anthologies, and the biographical essay included in this book. The first interview I conducted after I began working as a reporter for a news agency in Bonn in early 1956 was with Konrad Adenauer. Ludwig Erhard was the first to invite me to his discussion group with economic journalists, which later developed into the so-called "Erhard Brigade." I was twenty-four years

Konrad Adenauer and Ludwig Erhard with the editor, 1958.

Ludwig Erhard and the editor, 1965.

The editor with Kurt Georg Kiesinger, 1967.

Helmut Kohl and the editor, 1989.

old, and admittedly it was Erhard's warmth and openness that drew me to him rather than to the coolly reserved Adenauer. Previous to my work as a Bonn correspondent, I had been a journalist in Erhard's electoral district, and this fact contributed to our rapidly developing personal relationship. This relationship became closer during my years in Bonn and was the reason, after six years of work at German embassies in Amman, Damascus, Baghdad, and Jakarta, that I was asked to serve as press and political public relations officer on Erhard's staff.

By then the ideas and creative genius of the founder of the social market economy began to captivate me even more than the man himself. His profoundly humane ideas on thought and power, morality and politics, and economy and the state have never left me. Since the unification of Germany, it has become clear to all informed observers that the political players did what they had to do, but also that Erhard's theories deserve renewed attention that is long overdue.

As a journalist both before and after the time I spent in public service, and as a representative of the *Bundestag*, I got to know many people and maintained friendships with politicians of all stripes. Among them were three future chancellors, Kurt Georg Kiesinger, Willy Brandt, and Helmut Kohl. Ultimately I was named both minister for economic cooperation and minister for special tasks in Kohl's third cabinet, becoming government spokesman and chief of the Federal Press Office. Despite my professional respect for Helmut Schmidt's powerful gifts of oratory, no personal relationship developed between us.

It was during the years I spent as a political journalist in Bonn that I first came to know the co-authors of this book. For the essay on Kurt Georg Kiesinger, for example, I chose his knowledgeable associate, Günter Diehl, former ambassador to New Delhi and Tokyo and head of the Federal Press and Information Office during the Great Coalition. Diehl is known as an elegant writer. And as a research assistant in the Foreign Office, he knew Kiesinger during the war. This qualifies him to report on this part of Kiesinger's life, which was later to be the object of much controversy. At the same time, Diehl's intellectual autonomy is the guaranty for his historical objectivity.

Trying to match each chancellor to an author who viewed his subject with basic sympathy, and who was in agreement with that chancellor's politics without—for partisan reasons, for example—being unduly biased, I chose Bonn radio journalist Peter Zudeick for the Willy Brandt portrait. Zudeick did not work with Brandt, nor did

*Kurt Georg Kiesinger and
Günter Diehl, 1968.*

he have a close relationship with him, but he interviewed Brandt several times and authored a number of articles on him.

But Peter Zudeick, conscientious and serious journalist that he
is—as evidenced by his several published works—belongs to that
generation that was fascinated by Brandt's move to the left, and exercised criticism of the ex-chancellor only when Brandt failed to meet
that generation's expectations. I do not deny that I am only in partial
agreement with Zudeick's depiction. In my many private conversations with Brandt—when he was a young *Bundestag* representative,
the governing mayor of Berlin, the foreign minister of the Great
Coalition (whom I accompanied on his first trip to America), or my
Bundestag colleague following his resignation as chancellor—I came
to know another Willy Brandt.

But the appeal of this book lies in the diverse viewpoints from
which the six federal chancellors are represented and assessed. This
applies as well to the contribution on Helmut Schmidt by Reinhard
Appel, who chose to interview the sole surviving ex-chancellor.
Schmidt, as always, makes no secret of his opinions, doing justice to

his "Schmidt lip" that both political friend and enemy are familiar with. Appel knows Bonn and has done work in television, and his questions serve as a necessary jumping-off point. Helmut Schmidt has knowledge both of the world and of rhetoric, and spares neither friend nor foe. He admonishes Appel not to edit out his words of praise for Helmut Kohl. And he resists my request to reconsider a particularly harsh judgment he made concerning two incumbent ministers. In evaluating the processes of unification and European integration, he boasted of his "expert understanding of economics." These interviews are evidence that Schmidt has not been humbled by age.

Helmut Kohl—Who Else? was the title of a critical and partisan biography by Oskar Fehrenbach that appeared in 1990. His description of Kohl, his party, the political opposition, and the European scene was knowledgeable, reflective, empathetic, and comprehensive as he surveyed the relationship among them. His is the best of the current Kohl biographies.

This fact compelled the invitation to Fehrenbach, now an energetic retiree living in the Black Forest, to commit to paper what he had seen and experienced in his six years as a Bonn correspondent

Willy Brandt and the editor, 1968.

Helmut Schmidt and Reinhard Appel, 1980.

and seventeen years as editor-in-chief of the *Stuttgarter Zeitung*. His contribution is the most knowledgeable, the most reflective, the most empathetic, and informative of this book. His answer to the question, "Who else?" is equally unequivocal. But his depiction of the international political scene, the criticism surrounding unification, and the new challenges that Germany must meet conceal in part the political stature of the chancellor of unification, whose greatness Fehrenbach obviously never places in question. In times of great upheaval, when traditional structures are breaking apart and have not yet been replaced, it is the unavoidable fate of a political journalist to write in the face of the unknown. The constant is Helmut Kohl, with his almost un-German self-restraint, his secure understanding of the center path, his instinctive feel for new international developments, his ability to wait and to get things done, and his inexhaustible capacity for work.

Years ago Fehrenbach wrote: "Anyone who votes for Helmut Kohl goes against public opinion." Though the validity of such a statement disappears in election periods in which the cause and the candidate are one, it nevertheless could be applied in the broadest sense to all of the federal chancellors. And it applies in the figurative sense to the following statement, made by Thomas Mann in November 1926:

■ The great men of a people are not necessarily its "authentic" sons, and certainly not "representative." To a large degree they are strangers among their own people, and compel it to do things it would have no desire to do, left to its own devices. In this sense, they change their people, and their "authenticity" is established only later—after the educational cure they subject their reluctant people to has taken effect. This is particularly true in Germany, whose great men almost always appeared on a mission of national enlightenment that worked against the desire for national complacency and intractability, so that the newly forged accomplishments of such great "strangers" long are perceived as a violation, before it becomes spiritually possible to proclaim their "authenticity." ■

Of course, it was not only the federal chancellors who were the great shapers of German postwar history. Federal presidents, *Bundestag* presidents, minister-presidents, party chiefs—when not serv-

Helmut Kohl and Oskar Fehrenbach, 1984.

ing as federal chancellor at the same time—*Bundestag* caucus leaders, parliamentary secretaries, committee heads, ministers, and
undersecretaries are mentioned here only in relation to their respective heads of government, but this is not intended to diminish their
contributions. Leading political personalities such as Kurt Schumacher, Franz Josef Strauss, or Thomas Dehler exerted no less an
influence on the course of German postwar history that was in no
way inferior to that of the federal chancellors. And the chancellors
would have operated in isolation without the presence of employees
and employers, expellees, war victims, retirees, farmers, bureaucrats,
and white-collar workers, without, that is to say, the industrious and
resourceful German people, who possessed the will to rebuild their
country. And those Germans on the other side of the Iron Curtain?
Under disproportionately difficult conditions, they were equally
industrious, resourceful, and possessed of the will for reconstruction.

German unity has been re-established, and the effort to equalize
the standard of living in the new federal state is proceeding inex-
orably, despite the unforeseen magnitude of the great economic strain
to the west, and of high transitional unemployment in the east. European integration, with Germany as its motor, is irreversible, the
transatlantic relationship with the U.S. intact, and relations with the
rest of the world, particularly with Eastern Europe and the developing continents, is marked by a trust in unified Germany's sense of
responsibility and willingness to help. It is a good time for an overall
review, including that of the accomplishments of the first six federal
chancellors.

But the public manifestation of joy or even pride in Germany
appears to be permitted only on soccer fields, over a beer in pubs, or
on company outings. The role of the state, on the other hand, seems
to be to gnash its teeth, appear vulnerable, and acknowledge its
problems, and not to celebrate its successes. When on May 10, 1955,
the three High Commissioners of the Occupation Powers declared
that occupation was ended, a petty partisan squabble tarnished the
festive proclamation of this historical event. Even more pitiful was
the church district that on October 3, 1990, the day of German unification, prohibited the ringing of its bells in celebration.

The terms most often employed for this type of behavior are self-
abasement, self-vituperation, and self-defilement, all of which are
beside the point, for those who engage in such acts are not abasing,
vituperating, or defiling themselves. Rather, they point the finger at
others in order to elevate and praise themselves, to make themselves

appear particularly unsullied. If it has always been dangerous to point out the nakedness that passes for the emperor's new clothes, then within democratic politics—that arena of absolute rivalry, especially in postwar Germany—it appears to require superhuman courage to call national hypocrisy by its true name.

Years ago Charles de Gaulle said to the Germans: "You are a great people, even if you have erred! You again have a friend." Fortunately for us, and for Europe, we grasped the hand of friendship he extended. But we did not heed his appeal to our self-assurance. Perhaps we need not go so far as to emulate the French tendency toward the expressive gesture. But one would hope Germans will cultivate more graciousness, an easier relationship between intellect and politics, a bit more thoughtfulness in public appearances and warmth in private conversation, a bit more sensitivity to international developments and the peculiarities of other peoples, and more sense of the dignity and history of our own people.

1. Should Helmut Kohl serve his full term until 1998, he will have exceeded Adenauer's term of office by two years, and thus will have become Federal Germany's chancellor with the longest term in office.

[Top] *The "rose gardener of Rhöndorf" — With Charles de Gaulle in the garden of Ernich Castle, 1963 — At a session of the* Bundestag, *1958.*
[Center] *With Food Minister Heinrich Lübke and SPD chairman Erich Ollenhauer, 1955 — With (from left) General Hans Speidel and Defense Minister Franz Josef Strauss (with binoculars) inspecting troops*

and viewing tank model, 1958.
[Bottom] *Celebrating carnival in Palais Schaumburg, 1963 — The historic
Moscow visit in September 1955 with, left, Soviet prime minister Bulganin
and, right, Nikita Khrushchev, head of the Soviet Communist Party —
Playing boccia at the Italian vacation resort Cadenabbia, 1958.*

Chronology

1876	Konrad Adenauer born January 5 in Cologne.
1897	First state law examinations, followed in 1901 by second.
1904	Marries Emma Weyer (d. 1916), with whom he has three children.
1906	Cologne town councillor, deputy mayor in 1909.
1917–1933	Mayor of Cologne.
1919	Marries Gussie Zinsser (d. 1948), with whom he has four children.
1921–1933	President of the Prussian State Council.
1933	Removed from office by the National Socialists and expelled from Cologne.
1933–1945	Lives in seclusion in Neubabelsberg near Berlin, in Maria Laach, and from 1939 at his home in Rhöndorf. Arrested in 1934 and in 1944.
1945	Reinstated as mayor of Cologne in March, removed from office by the British on October 6.
1946	Chairman of the Christian Democratic Union in Northrhine-Westphalia.
1948	President of the Parliamentary Council.
1949	Elected federal chancellor.
1949–1953	First cabinet. As of 1951, also serves as foreign minister.
1953–1957	Appoints second cabinet.
1957–1961	Appoints third cabinet.
1961–1963	Appoints fourth cabinet.
1963	Retires from the *Bundestag* on October 15.
1967	Adenauer dies in Rhöndorf on April 19.

Konrad Adenauer

by Horst Osterheld

Konrad Adenauer was the first and founding chancellor of the Federal Republic of Germany. He led his country for fourteen years during a period that saw the western part of a devastated, defeated, and divided nation transformed into a flourishing member and partner of the free world. Adenauer was seventy-three years old when he was first elected chancellor in 1949. To understand the man who, like no other democratic German leader and statesman of his time, has placed his stamp on his country's future at home and abroad, a look at the first seventy-three years of his life is indispensable.

The German Reich was not yet five years old when Konrad Adenauer was born on January 5, 1876, in Cologne, a Prussian city on the Rhine with a history dating back to the Roman Empire and a predominantly Catholic population. He was the third of four children of Konrad Adenauer, a civil servant in the judicial department, and his wife Helene. Adenauer's father, a former Prussian officer, was a man of stern disposition. His mother had a sunnier nature, though like her husband she was short tempered. To their children they provided living models of hard work, piety, frugality, and, above all, a sense of duty. Adenauer later said his upbringing had been "very strict" and his way of life "very simple." But the family's feelings of love and warmth made up for it. All of the children attended secondary school, and the three boys even went on to university.

Konrad was a good if not exemplary student; though not unsociable, he was a serious and at times shy young man who was not particularly gregarious. Before exams, when he studied late into the night, he kept himself awake by putting his feet into buckets of cold water, which he replenished often so the temperature remained low. He studied law and economics in Freiburg, Munich, and Bonn from 1894 to 1897. While in Munich he visited the Pinakothek art museum almost daily, and he spent his vacations exploring Switzerland, Italy, and Bohemia, mostly on foot. In order not to prove an unnecessary burden to his parents, Adenauer took his first civil service exam after the shortest possible period of study.

After passing his second state examinations in 1901, he served briefly in the public prosecutor's office, and then went to work in a law office. During this time, in which he was more socially active than usual, he met Emma Weyer, the daughter of a respected Cologne family, and the two married in 1904.

Adenauer's career began to make rapid advances. In 1906 he became a city councillor of Cologne, and three years later was elected by a large majority to the position of deputy mayor in charge of finances and personnel. When war broke out in 1914 he was put in charge of the department of nutrition as well; a lung condition kept him out of the army. Unlike most Germans, Adenauer did not believe the war would end quickly, and as a result of his careful planning Cologne was able to provide for its population more successfully than most other cities, even during those periods of food shortages known as the "turnip winters." But the war demanded ever more sacrifices in Cologne as well, and the hardships became increasingly critical. Adenauer suffered a great loss in his private life during this time: his wife, and mother of his three children, died in 1916.

As a result of his exceptional accomplishments, Adenauer was unanimously elected *Oberbürgermeister*[1] (mayor) of Cologne in 1917. At forty-one years of age he was Germany's youngest mayor, responsible for a city of 650,000 people. When the Allies defeated Germany and the Kaiser abdicated in 1918, Adenauer faced a critical situation: hundreds of thousands of returning soldiers came flooding back, and revolutionary workers' and soldiers' councils were struggling for power in Cologne as they did in other cities. Adenauer persuaded the soldiers to turn in their weapons for money and rations. At the same time, he ordered 300,000 liters of alcohol stored in an army depot to be dumped into the Rhine at night, in all probability sparing Cologne any number of problems.

But the crisis extended beyond Cologne to all of the German Reich. The country was still without a constitution, its central powers were weak and barely reached the occupied territories west of the

Rhine. Separatist movements were emerging, and Adenauer himself considered the idea of secession from Prussia, but not from the German Reich. In June of 1919 he succeeded in preventing separatist attempts to take over Wiesbaden and Koblenz from spreading to Cologne, as a result of which a separatists' court condemned him to death. The National Socialists later attempted to tie him to the separatist movement, to no avail.

In September 1919, Adenauer's personal life took a new turn when he married Gussie Zinsser, daughter of a university professor who was a neighbor of Adenauer. They were to have four children together.

The extraordinary trials and tribulations of those years are well known—the Treaty of Versailles, the reparations, the harrowing inflation, the putsch attempts from both left and right, the occupation of the Ruhr by Allied forces. We must keep these events in mind to appreciate what Adenauer accomplished in Cologne—the reopening of the university, for instance, or the creation of a green belt around the city. To replace the city's defense fortifications, scheduled to be razed, Adenauer wished to create a park twelve miles long and six-tenths of a mile wide, a green lung, so to speak, an enterprise that was all but unknown at the time. The project met bitter resistance from many sides; there were protests and court proceedings, and even Adenauer's own party (the *Zentrumspartei*[2]) rejected the idea, but he refused to yield ground. "I wanted to free people from the alleyways and the streets," he later said, "and I knew that I was fighting for a good cause." His efforts were successful and Adenauer came to consider the green belt his greatest accomplishment in Cologne.

He also supported the construction of public housing. As he once said to a priest, "The Ten Commandments cannot be obeyed in inadequate housing." Adenauer built Germany's first large stadium and fifty other sports facilities. He established the Cologne Trade and Exhibition Fair to boost the economy, and a new harbor he constructed on the Rhine attracted major industry to Cologne. He incorporated so many suburbs into the city that Cologne grew to encompass the second largest area of any city in Germany, exceeded only by Berlin. After centuries of neglect, Cologne under Adenauer became a leading city almost overnight.

From 1921 to 1933 Adenauer served as president of the Prussian State Council. Beginning in 1921 he was considered for the office of Reich chancellor several times, coming closest to being named in 1926 when a letter of appointment had been drawn up for him. He planned to rule with a Great Coalition,[3] and to set a new direction in foreign policy; he opposed the Reich's "seesaw politics" between East and West, and already at that time pledged a closer relationship with the nations of the West. Gustav Stresemann[4] of the People's Party opposed him in this, and because Adenauer was not assured of parliamentary support he withdrew his name as candidate for chancellor. No one—neither he himself nor those who had half-heartedly summoned the irascible and determined Adenauer to Berlin—was aware of the consequences of this decision. Might he have kept Hitler from coming to power? The idea is staggering.

Adenauer stayed in Cologne and continued his impressive record of achievements, but encountered ever greater criticism on financial matters, due largely to his arbitrary and autocratic leadership. In 1929 he was reelected mayor by a very narrow margin. By then the somewhat illusory prosperity of the late 1920s was over and the worldwide economic depression came as a great blow to the long overtaxed Weimar Republic. Adenauer believed that Germany was headed for turmoil, and kept urging Reich Chancellor Heinrich Brüning[5] to create extensive job programs. When nothing happened, he began to make a start himself in Cologne. It was not Hitler but Adenauer who built the first section of the autobahn, running from Cologne to Bonn. But the situation in the Reich was worsening; unemployment rose over six million, and communists and Brownshirts ruled the streets. Democratic forces did not dare oppose them; and so Hitler came to power.

Adenauer, as well, had underestimated the Nazis. For a time he believed they could be brought under control, as he had the workers' and soldiers' councils in 1918–1919. More clearly than many other bourgeois politicians he saw just how dangerous they were, but even he did not anticipate the degree of brutality the Nazis would engage in after 1933.

In the *Reichstag* election of March 5, 1933, the National Socialists for the first time became the strongest party in Cologne. They attacked Adenauer as an enemy of the people and a criminal, and following the local elections held one week later on March 12, he knew that he faced arrest. When Hitler visited Cologne Adenauer ordered the Nazis' swastika flag taken down. Early on the morning of Monday, March 13, Adenauer stole past the sleeping SA guard posted at his home "for his protection," and went to Berlin to protest his removal from office. To no avail; his salary was cut off and his bank accounts were frozen. Without the generous support of a Jewish industrialist by the name of Heinemann, whom Adenauer did not even know well, his situation would have been quite grave. For ten months he went into hiding at the monastery of Maria Laach. Up until that point his life had been one of steady ascent, but now it had turned into dire adversity. His time at the cloisters was spent in isolation and loneliness, a period, he later said, which "strengthened my knowledge and my conscience."

Eventually his refuge was discovered. As Adenauer did not wish to endanger the order and—as his letters from that time attest—he suffered from being separated from his family, he moved with them to Neubabelsberg near Berlin in 1934. It was there that he was arrested following the "Röhm putsch"[6] of June 30, 1934, though Adenauer had no connection at all to the conspirators. He realized he might be "shot while trying to escape," but instead he was soon released. Now he knew the danger he was in and he moved around for a while until he found shelter in Unkel, a small town on the Rhine. His family visited him there regularly; but the vilification he had endured since 1933 had greatly shaken him, accustomed as he was to success. He had been forbidden to practice his profession, was almost sixty years old, and his hope of living to see the end of the Nazi dictatorship was beginning to fade. At times he experienced great despair, but he held out, and things improved. His brother was able to arrange for him to return to his family. Retroactive pension payments, and the compensation he received for his confiscated property in Cologne, supplied the funds to build his house in Rhöndorf, which was later expanded and still stands today, attracting up to 100,000 visitors annually.

With the completion of the house in 1937 began a quiet period in Adenauer's life. He cared for his family, occupied himself with "inventions"—he was later to astound his ministers with his knowledge of physics and chemistry—and devoted himself avidly to his large garden. Nature, his family, painting, and music were the most enduring sources of joy to him his entire life long. These could have been peaceful years for him had the political climate not become increasingly oppressive and hopeless. Should Adenauer have joined a resistance group? He met occasionally with a small circle in Bonn, but made no contact with those who planned to overthrow the Nazis by force. He doubted their discretion and their competence; he knew that Hitler was not to be brought down from within. Adenauer's mail, telephone, and visitors were under surveillance. He did not risk his life, he was not the martyr type, but neither did he leave the country. He wished to remain, come what may, "with my family and my people, and be a part of whatever the future holds."

The future held war, and Adenauer shared the same fate as did millions of others, until August 1944 when he was again arrested, in the wake of the July 20 assassination attempt on Hitler. Released a short time later he fled to a secluded mill in the Westerwald region, expecting the Allies to arrive soon thereafter. But he was wrong. When the Gestapo threatened to arrest their daughters for his crimes,[7] Adenauer's wife was forced to reveal his hiding place. Though it was the right decision, she never forgave herself. Her lifelong anguish over it crushed her spirits and hastened her demise. On September 25, 1944, their silver wedding anniversary, both Adenauer and his wife were taken to the same Gestapo prison in Brauweiler, unaware of each other's presence. Frau Adenauer was released earlier; Adenauer himself remained under arrest for nine weeks. Of the sixty men incarcerated with him, twenty-seven were hanged and one was shot. Adenauer, however, was allowed to return home at the end of November and finally, in the spring of 1945, the American tanks rolled in.

The U.S. Military Government placed Adenauer on their "white list,"[8] and on March 9, 1945, they reinstated him as mayor of Cologne. Adenauer must have felt satisfied and exonerated at this turn of events, but he was not given to ebullience, and conditions were too critical for that anyway. Of the 750,000 people who had lived in Cologne in 1939 there were only 32,000 remaining on the left bank of the Rhine. In the city's boroughs fighting was still raging between retreating German troops and pursuing American forces. More than half of the city's 59,000 buildings had been totally destroyed, a mere 300 had sustained no damage at all. Rubble was piled on top of rubble, there was enormous suffering among the population, and starvation was rampant. Adenauer worked sixteen hours a day with few assistants and practically no aid, but he took on the countless number of individual problems in the same spirit he did the great responsibilities. The vehicles remaining at the disposal of the municipal government were constantly underway delivering food supplies to the city from surrounding areas. Directly after the war Adenauer sent municipal buses to the concentration camps of

Buchenwald, Dachau, and Theresienstadt, "to bring the tortured survivors home." He worked to reconstruct the bridges over the Rhine, and made plans for a generous rebuilding of his native city.

In June, Cologne was assigned to the British occupation zone and on October 6 Adenauer was removed from office by the British. He had refused to allow the trees in the green belt to be cut down, because he felt it would do little to alleviate the fuel shortage and would create damage that would take decades to repair. Instead, he demanded that coal be brought in from the Ruhr district. Also, the British may well have suspected that Adenauer's ties to the Americans continued to be too close, and in all likelihood a former political opponent had denounced him to the ruling Labour party in London. Adenauer was relieved of his post as if dismissed in disgrace; he was ordered to leave Cologne within eight days and forbidden to take part in any political activity. With one blow this man, surrounded only shortly before by thousands of admirers, now was surrounded by the depressing void of fear. "When I left Cologne, no one bid me farewell," he wrote in his memoirs.

The humiliation may well have been worse than it had been twelve years before. The pendulum of history, as if in an act of great justice, had swung back, giving him a second opportunity to serve his native city, and he had engrossed himself in the task with everything he possessed. Now, without warning, totally unexpectedly, he again had been ousted from office, this time not by his enemies, but by the "liberators." He was not allowed to visit his wife who was confined to a hospital in Cologne. He was almost seventy years old and could not hope to survive the new masters. Wouldn't most people have given up in his place? Once again he experienced that, when the winds change, even the most strenuous efforts go unrecognized, without gratitude or reward. But the vitality that had had to lay dormant in him for twelve years now drove him to take action and assume responsibility. He wanted to set right what Nazi criminals had destroyed. He saw an opportunity to repair what had gone wrong in German history; he wanted to help build something that was healthy and solid. In December Adenauer again was permitted to participate in German politics, but not in Cologne. The only path remaining led him first to state, and later to federal politics.

What was Germany like in 1945–1946? The collapse was as total as war had been. One-fourth of the territory in the east of the former German Reich had been lost, and what was left was divided into four zones, which the victors believed should be placed under occupation for the next twenty years to come. Ten million Germans had died, an equal number of refugees was pouring in from the east. There were millions of wounded, widowed, and orphaned. Millions of young men still languished in captivity as prisoners of war. Industrial production was one-third of what it had been in 1938. Daily rations totaled only one thousand calories. Half of school-age children had tuberculosis. Housing, for the most part, was pitifully lacking; there was little protection against the cold and few medical supplies. Unemployment figures were high, and in addition to this were the black market, profiteering, and moral decline.

Adenauer, a devout Catholic, was convinced that this unparalleled catastrophe was the result of a decades-long rejection of spiritual values. Too many Germans had concerned themselves only with worldly matters, worshipping power and the state. It was time for this materialistic outlook to be replaced by a Christian one, which would bestow upon the individual, answerable only to God, a dignity and worth that the collective of necessity would respect. If Adenauer hated one thing it was totalitarian regimes like those of the National Socialists and the communists, which tyrannized their people unconscionably, promised them utopia, and deliberately deceived them. He had experienced that "a dictatorship can totally transform the human character, even in those of whom it would not have been believed possible."

Adenauer felt that these basic principles should be put forward by a party that included both Christian faiths and people of all classes and stations in life. He was not a founder of the Christian Democratic Union (CDU), but he soon became its leader in the British zone. He had decisively grabbed the reins at the first meeting of CDU representatives in January 1946. To many he was too decisive, but he handled himself so well that by the end of the meeting he had been elected CDU chairman of the British zone. The platform the assembly adopted agreed largely with those doctrines Adenauer had worked out in the course of twelve dark years. There was some disagreement on major economic issues, but over time the social market economy triumphed. It was not Adenauer, but Ludwig Erhard[9] who developed this policy. Erhard's bold and unprecedented decision simply to do away with rationing and price controls at the same time as he introduced the currency reform of June 1948 was the spark that ignited what the international community later would regard with awe as the

Meeting with leading representatives of the Catholic Church. Together with French politician André François-Poncet in conversation with Cardinals Frings and Spellman, Trier, 1953.

In conversation with Bishop Otto Dibelius, 1956.

German "economic miracle." Adenauer adopted Erhard's teachings to become part of his party's program.

During this same period Adenauer suffered a great loss in his private life. After a long illness his wife Gussie died on March 3, 1948, a loss which affected him profoundly. But he carried on, "because there was no one else to do so."

The Federal Republic

In addition to events in the British zone, it was also necessary to keep up with developments in the other occupation zones, and in the world at large. Tensions between the Soviet Union and the United States were growing. The West looked on as the communists seized power in Rumania and Hungary, but roused itself in February 1948, after the coup d'etat in Czechoslovakia. The blockade of Berlin by Stalin on April 1, 1948, led to international confrontation. Many, including Adenauer, feared a new world war.

It appeared that the Soviet Union wanted to annex Western Europe, or at the very least all of Germany. This moved the three Western powers in June of 1948 to allow the Germans in the Western zones to unite under a free and democratic federalist constitution. The eleven *Länder* (roughly equivalent to the states in the U.S.) of the three Western zones formed a Parliamentary Council that consisted of twenty-seven representatives from the CDU/CSU (Christian Social Union, the CDU's Bavarian counterpart), twenty-seven representatives from the Social Democratic Party (SPD), five from the liberal Free Democratic Party (FDP), and six from smaller parties.

Based on his "experience in leading a parliamentary commission" from his days on the Prussian State Council, Adenauer was elected president of the Parliamentary Council on September 1, 1948. The cosmopolitan SPD leader Carlo Schmid[10] became head of the steering committee, a position equal to that of president. The Council wished to draft a constitution that would avoid the mistakes of Weimar. There was considerable debate on many points, but the work progressed. Adenauer's reputation gained from his impressive service as president and his successful dealings with the occupying powers. On May 23, 1949, Adenauer announced that the Basic Law[11] (*Grundgesetz*, Germany's constitution) had come into effect, and with this the Federal Republic of Germany was born! The authors of the Basic Law did well; their work has stood the test of time.[12]

Meeting with U.S. general Lucius D. Clay in Bonn, 1962.

Almost simultaneously with the declaration of the Basic Law, the
Soviets ended their year-long blockade of Berlin.[13] The West, primarily
the Americans, had responded to the blockade with an airlift, a huge
and unprecedented undertaking. American and British pilots flew
roughly 280,000 missions, delivering close to two million tons of supplies to the beleaguered city and thus insuring its survival. The Allied

airlift became symbolic of the fact that America would, even at great risk, protect the freedom of those who relied on it; this forged the nearly unshakable liking Germans felt for Americans.

In the meantime, election campaigns for the first West German parliament (*Bundestag*) were under way. The primary issue was whether the voters would support the CDU social market economic policy (essentially a free market with governmental tax-credit and loan incentives for home construction, industry, and business) against the planned economy the Socialists wanted. In foreign policy the two opposing views were strong ties to the West on the one hand and independence in the tug-of-war between East and West on the other, something the Socialists favored. The SPD with its support by the labor-friendly British Military Government, was widely favored to win. So it came as a great surprise on August 14, 1949, when the CDU/CSU received 31 percent of the vote, as opposed to 29.2 percent for the SPD. The FDP received 11.9 percent, the nationalistic German Party (*Deutsche Partei*, DP) 4 percent, with the rest of the votes divided among a number of smaller parties. It was Germany's first free election in seventeen years.

The election results, however, did not settle the question of who would form the new federal government. Since the CDU/CSU did not win enough votes to govern alone, it would have to form a coalition with one or more of the other parties. But would it be a Great Coalition bringing the CDU/CSU together with its rival, the SPD, or a Small Coalition in which the CDU/CSU would link up with the Free Democrats and several others? Most of the minister-presidents (roughly equivalent to the governors of U.S. states) of the eleven *Länder*, as well as the three occupation powers, were in favor of a Great Coalition. Moreover, most of the leaders in the two Union parties felt the terrible burdens created by the Third Reich and the war should be borne on as many shoulders as possible. But the SPD refused to enter into a coalition unless it was promised the Ministry of Economics. In Adenauer's eyes, this would have been an affront to the many voters who had elected the Union parties chiefly because they supported a social market economy; it would have meant breaking a campaign pledge.

Clearly, Adenauer's main reason for not giving in to the demands of the SPD was that the enormous economic problems the first federal government would face could not be resolved by a planned state economy. Moreover, Adenauer considered any policy that played the

East against the West to be a reckless one. Just as Germany had lost, had been destined to lose, both world wars when they became wars fought on two fronts, so any tactical attempt to deal first with the one major power and then with the other would lead first to isolation, then to dependency, and perhaps to new catastrophe.

Today, many people view the decision in favor of a social market economy and ties to the West to be obvious, almost self-evident. But at the time it wasn't. Adenauer knew how difficult it would be to get others to accept his view, but he risked his political future on it. One week after the federal elections he made his move: he invited twenty-five CDU/CSU politicians to meet at his home in Rhöndorf on August 21, 1949. The evening before, he met in Frankfurt with the minister-president of Bavaria, Hans Ehard (CSU), and won this widely respected politician over to the idea of an alliance with the liberals without the socialists. In the detailed and dogged debate with his guests the following day, Adenauer argued that only a fairly homogenous group could make the bold decisions needed to achieve the goals the Union parties had fought for. Constantly introducing new arguments and skillfully lobbying individual politicians, he was able to get the majority of those present to vote for the Small Coalition and—a daring accomplishment—to agree in advance to choose Theodor Heuss[14] of the FDP as federal president and himself as federal chancellor. Two days later he held a press conference to impress this endorsement on the public awareness.

The Rhöndorf conference was Adenauer's most successful political ploy. He himself called it the most important achievement of his time in office; it totally determined German politics of the years to follow.

On September 12 the *Bundesversammlung* (a joint session of the *Bundestag* and members of the state legislatures, the *Landtage*) elected Theodor Heuss the first federal president. Three days later Konrad Adenauer became the first federal chancellor in a *Bundestag* vote which gave him 202 out of a total of 402 ballots. With a bare majority of one, Adenauer had cast the decisive vote for himself. "Since I was determined to accept the appointment," he later said to his son, "I should have felt it sheer hypocrisy not to have voted for myself."[15]

Adenauer at seventy-three was the oldest head of state in memory. Nicknamed "Der Alte" (The Old Man), he had been born before most of the men who served as chancellors of the Weimar Republic; he was

Taking the oath of office as first federal chancellor, administered by Erich Köhler, president of the Bundestag, *on September 15, 1949.*

Adenauer's first cabinet assembled at the Bundestag *for a photograph on September 15, 1949. From bottom left: Anton Storch, Ludwig Erhard, Wilhelm Niklas (behind Erhard), Adenauer, Franz Blücher (partially concealed), Eberhard Wildermuth, Jakob Kaiser, Thomas Dehler, Hans Lukaschek. From top left: Heinz-Peter Hellwege, Hans Schuberth, Gustav Heinemann, Fritz Schäffer, Hans-Christoph Seebohm.*

thirteen years older than Hitler, and became chancellor at the same age that Bismarck[16] had been dismissed from office. At the Rhöndorf conference Adenauer announced that his physician, Professor Paul Martini, had assured him he would be able to fulfill the duties of chancellor for a good year or two. In fact, Adenauer went on to govern longer than all twenty-one cabinets of the Weimar Republic put together, and longer than the "Thousand-Year Reich" had existed. But, in September 1949, no one, not even Adenauer himself, would have considered such a thing possible, just as no one could have anticipated the Federal Republic's phenomenal recovery in the fourteen years Adenauer governed.

But he did not lose any time. After his cabinet was sworn in, twenty-four hours after delivering his first "statement of government policy" on September 20, 1949, he summoned several of his ministers for a pilgrimage to the feudal castle atop the Petersberg across from Bonn, seat of the High Commissioners representing the United States, Great Britain, and France. As occupying powers, they, together with the Soviet Union, still held ultimate control over all Germany, and within the city of Berlin. Adenauer accepted this, but he regarded himself as the man mainly responsible for the German people.

His four major goals were as follows:
- restarting the German economy;
- establishing a stable domestic order;
- reestablishing Germany's sovereignty;
- securing Germany's position within the community of free nations.

He never let these goals out of his sight, but in the fall of 1949 his major concern was halting the dismantling of German industry.

A great many factories already had been dismantled in the Western zones, and according to the plan decided upon in 1947 an additional 918 plants were on the list. Had this continued, the situation for the German economy would have been close to irreparable. Adenauer fought for each shop, each machine. Within eight weeks he achieved something no one would have believed possible. According to the Petersberg Agreements of November 22, 1949, with the three Western occupying powers, eighteen large firms were saved from dismantling, among them the industrial giants Bayer Chemiewerke Hüls and Gelsenberg, Thyssen, Klöckner, Bochumer Verein, and Ruhrstahl AG. All of the targeted factories in West Berlin were saved. It was an enormous victory, economically as well as psychologically. In addition, Adenauer succeeded in getting permission for the federal government to reestablish diplomatic relations with several foreign nations, and to work together with international organizations.

One might assume that this extraordinary accomplishment would have been met with wide approval in the *Bundestag*. But the Allies had given Adenauer no choice but to negotiate the Ruhr Statute,[17] which internationalized oversight of Germany's richest coal-mining region. This was considered by many an affront to the German nation. At three o'clock in the morning of November 25, after long and intense debate in the *Bundestag*, the socialist leader Kurt Schumacher accused Adenauer of being the "Chancellor of the Allies." This caused an uproar, but things were resolved when the Federation of German Trade Unions sided with Adenauer. Schumacher accepted the view of the Federation, for it was as resolute an opponent of communism as he himself.

The Petersberg Agreements not only carried great economic significance, they were also a strong link connecting the fledgling republic to the democracies of the West. To advance his fourth goal—to anchor Germany in the safe haven fortified by the Western alliance—Adenauer took an even more daring and, for him, riskier step only two weeks later. In two interviews in November and December 1949 he opened up for debate the issue of a West German defense contribution, and with this stirred up a hornet's nest. The East exploded in rage and fulminations, but there were those in the West who were also upset. Hadn't Germany just been demilitarized and its arms industry dismantled? The reaction in Germany itself was even more vehement, and considering all that had occurred since 1945 this was not surprising.

Adenauer was no militarist, but he was a realist par excellence. The Germans wanted the West to guarantee their safety, and so did Adenauer. But he knew the Western powers were not about to endanger their sons' lives for Germany's freedom unless Germans were also prepared to defend themselves. The participation of German troops would ensure that the line of defense would run along the Federal Republic's eastern border, instead of along the Rhine. Adenauer was not interested in a West German national army but in a German contingent, without general staff, within a European army. For he considered European unity a goal.

Before it could be accomplished, an understanding was necessary with the "archenemy," France. This was inherently problematic, and made more so by the thorny issue of the Saar. But, in December 1949 and in March 1950, Adenauer made overtures to initiate closer cooperation with France. He continued to work for an understanding between the two countries despite strong resistance on both sides of the Rhine, and his efforts bore fruit. On May 9, 1950, Robert Schuman, France's foreign minister, sent Adenauer his famous letter suggesting the formation of a joint agency for the German and French coal and steel industry.[18]

In the preceding four hundred years, twenty-five wars had been fought between Germany and France. Bilateral control of the armament industry was one way to put a stop to this destructive cycle, and at the same time look to the future. Italy and the Benelux[19] countries were asked to join, and the European Coal and Steel Community (*Montanunion*) became the nucleus of European federation.

The domestic situation in the Federal Republic was progressing as well. The Petersberg Agreements had saved more than one million jobs, and an equal number of new jobs were created during Adenauer's first year in office. In the same time period, 550,000 new housing units were created, a number that was repeatedly matched in the years that followed. Roads and highways were energetically rebuilt, and federal postal and rail services—*Bundespost* and *Bundesbahn*—established. The Federal Constitutional Court convened on February 1, 1951. Huge responsibilities were being met, and in the beginning even the most basic materials, including tables and telephones, were lacking.

One major trouble spot was a proposed law for the right of codetermination[20] (*Mitbestimmungsrecht*) by owners and unions in the coal and steel industry. Foreign interests were intervening, and major strikes threatened, with possibly far-reaching consequences. Quick and farsighted action was called for. The Law on Codetermination was passed on May 21, 1951, granting Germany for twenty years to come a measure of stability and success unknown in any other Western European country. It does no disservice to the contributions of Hans Böckler, the head of the German Trade Union Federation, or Kurt Schumacher and others to say that this framework for coexistence between the "social partners" of industry and labor became possible only after Adenauer applied himself to the issue. It was universally regarded as "one of his most brilliant achievements as a statesman."

Another plan without precedent was an "equalization of burdens" (*Lastenausgleich*) scheme, compensating those who had lost everything in the war with the help of those who had retained most of their property and belongings. The latter were to give up 50 percent of their property over the next thirty years. The proposal was met with vehement protests from all sides, but Adenauer persisted: "He who gives quickly gives doubly!" Following a bitter struggle, The Equalization of Burdens Law was passed on August 14, 1952, "a unique achievement of exemplary solidarity, which is greatly underappreciated." Total compensation amounted to 115 billion Deutsche Mark.

By then the ten million refugees that had been expelled from Poland, Czechoslovakia, Hungary, and the Soviet-occupied zone, a number that grew to roughly thirteen million by 1963, had found a home in Western Germany. One need only consider other refugee groups the world over to realize the suffering these refugees and expellees were spared. Two of the Allied High Commissioners wanted to close the borders, due to the high number of unemployed in the Federal Republic and because Stalin apparently had planned the expulsions and deportations to create permanent economic difficulties for the country. But Adenauer stood firm and kept the borders open. The Charter of the Expellees (*Charta der Heimatvertriebenen*), issued on August 5, 1959, expressly rejected the concepts of reprisals and restoration,[21] and had a conciliatory effect.

Moral principle also demanded that reparations be made to those persecuted by the Nazis for reasons of race or political or religious beliefs. The dead could not be brought back to life, the unspeakable suffering could not be undone. The only possible compensation was a material one, and this too led to much dissent, above all surrounding the issue of reparations made to Israel. The Arab countries threatened an economic boycott and sanctions. Influential Jewish groups rejected the idea of making any agreement with Germany. The German Party (DP), one of Adenauer's coalition partners, was resolutely opposed to reparations, as were most members of the Free Democratic Party. Had the DP withdrawn from the coalition, Adenauer would have lost control of parliament, but he decided to risk it. "One must simply stick it out!" he noted in 1965, looking back at that critical period. Reparations, also made to twelve European countries and to hundreds of thousands of individuals, were critical in reestablishing Germany's standing in the eyes of the world, and to its readmittance to the family of free nations.

Adenauer's progress in the first eighteen months of his term surpassed all expectations. His resolute yet flexible attitude toward the occupying powers, and his tireless pursuit of his goals led, on March 6, 1951, to a major revision in the Occupation Statute. As a result, lawmaking was almost entirely turned over to the Federal Republic and to the *Länder*. The remaining economic restraints were relaxed to a large degree, and the authority of the federal government in matters of foreign affairs greatly expanded. This led to the establishment of the Foreign Office, and on March 15, 1951, Konrad Adenauer became the Federal Republic's first foreign minister.

He tackled this additional and immense responsibility with his usual prudence and farsightedness, and with an almost palpable intensity. It was an era of tumultuous beginnings, with practically each day bringing new advances. Adenauer held innumerable meetings with his advisors, his cabinet, the various political caucuses, the press, and—often for days at a time—with the High Commissioners. "To be successful in politics," he once said, "you have to be able to sit longer than others." John McCloy, the American High Commissioner, recalled many meetings at Petersberg that continued "deep into the night. Sometimes we watched the sun come up. Adenauer would still be wide awake, while the rest of us were beginning to grow weary." His final meeting with the High Commissioners on the *Deutschlandvertrag* [22](or General Treaty), held in May 1952, lasted for seventeen hours without pause.

One must keep in mind the sheer volume of Adenauer's accomplishments in these years: the passage of hundreds of statutes and laws designed to spur the economy and promote social welfare; the formation of the federal government, the administration, and countless institutions; the agreements concluded with other nations, West Germany's joining the Council of Europe (*Europa Rat*) and GATT (General Agreement on Tariffs and Trade). Those familiar with the scene in Bonn of those days will attest that Adenauer was "70 percent of his cabinet." It was undoubtedly his best period, a time when all of his skills were put to optimal use: his vision, keen perception, creative imagination, courage, and, above all, his tenacity.

He himself considered his greatest virtue to be "constant and determined work from childhood on." Not for him the standard forty-eight-hour work week; his lasted eighty-four hours, exceeded only by the intensity and speed with which he worked. It is hard to imagine anyone who labored more steadfastly and relentlessly than Adenauer. He owed this to his constant good health and uncommon regenerative powers. He took the fifty-eight steps leading up to his house in Rhöndorf briskly. He required no rejuvenating injections, for, as his physicians attested, he had a "heart like a horse" and the "arteries of a young man." This explains the remarkable stamina he exhibited in conference rooms, and during election campaigns and weeks of stressful activity—to the amazement of the domestic and foreign journalists covering him, his negotiation partners and, though they were familiar with it, his colleagues.

He was an early riser who ate and drank in moderation. Order played a great role in his life; he required it, and he imposed it upon his surroundings. He turned his undivided attention to each and every matter, hundreds daily. He had the ability to defer problems, an example being the time he was handed a message during a conference: "I have to make an important decision here, I can't be upset at the moment. There's time for that tomorrow!" He was a very skeptical man, but when the situation called for it he could exhibit trust. He had an iron discipline; well into advanced age he could summon his strength at will, restrain or focus it and put it to optimal use. It should not be surprising that a man with such self-control would exert power over others. He knew how to lead.

He never enjoyed an idle moment, yet despite the pace at which he worked he never gave the impression of being harried. "Even if everyone else is going crazy," he said to his receptionists, "we shall remain calm!"

Adenauer was not overly sensitive. He remarked that a politician needed "a thick skin." This didn't keep him from being sensitive to whatever was going on around him, but it did protect him from the constant gibes and more strenuous attacks he had to endure. Disappointment no longer affected him deeply, and he rarely allowed his compassion to affect his policymaking. Which is not to say that he did not have feelings; his emotions could run quite deep, his sense of responsibility, for example, or his desire to follow his own conscience. But in the daily political arena he was ruled by intelligence and reason. Churchill, Ben-Gurion, de Gaulle—all were more impassioned than he, and better able to inspire people, as well.

His basic attitude was one of seriousness, but he could smile if the sublime became all too human or comical. He enjoyed banter—he was a true Rhinelander in this—and many of his speeches, no matter how serious, included an amusing touch. This was evident even in his farewell speech of October 15, 1963, when, in taking leave of members of parliament, he expressed his thanks "to this member somewhat more—and to that member, of course, somewhat less." His repartee enlivened many a meeting, and at press conferences journalists eagerly anticipated his bon mots and his irony. His humor mitigated his authoritativeness and served as a conciliatory influence, winning sympathy. It ranks high among the reasons for his political success.

By the end of 1951, two complex problems dominated the political scene: the General Treaty (on regaining German sovereignty), and the European Defense Community Treaty, concerning European security and unity. These two sets of negotiations ran parallel and were proceeding well, when on March 10, 1952, a note—the so-called "Stalin note"—from the Soviets addressed to the three Western powers threatened to call everything in question. Stalin suggested entering negotiations for a peace treaty under which Germany would be reunified as a neutral nation. The note was a bombshell. Many German politicians favored the proposal, but Adenauer immediately saw in it a cleverly disguised attempt to block both the General Treaty and, above all, the European Defense Community Treaty. He was able to convince an increasing number of German politicians that a neutral Germany would inevitably be drawn into the Soviet sphere of influence. The connection to the free nations of the West would be severed, and European unity hindered. The Iron Curtain would descend on the Federal Republic's western border.

Once again Adenauer's excellent sense of reality prevailed. American secretary of state Dean Acheson shared Adenauer's point of view, and the three Western powers demanded that free elections, monitored by the United Nations, be held throughout Germany as a precondition of the peace negotiations. Moscow rejected having controls imposed upon the Soviet-occupied zone, and did not follow up on its own proposal.

The Stalin note was the most serious obstacle to achieving agreement on the two treaties, but it was not the final one. The SPD rejected both treaties; Adenauer's own faction made difficulties; France set conditions. But Adenauer and Acheson together managed to advance the treaties to the signing stage. On May 26, 1952, Adenauer, the French and British foreign ministers, and the American secretary of state signed the General Treaty in Bonn. That afternoon they flew with their delegations to Paris, where on May 27, together with the foreign ministers of Italy and the Benelux countries, the European Defense Community Treaty was formally signed.

Though the treaties still faced ratification battles, the fact that they had been signed represented a great step forward. In practice, the Federal Republic would be treated as a sovereign and equal country.

The German public felt the difference: according to an opinion poll of July 1952, 53 percent of the population agreed with Adenauer's policies. One year earlier the number had been 30 percent.

Among the numerous major events of that period were the negotiations resulting in the London Debt Treaty[23] and the Saar Treaty,[24] the creation of the *Land* of Baden-Württemberg, and trailblazing *Bundestag* debates, as well as major declarations and letters by Adenauer. That September, in Luxembourg, Adenauer and Israeli foreign minister Moshe Sharett signed the Reparations Agreement with Israel.[25] And, in December, the second reading of the European Defense Community Treaty in the *Bundestag* turned into one of the longest, most tumultuous and vociferous battles up to that time.

In January 1953 Dwight D. Eisenhower took office as president of the United States. The Federal Republic, and especially Berlin, owed a great debt of gratitude to departing President Harry S. Truman, as well as to his secretary of state, Dean Acheson. Acheson had provided decisive support to the policies of the Federal Republic at crucial moments, and made no secret of his wish to see Adenauer reelected in the fall of 1953. On February 3 his successor as secretary of state, John Foster Dulles, arrived in Bonn on a trip through Europe. Adenauer was concerned about how he would get along with the new man, but he needn't have worried. Both men abhorred communist totalitarianism; their ideals and standards were similar, as were their goals and points of focus. In the course of their fourteen subsequent encounters the two statesmen developed a rare and highly constructive relationship of trust.

When Stalin died on March 5, 1953, the world held its breath. Stalin had exerted immense power; he was unpredictable, and feared. Would another individual in the Kremlin now assume the same absolute power? This turned out not to be the case; several men took power jointly. It was a reassuring development, but no reason to lower one's guard. Certainly not in the Federal Republic, which shared a border with the gigantic and unfathomable Soviet empire. Regardless of the shift in power in Moscow, the Federal Republic's ties to the West remained a priority. To Adenauer, continuity and dependability were the basis for true trust.

During his first visit to the United States, in April 1953, Adenauer did everything in his power to strengthen the bonds between Germans and Americans, and to make them more dependable and

On the first visit by a U.S. president to the Federal Republic, Adenauer receives Dwight D. Eisenhower at the Wahn Airport in July 1959. Behind them stands Adolf Heusinger, chief of the German armed forces.

In conversation with U.S. secretary of state John Foster Dulles in September 1954.

cordial. In his speeches and conversations he expressed gratitude to
Americans for the assistance they had provided since 1945, and conveyed his appreciation of that rare moment in history when a vastly
superior victor generously offers the vanquished a helping hand.
There was continuing consensus between the two governments on
concrete political and economic issues, and an agreement to work
together more closely in the future. Adenauer's visit was a great success, with numerous important encounters and a remarkable public
response.

The high point of Adenauer's trip was his visit to Arlington
National Cemetery. As he laid a wreath at the Tomb of the Unknown
Soldier for those who had fallen on both sides, the German national
anthem sounded and the German flag was given a military salute.
Adenauer, as he reported, was deeply moved. At that moment it was
as if those German soldiers who had fallen in the war had been given
back their honor by a world that had reviled them. "It was a long
and hard path from total collapse in 1945 to this moment in 1953,"
he said, viewing his visit to America as "a major step for a defeated
people on the path to the community of nations."

For nations as for individuals, life does not stand still even in the
happiest of moments. More and more refugees from the German
Democratic Republic continued to pour into the Federal Republic.
Fifty-eight thousand arrived in March of 1953 alone, in all likelihood
due to the power shift in Moscow. The assumption that the iron fist of
the Soviet Union had relaxed a bit might also have been what spurred
workers in East Berlin to take to the streets on June 17, 1953, to
protest a rise in production quotas. Protests against the ruling Socialist Unity Party of Germany (*Sozialistische Einheitspartei Deutschlands*, SED) spread like wildfire throughout East Germany, sparking
a people's revolt that was contained only with the use of Russian
tanks on the streets of East Berlin. With such draconian measures,
Moscow and the East German regime suppressed the revolt and
reestablished control. The world learned that the new regime was
determined to uphold the old system, with force and terror if need be.

The uprising of June 17 deeply moved the population of the Federal Republic. Many had relatives and friends in the East for whom
they feared. More than ever, West Germans were aware of how much
better off they were, of the value of personal and economic freedom,
of the meaning of human rights and true democracy, and of how fortunate they were to be with the West. This perception surely strength-

ened support for Adenauer's policies in the coming *Bundestag* (federal parliament) elections. And a number of new laws and measures, such as those on expellees, the Federal Law on Pensions to War Victims, and laws on the procurement of work and on unemployment had a similar effect. Between 1950 and 1953 the gross national product rose from 98 billion to 152.5 billion Deutsche Mark. Unemployment fell from 8.2 percent to 5.5 percent, despite the integration of millions of refugees into the national economy.

The second *Bundestag* elections took place on September 6, 1953, with 86 percent of eligible voters turning out at the polls. The two Christian Union parties received 45.2 percent of the vote, the Social Democrats 29 percent, the Free Democrats 9.5 percent, and the nine other parties (of which only three won seats) 16.5 percent.[26]

The second *Bundestag* convened on October 6, 1953, and the next day Konrad Adenauer was reelected federal chancellor with 304 votes; 148 were against, and there were 14 abstentions.[27] This was a great victory—the extent of it surprised even Adenauer. Any other man might have let this go to his head.

Adenauer was aware of his gifts, his abilities, and his importance. But he did not overestimate himself; indeed, he seemed almost unnaturally immune to an inflated view of himself. This was due to his sober outlook on life and to his long personal experience. The two major setbacks in his life, the loss of two wives, had taught him that "bitter experience forms the man." He often said this to console those who had been hard hit.

In terms of self-assurance, there were two maxims he followed. "One should constantly test oneself," he said repeatedly, "but never doubt oneself, neither one's own abilities nor one's own worth. Even in the worst of situations, one should maintain one's self-respect." That was one side; the other cautioned against inflated self-importance. Adenauer had no missionary pretensions of having been personally chosen. But he was aware of his great gifts, and he had a great sense of responsibility. He believed "one must do one's best to see that the future is more tranquil, more balanced, and more peaceful," so that "others may have a greater opportunity for happiness." In one campaign speech he stated, "I have the hope that someday, when people look out beyond the fog and dust of our time, they will say of me that I did my duty." Adenauer called his sense of duty his highest law. And so he began his second term as chancellor.

President of the Federal Republic Theodor Heuss receives Adenauer's second cabinet on October 20, 1953. First row, from left: Hermann Schäfer, Jakob Kaiser, Anton Storch, Heuss, Adenauer, Gerhard Schröder, Waldemar Kraft. Second row, from left: Heinrich Lübke, Heinz-Peter Hellwege, Theodor Oberländer, Victor Emanuel Preusker, Ludwig Erhard, Robert Tillmans. Third row, from left: Franz-Josef Würmeling, Hans-Christoph Seebohm, Fritz Neumayer, Franz Josef Strauss, Fritz Schäffer.

Immediately after reelection he declared, "We shall continue on the path we have cleared, which has proved to be right. We want peace; we want the reunification of Germany; we want Europe, and we want to be equal among the nations of the free world." In his statement of government policy of October 20 he announced a comprehensive social-political program, and declared that Germans would never accept the division of their country.

On February 26, 1954, 334 members of the *Bundestag* voted in favor of a constitutional amendment (with 144 SPD votes against) of Article 73 establishing the Federal Republic's military sovereignty. This was followed by a more tranquil period in domestic policy. The great battles of the *Bundestag* had been fought and Adenauer, to a great extent, had been able to exert his ideas.

But there was trouble ahead on the foreign policy front. It had long been doubtful whether the French parliament would ratify the European Defense Community Treaty. On August 30, 1954, the situation took a serious turn. Following impassioned debate, the French National Assembly voted against ratification by a vote of 319 to 264, with twelve abstentions. This came as a great shock, and Adenauer referred to it as the bitterest disappointment of his time in office—a tragedy, a crisis, a heavy setback for Europe. The goal of the treaty, he added, was correct, and remained so, and must continue to be pursued. The consolidation of Europe was not only a matter of the heart but of reason as well, particularly to the Germans.

One day later, Secretary of State Dulles declared that the Federal Republic of Germany could no longer be denied the right to individual and collective defense. On September 12 and 13, 1954, British foreign minister Eden came to Bonn to seek a resolution to the crisis. Dulles followed four days later. These talks resulted in the foreign ministers of the six EDC countries plus those of the U.S., Great Britain, and Canada meeting in London for a "Nine Powers Conference." It was at this meeting that Adenauer uttered his famous off-the-cuff remark after declaring that Germany would never produce and use nuclear, biological, or chemical weapons: "*rebus sic stantibus*" (as long as the situation remains the same).

The discussions held in London were epoch-making, but the final agreements came later, at the Paris conference of October 20 to 23, 1954, where the three Western powers and the Federal Republic signed a series of agreements known as the Paris Treaties. They established a West European Union (WEU) and accepted the Federal Republic into NATO. Bonn and Paris finally agreed on the Saar Treaty, which was to be voted on by the Saarlanders themselves.

Adenauer could be well satisfied with all of this. While it was true that the ratification of the original EDC Treaty would have led to consolidation in Europe, its acceptance was impossible in the face of opposition from such an important partner as France.

The degree of trust that developed between the Western democracies and the Federal Republic—the Germany the West had viewed with such distrust—within the first five years of its existence is astounding. This above all was due to the policies and personality of Konrad Adenauer, a man who had succeeded in establishing positive, even cordial relations with many leading politicians and statesmen, a fact that cannot be overstated. The list includes a Who's Who of world leaders: Winston Churchill and his successor Anthony Eden; Charles de Gaulle; the French foreign secretaries Robert Schuman and Antoine Pinay; the influential Jean Monnet, general secretary of the European Coal and Steel Community; Paul Henri Spaak, as Belgian foreign minister and NATO general secretary, a tireless advocate of European unity; foreign ministers Dirk Kipko Stikker from the Netherlands and Halvard Lange from Norway; the Italian statesman Alcide De Gasperi; the president of the Jewish World Congress Nahum Goldman; Pakistan's president Ayub Khan and Israel's "Grand Old Man," David Ben-Gurion; Shigeru Yoshida, who at the same time piloted Japan, the other country defeated in World War II and subsequently occupied, through rough currents, into the Western mainstream; Pope Pius XII, Dwight D. Eisenhower, John Foster Dulles and the American High Commissioners Lucius D. Clay and John J. McCloy.

"To earn respect," Adenauer said, "one must be a reliable and dependable partner—To be a friend, one must agree on political principles and ethical conviction, openly and honestly—and not disappoint one another!"

Adenauer was fortunate to encounter such men. Still, much effort went into maintaining strong relations with them. Few statesmen kept up the active correspondence that Adenauer did. He was attentive to those he dealt with and valued frequent meetings, for which he carefully prepared. His friendships with the above-named individuals benefitted all Germans.

On February 27, 1955, the *Bundestag* passed the Paris Treaties by an overwhelming majority, and on May 5, 1955, the three High Commissioners declared the occupation ended. Ten years after the total defeat of Germany, the Federal Republic was declared a sovereign state. Due to partisan differences, a formal proclamation of the event could not be made in the parliament. Instead, Adenauer had the German flag raised ceremoniously at the Federal Chancellor's Office. With deep satisfaction he declared that "we now stand as free human beings among free human beings, bound in true partnership to the former occupying powers." To the East Germans he declared, "You

Adenauer received Jawaharlal Nehru, prime minister of India, at the Schaumburg Palace in July 1956.

Meeting with Israeli prime minister David Ben-Gurion at the Waldorf-Astoria Hotel in New York, March 1960.

belong to us! We belong to you! . . . Together with the free world we will not rest until you, too, are granted human rights and may live peacefully with us, united as one nation." He also promised to do everything in his power to see that all German prisoners of war were released from captivity.

In Paris, on Monday, May 9, 1955, West Germany was formally admitted to NATO. It was the last major event that Adenauer would attend as both chancellor and foreign minister. On June 7 Heinrich von Brentano was named foreign minister.

On September 8, 1955, Adenauer, accompanied by a large delegation, left for Moscow in response to an invitation by the Soviet leadership. There are a number of colorful reports on this memorable six-day visit. The Germans and the Soviets occasionally clashed in their points of view: "You cannot equate Hitler and his followers with the German people!" Adenauer responded to Soviet attacks. When Nikita S. Khrushchev, the new head of the Soviet Communist Party, sharply criticized German war crimes, Adenauer countered with the wrongs that the Soviet army had committed when they marched into Germany. When Khrushchev shook his fists at the chancellor, Adenauer returned the gesture. When Molotov asserted that it was the German people who were responsible for the war because they had brought Hitler to power, Adenauer shot back, "Who signed the 1939 agreement with Ribbentrop? You or I?" Adenauer simply deflected ideological slurs. "I am not going to convert you and you are not going to convert me. Nor should we undertake to do so!"

In private the Soviet leadership respected Adenauer for laying his cards on the table and not being afraid to openly state his opinion. And a more peaceful discussion did take place at the dacha Adenauer was staying at outside Moscow. Adenauer's conciliatory handshake with Nikolai Bulganin[28] at the Bolshoi Theater was greeted with prolonged applause, but the next day their disagreements reached the point where Adenauer felt further negotiation to be inappropriate and futile, and scheduled German planes to take his entourage back to Bonn ahead of schedule. That evening, however, he appeared at the reception given by the Soviets, which he felt he could not politely fail to attend. And it was at this reception that the tide turned: Bulganin gave his word of honor that all German prisoners of war would be returned in exchange for the resumption of diplomatic relations between Moscow and Bonn.

This led to strong differences of opinion within the German delegation. Foreign Minister von Brentano feared that resumption of diplomatic relations would signify recognition of the Oder-Neisse Line[29] and of East Germany as a sovereign state. He did not feel that Bulganin's word alone was a sufficient basis for action. But Adenauer stood by his decision. To counter von Brentano's fears, he wrote a letter to Bulganin concerning the former German territories now under Soviet control, and "our right to sole representation." The deciding factor for Adenauer had been the promise of the return home of those Germans who had suffered so terribly in captivity.

On October 7, 1955, the last transport carrying ten thousand German prisoners-of-war landed in Camp Friedland. No one who was present, or who experienced it through the media, could forget the crowd singing *"Nun danket alle Gott. . . ."*[30] Many Germans today still consider the return of German prisoners of war to be one of Adenauer's greatest achievements.

On October 23, 1955, 67.7 percent of the population of the Saar voted to reject the Saar Statute with its prolonged timetable for restoration to Germany. At the end of January 1956, its Parliament voted for the Saar to become part of the Federal Republic.

When Adenauer turned eighty years old on January 5, 1956, his birthday was celebrated in great style for two days. The thousands of birthday wishes that poured in from both inside and outside the country were evidence of the respect Adenauer had earned, but they also demonstrated just how important the Federal Republic had become.

The celebration ended and the lively business of politics resumed. In the course of 1955 tensions had increased between Thomas Dehler[31] and elements within his Free Democratic Party on the one side, and Adenauer and the CDU/CSU on the other. Dehler was critical of Adenauer's handling of the Saar question, and of his policies on Germany and Europe. He supported a more flexible policy toward the East, and several FDP members advocated withdrawal from NATO. Such statements caused both East and West to call into question the Federal Republic's straightforwardness concerning its policies. Adenauer demanded total support from the FDP, his coalition partner, on governmental policies.

The crisis came to a head on February 25, when the FDP withdrew from the coalition. It joined the opposition one month later. Both sides were at fault; both had reacted rashly. But to Adenauer it was imperative that the federal government follow a clear and unmistakable course. Before the year was over it became clear how important this was.

The elections of January 1956, which brought socialist Guy Mollet to power in France, raised doubts about that nation's future policies.[32] Meanwhile, the increasing effects of unrest in Algeria threatened France's internal stability. But even more worthy of close attention from Adenauer's perspective was the Twentieth Party Congress of the Soviet Communist Party, the "de-Stalinization" congress which met from February 14 to 25, 1956, in Moscow. The Soviet leadership accused Stalin posthumously of gross political miscalculations and of diverging from the doctrines of Lenin. It criticized the terror of the purges and the cult surrounding Stalin's person. The toppling of an idol, this posthumous condemnation of Stalin behind which the hand of Khrushchev became ever more visible, came as a powerful shock to the Soviet Union, and sent a tremor through communist parties and regimes throughout the world.

The West, too, found these disclosures extraordinary. Indeed, they caused renewed optimism in many circles. But Adenauer remained skeptical about the new rulers in the Kremlin—he had dealt with them, after all. They, like their predecessors, were working for the victory of international communism. Their methods might be more flexible, but their goals remained the same. Adenauer knew human nature, and the experiences of his long life had only made his vision sharper. "If one goes through life with one's eyes open," he said, "then there is no substitute for experience, neither science nor education nor native intelligence. . . ." At this time in Europe, there was no other politician with as much experience as Adenauer. Nor were there many who possessed his honesty of vision.

When Bulganin and Khrushchev were received in London at the end of April, many feared a "friendlier" Kremlin might lull the West into a false sense of security. In mid-May French prime minister Guy Mollet traveled to Moscow. The highly regarded U.S. diplomat George F. Kennan[33] argued that now was the time for the two blocks in Europe to move apart, to be separated geographically. There were others who similarly called for a zone of detente in the middle of Europe which might perhaps lead to the reunification of Germany—a Germany which of course would remain neutral. But Adenauer held to his view that a neutral Germany would undermine the freedom and security of the Federal Republic and weaken the position of the West. Whenever possible, he opposed plans for appeasement.

With presidential elections approaching in the U.S., Eisenhower also issued several statements that could have impacted adversely on West Germany. But Dulles sided with the Federal Republic, taking

the risk that his opinions would be perceived as contradicting Eisenhower. "Neutrality is an outdated issue," he said. "In order to protect
the free world from communism the system of collective security,
based in military alliances, must be further reinforced." It is not surprising that this strengthened the bond of friendship between Adenauer and Dulles. "Based on my activities, which have brought me
together with a great many people," Adenauer once wrote, "I have
learned to judge people well, inasmuch as that is possible. I valued
Dulles greatly. We became close friends." And on a hurried visit to
the United States from June 8 to 15 designed to deflect a potential
political catastrophe, Adenauer vehemently defended Dulles, who
was under heavy fire himself, and ceaselessly pleaded the case for the
free nations sticking together.

Adenauer returned to Bonn somewhat reassured. On July 6 and
7, to reinforce the barrier against Communism from the German side,
he, arch-civilian that he was, introduced universal conscription, preceded by a long and impassioned debate in the *Bundestag.*

Meanwhile, other trouble spots flared up. In Cypress, the Greeks
and Turks remained intransigent despite British attempts to mediate
their conflict. Situations in the Suez and Hungary had become critical. The countries of Eastern Europe had reacted to the Soviet leadership's renunciation of Stalin with demands for more autonomy. In
Poland, Wladyslaw Gomulka, the former head of the Communist
Party who had fallen out of grace with Stalin, was rehabilitated. He
was and remained a communist, but he was also a Pole who thought
along national lines. He replaced Soviet-influenced officials with men
who held views similar to his own, halted the collectivization of agriculture, and reinstated dissident Cardinal Stefan Wyszynski. Though
Moscow was furious, it did not attack Gomulka directly, as he was
not outspokenly anti-Russian, but offered continued cooperation with
Moscow instead.

In Hungary things took a different turn. The mood there was not
only nationalistic, but also anti-Russian and anti-communist. The
leaders of this movement were intellectuals for the most part, and
massive student demonstrations on October 23 led to open revolt. As
had happened three years earlier in East Berlin, Soviet tanks now
rolled into Budapest and other cities to square off against the population. But the Hungarian army joined the demonstrators and forced
back the Soviets, and by the end of October 1956, parts of Hungary
had been liberated. The Hungarians had counted on the support
of the United States, but America had its hands full with the situation

at the Suez Canal. The Soviet Union returned to Hungary with reinforcements and the revolt was suppressed in a bloody confrontation. By the end of November the country was once again under Soviet control.

The Suez crisis arose in the summer of 1956, when Egypt swept aside the vested rights of Great Britain in the Canal Zone and tried to drive the British out. Egypt was backed in this by the Soviet Union, which placed massive arms at its disposal. The Canal was vital to Britain's economic and military interests, and France sided with Britain because of Egypt's role in inciting the Algerian revolt. Both Britain and France found a natural ally in Israel, struggling against its neighbors. Circumstances converged to bring fighting at the Suez Canal.

It was suggested that London and Paris had lent Israel encouragement in order to justify their own intervention. Military errors were made. But, most important of all, Britain, France, and Israel committed the political error of acting on their own without first informing the United States. The United Nations condemned the Israeli-British-French attack, and Moscow threatened to intervene with all military means, including nuclear arms. The U.S.S.R. had already sent so many weapons to the region that all it needed to establish military bases there was to fly in Russian soldiers—right into the middle of a major oil region on the Mediterranean. The situation was critical, and the British and French had no choice but to withdraw their troops.

"It is a tragic chapter in history," Adenauer wrote, "that at the same moment an Eastern European nation was carrying on an incredibly courageous battle for its freedom, events in the Near East allowed the Soviet Union to silence the voice of freedom mercilessly, with tanks and machine guns." It was tragic as well for Dulles, who so desired autonomy for Eastern Europe, and who was forced to look on as Hungarian freedom fighters went down in defeat. And at the same time he had to restrain Israel and two long-standing allies of the United States. Many were of the opinion that the fatal illness to which Dulles succumbed two years later had its beginnings in this agonizing situation.

The American presidential election was held on November 6, 1956, and Eisenhower was reelected. This meant that Dulles would continue as secretary of state, an enormous relief to Adenauer. He could now concentrate on the completion of two major projects—a progressive pension plan and the European Economic Community

(EEC), or Common Market. It is well-known how highly Adenauer valued foreign policy. Less well-known is the fact that he considered domestic policy to be equally important. Witness the millions of jobs created during his term in office, the housing construction, the establishment of the government and administration, the Codetermination and the Equalization of Burdens Laws, the aid to families, and now, the pension plan.

Adenauer had been influenced by the ideas of Wilfrid Schreiber,[34] who wanted an old-age pension plan based not on compulsory savings, the only alternative discussed up to that point, but on a generational contract, an entirely new concept. Pension payments were to be adjusted to prevailing wages and salaries. Adenauer supported this idea, but almost everyone else opposed it: the FDP and the DP rejected it categorically, and academic, economic, and trade union circles attacked it as well. Even the majority of the CDU/CSU argued that over the long run the cost of such a plan would become prohibitive. But Adenauer wouldn't let go of the idea, and supported its basic premise of true solidarity.

There is no doubt that without Adenauer there would have been no progressive pension plan. The *Bundestag* approved such a measure by an overwhelming majority on January 21, 1957. Polls have indicated that no previous official act, constitutional measure, law, or symbol of state was received with more appreciation by the populace.

Two months later Adenauer celebrated another success equally important to his nation's future: the signing of the treaties that established the European Economic Community (EEC) and the European Atomic Energy Community (EURATOM). The basic concepts of these treaties had been worked out in the summer of 1955 at the conference of foreign ministers in Messina. Adenauer was hesitant at first because he feared that many Europeans would be satisfied with economic regulations and no longer push for the political unification of Europe. But "one should not refrain from doing what is good," he said, "just because one wants to do what is better."

These two treaties caused great debate in all participating countries, including the Federal Republic. The Ministry of Economics championed international free trade and feared any form of central control. But Adenauer urged passage. He was apprehensive about the future attitude of the United States, but he saw the future as, above all, residing in Europe. The final, arduous negotiations took place in Paris on February 19 and 20, 1957. Both treaties were signed in Rome on March 25. They would be known collectively as the Rome

Treaty. "It is very difficult to make political pronouncements when everything is in flux," Adenauer said. "But this agreement is perhaps the most significant event of the postwar era." And then he added something that took on particular weight because it was uttered by such a rational man: "In politics, one must indeed sometimes have visions."

The fulfillment of this particular vision has become a main current in the lives of 340 million Europeans. Its impact extends to many parts of the globe. Many European thinkers and statesmen worked together to plan and shape it. But although it was not Adenauer's vision alone, without him the EEC in its present form would not have existed.

The Great Victory

The progressive pension plan and the Rome Treaty were remarkable achievements, perhaps more than enough for one year. But Adenauer was directly involved in the many things that occurred in 1957. When it was suggested he delegate more responsibility in order to preserve his strength, he answered, "It's all right, I enjoy taking care of the details!" Once the larger issues were resolved he tended to the smaller, for they held his interest as well; he kept his eye on everything. Other men take walks or hold discussions to stimulate their thinking; Adenauer needed no such thing. He utilized every minute—in his automobile, while he was eating, and even as he rested—drawing parallels, conceptualizing, making connections, and then starting again from another direction. He inundated colleagues with questions and plans, but worse, the questions and plans inundated him, intruding upon his few precious hours of sleep.

"A statesman must be pessimistic, he must see the dangers that are everywhere present," he said. As level-headed as Adenauer was, his outlook nevertheless was often dismal before major conferences. He sometimes would abruptly break off final internal discussions held before these conferences with: "The negotiations will fail!" He then would once again immerse himself in the issues, thinking through all eventualities. These waves of apprehension that came over him were to some degree a trick he played on himself, designed to mobilize his last reserves of acumen and imagination. Suitably energized, Adenauer would enter the conference and, as often as not, perform brilliantly. Those who knew him understood that the conferences he was particularly troubled by were precisely those he succeeded best at.

He was old in years, but not in spirit. He did not spend time reminiscing, and always came right to the point. He lived in the here and now, he was concise and worked almost without interruption. He did his "homework" as few other politicians, and appeared at meetings well-prepared. His detailed knowledge gave him an advantage at most conferences. Adenauer never appeared to be driven, but he often processed files practically before they landed on his desk. Every evening he would take home with him to Rhöndorf a briefcase full of files, and work on them until late in the night or early the next morning. But now he no longer needed to resort to the cold water tricks which kept him awake as a student. Even on vacation he accomplished more than most politicians during their working hours. He governed from wherever he was. His energy appeared inexhaustible. There were many hard workers in the chancellor's office, but none who matched him.

In the summer of 1957, Adenauer's energy was applied once again to the question of German unity. On July 29, Foreign Minister von Brentano and his British, French, and American counterparts signed the "Berlin Proclamation,"[35] reaffirming their commitment to reunification.

The election campaign was beginning. The Social Democrats, who did not object to a neutral Germany, promised to rescind compulsory military service, stop German participation in nuclear defense, and even prohibit the placement of American and British nuclear weapons on German soil. Adenauer kept repeating his warning that "our freedom and security are greatly jeopardized by such measures." They were, he said, an invitation to the Soviet Union to extend its sphere of influence to the West. As opposed to the fears of many others, Adenauer said, he himself believed that another great war was avoidable, but only if the West was in agreement on the issue and stood united, and only—and this was the *ceterum censeo* of his speeches—"if we make the necessary contribution as well."

Adenauer hoped to convince the West Germans of these views, despite vociferous opposition. He also hoped the public would recognize what his government had achieved. Over the four years preceding, the gross national product had jumped from 152 to 225 billion

Deutsche Mark, and per capita income had risen from 2300 to 3300 Deutsche Mark annually. Unemployment had dropped from 5.5 percent to a remarkable 1.9 percent.

On September 15, 1957, 87.7 percent of all eligible voters went to the polls. When the votes were counted, 50.2 percent had voted for the CDU/CSU, 31.8 percent for the SPD, and 7.7 percent for the FDP, with the smaller parties sharing 10.3 percent of the vote. It was a tremendous victory for the Union parties. To the present day it remains the sole *Bundestag* election in which one party won an absolute majority. (In his own election district, Adenauer won an absolute majority three consecutive times.) Adenauer was happy that "the stability of foreign policy is guaranteed for the next four years," and he was glad, as he wrote, "that this time the Union was voted in by a large number of workers, particularly the young."

It took Adenauer more than seven weeks to appoint his third cabinet, an unexpectedly long time in view of his decisive victory. His second cabinet, which continued to serve during this interim, was faced with a new crisis when, on October 15, Yugoslavia established diplomatic relations with the GDR (East Germany). The world anxiously awaited West Germany's response. Would the federal government break off relations with Belgrade, as the prevailing Hallstein Doctrine[36] stipulated? Or would a less drastic solution be found? A number of powerful German politicians called for the latter. Von Brentano and a majority in the Union parties, however, demanded a break in relations, designed to prevent a chain reaction occurring in roughly thirty other countries that might follow Yugoslavia's lead.

Adenauer adopted von Brentano's position. He thought that a tough stance would reassure the West, which had been caught off guard by the Soviets' imposing armaments build-up. The Soviet Union had possessed the atomic bomb since 1949, and the hydrogen bomb since 1953, but the United States had always maintained the lead in both the development and number of weapons. Then, on October 4, 1957, the Soviet Union's first Sputnik orbited the earth, revealing that the U.S.S.R. had gained the lead in rocket technology. This became even more obvious when Sputnik II was launched one month later. Substantially heavier than its predecessor, this space capsule also carried a living creature—a dog named Laika.

The government's decision to break off diplomatic relations with Belgrade was greeted by the free world with understanding and approval, and may have had a stabilizing effect on the West. It became a cornerstone of Bonn's Germany policy: the claim to sole representation remained unchallenged until 1962, and as evidenced by a similar governmental reaction against Cuba, it continued in effect during the Great Coalition.

On October 22, 1957, Adenauer was again reelected federal chancellor and his cabinet, consisting solely of members of the CDU/CSU and the DP, was sworn in one week later. Domestic and foreign policy continued on its set course. But Soviet military strength was growing.

Federal President Theodor Heuss receives Adenauer's third cabinet on October 28, 1957. First row from left: Heinrich von Brentano, Adenauer, Heuss, Gerhard Schröder. Second row from left: Theodor Oberländer, Richard Stücklen, Heinrich Lübke, Ludwig Erhard (partially concealed), Franz Etzel, Fritz Schäffer. Third row from left: Siegfried Balke, Paul Lücke (behind him), Hermann Lindrath, Ernst Lemmer, Theodor Blank, Franz-Josef Würmeling, Franz Josef Strauss (in front), Hans-Christoph Seebohm.

Pressure from the East was escalating, and, with it, the West's willingness to compromise.

In December the second Rapacki Plan (devised by Gromyko) was introduced, proposing a nuclear-free zone in Germany. From the U.S. came renewed suggestions of Western disengagement. The Soviets suggested a confederation of the two German states. There was strident discussion in Germany about which was more important—reunification or secure freedom for the Federal Republic.

Adenauer's response was succinct: "We can concentrate on the liberation of the seventeen million (Germans) living behind the Iron Curtain only when we have secured the freedom of the fifty-two million (living in the Federal Republic)." Leading Union politicians shared this opinion. But they too knew that remonstration was not enough; they had to come up with concrete suggestions for easing the tension between East and West.

On March 19, 1958, Adenauer surprised the Soviet ambassador by asking whether Moscow was prepared to grant the Soviet-occupied zone the same status as it did Austria. For Adenauer the issue was obtaining for East Germans the right of self-determination, and an improvement in their living conditions, even if this meant the postponement of reunification. Adenauer's suggestion irritated the Soviets. They never responded.

On March 27 Bulganin was removed from office. Khrushchev, then secretary general of the Soviet Communist Party, became premier as well. This put Khrushchev in a position of power comparable to Stalin's, a fact closely noted by Bonn. Soon it became clear that the Kremlin's new leader would not hesitate to exert pressure and force to achieve his goals.

France, at the same time, was seriously shaken by crisis. The war in Algeria weighed heavily upon the country, sending many of its young men to their deaths, and splitting the heart and soul of the population. When it became increasingly clear that France would have to give up Algeria, French officers there staged a coup d'etat on May 13, 1958. The situation could not be contained, and those in power soon concluded that only de Gaulle could save France. On June 1, 1958, de Gaulle was named prime minister.

Adenauer was not pleased by this; he had considerable reservations concerning de Gaulle. The general was known to oppose NATO and European integration, and Adenauer feared that de Gaulle would soon establish closer ties with Moscow. But the chancellor had to meet with the new prime minister, and following cautious inquiries it was decided the meeting should take place on September 14 and 15, at de Gaulle's country estate.

The two men met in private. Both elaborated their opinions on major policy questions, and on their own concrete plans for the future. In the process they became acquainted with each other as individuals and as politicians. Adenauer was eighty-two years old, and de Gaulle sixty-seven. Both had served their countries in extraordinary fashion; both had gained respect and come to power at an early age; and both had suffered crushing defeat and spent twelve years removed from public life. Both were practicing Christians, placed a high value on the individual, rejected totalitarianism, and honored the spiritual above the material.

It would not be an overstatement to call this an historic encounter. The first Adenauer–de Gaulle meeting became the basis for Franco-German reconciliation and cooperation.

Only ten weeks later, on November 26, 1958, de Gaulle visited Adenauer at Bad Kreuznach. This time large delegations represented both sides, and the political dialogue covered a broad spectrum. De Gaulle declared his support for Europe, and of particular significance was the exchange of ideas on the approach to the Soviet Union. On November 10, Khrushchev had demanded that the Western powers renounce their right to occupy Berlin and withdraw their troops immediately. The West rejected this, but felt that Khrushchev's demand had merely signaled the beginning of a serious attack on the West's position. Indeed, on November 27, the day after the meeting in Kreuznach ended, the Soviet Union called for the three major Western powers to agree within the next six months to a new status for Berlin, that of a free and demilitarized city. If this did not occur, the Soviet Union would enter into a separate peace with the German Democratic Republic and transfer the Soviet right to Berlin to the GDR.

This, as Adenauer wrote, plunged the world's barometer to a level seldom before seen. Many in the West feared a recurrence of the Berlin Blockade, or worse. Clearly the situation was critical. Adenauer believed the West should prepare for a long battle and remain calm. Not succumbing to fear of Khrushchev, it must hold and defend its own position, united. He warned against entering into a new agreement with Moscow out of a desire for security. The Soviet Union had broken ten of the eleven non-aggression pacts it had concluded since 1925, four of them after 1945. Of the six peace treaties it had signed following 1946, it had already broken three.

On January 10, 1959, Moscow offered yet another peace treaty, this time between all the countries that had fought against Germany on the one side, and the two German states on the other. It called for the Federal Republic to withdraw from NATO and from the European Community, and for both German states to be declared neutral and put under supervision. The three Western powers and the Federal Republic rejected the proposal.

Dulles spent February 7 and 8 in Bonn, following conferences in Paris and London. He was of Adenauer's opinion that "once you begin to make concessions to the Soviets because they have threatened war, they will continue with their threats and the West will be forced to make one concession after another." Adenauer was shocked when he greeted Dulles at the airport, for Dulles looked very ill. Indeed, he was already suffering from cancer, but would find this out only after his return to the United States. He died on May 24, 1959. Adenauer attended his funeral in Washington. He had lost a close friend, one who had done much for freedom and for Germany.

Dulles' death influenced a major decision Adenauer was called upon to make around that time—whether he would agree to become federal president. Much has been written on the presidential crisis of 1959. There were many who preferred Ludwig Erhard for the position, but he withdrew his name in March. The question was eventually posed to Adenauer, who began to look more closely at the president's powers. Perhaps he thought he might be offered a position similar to that which de Gaulle had recently occupied under the new French constitution. He also may have hoped that he could take it a bit easier after ten years of exceptional service to his country; he was now eighty-four years old, after all. Opinions on the state of his health at that point varied. Hans Globke, his chief of staff, confirmed that in 1959 Adenauer went through a period of fatigue and exhaustion as never before and never since.

Nevertheless, at the beginning of April Adenauer announced his availability as a candidate. He believed he could determine who then would succeed him as chancellor; he preferred Franz Etzel[37] and under no circumstances wanted the position to go to Economy Minister and Vice Chancellor Ludwig Erhard. But leading members of the CDU/CSU and of the parliamentary caucus were insisting on Erhard. Adenauer was not sure his choice would prevail and he considered withdrawing his name as candidate for president. On top of which there were foreign policy concerns to attend to. British prime minister

Harold Macmillan had gone to Moscow at the end of February, and while there had declared support of many things which would have proven disadvantageous to the Germans. And the SPD's Germany Plan[38] for a demilitarized Central Europe was evidence that the opposition had not distanced itself from what, in Adenauer's eyes, were quite dangerous ideas.

Dulles' death was the deciding factor. "As practically no one else, Dulles recognized the danger that Bolshevism posed to the free world," Adenauer wrote. He feared that Eisenhower and his new secretary of state, Christian Herter, might soften their positions. Was it then advisable that he himself withdraw from the front lines? He decided not to and so, out of a sense of responsibility—"for reasons of conscience," as he put it—he withdrew his name as a presidential candidate on June 5.

He believed that the German people would not resent this change of mind and he was correct, as an Allensbach poll showed. But many leading politicians and above all journalists, the opinion makers, were irate—some extremely so. And not a few members of Adenauer's faction complained that once again they had been forced to yield to Adenauer's iron will. One can only imagine the indignation of Erhard and his "brigade"; "undemocratic" and "cynical powermonger" were words that were bandied about.

Were these critical assessments totally unjustified? Adenauer considered himself a good judge of human nature, and he was. But his treatment of people was not always positive. It is true that he enjoyed good, even cordial relationships with a number of foreign statesmen. But his attitude toward those he governed could be hard and unyielding, nowhere more so than with members of his own party. He demanded a great deal of them, and the closer they were to him, the more he demanded. Most of the time they received the velvet-glove treatment, but it concealed an iron fist. He was quite intent on being master of the house and head of the Federal Republic. His strong personality, monumental energy, superior intelligence, and enormous resolve made him an imposing figure. But Adenauer was capable not only of drawing people to him, but of pushing them away, at times quite pointedly. He was particularly hard on rivals and presumptive successors. He "let them have it" now and then to keep them at a distance. Anyone who made difficulties, deviated from the path, or went so far as to conspire against him was quickly brought back into line.

Adenauer had a strong attachment to nature, to painting and music, to family and a few close acquaintances—but he kept all of that quite separate from politics and governing. "My experience with people has made me hard," he said occasionally. He was not good-natured. He was closest to those who worked hard, were loyal, and devoted themselves to the cause, and he seldom slighted them. But even with them he could be severe, and the sensitive among them were slow to recover. Adenauer knew his harshness was unwise, but at times he simply could not control himself. He had a sharp tongue, and was sometimes inclined to coldness and insult. In matters of import, his decency prevailed.

Adenauer acted in good faith at crucial moments. He could have accomplished even more had he made more of an effort with others; his weakness in this area eventually contributed to his downfall. But it had not yet come to that in 1959. He told his most vehement critics that if they wished to get rid of him they could call for a vote of no-confidence in the *Bundestag*. And with this, the federal-presidency controversy was over. But Adenauer had made enemies, who were only waiting for the moment when they could strike back at him.

Adenauer remained chancellor, and welcomed Eisenhower to Bonn on August 25. The U.S. president declared that the issue of the division of Germany should be resolved according to the wishes of the German people, and he renewed his promise to protect the freedom and welfare of Berlin. The mutual communique issued after this meeting affirmed that the collaboration between the two countries within the Atlantic Alliance was the cornerstone of their respective foreign policies.

On August 31, 1959, the twentieth anniversary of Nazi Germany's attack on Poland, Adenauer declared that the Federal Republic wanted friendly relations with that country; this overture led to the eventual establishment of mutual trade missions in March of 1963.

On November 15 the SPD approved by overwhelming majority their Godesberg Program,[39] in which they clearly distanced themselves from Marxist theories of class struggle. Seven months later the SPD announced that it was prepared to support the underlying principles of the federal government's foreign policy. Could there have been any greater confirmation that Adenauer's policies had been wise?

A summit conference between the three Western powers and the Soviet Union was scheduled in Paris on May 17 and 18, 1960. Many in the West, Adenauer wrote, expected miracles of this conference; others, like himself, were inclined to be apprehensive. Preliminary talks were arranged for May 15 and 16, to be attended by Eisenhower, de Gaulle, Macmillan, and Adenauer. Adenauer flew to Paris on May 14. During his visits to London and Washington that April, de Gaulle had resolutely supported German interests. He and Adenauer agreed that the West must stand firm. "To make concessions in Berlin is, to me, the same as unleashing the demons of crisis," de Gaulle commented to Eisenhower and Macmillan during the preliminary talks. He had no desire, he said, to wake up one morning and hear that the Russians were at the Rhine.

But the summit conference took an unexpected turn: Khrushchev demanded an apology from Eisenhower for sending aircraft over Soviet territory to spy on the Russians (a U-2 plane operating at high altitude had been shot down over Sverdlovsk on May 1). Eisenhower refused, and that was the end of the conference. Adenauer was greatly relieved, for he had found what Eisenhower and Macmillan said during the preliminary talks to be "very vague." But his private discussions with de Gaulle had made him hopeful nevertheless. Perhaps in de Gaulle he had found someone strong enough to replace Dulles as a dependable ally against the Soviet threat in Europe. He was particularly receptive to de Gaulle's suggestion "to make even tighter the bonds between Germany and France."

Three developments marked the end of the fifties: the Soviet Union's growth in power; the United States' signs of weariness; and France's return to world politics. The first two held dangers for the Federal Republic, and even the third had its drawbacks. De Gaulle supported Adenauer's policies on Germany and Berlin, and would later make a promising offer of collaboration between the two countries. But he also shook two solid foundations of West German policy—NATO and the EEC. De Gaulle wanted to maintain his ties to the United States, but he did not want France to be dependent. NATO for him was a "branch of the U.S." For Europe as well, de Gaulle's priority was national autonomy, particularly that of his own nation. He wanted European cooperation, not supranationalism; he believed only in confederation, with national governments remaining the primary centers of power.

The difficulty of reconciling this with German policy was reflected in Adenauer's meeting with de Gaulle in Rambouillet at the end of June 1960. But Adenauer was willing to concede much to a partner he could depend on, for the pressure from the East was not lessening. There were repeated incidents in the air corridors above, and on the roads leading into, Berlin, as well as at the border to the Soviet zone. But the West stood together and—not least due to France—agreed on a response to Moscow.

Adenauer turned eighty-five on January 5, 1961. It was the biggest birthday celebration of his life. Congratulations poured in for two days, beginning with the leading figures of the Federal Republic. They were followed by one group after another, the diplomatic corps, musical interludes, and a festive tattoo. Adenauer never tired; he spent both days on his feet—a marvelous demonstration of his stamina and his animated, quick-witted presence. He enjoyed the two days enormously, but he remained alert. "It is hard to sleep on one's laurels," as he liked to say.

As always, he was keeping his eye on the world; above all on Washington, where on January 20, John F. Kennedy assumed the office of president of the United States. Kennedy was now the most powerful man on earth, and a great deal depended on him, especially for the Germans. He was half Adenauer's age and little known in Germany. His position on the issues of Germany and Berlin was not clear, but his initial statements were reassuring. On April 9, Dean Acheson, whom Kennedy had sent to Germany as a special envoy, told Adenauer at Rhöndorf that America's new government would, for the most part, continue the prevailing policy. The following day Adenauer announced to the press that the major issues discussed with Acheson had been NATO's military and political structure and the leadership role of the U.S. "To lead," he added, "is not to command, but to convince, and to make clear one's own will."

During his trip to the United States from April 11 to 17, 1961, Adenauer conveyed this message to Kennedy. Whether the light of freedom would continue to shine throughout the world would depend, above all, on the United States—this he repeated before the Senate, the press, and in the course of numerous talks. He added that, in Europe, the fate of the United States was also being decided. And he reminded the new U.S. government that according to the Paris Treaties it was obliged to support the reunification of Germany. Kennedy reiterated previous U.S. commitments. The contact between the two was satisfactory, and following his discussions with the president, Adenauer flew to Texas to visit Vice President Lyndon Johnson. It was a happy, spirited time. Here, as in Washington, the media were full of admiration. Adenauer's amazing stamina made a lasting impression on the American people.

On May 20, de Gaulle visited Adenauer in Rhöndorf and Bonn. It was the first official visit to Germany by a French head of state. The two men agreed to bring about closer political cooperation in Europe.

Kennedy's meeting with Khrushchev in Vienna on July 3 and 4 was of monumental importance. When in Rhöndorf, de Gaulle had expressed his fear that the American president would allow himself to be duped by the Russian. When Kennedy visited France, just before the meeting in Vienna, de Gaulle advised him to stand firm on the issue of Berlin: "There is no greater service you could perform for the world, including Russia."

The meeting did not go well. Kennedy wanted a standstill agreement, by which troop strengths would be frozen and deployment of new weapons halted. Khrushchev wasn't ready for this. He wanted to stabilize the GDR to ensure the cohesion of the Soviet empire. In practical terms this meant that Berlin—the "bone stuck in Russia's throat," the "escape hatch" for an ever growing number of refugees from East Germany—would be brought totally under East-bloc control. West Berlin would become a free city, but entry to it would be regulated by the GDR, and Soviet troops would be stationed within its boundaries. By the end of 1961 at the latest, Khrushchev said, he would conclude a separate peace with the GDR, and if the Western powers attempted to assert their position militarily, there would be a "major collision." Kennedy had not anticipated such ruthlessness; he argued his case, but Khrushchev had detected that Kennedy would go to battle only for West Berlin. Khrushchev was quite satisfied with the meeting, and exuberantly celebrated his "victory."

The Berlin crisis that broke out forty days later, and that altered global politics, had its beginnings here. A succession of precipitous major events followed, among them: de Gaulle's statement of July 12 that the Soviet Union alone bore responsibility for the Berlin crisis; the July 17 response of the Western powers to Khrushchev's ultimatum in Vienna, asserting their original rights in Berlin, but also letting it be known that they were prepared to negotiate; Kennedy's major speech of July 25, with its essential statement: "We want peace, but we will not capitulate. . . . The source of unrest in the world is Moscow, and not Berlin!" The leaders of the Warsaw Pact met in Moscow from August 3 to 5. On August 5 and 6 the French foreign minister, British foreign secretary, and American secretary of state met with Germany's foreign minister von Brentano in Paris to decide upon countermeasures to potential violent acts from the East. They anticipated the closing of access roads and air corridors, and something resembling a surprise attack in an attempt to occupy West Berlin, and agreed upon contingency plans.

But contingency plans proved useless. The West was prepared for a direct military confrontation, but not for the closing of the eastern sector of Berlin. The West's intelligence services had noted nothing of the preparations, nor had the Berlin senate. But in the early hours of August 13, a Sunday, barbed wire was set up at the border crossing, East German police blocked traffic to and from West Berlin, and tanks rolled onto the major arteries. Groups of people slowly gathered on the western side, but no action was taken against the setting up of the barrier.

East Berlin did not belong to the GDR; the three Western powers were responsible for all of Berlin, and for the unrestricted movement within the city. But they did nothing. Kennedy had chosen to simply neglect this joint responsibility without a word; but Germans and Berliners didn't know this, and now the people of West Berlin were forced to look on helplessly as those on the other side of the barrier were locked in once and for all. West Berliners stood confused and enraged at the cruel injustice being perpetrated in the east. But they were also filled with disappointment and anger at the passivity of the Western Allies and their own leadership.

Many West Germans urged Adenauer to fly to Berlin immediately. But he didn't, and this brought the greatest disapproval registered by opinion polls of the postwar era: support for the Union parties dropped from 49 percent to 35 percent.

Adenauer wished to avoid any action that might lead to major disturbances in Berlin and East Germany. It now seems unlikely that an immediate visit to Berlin would have done this. Adenauer had called for calm in an address to the nation on the evening of August 13, and again before the *Bundestag* five days later. Many believed he needed to do so in Berlin, so the deeply shaken people there would see that he shared this difficult hour with them, and feel less helpless.

For the East, the building of the Wall was a great success. The constant loss of refugees to the West was stanched, the hold on its satellite states was strengthened, and the West had suffered a defeat in the eyes of the world.

The West, and the United States above all, had allowed a setback to its prestige—not decisive, but discernible. The boundless, almost childlike trust that Germans felt for their omnipotent American friend, especially since the Berlin airlift, suffered a major blow.

It was also a major blow for Adenauer. Not because he had allowed the Wall to be built—he could not have prevented it. And not because of how the Wall reflected on his policies—if anything, it had confirmed them. The problem lay elsewhere. In a moment of national crisis, Adenauer had been preoccupied with his reelection campaign. He made the grave psychological mistake of underestimating the distress of the German people. They had felt helpless in the face of cruel injustice and brutality from the East. Adenauer had seemed out of touch. This was to signify the turning point for Adenauer, the beginning of his descent from the heights. The end of his chancellorship was in sight.

The Cornerstone of New Construction

In the *Bundestag* elections of September 17, 1961, the CDU/CSU received 45.4 percent of the vote, the SPD 36.2 percent, and FDP 12.8 percent. The formation of the government was unusually difficult and took fifty-eight days. The choice was between a Small (CDU/CSU–FDP), a Great (CDU/CSU–SPD), and an all-party Coalition. It was a bitter battle, fought with all means. At the end, the Union parties again joined their proven junior party, the FDP. Adenauer was reelected chancellor on November 7, but he had to pledge in a letter to CDU chairman Heinrich Krone, with a copy to FDP leader Erich Mende, that he would resign in time for his successor to prepare for the 1965 elections.

As unwelcome, critical, and enervating as this domestic political struggle had been, an international development of September 1961 proved even more troubling to Adenauer. The American government began to negotiate with the Soviets about Berlin, Germany, and Europe. The U.S. may have feared that Khrushchev viewed the Wall as the first step of many. In any case, the Americans wanted peace in Central Europe, and Adenauer's nightmare was that this peace would be bought at the expense of the Federal Republic of Germany. He wrote to Kennedy several times, warning against making any concessions, and, following his reelection, flew to Washington at the first opportunity. He advocated re-establishing a unified Berlin policy, argued against disengagement in Central Europe, and insisted: "The Wall must go!" He masterfully succeeded in getting Kennedy to agree to all points. "Adenauer has achieved what no one actually considered possible," wrote the *New York Times* on November 23, "namely,

Federal President Heinrich Lübke receives Adenauer's fourth cabinet on November 14, 1961. First row from left: Ludwig Erhard, Lübke, Adenauer. Second row from left: Hans-Joachim von Merkatz, Hans-Christoph See-bohm, Hans Lenz, Paul Lücke, Gerhard Schröder, Hermann Höcherl, Franz Josef Strauss, Wolfgang Stammberger. Third row from left: Heinz Starke, Heinrich Krone, Werner Schwarz, Elisabeth Schwarzhaupt, Richard Stücklen, Theodor Blank (partially concealed), Ernst Lemmer, Franz-Josef Würmeling, Wolfgang Mischnick, Walter Scheel, Siegfried Balke.

no disengagement, no recognition of the GDR, the continuing presence of the Allies in Berlin, free access to and protection of the life of the city." Adenauer managed the situation with Kennedy so splendidly that Kennedy later called it the best dialogue he had had with a foreign politician since he took office.

Unfortunately, Adenauer's triumph was short-lived. Many leading

Americans continued to press ceaselessly for a modus vivendi with the Soviet Union. Meetings took place at various levels in Moscow, Washington, and elsewhere, between U.S. secretary of state Dean Rusk and Soviet foreign minister Andrei Gromyko. Adenauer followed these negotiations with great uneasiness. But it was difficult to stay informed about them, still harder to hinder their progress. At the beginning of April Bonn was called upon to reply to American proposals within a twenty-four-hour period; a close-to-unreasonable demand. The press got wind of it and this led to ill will between Washington and Bonn. But Adenauer, who had grave misgivings about the proposals, wrote a letter to Kennedy clearly stating his views and strongly asked for a delay in the negotiations. The Americans, however, simply proceeded. Their proposals included the following:

- an international agency to control access to Berlin;
- a nonproliferation agreement on nuclear weapons;
- non-aggression agreements between NATO and the Warsaw Pact;
- "technical commissions" with an equal number of members from the FRG and the GDR.

Washington had promised not to recognize the East German government, but Adenauer feared that, in practice, the entire package would be interpreted as de facto recognition. In a letter to Kennedy he requested that the American president hold to the agreements of November 1961, and not make any further proposals of this kind.

When nothing came of this, and because influential Germans were giving in to pressure from the West, Adenauer decided on a dramatic step. He called a press conference for May 7, 1962, in Berlin. He first took aim at the proposed international agency that was to control access to Berlin. The proposal called for five representatives from Eastern countries, five from Western, and three from neutral countries. "How is this supposed to work," Adenauer asked, "when decisions will depend on neutral countries who have no interest in us or in Berlin? That can only lead to catastrophe!" And once again he called for a delay in the negotiations, this time before the whole world.

The Americans were furious. But the agency in question never came into being, and access to Berlin remained under prior regulations, an enormous achievement for Adenauer. The chancellor had stepped in front of an apparently unstoppable steamroller and brought it to a halt. Without Adenauer's spectacular intervention

Berlin slowly would have died; it was he who saved it. And that alone more than justified his 1961 reelection.

In the spring of 1962 the process of political integration in Europe suffered a serious setback. On April 17 Holland and Belgium refused to negotiate further on the long-discussed political unity of the Six (France, West Germany, Italy, and Luxembourg complete the list). The Federal Republic had great hopes for the political unity of Europe and would have accepted it in various forms; West Germany was prepared, as it had been earlier, to make great sacrifices to see unity achieved. But on April 17, 1962, "Black Tuesday for Europe," it became clear once and for all that the integration of the six nations was not going to succeed. And this led to the revival of the idea of a closer relationship with France.

On July 2, 1962, Adenauer set out on a major visit to France, one equal in significance to his earlier visits to Arlington and Moscow. Adenauer and de Gaulle met for extensive talks, including, of course, those on the political integration of Europe. De Gaulle asked Adenauer whether the West Germans would enter into a closer relationship with France alone if the other nations would not participate. Adenauer hesitated, suggesting a variety of possible third partners. Finally, de Gaulle pressed for a direct answer. Adenauer said, "Yes."

The visit was a splendid one, rich in lasting impressions, proceeding from Paris to Rouen to Bordeaux to Reims. On the morning of July 8 a bipartite military review took place in the Champagne, the site of so many bloody battles between the Germans and the French. The high point was a service held at the Cathedral of Reims, attended by members of both countries. De Gaulle and Adenauer stood side by side under the magnificent, seemingly infinite dome of the cathedral for a Franco-German *Te Deum*. Both men knew that "the Old Continent," as de Gaulle put it, "can never come together if the two peoples whose land, labor, and genius complement each other so well remain divided." At that moment in Reims, the two men affirmed that reconciliation finally had been achieved. "An immeasurable transformation has turned archenemies into fast friends."

De Gaulle travelled to West Germany in September, and it was a triumphant visit. His speeches, delivered in German to huge crowds, were lavish in pathos and emotion. To Germans, accustomed since the end of the war to being told the worst about themselves, it was infinitely liberating to hear: "You are a great people! Even if you have erred. You once again have a friend in the world!"

De Gaulle envisioned the French and Germans henceforth stand-ing side by side, as blood brothers. By mid-September he had already sent Adenauer a memorandum on future collaboration between the two governments.

Meanwhile, on June 6, 1962, Adenauer had proposed a "truce" to the Soviet government. By its terms, the two nations would agree to leave the situation in Germany and in Berlin as it was for ten years. During the same period East Germans would be allowed to lead freer lives. Years later, when it was made public, this proposal aroused considerable notice, not least due to the flexibility it revealed in Ade-nauer. But in 1962 the Russians did not respond.

Dean Rusk visited Berlin on June 21 and went to Bonn the fol-lowing day, where he had a lengthy exchange of ideas with the chan-cellor. Their discussions covered a full range of topics. More impor-tantly, they got along well, and cleared the air concerning the conflicts of April and May.

On October 9, 1962, Adenauer stated in the *Bundestag* that "the Federal Government is prepared to discuss many issues openly, as long as our brothers in the (Soviet) zone are allowed to live their lives as they wish. . . . Human considerations play a more important role for us than national ones." This speech greatly impressed the *Bun-destag*, as it did the rest of the world, and it succeeded in creating breathing space for the chancellor. It demonstrated that Adenauer was not as rigid as many had believed. This of course would have been obvious earlier had the Globke Plans of 1959 and 1960[40] and the 1962 proposal of a standstill agreement been made public. These were Adenauer's blueprints for how reunification could be achieved. President Kennedy had requested the latest version of the standstill agreement, but this had been overshadowed by the Cuban missile cri-sis, which shook the world and transformed it.

In the summer of 1962 the Soviets began setting up missile bases in Cuba, from which almost any large American city could be directly targeted. Initially, the Americans underestimated the danger because they could not believe that Khrushchev would be so foolhardy. When, in mid-October, they recognized the risk, they turned to their allies, among them Adenauer. Acheson himself went to Bonn. Without a moment's hesitation, Adenauer placed himself firmly on the side of the Americans and made several valuable suggestions. From October 23, the crisis escalated daily. Kennedy imposed a blockade on all Soviet ships, demanding the unconditional withdrawal and dis-mantling of the deployed missiles, and threatening a crushing counter-attack if a single missile were to be fired from Cuban soil. For a while the situation remained unpredictable, rumors circulated wildly, information was contradictory. Finally, however, on October 28, Khrushchev decided to relent.

Adenauer expressed his thanks to Kennedy in writing: "You have done the free world a great service." And in truth, the world had escaped an incalculable threat. Had the situation turned out differently, Khrushchev might have been able to dictate the course of future events in Central Europe, as well as around the globe. At the height of the crisis the world had held its breath; now it expressed its approval of the Americans. They in turn acknowledged the solidarity that Adenauer and de Gaulle had offered.

For Adenauer, however, the Cuban missile crisis was soon pushed into the background by governmental upheaval at home. The crisis was touched off by the arrest of several leading members of the press in what came to be known as the "*Spiegel* Affair."[41]

Adenauer had just returned to Bonn in November from his eleventh U.S. journey when the volcano erupted. The FDP announced that it could no longer work together in a cabinet that included Defense Minister Strauss, because of his role in the episode. On November 19, all FDP ministers resigned. A brutal battle ensued and tensions soared to the boiling point. Serious negotiations were held for an entire week on whether a Great Coalition should be formed with Adenauer as chancellor for an unlimited term. But in the end misgivings in both major parties won the upper hand. Reestablishment of the original Small Coalition was made possible by Strauss's resignation on November 30. On December 2, Adenauer presented the retirement schedule he had agreed upon the previous spring. It would go into effect in the fall of 1963. His fifth cabinet was sworn in on December 14, but the end was now in sight.

Adenauer had said that in the time that remained him he wished, above all, "to accomplish the matter with France." And that now became central, despite the all-consuming formation of a new government and other equally pressing matters and a dizzying schedule of meetings. On December 16 and 17, the German and French foreign ministers agreed on future cooperation, based on de Gaulle's memorandum of September. Originally this agreement was to be transacted by letter, but the German Constitutional Court required a formally ratifiable treaty. The French agreed to this. The treaty, drawn up for purely constitutional reasons, proved to be the central force that held the entire policy in place over the decades.

On January 14, 1963, eight days before the treaty was scheduled for signing, de Gaulle held a press conference that appeared to call everything into question. Furious about the Nassau Agreement[42] recently concluded between Kennedy and Macmillan, and determined to demonstrate that France would go its own way, de Gaulle replied to the United Kingdom's wish to join the EEC with a sharp, "Not yet!" He then categorically rejected Kennedy's plan to put French nuclear arms under American command. This unleashed a storm of protest in London, Washington, and other international capitals, including Bonn. The SPD caucus demanded that Adenauer postpone his scheduled visit to Paris. Should Adenauer decide not to postpone the visit, Union politicians demanded that he under no circumstances sign the treaty. Various other organizations responded similarly, as did the majority of the media and many foreign politicians.

Adenauer himself was not pleased by de Gaulle's statements, but he knew that this particular moment in history would not come around again. "I will not postpone," he said, and went to Paris on January 20, 1963. No one but Adenauer would have had the fortitude and the deep-seated conviction to withstand opposition from all sides—there were those who were practically hanging onto his coattails up to the last minute, trying to convince him not to go. On January 22 the Franco-German Treaty on Organization and Principles of Cooperation, known as the Friendship Treaty, was signed at the Elysee Palace. After the signing, de Gaulle embraced the German chancellor.

Among the treaty's important provisions were a semi-annual meeting of the heads of state and government, and frequent meetings between the foreign ministers and other ministers as well. All major issues were to be broached at these meetings, and an effort made to reach parallel positions.

The treaty would never have come about without de Gaulle. No other French statesman possessed his power of persuasion, his ability to get the French people to put aside their fear and distrust of the Germans and risk agreement with their previous "archenemy." In turn, the French would never have trusted any other German politician as they did Adenauer. Nor could any other politician have convinced the Germans to enter into the treaty, or steered it past the rocky cliffs of 1963.

The signing of the Franco-German Friendship Treaty did nothing to calm the storm that had been raging since de Gaulle's defiant press conference. American and British politicians and media now fumed against the "conspiracy." British ministers declared that their own and the American government would see to it that Adenauer soon would find himself out of office. Because little could be done against France, opponents concentrated on the more vulnerable Germany. It was decided that the treaty could be undermined through the addition of a preamble, one which would place the EEC, NATO, and, above all, friendly relations with the United States above Franco-German cooperation. Under massive pressure from many sides, and fearing damage to cordial relations with America, the majority of the *Bundestag* fell into line. Adenauer could not prevent the preamble; he no longer possessed either the power or the time to do so. His only choice was between a treaty with preamble and no treaty at all. He accepted compromise. On May 16, 1963, the *Bundestag* ratified the Franco-German Friendship Treaty, with preamble, almost unanimously.

For France and for de Gaulle the preamble was a strong blow, a grievous disappointment. But Adenauer also suffered a defeat of a different sort—on April 24, 1963, the CSU/CDU caucus elected Ludwig Erhard as Adenauer's presumptive successor. Adenauer had sought to prevent this, and had spoken out directly against Erhard at a caucus meeting. When Erhard was elected anyway, Adenauer then declared himself prepared to work together with him. "In the end there was something conciliatory about it," he commented that evening to his closest associates. "After all, it had to happen sometime."

To the world, Erhard's election was an event of first rank, and to Germans too, of course. Many who had paid lip service to the chancellor before now felt they could slight him. But Adenauer continued to govern. The few months remaining in his term were filled with appointments, and there were still three important events to come: Kennedy's visit to Germany, keeping alive the Franco-German Friendship Treaty, and one last, passionate defense of his policy on Germany.

John F. Kennedy visited the Federal Republic of Germany from June 23 to 26. He wanted to win back support for the United States among those Germans who were wavering. In this, he succeeded magnificently. His blend of charm, earnestness, and idealism lent the visit an extraordinary excitement. The streets were lined with people wherever he went. Huge crowds applauded his speeches, which focused on friendship and delivered an unmistakable message—that an attack on Germany and Berlin was an attack on the United States of America. Kennedy's climactic statement of this message fell on waiting German ears with the inevitability of logic and the power of pure poetry. The words, *"Ich bin ein Berliner!"* uttered before the Schöneberg Rathaus, are remembered to this day. For Kennedy the visit was a triumph. For Adenauer it was an accomplishment. He had succeeded in arousing in the president of the United States a greater understanding and sympathy for the Germans.

Another matter entirely was de Gaulle's visit to Bonn from June 4 to 7, the first semi-annual meeting called for in the Franco-German treaty. De Gaulle had let it be known through his ambassador that many German parliamentarians and the German public apparently had not appreciated what the French people and de Gaulle's party had had to overcome in order to accept the treaty. Many Germans, he said, had felt it necessary to apologize to Washington and to London for the treaty, and had disparaged it to the point of distortion. De Gaulle was quoted as saying, "Many treaties last no longer than roses and young girls." There was fear that de Gaulle would give up in despair, or at the least make very little show of support for the treaty, but Adenauer would not allow that.

Adenauer's expectations for the treaty were less lofty than de Gaulle's; important to him was that the Federal Republic not stand alone in the world, but together with staunch and dependable friends. The United States was a powerful country in comparison to West Germany, but separated from it by an ocean. France was a close neighbor, equal in strength to the Federal Republic. The two nations seemed bound by common circumstances to a common destiny. To Adenauer, this implied the necessity of mutual commitment. To that end, he fought tenaciously to save the treaty. And because of one salient feature that boded well for the future—the establishment of a Franco-German Youth Services Organization—de Gaulle agreed to the treaty's continuance. He was realist enough to see that even a limited, truncated treaty was better than none.

Adenauer had delivered on the treaty. The frequent meetings it provided for kept the two neighbors from drifting apart anew. Despite all dire predictions the treaty harmed neither the EEC nor

NATO; indeed, it benefitted both. "It quite decidedly brought Europe forward," Helmut Kohl, Germany's future chancellor, said. "Franco-German friendship is the most important accomplishment achieved by the German people after the war." And what would this friendship have looked like without the treaty? It was not the idée fixe of an old man, as some critics maintained. Rather, as Adenauer himself rightly said, it was the most important achievement, together with the Rhön-dorf Conference of 1949, of his chancellorship.

Only two weeks after meeting with de Gaulle and salvaging the Franco-German Friendship Treaty, Adenauer once again had to wage a defensive battle on the German question. Washington and Moscow wanted an agreement banning the testing of nuclear weapons in the atmosphere, in space, and underwater, and they wanted the agreement to be entered into by all the countries in the world. The proposal was welcomed by the Federal Republic as well. But Moscow wanted to exploit the Kennedy administration's urgency on the issue in order to force international recognition of the German Demo-cratic Republic. To thwart any objection, the United States informed Bonn of this condition only after the agreement had been initialed on July 25.

Adenauer had been suspicious of the agreement. Now the major-ity of German politicians and journalists recognized the danger as well. They were furious with the Americans, and this time the major-ity sided with Adenauer. At the same time they believed that little could be done and they would be forced to swallow the bitter pill. But Adenauer refused to give in. "Never before has our policy of reunifi-cation, which benefits not only us, but the entire free world as well, been so endangered as it has by this agreement," he said. "And I will not abandon [our policy]." German suggestions for changes and additions were rejected, but Adenauer continued the struggle in two long talks, first meeting with the American defense secretary, Robert McNamara, and then with Secretary of State Rusk.

Adenauer asked that East Germany not be allowed to become party to a treaty with the United States, and that the American gov-ernment announce to the world that it did not recognize the East German government. Rusk agreed, and made such a statement before the U.S. Senate on August 12. Once again Adenauer had achieved something no one had considered possible: he had halted the progress of an agreement already set in motion. "This was so important to me," he said to his cabinet, "that I, who had been labelled at the outset as 'Chancellor of the Allies,' was willing to risk leaving office as 'Chancellor Against the Allies'—A nation in such a precarious situation as we must be willing to risk the anger of others."

Though it was made increasingly difficult for Adenauer to govern, the chancellor had one final and unexpected opportunity to avert another grave situation before he left office. A massive crop failure forced the Soviet Union to import huge amounts of wheat from the U.S., Canada, and Australia. The news of this inspired Adenauer to suggest that, in exchange, the Soviets could be required to lessen the pressure they were exerting on Berlin, and to grant East Germans more freedom. "If we don't use this opportunity, we will have made a serious mistake!" he said. But Adenauer could not convince the three Western Allies to agree to this. And even powerful leaders in his own country offered only half-hearted support; they were more concerned about their own positions under a new chancellor.

Following his farewell visits to Rome and to de Gaulle in Rambouillet, Adenauer also began to take his leave in Germany. This did not take the form of a quiet stepping aside, but of a grand finale, with full orchestra before a packed house. Farewell ceremonies were held in Hamburg, Munich, Berlin, Cologne, and Bonn; others were organized by the party, the caucus, the army, and the press. In addition, there were the many individual events—afternoon speeches and evening speeches, handshaking and smiles, interviews, photo engagements, and continual demands for appearances. Adenauer went on with the business of governing through it all, conscious of his responsibilities up to his last day in office. His calendar was full to bursting, and he was in top form. It was an impressive display to anyone who witnessed it.

On October 14 a Pontifical Mass was held in his honor at the cathedral in Bonn, "for the people and the fatherland, and especially for the end of the division of Germany." There followed on October 15, 1963, the great farewell ceremony in the *Bundestag*. Eugen Gerstenmaier, president of the *Bundestag*, delivered an enthusiastic speech and Adenauer stood erect throughout the entire forty minutes of its duration, expressionless, as if carved of stone. Following his own farewell speech he walked with sure step down into the plenum and took his appointed seat as a delegate.

What must Adenauer have felt at this forced retirement from office after fourteen years of unprecedented effort at the top? "It is," he said, "as if someone had chopped off my arms and legs." But he did not allow himself to become paralyzed. He set himself new tasks, and created a new pattern for his life at eighty-eight years of age. Forcing himself not to become bitter, he wrote his memoirs and continued to participate in political life. He persevered in his support of friendship and close cooperation with France, not as a one-sided option, but as counterbalance to Erhard's policies, which were solely geared toward the United States. Adenauer supported NATO and West Germany's alliance with the U.S., but not to the exclusion of everything else. The alliance with France was equally important, and the Federal Republic was strong enough to maintain cordial relations with both countries.

Adenauer made many speeches in the election campaign of 1965; he was tireless, and inspired those accompanying him with his stamina and willpower. He remained head of the Christian Democratic Union until past his ninetieth birthday. During a visit to Israel in 1966 Adenauer argued against condemning the Germans as a people, and on his last visit to Spain, in February 1967, he urgently pushed for the political union of Europe.

On March 29, 1967, Adenauer suffered his second heart attack, and bronchitis, which developed into pneumonia. He remained in his house in Rhöndorf still exchanging telegrams with de Gaulle. A team of seven doctors attended to him around the clock. On April 16, after suffering another heart attack, he lost consciousness, regaining it only intermittently. His son Paul performed the last rites on April 19, when his condition had clearly become critical. His last words, spoken in unmistakable Rhineland dialect, were directed to his sons and daughters: *"Do jitt et nix zo kriesche."* There's nothing to cry about. He died at 1:21 P.M.

Never before had any German's death affected so many people. Hundreds of thousands filed by his coffin in Bonn and then in Cologne. Twenty-one heads of state attended his funeral, among them de Gaulle, Johnson, and Ben-Gurion. Ninety special delegations and close to one thousand guests of honor from friendly nations paid their final respects. Roughly 400 million people throughout the world viewed the funeral ceremonies on television. Media the world over paid tribute. And historians and political scientists have been kept busy ever since, analyzing in ever greater detail his accomplishments and significance.

He was "both restorational and modern," a man open to the future, a "stabilizing force and, in equal measure, an innovative one,"

wrote Hans-Peter Schwarz.[43] His tactical virtuosity was acknowledged as well as his visionary views. He was criticized for his micro-
management style and his cunning. But there is agreement on the fact
that his ultimate goals were always honorable. Gordon A. Craig calls
him a "parliamentary politician of almost uncanny quality, a unique
figure among the prominent statesmen of the twentieth century."[44]

In polls taken on which great German had achieved the most for
his country, Adenauer placed first on the list for years following his
death; as late as 1989 he was named by 33 percent of those respond-
ing to an Allensbach poll. Bismarck ranked second, with 8 percent.

The greatest of his talents was that of lifting up a community of
people—of contributing to its development and constantly improving
it. So it was in his days as mayor of Cologne, and so it remained in a
much more all-encompassing way as chancellor of the Federal
Republic. When Adenauer took office Germany was a country in
defeat—devastated, dejected, and without much hope. Adenauer
helped it to its feet and it went forward, making great strides in an
amazingly short period of time. The entire world was soon talking
about the "German economic miracle." In looking back at that period
the historian Golo Mann wrote: "The extent of his success was almost
incomprehensible."

Economic recovery and domestic order comprised one aspect of
Adenauer's incredible achievement. The other was the reentry of Germany into the family of nations. When Adenauer began governing,
the German people were surrounded by a sea of loathing, hatred, and
enmity. Only someone as strong and decent as he could have
breached the waves. Adenauer had gone through trial by fire in Nazi
Germany, and the entire nation benefitted from it. "It is wholly and
solely due to the policies, the intellect, and the moral character of
Konrad Adenauer," said Robert Schuman, "that Germany was
accepted again so quickly into the family of nations."

Adenauer's magnificent accomplishments, both domestically and
abroad, were possible only because he possessed the vision to see
through the often thick fog that enveloped events. He kept his eye on
ten or twelve time clocks simultaneously. His clear standards enabled
him to come to quick and judicious decisions. He was energetic, and
had inexhaustible stamina. He remained a great warrior to the end.

Adenauer was ambitious, and he enjoyed his power. But what
drove him most was what he called his "pragmatic ambition," namely,
his absolutely unrestrainable will to perform his work as perfectly as
possible, and in that, to give his all, day after day.

Adenauer was not a mild man, he was severe and demanding and solemn. But he wanted for his people a better and more secure future. His conscience demanded it, and his conscience was grounded in the spiritual.

Adenauer considered the Germans to be an ailing people. The last generations had been forced to go through too much: two lost wars involving incredible adversity and millions of dead; totally disparate forms of government; the most contradictory value systems—all of this, Adenauer believed, would have proved too much for any people. He felt it was important that the people have a chance to rest, that healing forces be allowed to develop so that the Germans could recover from within. Adenauer stood up for his people. To Kennedy he said,

In prayer during the Corpus Christi procession of 1964
on the island of Grafenwerth bei Honnef.

"If the Germans commit no new sins, they should be forgiven the old ones." Even in his last public speech, delivered in Munich on February 28, 1967, Adenauer asked the world not to judge the German people too harshly. And he closed with the words, "From the depths of my soul I wish for the recovery of the German nation, that it might rise again, not to material heights—I am not thinking of that—but to spiritual ones!"

Since the Germans first stepped into the light of history they have experienced good times and bad, greatness and ruin. By the measure of these diverse epochs, the Adenauer era must be seen as a landmark of accomplishment. For many Germans, it will be remembered as a happy time.

Notes

1. Cologne's *Oberbürgermeister* (mayor), unlike his counterpart in the Anglo-Saxon civic system, is also the town clerk, chief of police, and permanent head of every municipal department.

2. The *Zentrumspartei*, the Catholic Center Party, was an avowedly confessional party founded in 1870 to protect the rights of Catholics in a predominantly Protestant country.

3. The Great Coalition under Adenauer would have brought together the Social Democrats (SPD) and the People's Party (*Deutsche Volkspartei*, DVP) along with other parties of the center and the moderate right. It was perhaps the last chance to hold off the extreme right and the eventual rise of Hitler, and it failed because the People's Party was unwilling to join a Socialist-dominated government.

4. Gustav Stresemann, founder of the DVP, was one of the Weimar Republic's most prominent politicians. He was chancellor in 1923 and foreign minister from 1923 to 1929. In 1926 he shared the Nobel Peace Prize with Aristide Briand.

5. Heinrich Brüning, a Westphalian Catholic Center deputy, served as chancellor from 1930 to 1932, a period in which the Nazis continued their gains at the polls.

6. In the infamous "Night of the Long Knives," Ernst Röhm, chief of the SA, and dozens of other brownshirt leaders were snatched from their beds and shot without trial by SS troopers. Among the other suspected dissidents murdered that night were Gregor Strasser and the last chancellor before Hitler, General Kurt von Schleicher.

7. Under *Sippenhaft*, a common Nazi practice, close relatives of anti-Nazis on the run were incarcerated in order to find out the hiding places of the fugitives.

8. The U.S. Military Government, in addition to having prepared lists of prominent Nazis and war criminals to be apprehended, also had the names of known leading anti-Nazis who were likely to cooperate with the occupiers.

9. Ludwig Erhard (1897–1977). Bavarian economist, economics minister of Bavaria from 1945 to 1946, economics minister in Adenauer's cabinet from 1949 to 1963, federal chancellor from 1963 to 1966.

10. Carlo Schmid, prominent leader of the SPD, a distinguished legal scholar from southern Germany. He is generally credited with much of the work which went into the final draft of the Basic Law.

11. The Basic Law, its "temporary" nature notwithstanding (pending the reunification of Germany), proved a sturdy foundation for the new democratic state, and when the two parts of Germany were finally reunited in 1990 it went into force for the whole German nation.

12. With Adenauer's strong support, the Parliamentary Council, before it ceased to exist, also chose Bonn over Frankfurt as the "temporary" site for the Federal Republic's new capital. Adenauer's argument—the choice of a small university town, unlike a larger city like Frankfurt, would not pose the danger of becoming permanent—won the day. A recently confirmed, hotly contested decision of the *Bundestag* again made Berlin the capital and seat of the Federal Government, with the move from Bonn to be completed by mid-2000.

13. With Berlin, in the heart of the Russian-occupied zone more than 100 miles from the nearest point in West Germany, the Soviets on June 23, 1948, halted all supplies shipped by land from reaching Berlin's Western zones. They also cut off all food and energy supplies from the eastern sector of Berlin and the surrounding Soviet zone.

14. Theodor Heuss, co-founder and chairman of the liberal FDP, had been minister of culture of Württemberg-Baden for a short time after World War II. He was a highly respected professor of political science, author, journalist, and a former member of the *Reichstag* during the Weimar Republic. He served one five-year term as president until 1954.

15. Paul Weymar. *Konrad Adenauer: The Authorised Biography.* Trans: Peter de Mendelsohn (London: André Deutsch, 1957), p. 292.

16. Prince Otto von Bismarck (1815–1898). German statesman, creator of a united, imperial Germany, and its first chancellor, known as *Der Eiserne Kanzler* (The Iron Chancellor).

17. The Ruhr Statute established an international Ruhr Authority, with Britain, France, the U.S., and the Benelux countries as members, to control the coal and steel production of the Ruhr and to set user allocations, export quotas, and prices. The German Federal Republic, by becoming a member in November 1949, was given equal voting rights.

18. Schuman's letter contained the legendary proposals with which the French foreign minister would electrify the French parliament and the world two days later—a plan to bring together French and German heavy industry under an international authority which became known as the Schuman Plan. It was the first step toward European unity via the European Community for Coal and Steel and, eventually, the European Common Market. Adenauer agreed to the proposal the same day he received Schuman's letter.

19. The Benelux countries are comprised of Belgium, the Netherlands, and Luxembourg.

20. Codetermination provides for a system of joint management by management and labor of industrial enterprises of a certain size with the help of supervisory boards comprising an equal number of representatives of each to set policy on a variety of such matters as wages and management personnel.

21. The Charter of the refugees who had been expelled from former territories in the east renounced all thought of vengeance and retribution, embraced a free, united Europe, and urged the right to a homeland as one of God's basic human rights.

22. The General Treaty or Treaty of Germany, along with the Contractual Agreement, were to have put an end to the occupation of Western Germany and established the Federal Republic as a sovereign state. These agreements were to have come into force at the same time as the EDC Treaty, which had still to be ratified. When the French Assembly rejected the EDC in March 1954 and the Federal Republic subsequently joined NATO, the Paris Treaties, effective May 5, 1955, included the provisions for the Federal Republic's full sovereignty originally in the General Treaty. From then on the Allies could claim special privileges only relating to: 1. The stationing of troops; 2. Berlin; 3. Germany as a whole, including all questions of reunification.

23. The London Debt Agreement of February 23, 1953, between the Federal Republic and twenty countries (eventually extended to thirty-two countries) set Western Germany's total debt (both prewar and postwar, including postwar reconstruction loans and the Marshall Plan) at a total of 15 billion Deutsche Mark. By making its debt payments on time the Federal government did much to earn the trust of the Western democracies.

24. The Saar Treaty between the Federal Republic and France returned the Saar to Western Germany in two stages—politically on January 1, 1957, and economically on December 31, 1959 (later advanced to July 1959).

25. This agreement obligated the Federal Republic to pay collective reparations in goods and services to Israel, valued at three billion Deutsche Mark, and to the Conference on Jewish Material Claims Against Germany, valued at 450 million. The Federal Republic entered into similar reparations agreements in favor of victims of National Socialism with twelve European countries.

26. The new "Five-Percent Rule" adopted before the 1953 election denied parliamentary representation to parties polling less than five percent of the total votes counted in order to avoid fragmentation of the parliamentary process. However, a party winning a majority for one deputy in an election district (later increased to three) may nevertheless be represented in the *Bundestag*.

27. Adenauer's cabinet was based on a coalition of the CDU/CSU, FDP, DP, and BHE (*Bund der Heimatvertriebenen*), a party representing the interests of refugees expelled from former German territories.

28. Nikolai A. Bulganin, Soviet prime minister from 1955 to 1958, chairman of Council of Ministers.

29. The line formed by the rivers Oder and Neisse was adopted by the Potsdam Agreement in 1945 as the border between Poland and Germany. The East German government in 1950 confirmed the Oder-Neisse line as an "inviolable" border between Poland and Germany. This prompted the West German Federal

government to declare all "border accords of the Soviet zone" as "null and void." However, West Germany under Chancellor Willy Brandt officially acknowledged the Oder-Neisse line in 1970.

30. "Now let us all thank God. . . ." church hymn by Martin Pinckart (1644).

31. Thomas Dehler, FDP chairman and parliamentary leader, former minister of justice and attorney general.

32. With Guy Mollet's Socialist government now in power, Adenauer's faith in France began to weaken. "Italy's minister president Segni was told by him it would be wrong to wait too long for France, which had lost the leadership of the European movement." (Schwarz, *Konrad Adenauer, der Staatsmann*, see Note 43).

33. George F. Kennan, U.S. Department of State official and diplomat, former U.S. ambassador to the Soviet Union; credited with formulating the containment policy to prevent Soviet expansion after World War II.

34. Wilfrid Schreiber, president of the Catholic Industrialists Federation and professor of social science.

35. The Declaration on German Unification by France, the Federal Republic of Germany, the United Kingdom, and the United States.

36. In order to keep the door to reunification ajar, Bonn under the Hallstein Doctrine refused to maintain diplomatic relations with any state that recognized what was then referred to as the "so-called" German Democratic Republic. Walter Hallstein was then undersecretary in the Foreign Office. Later he became president of the European Common Market.

37. Franz Etzel (CDU) served as finance minister in Adenauer's third cabinet from 1957 to 1961.

38. The *Deutschlandplan*, passed on March 18, 1953, called for a demilitarized, nuclear-free zone in Central Europe (both German states, Czechoslovakia, Poland, and Hungary) in the hope that this would lead in stages to the restoration of German unity. The SPD dropped the plan in 1960.

39. The Godesberg Program, adopted at a special SPD conference at Bad Godesberg, November 13 to 15, 1959, abandoned all ideological Marxist doctrines, embraced the free market economy, religious tolerance, parliamentary democracy, and the defense of a free, democratic order.

40. Hans Globke, Adenauer's controversial chief of staff (because of his Nazi past), drafted his plans in response to Khrushchev's Berlin ultimatum and in preparation for consultations with the Western powers. Its provisions sought an interim solution to the thorny issues of Berlin and Germany.

41. On October 26, 1962, police occupied and searched the offices of *Der Spiegel* (West Germany's largest and most influential news magazine) in Munich and Hamburg, remaining in occupation for over a month. Its publisher, Rudolf Augstein, was arrested along with Conrad Ahlers and several of his other editors and charged with "suspicion of high treason" because of an article drawing attention to the inadequacy of the national defenses. The Federal High Court eventually dismissed all charges against Augstein and Ahlers owing to insufficient evidence. Defense Minister Franz Josef Strauss was compelled to admit before the *Bundestag* that he had played a vital part in the arrest of Ahlers.

42. The Nassau Agreement of December 1962 between Macmillan and Kennedy, which stated that the U.S. was to furnish nuclear missiles for British submarines, enraged Charles de Gaulle, who insisted on a Europe uncontrolled by the U.S. (*Encyclopedia Britannica*, Macmillan).

43. Hans-Peter Schwarz, *Konrad Adenauer. Vol 1. Der Aufstieg* (Stuttgart: DVA, 1986). *Vol 2. Der Staatsmann* (Stuttgart: DVA, 1991).

44. Gordon A. Craig, *Germany and the West: The Ambivalent Relationship* (London: German Historical Institute, 1982).

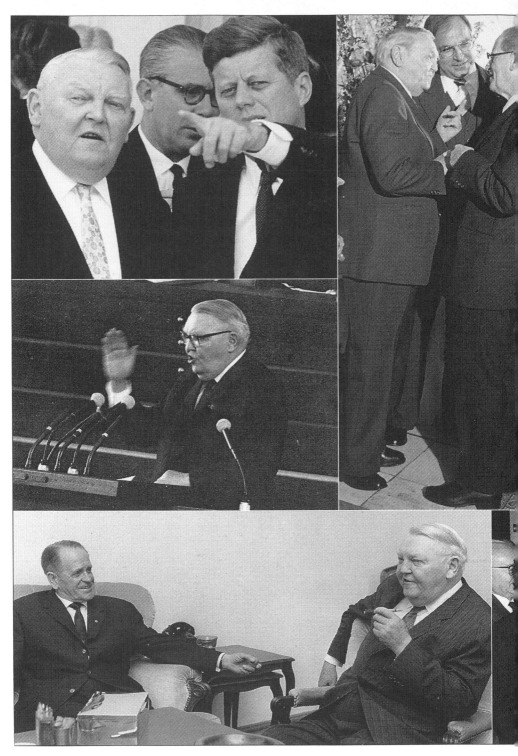

[Top] *With John F. Kennedy in Bonn, 1963 — Helmut Kohl and Herbert Wehner congratulate Erhardt on his eightieth birthday, 1977 — With Adenauer and de Gaulle in Bonn, 1966—Delivering a campaign speech in the Saarland, 1965.* [Center] *Addressing* a Bundestag *session, 1964 — With his bestselling* Wohl- stand für Alle *(Prosperity for Everyone), 1957 — With the executive committee*

of the Trade Union Federation, from left: Heinrich Gutermuth, Georg Leber, Otto Brenner.
[Bottom] *With West German soccer-team trainer Sepp Herberger, 1965 — Voting in the federal elections in 1965 — Visiting the Bonn orphanage Maria im Walde in 1963.*

Chronology

1897	Ludwig Erhard born February 7 in Fürth.
1903–1916	Attends Volksschule and Realschule; commercial apprenticeship.
1916–1919	Enlists and is wounded; finishes military service in a hospital.
1919–1922	Attends Nuremberg School of Business.
1922–1925	University of Frankfurt, completes doctoral studies with Franz Oppenheimer.
1923	Marries widowed Luise Schuster, née Lotter.
1925–1928	Manages parents' dry goods business.
1928–1942	Joins the Institute for Economic Research of the Nuremberg School of Business, working with Wilhelm Vershofen.
1942	Founds the Institute for Industrial Research.
1944	Writes the memorandum "Financing Wars and Consolidating Debts."
1945–1946	Bavarian minister of economic affairs.
1947	Head of Special Bureau for Money and Credit.
1948	Director of economic administration; as part of the currency reform of June 20, announces lifting of all price controls.
1949	Elected CDU representative to the *Bundestag*; minister for economic affairs.
1952	Member of the Ministerial Council of the European Coal and Steel Community, and governor of the World Bank.
1957	Federal vice-chancellor.
1963	Federal chancellor. Names first cabinet.
1965	Announces concept of a *Formierte Gesellschaft*. Re-elected federal chancellor. Names second cabinet.
1966	Named head of CDU. FDP ministers withdraw from cabinet; resigns office on December 1.
1972 and 1976	Chairman emeritus of the seventh and eighth *Bundestag*.
1977	Dies in Bonn on May 5.

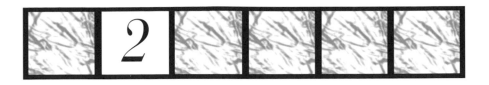

Ludwig Erhard

by Hans Klein

Ludwig Erhard was a singular phenomenon of this century. He showed a German people searching for an identity the road to a free economy; and the people in its hour of dire need after total defeat gave him its trust. It placed its hopes in this new type of politician, a man capable of abstract thought who also knew how to take concrete action—a man who set wit and morality against traditional power politics, who gave voice to the longing, buried by two devastating world wars, to overcome national, social, and ideological conflicts, and who promised success to the striving for reconciliation, both in and outside Germany. Erhard's social market economy was not a synthesis of capitalism and socialism, but a modern, democratic refutation of both, its goal prosperity for everyone. It succeeded to a degree never known before, and in the process became the signature mark of the Federal Republic of Germany.

Thirteen years after Erhard's death, socialism, having ossified into the idea of the totalitarian state, came crashing down all over the world. Ludwig Erhard's work has survived the "specter" of Marx and Engels. Suddenly politicians and economists are mentioning his name again, though often in the support of ideas that run counter to Erhard's own.

During the difficult process of reunification, an older generation of Germans remembered him as the creator of the social market economy. But his principles had been suppressed by party and state in the former East German GDR (*Deutsche Demokratische Republik*—German Democratic Republic), while in the old West Germany many years of welfare mentality had buried them under a thicket of laws and regulations. Though West Germany's situation at the end of the forties little resembled that of East Germany at the beginning of the nineties, Erhard's image once again gripped public imagination as that of a man who confidently and intuitively had fought for the right answers, whose radiant optimism carried a free Germany along with him. But the fact that Ludwig Erhard also had once been chancellor of the Federal Republic was something many Germans almost seemed to have forgotten.

Was this because since then the dizzying sequence of political change has smothered the impact of day-to-day events? Or was the memory of Erhard's chancellorship simply erased by his relatively short time in office? Did perhaps both Konrad Adenauer, Erhard's predecessor, and Kurt Kiesinger, Erhard's successor, see to it, for totally disparate reasons, of course, that the years 1963 to 1966 appeared to be merely transitional? Did the rather heterogeneous alliance within his own Union parties, having brought about Erhard's fall, try to ennoble its own motives by calling into question Erhard's achievements as federal chancellor? Or was his chancellorship merely the final, lackluster chapter of the Adenauer era, or perhaps the inadvertent prelude, barely noticed at first, to postwar Germany's change of political course?

Each of the above is a partial answer to why so few Germans remember Erhard as head of state—but only a partial one. Konrad Adenauer's chancellorship lies further back in the past, yet Adenauer still casts a patriarchal shadow on the present. Kurt Georg Kiesinger and Willy Brandt each served as head of state for only a short time, but their roles as federal chancellors remain strong in memory. If nothing else, Erhard's absolute power to draw voters and his consensual style of governing, which earned him the honorary title of "chancellor of the people," argue against judging his chancellorship as transitory. No matter how much his enemies within his own party were said to be plotting and conspiring against him, word of their ambitions and intrigues always reached his ears and was made public by the media. And finally, Ludwig Erhard, who became chancellor despite the explicit and often publicly expressed wishes of Adenauer, and who fought with great determination against a Great Coalition, cannot seriously be accused either of prolonging the Adenauer era or of paving the way for the Brandt-Scheel or Schmidt-Genscher epochs.

In truth it is the social market system, Ludwig Erhard's momentous life's work, which serves to diminish, supplant, and eclipse his notable achievements as chancellor. This "third path" in political-economic policy is inseparable from his name. It led to prosperity for all and not merely a wealthy or powerful ruling caste. It brought about the rapid economic recovery of West Germany and stimulated new socio-political developments in all western industrial nations. And it gave the peoples of eastern Europe and of the southern continents concrete hope for overcoming oppression and economic woes in their own countries.

For almost two decades, including the three years he spent as federal chancellor, Ludwig Erhard lived in almost magical harmony with the great majority of the German people. Rolf Zundel of *Die Zeit*[1] labeled this rapport a "unio mystica," a "pseudo-religious relationship."

Erhard engaged in a permanent dialogue with the masses; it was the style of political leadership he preferred. Never before had any German politician held so many public meetings, granted so many radio interviews, appeared in so many televised discussions, contributed so many articles to newspapers and magazines, or written so many books. He drew strength and conviction from the response to all of this, whether it took the form of approval or of protest. He was persuasive because his intentions were sincere, his insights were right, and his policies successful. He appealed both to people's reason and to their emotions. His arguments were based on his solid theoretical knowledge, acquired through study and his own research. Even as federal chancellor he felt he was "Otto Average-Consumer"[2] because the consistent lower middle-class pattern of his life enabled him instinctively to grasp the needs and yearnings of the broad mass of people.

Most of his public speeches consisted of economic excursus with a sprinkling of technical terminology. But he deliberately interspersed this with homespun popular expressions and sayings from his native Franconia, so that all of his listeners understood, or at least felt what he meant. He had a deep voice and rolled his "r's." When he appealed to civic moral principles he employed the stilted vocabulary of sociologists of the nineteen twenties. He was not witty but a master of the quick retort, especially when provoked.

His physical appearance—round face, silver-gray hair, piercing blue eyes, and ever-present cigar—inspired sympathy and trust. People affectionately referred to him as *"der Dicke"* ("Chubby"), though he was not particularly overweight. But his hunched shoulders made his neck disappear, which made his body appear massive. This anomaly was due to a physical impediment. As a two-year-old he was stricken with infantile paralysis, which had left him with a slightly deformed right foot. In the First World War, in which he was promoted from gunner to artillery sergeant to officer candidate, he was wounded so seriously that he spent almost an entire year in a military hospital. It would take decades to reveal how profoundly his life would be changed by the injury that kept him from taking over his parents' business.

Though Erhard could not take part in sports himself due to his foot impediment, he was an enthusiastic soccer fan. He kept up weekly with the scores of "his" *Spielvereinigung Fürth* (Fürth Sports Club).[3] And now and then he organized a card game in the chancellor's bungalow. Erhard followed a moderate and simple diet, but liked to drink a glass of scotch whiskey in the company of his small circle of friends. He was a family man who called his wife, Luise, "Lu." She in turn called him "Lulu." His daughters-in-law were as dear to him as his own daughters and their husbands, and he devoted many rare private hours to his two granddaughters.

Johannes Gross, the most original of Erhard's critics, who belonged to his circle of advisors and occasionally served as his ghostwriter, is credited with having said, "Politics ruins character. And since Ludwig Erhard's chancellorship we know that character also ruins politics." And Hermann Schreiber, in a 1965 portrait of Erhard in *Spiegel*, noted, "The most intimate bond between Ludwig Erhard and the German people is their common dislike of politics."

But these sentiments do justice to Erhard only if the word "politics" is applied strictly to party politics. One of Erhard's favorite phrases as chancellor was "beyond and above all parties." Despite his zest for attack, his pugnacity, even his stinging ferocity in the defense of his policies, he was incapable of giving his wholehearted support to the kind of half-truths that parties espouse as pure gospel.

So it was also consistent with his personality that on October 18, 1963, two days after his election as federal chancellor, Ludwig Erhard delivered a statement of government policy before the *Bundestag* that was interrupted by applause 112 times. Forty-five of these originated with, or were joined in by, members of the opposition SPD, which fifteen years before had termed Erhard a "charlatan and a gambler," and his social market economy a "slogan of lies."

The election of a new chancellor, viewed by many concerned observers both in and outside the Federal Republic as the greatest

test of German postwar democracy, took place relatively smoothly. It was the transition from a head of government who had held high-ranking offices both under the German monarchy and during the Weimar Republic to a successor who had set out on the political path only following the Second World War.

The anticipated shift in focus from foreign to economic policy, based on the two men's diverse spheres of experience, never came about. To the contrary, Konrad Adenauer emphasized domestic issues in his last statement of government policy on November 29, 1961, whereas Ludwig Erhard placed all German and foreign policy in the foreground of his first policy statement two years later. Like Adenauer, he condemned continuing Soviet aggression, considered the

Taking the oath as federal chancellor, administered by Bundestag *president Eugen Gerstenmaier, on October 16, 1963.*

"German Question" the core of East-West relations, referred to Germany's membership in NATO as the basis of the country's security, placed close cooperation with the United States on equal footing with the endeavor to strengthen Germany's accord with France, and emphasized Germany's positive relations with the friendly nations of the Near and Far East, Africa, and South America. He pursued these policies, however, not just because of mere reverence for the success of his predecessor's astute and steadfast diplomacy.

Nevertheless, it wasn't long before the *simplificateurs terribles* were labeling Erhard's chancellorship in terms that had less to do with political reality than with ancient battle lines, some going back as far as the Reformation. From the trauma of National Socialism, the war, and the postwar period emerged the great movement toward political union of the two Christian denominations, which brought Catholics and Protestants together. Nevertheless, some sought to create a division, no matter how irrelevant, placing "Catholic-conservatives" on one side and "Protestant-liberals" on the other. Those who advocated closer relations between France and Germany distrusted and opposed those who sought comparably strong relations with the United States and Great Britain. The front line between the Gaullists and the supporters of "Atlanticism"—an alternative harmful to German interests—was drawn within the party and personified by Adenauer and Strauss on the one side, and Erhard and Schröder on the other.

The pivotal reason for the abrupt end to Ludwig Erhard's chancellorship was the same as for his brilliant rise to the highest government office—his attitude toward power. Only future developments will determine whether it was one of uncommon guilelessness or farsighted wisdom.

Democracy and Power

Jacob Burckhardt's[4] dictum, "Power in itself is evil," corresponded largely to Erhard's own views. But he considered the concept of power in a democracy as a *contradictio in adjecto*, even by the Anglo-Saxon definition, which established temporal limits and parliamentary control. Erhard felt that within a democracy individual self-esteem opposed being ruled, even if the power that ruled was elected. In modern-day enlightened industrial society people would demand a mutual give-and-take rather than a relationship of command-and-obey dictated by power.

This view was the basis of the difference between Erhard and Adenauer. Their understanding of the art of governing, and of the methods required both to create majorities and to use them to achieve political goals, was diametrically opposed. Adenauer thought in terms of dynastic power and knew how to skillfully play opposing interest groups off against each other. He used almost every management strategy imaginable and—though mindful of his reputation as an authoritarian chancellor who arrived at his decisions alone—was always prepared to go to the very limit of the justifiable, and beyond, in order to achieve compromise. In doing so he capitalized on his advanced age, enlisting his Rhineland charm to defuse negative reactions to his frequent wiles and the willful way he often arranged the facts.

Erhard trusted people's insights and sense of responsibility; he encouraged individuals and social groups as a whole to work toward the common good. And he imputed to the Germans—and rightly so in the first two decades after the war—a particularly high degree of social maturity due to their unique historical experience.

Adenauer applied his political virtuosity to implementing the social market economy, just as Erhard's successful economic policies had contributed decisively to Adenauer's election victories. Both men were aware of these facts. Franz Josef Strauss was right when, a few months after the change of government in 1963, he wrote, "The Adenauer era was also an Erhard era."

Adenauer was not the cynical misanthrope his critics considered him. Nor was Erhard the dreamy-eyed do-gooder even many of his friends believed him to be. Both firmly believed in Christian values—Adenauer Catholic and Erhard Protestant. Society's religious undercurrents, which were even more distinct in those days, must be understood in order to decode the personalities of these two most important statesmen in postwar German history. Konrad Adenauer and Ludwig Erhard personified the great concept of Christian community as an answer to the challenge of Germany's defeat, much as resisters like Niemöller of the *Bekennende Kirche*[5] had drawn on Chistianity in their response to the evils of Naziism itself.

For fourteen years the government of the Federal Republic was headed by a Catholic chancellor and a Protestant minister of economics—and the experiment succeeded. Their joint success in drafting the political blueprint for German postwar democracy, and its acceptance into the community of free nations, was due to a great extent to the differing but complementary skills of these two men. But the fact that they worked together for so long, despite their often troubled personal relationship and their many conflicting views, was no doubt due to the character and life of Ludwig Erhard.

When Ludwig Erhard was born in Fürth, near Nuremberg, on February 4, 1897, no one could have predicted that a half century later he would embody the hopes, and shape the economy, of a nation crushed in defeat in two world wars. Erhard had a sister and two brothers, the elder of whom was killed in the First World War. His Protestant mother came from a family of craftsmen in nearby Rothenburg, a picturesque "fairy-tale" town of Franconia, his Catholic father from a small farmstead in the Rhön mountain range, south of Hanover. His parents owned a lingerie and accessories shop, "Wilhelm Erhard Dry Goods en gros and en detail." Ludwig Erhard grew up in the security of modest, lower middle-class prosperity. Religious tolerance, taken for granted both at home and in the mercantile city of Fürth, with its uncommonly large Jewish population, had a marked influence on him. In the year Erhard was born, Jakob Wassermann, a fellow citizen of Fürth, published an explosive novel entitled *Die Juden von Zirndorf* (The Jews of Zirndorf).[6]

Erhard's two salient and seemingly contradictory characteristics—his penchant for reflection, and his enjoyment of public appearances and political struggle—he owed to his quiet, peace-loving mother and his ambitious, activist father. The seed of his independent thinking was also planted at home, for though his father was an upstanding patriot, loyal to king and emperor, he was also a dedicated freethinker who adhered to the liberal principles of Eugen Richter,[7] Baron Franz August Schenk von Stauffenberg,[8] and later, as Germany's social problems increased, of Friedrich Naumann.[9]

Since Ludwig Erhard was meant one day to take over the family business, he completed a commercial apprenticeship after receiving his middle school certificate. After enlisting in 1916, he was sent as an artillery gunner to the Vosges Mountains, then to Rumania, and finally to Flanders, where he was wounded. Once army doctors had sewn him back together in the course of several operations, he was sent home in 1919. A livelihood standing behind a counter was no longer feasible.

To make the best use of time spent convalescing at home in Fürth, Erhard enrolled at the newly established School of Economics and

Social Sciences in Nuremberg. He attended lectures on political economy. Wilhelm Rieger, rector of the college, soon recognized Erhard's academic talent and talked Erhard's father into allowing his son to study for the full four semesters.

Several things occurred in those years which furthered Erhard's development. He received a mark of "very good" for his thesis, "The Economic Significance of Cashless Transactions." And at university he became reacquainted with Luise Schuster, née Lotter, a childhood friend. Her husband, with whom she had a daughter, had been killed in the war, and she was studying in order to pursue a professional career and support herself and her daughter. Because the Nuremberg School of Economics did not offer a doctorate both Erhard and Luise Schuster matriculated at the University of Frankfurt. They married in the winter of 1923. This was the period of the worst inflation, in which Erhard's parents lost all their savings and Luise found it impossible to both study and take care of her child. Ludwig Erhard, who in the course of his education was beginning to realize his calling, continued his studies alone.

Erhard's most important mentor was Franz Oppenheimer, the great Jewish thinker whose roots were firmly embedded in German culture, and who advocated a "liberal socialism." Erhard was more fascinated by the compelling logic of Oppenheimer's thought, the practical application of theory, and the judicious and down-to-earth humanity in which these were grounded, than by proposals for action based on then-current social conditions, à la Marx. In 1924 he graduated cum laude as *Dr. rer pol.* (Doctor of Political Science). On a hike with Erhard in the Swiss Alps, Oppenheimer, who had served as his doctoral supervisor, concluded his oral examinations by joking, "I herewith award you the 'highest' academic degree."

In 1928, following a brief stint as manager of his father's stagnating business, Ludwig Erhard found the first position to suit his interests, as academic assistant at the Institute for Economic Research of German Products, with a beginning salary of 150 marks. His daughter Elisabeth had been born two years before and Erhard, who had turned thirty in the meantime, had a family of four to support.

The director of the institute was Wilhelm Vershofen, a writer and economist who had authored several novels set in the world of business and industry, as well as philosophical works and countless titles in the field of economics. His market research institute, associated with the Nuremberg School of Economics, appeared to Erhard to open the door to an academic career. But this door was slammed shut

due to political developments Erhard was unwilling to go along with.
Five months before Hitler seized power Erhard wrote an article which
strongly attacked the financial theorist Hjalmar Schacht.[10] Erhard
called Schacht's economic program a "mix of banal truisms, plain
ignorance and heated contradictions." It was "beyond discussion.
One can only reject it, enraged and embittered at such a violation of
thought . . . designed to serve a political career." Schacht was to gain
early favor in the Nazi period.

Yet the years that followed at the Institute were not lost to Ludwig
Erhard. The market inquiries, studies on cost and profit ratios, and
empirical research on the effects and countereffects of the economic
process, provided him with comprehensive and well-tested knowledge
of the laws of economics, and later gave him penetrating insight into
the state of Germany's war economy. In 1942 anti-Nazi industrialists
that long had respected his name helped him set up his own Institute
for Industrial Research in Nuremberg.

Among the more enigmatic features of totalitarian regimes that
often confound superficial observers are the internal battles for power
among dissenting factions. Characteristically, such regimes practice,
or at least tolerate, many things that publicly they punish. In the last
years of the Third Reich theoretical preoccupation with the anticipated consequences of the war and the reorganization of the postwar
economy was a case in point. Though postwar planning was strictly
forbidden by Hitler in his Decree on Total War of January 25, 1942,
Erhard's own Institute for Industrial Research cooperated with the
so-called "steel circle" within the Reichs Group on Industry[11]
to pursue just such planning. A highly placed SS officer in the
Reichs Ministry of Economics, who was critical of the Nazis, protected Erhard's research into problems of war debt and of fiscal and
monetary policy in a defeated Germany. The result was a volum-
inous paper.

The bluntness with which Erhard outlined a German defeat meant
that it was hardly advisable to disseminate his paper. But Erhard sent
his explosive memo on postwar economic planning to Carl Friedrich
Goerdeler, with whom he had been corresponding and meeting for
years. Goerdeler was a former mayor of Leipzig and Reichs Commissioner for Price Controls, whom non-communist conspirators against
Hitler had chosen as provisional successor to the office of chancellor
of the German Reich. When Erhard mailed him the memo Goerdeler
was already being hunted by the Gestapo. But he took time to read it

and to express his support in an eleven-page memorandum, which historian Gerhard Ritter has described as "a kind of political testament." In it he expressly recommended that "Dr. Erhard," the sole name mentioned in the original memorandum, serve as advisor to his co-conspirators, who were to make an attempt on Hitler's life on July 20, 1944.[12] Goerdeler was arrested shortly thereafter, sentenced to death, and executed. But the memorandum did not fall into the hands of the Nazis.

Erhard's lack of concern for his own personal safety is also mentioned by Theodor Eschenburg, who gained prominence after the war as a professor of political science in Tübingen. Eschenburg had found shelter during a bombing attack on Berlin in the same building where Erhard was staying during his frequent trips. Eschenburg recalled:

> ■ One evening in October 1944 we met again. Erhard was sitting next to me and I noticed that his shirt was missing two mother-of-pearl buttons. I was a corporate lawyer at the time, for the button industry among others, and I went to my room and got a card of a dozen buttons for him. At this, Erhard reached into the large, shapeless, much-used briefcase he always carried with him and pulled out a manuscript. He had a great number of copies with him, about thirty in all, and he gave me one and told me to read it. "We can discuss it the next time we meet," he said. ■

Back in his room, Eschenburg read the text immediately. It was a precisely formulated shorter version of Erhard's explosive memorandum. He didn't want to keep the paper in his possession one minute longer than necessary, and immediately went to Erhard's room to return it. But Erhard was in a deep sleep by then, and only after Eschenburg knocked loudly and called out to him did Erhard angrily open the door. Eschenburg's warnings about Erhard's risk of exposure and the possibility of a house search and arrest were met by Erhard with a sleepy growl: "And for this you woke me up?" The next evening, when the two met on a commuter train, Erhard was still unworriedly carrying the exposé around with him in his beat-up briefcase.[13]

In the memorandum Erhard first analyzed the strategy used in financing the war, and then described ways in which the war debt could be paid off. He concluded that the existing financial system would have to be abolished; it was ruining the economy and the currency, and robbing people of the profit of their labor. His proposal also included a goal important to the morale of Germany and its citizens—the equitable distribution of the debt burden. When the memorandum surfaced again in 1977, experts found it amazing that at the midpoint of the war Erhard had accurately anticipated a war debt of close to four hundred billion Deutsche Mark. And he had done so without benefit of data from either the Nazi Office of Statistics or the Audit Office. The war budget and financing were kept secret.

A copy of Erhard's memorandum came into American hands after the war. They located its author and named Erhard advisor to the occupation authorities in Nuremberg, and then advanced him to the position of Bavarian minister of economic affairs. Organized rationing was not what Erhard favored, nor did he get along with the old-time political hacks in Wilhelm Hoegner's cabinet.[14] He served as a Bavarian minister from October 1945 to December 1946.

Erhard's management style as minister of economic affairs was clearly marked by his great aversion to the rationing bureaucracy, and by his total impatience with the type of politician exemplified by Dr. Alois Schlögl, Bavarian minister of agriculture. A loyal Farmers' Association functionary and member of the Bavarian People's Party, Schlögl had served for years as a representative in the Bavarian parliament (*Landtag*). He correctly saw in Erhard an enemy of political patronage, and following the *Landtag* elections in December 1946 he headed an investigatory committee to expose "the deplorable state of the Bavarian Ministry of Economic Affairs under Erhard." After nine months, the committee's final report attested to Erhard's moral integrity while criticizing administrative problems in the ministry. Erhard took his revenge in an angry radio broadcast, terming the entire investigation "grandiose nonsense."

Following this he strengthened his ties to political economist Adolf Weber and his circle in Munich, which devoted itself primarily to the transitional economy and to currency reform. At the end of 1947 the University of Munich named him honorary professor. But once again his hopes for an academic career were dashed when the Americans summoned him to head the Special Bureau for Money and Credit, established to assist the occupation powers in preparing for the currency reform.

This group of German financial experts provided the supporting cast for Project D-Mark, which for a time took on elements of a mystery novel. Its hero was Edward Tenenbaum, a twenty-eight-year-old New

At the opening of the first Bavarian Export Show in Munich, August 1946, together with British general Sir Cecil Weird and wife of U.S. general Lucius D. Clay.

York banking expert, who at the time was serving as assistant and financial advisor to the American military governor, General Lucius D. Clay. The German experts were sequestered and subjected to the most exacting security measures, as if they held the formula to nuclear fission. At the same time, the Allies kept them in the dark about what was going on.

The members of this Special Bureau for Money and Credit—who at best could only vaguely divine from cautious hints and reactions what their Allied partners intended—were only supposed to work out the technical and administrative details for the planned currency exchange. But Erhard somehow got wind of what the Americans had in mind—the Colm-Dodge-Goldsmith Plan[15] for a new Deutsche Mark. This enabled him to lobby for a more comprehensive economic reform. "For if there's nothing for people to buy with the new money," he said to Tenenbaum at a hearing on November 6, 1947, "then the new currency won't be viable either."

Several months before the currency reform, Erhard was elected director of economic administration of the United Economic Areas (Bizone), the recently amalgamated U.S. and British occupation zones. In effect, this made Erhard the minister of economics of the German administration. He was the head of the *Wirtschaftsrat*[16] (Economic Council), made up of members of the various parliaments of the *Länder* (states) within the U.S. and British zones—the precursor of a West German parliament with limited legislative authority, governed by the directors it elected.

Coincidence had landed Ludwig Erhard in a very influential office. His predecessor, Johannes Semmler, had been dismissed by the Allies following an imprudent and aggressive speech in which he labeled the food supplies that Americans were sending to Germany "chicken feed." Victor-Emanuel Preusker, general secretary of the Free Democratic Party in Hesse, had then brought up Erhard's name. Theodor Blank[17] and others squashed the opposition to Erhard's election within the workers' wing of the Christian Democratic Union, and Josef Müller,[18] among others, did the same within the agricultural wing of the Christian Social Union.

Erhard threw himself into his new task with unparalleled energy. He argued, reasoned, pleaded, and fought. He conferred with prominent leaders of the economy and with experienced members of the Economic Council. He reached new rhetorical heights in parliamentary debates and his public speeches grew in effectiveness. On April 21, 1948, he introduced his program to the Economic Council. On June 17 and 18 parliamentary debate was held on the "Law on Guidelines for Controls and Price Policies Following the Currency Reform," a law which reflected Erhard's spirit. In the early morning hours of June 18 it was passed at its third reading, by a vote of fifty-two to thirty-seven.

The *Länderrat* (Council of States), controlled by a Social Democratic majority, still had to approve, and the military authorities still had not given their formal endorsement when, only a few hours after the law was passed, the three military governments made public their own Law of Currency Reform. June 18 was a Friday. On Sunday every German was to receive forty Deutsche Mark (German marks, DM), two-thirds of the planned "per capita quota." As of Monday only the new currency would be valid.

The twenty-six paragraphs of Allied Law No. 61 were essentially the work of Edward Tenenbaum. They set the value of the new Deutsche Mark at one-tenth of the old Reichsmark, with wages and salaries, rents, and retirement and social insurance pensions remaining at a ratio of 1:1. There were also regulations for most other forms of money ownership, all beneficial to the economy. The young American, self-assured and knowledgeable, acted entirely by himself. He made the painful incision that would have been impossible had those affected by it been included in the decision process, the midwife in the birth of a currency that was to become one of the most stable in the world. But what turned the currency reform into the initial spark which set off West Germany's runaway recovery was the achievement of Ludwig Erhard. Without worrying about the Allied occupation laws, he simply cut through the Gordian Knot of the command economy, which dealt with scarcity by rationing its resources.

The timing of the currency exchange took Ludwig Erhard by surprise as much as it did every other German. Privately, he had expected to be given at least a few days advance notice. But rather than being offended at the Allies he immediately went into action. Ignoring the fact that the "Law on Guidelines" was not yet in effect, Erhard gave the public the impression that currency reform and economic reform were one and the same thing.

On Sunday he arranged for his press spokesman, Kuno Ockhardt, to announce over the radio the abolition of price controls and of the rationing of a great number of goods, as well as other consumer-friendly measures. Controls would be maintained only over food staples and raw materials. This was technically correct, but Erhard intentionally implied that all of these measures had been arrived at simultaneously.

Then on Monday Erhard delivered his historic radio broadcast. In it he announced an "end to price controls" and a "decisive break with the principle of a controlled economy," and castigated the "specter of mass hysteria" and the "lunatic financial swindle of price-frozen inflation." His speech achieved the hoped-for effect; in no time, store windows and shelves suddenly were filled with hoarded consumer goods, and for the new money there was something to buy—at pre-war prices.

The occupation powers were furious at Erhard for taking matters into his own hands. But his independence was evidence as well that the regulations for a social market economy were in no way the inevitable consequence of West Germany being under the "dominion of the capitalistic occupation powers."[19] France, which until shortly before had been governed by socialists, communists, and "peoples' republicans," had nationalized its credit and insurance institutions, energy sources, merchant marine, and countless industrial enterprises. Great Britain's Labour Party was also betting on its nationalization policy, which affected the Bank of England, Cable & Wireless, the airlines, gas and electric utilities, railroads, the mining industry, and large sectors of the iron and steel industries. And the Americans? Military officers are trained to think in terms of logistics and distribution rather than production and consumption. And not a few of the Germany experts among the American occupation officers were German émigrés who had come from a socialist background. Only General Clay, with his understanding of political-economic connections, met Erhard's ideas with a high degree of sympathy.

But even Clay was not pleased by Erhard's striking out on his own, and at the urging of the other military governors called him onto the carpet. He rebuked Erhard in strong language, even threatening to dismiss him should such a thing happen again. Erhard, for his part, complained that he had not been notified early enough, and again stressed the inseparable bond between the value of the currency and the supply of goods. Clay then asked: "What makes you think you can alter Allied decisions?" To which Erhard wryly and courageously replied, "Herr General, I did not alter them, I did away with them."[20]

Following Erhard's fait accompli the *Länderrat* and the military authorities passed the "Law on Guidelines for Control and Price Policies Following the Currency Reform." The social market economy—though it took a while for this expression first coined by Alfred Müller-Armack[21] to sink into public consciousness—began to work; the German economy took off at a pace no one would have considered possible.

In the final months of 1948 and the first months of 1949 a series of further developments helped bring about a total breakthrough for Erhard's economic ideas. When German unions called a twenty-four-hour strike for November 12, 1948, and 9.25 million workers in the Bizone walked out in protest against Erhard's economic policy, it was the first time he was confronted with the full force of an interest group. But just as workers had ignored his radio broadcast appeal—in which Erhard warned not to let economic policy become subject to the dictates of social, economic, or political groups if democracy was not to become a farce—Erhard refused to be influenced by the general strike.

Erhard's first encounter with Konrad Adenauer's pragmatic power politics came on February 24 and 25, 1949, when in Königswinter the CDU willy-nilly replaced their Ahlener Program[22] with Erhard's social market economy. The Ahlener Program included distinctly socialist elements and called for the nationalization of major industries. Adenauer disingenuously maintained that the CDU's adoption of the social market economy did not affect the Ahlener Program, which he totally supported. And Erhard came to his support when he accepted the program's moral precepts, derived from the social teachings of the Catholic Church. In later years Erhard liked to joke that the CDU had "arrived at its economic program by way of immaculate conception."

Actually, soon after the Americans, it was Konrad Adenauer who discovered Ludwig Erhard. Adenauer had begun to notice him early on, talked with him a few times, and offered him the platform at Königswinter to present his ideas to the economic experts of the CDU, which Erhard did persuasively in a three-hour lecture.

It was the FDP that had introduced Erhard to the Frankfurt Economic Council, and in fact Erhard most closely identified with the liberal economic policies of that party. But he soon came to realize that he needed the much broader middle-class base of the CDU to carry out his program. He didn't join the CDU for some years to come, but in 1949 he "declared himself prepared" to lead the CDU slate in Baden-Württemberg, and to campaign as a CDU candidate in the Ulm/Heidenheim electoral district without yet being a member of the party.

What followed had a certain logic. The all-important issue of economic revitalization, and with it the personality of the feisty, dynamic professor of economics, dominated the first federal election campaign to a great extent. Consistent with his cautious fairness, Adenauer brought Erhard—who admired Adenauer without reservation as a prudent and experienced father figure—into his cabinet and entrusted him with the Ministry of Economics, but did not grant him a higher office. Erhard would not become vice-chancellor until 1957.

A series of events during his first years in federal government helped define Erhard's public personality. The hard winter of 1949–1950, with two million Germans unemployed, the crisis in Korea, the devaluation of the British pound and the Deutsche Mark, the liberalization of imports, and the unstoppable success of Erhard's economic policy—each played its part. The European Coal and Steel Community was established, the Federal Republic was accepted into the World Bank and International Monetary Fund, and the second, third, and fourth *Bundestag* elections took place with the selection of the cabinets. The *Spiegel* Affair was followed by the standoffish attitude of the liberal coalition partner. Adenauer made overt and covert attempts to curtail his successful minister of economics, and a growing anti-Adenauer movement was openly led by the FDP, with more and more Union party politicians joining in.

Erhard was able to achieve most of his antitrust objectives in the first legislative period of his tenure as minister with a draft of the Cartel Act,[23] which he considered the core of his social market economy because it would ensure unhindered competition. He was critical of the EEC Treaty, but its overriding goal of European integration was more important to him than the treaty's troublesome details. Erhard always thought in terms of a larger European economy—in truth, of an international economy. When negotiations on Great Britain's admission to the EEC broke off in January 1963, he called it "a black hour for Europe."

Time and again Erhard was forced to acquiesce to the political tactics of both Adenauer and parliament, and to keep his own ideas in check, to avoid fierce internal clashes that might jeopardize the government's majority in parliament and with it his own political objectives.

His social market economy suffered its first serious blow in January 1957, with the passage of a progressive pension plan linked to income growth and not, as Erhard had wanted, to productivity. Decades later, in the face of demographic changes, those elements of the plan that had been left unexamined in the general euphoria over this truly vast reform had to be given another look.

Aside from such developments, which ran counter to Erhard's economic policies but were supported by a broad majority in parliament, most of Adenauer's maneuvering against his vice-chancellor and minister of economics merely served to increase Erhard's popularity. One example was the hullabaloo in 1959, when Adenauer nominated Erhard for the office of federal president against the latter's will. Erhard turned down the nomination, at which Adenauer nominated himself, only later to withdraw his candidacy. Heinrich Lübke was then elected federal president.

Erhard's aspiration to succeed Adenauer as federal chancellor reflected not only his own ambition, but also the widely held belief that his candidacy was a foregone conclusion. He was encouraged in this by most of the leading CDU/CSU politicians, by the majority of his party, and by public opinion. Karl Hohmann was the strategist who was working quietly behind the scenes to prepare the press and politicians for his election. Born in 1916, Hohmann served in the military through the period of the Second World War and was discharged, after seven years, as a captain. He spent three years in the Ministry of Economics of Württemberg-Hohenzollern, and joined the Federal Ministry of Economics in 1951. As head of the Press and Public Affairs Department, he quickly succeeded in winning over to Erhard's policies first Bonn's economic correspondents, then a growing circle of journalists, and finally a group of influential politicians. In doing so he employed the most effective means of dealing with journalists and politicians—immediate, interesting, and invariably dependable information.

Prominent Bonn economics correspondents were regularly invited for evening interviews with Erhard, and before long they had formed the "Erhard Brigade." Their influence with other members of the press was extensive. And when Hohmann became director of the chancellor's office he created the so-called Special Circle, which included several astute journalists especially critical of Erhard. In the beginning they served as challenging discussion partners, then as advisors, and in the end they became, in the best sense of the word, propagandists for Erhard's policies. Hohmann's foresight, together with Erhard's ability to expand his sphere of influence, exemplified Karl Jasper's statement that "Whatever fails to touch the masses, fails."

The great majority of West German politicians and officials understood and supported freedom of the press as a constituent of democracy. But dealing with the media came hard—to many politicians for subjective reasons, and to many officials for objective ones.

Clearly, Ludwig Erhard's unparalleled impact on the public mind unleashed in some politicians something resembling jealousy. Others less dependent on the public's approval were condescending and hostile toward the media who they felt were obstructing their work. Any official, even if, like Hohmann, he held academic degrees in economy and political science, could expect the contempt of those members of the bureaucracy.

Ludwig Erhard maintained a close, almost familiar relationship with many scientists, academics, and politicians as well with members of his staff. Some of these ties were undoubtedly warmer than the one he enjoyed with Hohmann, a man whose reserve made it difficult to get close to him. And yet it was Hohmann who comprehended and fostered the work and personality of Ludwig Erhard as did no one else. The Ludwig Erhard Foundation, for which Hohmann served as director for many years following Erhard's death, and the posthumous dissemination of Erhard's ideas were largely Hohmann's achievements.

But it little benefits a politician to maintain the best of public relations if there are misgivings within his own ranks. In the beginning

The federal chancellor with Karl Hohmann, head of the chancellor's office.

The federal minister of economics in a plenary session of the Bundestag, *October 1962.*

only a few individual politicians presented a distorted picture of Erhard, but with time their number grew, and then the media joined in as well, depicting him as too dependent on consensus and therefore no match for Adenauer's cool toughness. But Adenauer's own antagonism toward Erhard was not rooted in toughness. Erhard's relaxed self-confidence, rhetorical brilliance, and popularity evidently kindled a feeling of defensiveness in the domineering Adenauer, who might well have identified with the speaker of the Old Testament pronouncement, "Thou shalt have no other gods before me."

Adenauer doubtlessly was alarmed by the Emnid Poll of June 1949. When three thousand Germans in the Western occupation zones were asked to name a politician they wished to see govern Germany in the future, thirteen percent named Ludwig Erhard, another thirteen percent responded with Kurt Schumacher, and only eleven percent mentioned Konrad Adenauer's name.

Adenauer's penchant for power may have allowed him to exploit Erhard's popularity to the good of the CDU in the first federal elections, but he must have been unsettled by a campaign pamphlet put out by his own party that stated: "If Professor Erhard puts his trust in CDU, so can you!" And the statement Erhard gave on August 19, 1949, five days after the Union victory at the polls, scarcely sounded like that of a junior partner: "I am in total agreement with Dr. Adenauer that regardless of which solution (to forming a government) is found, our clear line on economic policy shall not be affected."

In this light, one can understand Adenauer's attempts to prevent Erhard from becoming chancellor, assigning the role of "crown prince" instead to a long list of cabinet members: Franz Etzel, Fritz Schäffer, Heinrich Krone, Heinrich von Brentano, and Gerhard Schröder. Even up to April 23, 1963, when the CDU/CSU voted 159 to 47 to nominate Erhard to the office, Adenauer had gone down his list of favorites and asked each if he would accept the office. They all declined, with only Gerhard Schröder qualifying his answer by saying that in his case the question was premature.

New Wine in Old Bottles

When Ludwig Erhard became chancellor in 1963 he assumed an office that had been marked by a chancellor with broad administrative experience and a passion for the political exploitation of the office's administrative possibilities. The chancellor's office was run by Undersecretary of State Hans Globke, who maintained a cordial but aloof relationship to everyone, both professionally and personally. The pattern of the office was set; the administration's gears had been well-oiled in fourteen years of bureaucratic routine.

In keeping with Adenauer's guidelines, section and departmental chiefs in the chancellor's office viewed their role as a kind of supervisory post over the various cabinet offices. The fact that the "shadowed" ministries rarely if ever protested against this system was presumably due to Adenauer's power, but also perhaps to Globke's skillful circumspection in dealing with delegated authority.

The "regime of administrators," a universal phenomenon perhaps much more relevant than the "regime of managers" so much dis-

Federal President Heinrich Lübke receives Erhard's first cabinet on October 17, 1963. First row, from left: Rolf Dahlgrün, Gerhard Schröder, Lübke, Elisabeth Schwarzhaupt, Kai-Uwe von Hassel, Erich Mende. Second row, from left: Walter Scheel, Richard Stücklen, Hermann Höcherl, Werner Dollinger, Hans Krüger, Werner Schwarz. Third row, from left: Paul Lücke, Bruno Heck, Alois Niederalt, Kurt Schmücker, Hans-Christoph Seebohm. Fourth row, from left: Theodor Blank, Hans Lenz, Ewald Bucher, Heinrich Krone.

cussed in books, was tailored to the roles of Adenauer and Globke in the chancellor's office of 1963. When Erhard took over the office, two very different administrative styles faced off against each other. That Erhard brought a few of his own staff with him changed little at first. They were accustomed to Erhard's style, but the perfectly functioning apparatus Adenauer had created needed time to turn around. Slight corrections in course, minor shifts in power, or small internal changes were not what was needed, but, rather, a totally new concept of governing. The chancellor's office would have to be transformed from an instrument of control into an instrument of coordination.

Ludger Westrick, with his eloquent charm and solid economic experience, played a dual role as Adenauer's confidante and Erhard's friend. He was chosen to be minister of the chancellery. Karl Hohmann, Erhard's taciturn, prudent, and perceptive promoter, was named head of the chancellor's office.

In his first weeks in office Erhard set a breathtaking pace. Elected chancellor on October 16, 1963, he introduced his cabinet the very next day, and issued his statement of government policy a day later. On November 1 he described in detail the proposals he had made in his governmental policy statement to the communist East. In a televised discussion broadcast in America over CBS, he stated that the German federal government was prepared to make great sacrifices if the end result was reunification. On November 9 a long-term trade and finance agreement providing for the exchange of commercial missions was signed in Budapest by representatives of the Federal Republic and Hungary. This was followed on December 24 by a long-term German-Rumanian trade agreement. On March 6, 1964, after a month-long negotiation, the Federal Republic and the People's Republic of Bulgaria reached a trade and payments accord and agreed to establish commercial agencies in Bonn and Sofia.

On December 17 in Berlin, the government signed an agreement to issue passes to roughly 1.2 million West Berliners allowing them to visit relatives in East Berlin from December 18, 1963, to January 5, 1964.

Erhard made his first official visit as federal chancellor to Paris, from November 21 to 23. On November 25, at President John F. Kennedy's funeral, he met with the heads of the U.S. government. And on December 28 and 29 he flew to Texas to visit the new American president, Lyndon B. Johnson. On January 9, 1964, he delivered a special report of his activities, in which he particularly stressed West Germany's cordial relations with France and the United States. He visited Great Britain on January 15 and 16, and Italy from January 27 to 29. Returning to France on February 14 and 15, he participated in Franco-German talks, and on March 2 and 3, he paid the first official visit by a German federal chancellor to the Netherlands. On April 23 and 24 he became the first German head of state officially to visit Belgium since the First World War.

Erhard was never blinded by the recorded successes of such high-level international encounters. As federal chancellor he was always conscious that the support of the free world for the interests of divided Germany could not be taken for granted.

The carefully fabricated SPD myth that it was international socialist connections that reestablished respect for Germany in the eyes of the world is belied by the following list of government officials who paid state visits to Germany during Erhard's term in office: In 1964, Swedish prime minister Tage Erlander, Luxembourg's premier Pierre Werner, Dutch prime minister Victor Marijnen, and Jordan's King Hussein. In 1965 came newly elected British prime minister Harold Wilson, Queen Elizabeth and the Duke of Edinburgh, Italian president Giuseppe Saragat, Chilean president Eduardo Frei, and King Hassan II of Morocco; and, in 1966, Rumanian minister of foreign trade Gheorge Cioara, Italian prime minister Aldo Moro, and Tunisian prime minister Habib Bourgiba. As federal chancellor, Erhard also visited Great Britain, Italy (where he met with the Pope), Belgium, the Netherlands, Luxembourg, Canada, Denmark, Norway, and Sweden.

State visit of Elizabeth II, Queen of England, and the Duke of Edinburgh, Bonn, May 1965. Luise Erhard is standing to the right; behind her is Hans Klein, political press officer.

Erhard also established close contacts with scientists, artists, musicians, writers, journalists, actors, and cabaret performers, whom he officially received at the Schaumburg Palace though he preferred to invite them to the more convivial chancellor's bungalow. Even Munich's *Lach-und-Schiessgesellschaft*,[24] which was not in particularly good standing with the conservative CDU/CSU, paid Erhard a visit. It's sarcastic star, Dieter Hildebrandt, left a record of the occasion: "Our satirical temperament was totally disarmed when the chancellor entered the room and initiated a friendly conversation. It immediately became clear to me why Adenauer, even today, considers his successor unsuited to the job: Ludwig Erhard's political activity might suffer from his human emotions."

As much as he sought out encounters, conversations, and exchanges of ideas with ordinary people, Erhard also needed the stimulation that the intellectual world offered, and the opportunity to put his own thoughts and ideas on the table for discussion. He publicly expressed his resentment of censure only rarely, as in the case of author and playwright Rolf Hochhuth.[25] Erhard referred disparagingly to Hochhuth as "pinscher," not to belittle his literary work, but because Hochhuth's criticism of the government's policies was uninformed. Pinschers, Erhard explained, are a breed of dogs known as rat catchers, and since "The Pied Piper of Hamelin" rat catchers have had the reputation of luring the unsuspecting to their demise by playing seductive tunes. Erhard was charged with anti-intellectualism in this fracas, and though the accusation might have been politically effective, he remained personally unmoved.

Herbert Weichmann, a noted Social Democratic leader who said of Erhard that he was "resolutely paving the way to a new epoch," rhetorically asked whether the word *"pinscher* was really so wrong, given the context." Weichmann had lived through the Weimar Republic and recalled "the calamitous role of those loafers who lounged around at the *Romanisches Café*, whom historian Walter Laqueur branded 'totally negative.' Their contemptuous dismissal of Friedrich Ebert, Otto Braun, and Gustav Stresemann[26] as loathsome representatives of a loathsome system contributed to undermining the [Weimar] Republic."

Another of Erhard's brushes with the intelligentsia occurred when the leftist novelist Günter Grass requested a meeting with the chancellor following the defeat of the SPD in the elections of September 19, 1965. Erhard did not hesitate to invite him. He believed Grass would behave as any civilized man would—as a good loser. This turned out to be a mistake. The author arrived to accuse Erhard, as television cameras were rolling, of the strange and preposterous crime of having set his own house on fire. It was so crude an overreaction that when Grass later became politically active on behalf of Willy Brandt many voters viewed the author's politicking as unconvincing, more deliberate self-promotion than anything else.

The relationship between intellect and politics doubtlessly occupied Ludwig Erhard more than it did most of his critics. It had been the subject of many a conversation with his greatly admired, respected, and beloved teacher, Franz Oppenheimer. The theoretical structure of the social market economy was charged, after all, by the tension between intellect and politics, morality and power. And its development was decisively influenced by the dialogues Ludwig Erhard held with the forerunners of neo-liberalism—authoritative thinkers such as Franz Böhm, Friedrich August von Hayek, Walter Eucken, Wilhelm Röpcke, and Alexander Rüstow.[27]

In an essay commemorating Eugen Gerstenmaier's[28] sixtieth birthday, Erhard wrote: "The economy is as dependent on the creative energy of the politicians as the culture is on the economy. But the economy will know soon enough if society fails to receive new ideas and impulses from the cultural sphere. No sector of our society can forgo the creative force, the active intellect, of any other sector. We are constantly reminded that the spirit of the intellect hovers everywhere."

Several major domestic policy decisions were made during Erhard's chancellorship—the agreement with the minister-presidents of the *Länder* on comprehensive financial reform embodied in the Developmental Aid Tax Law; the Proclamation on the Exploration and Exploitation of the Continental Shelf Off the German Coast; and the establishment of a council of experts to assess economic development, among others.

At the beginning of the sixties the CDU/CSU was firmly in place as West Germany's ruling party, not least due to Adenauer. This may have ensured certain perquisites for its members in government, but it also meant that the party had to expend a great deal of energy, at the very least, to hold in check the grassroots political gains the opposition SPD was making with its strict party organization, its committed party workers, and its burgeoning membership. The situation also meant that interest groups within the two Union parties saw themselves as direct partners of the government, and as such lobbied "their" respective ministers. Up to a point this reflected the image of both CDU and CSU as people's parties, and mirrored a pluralistic society.

In economic and social matters, Erhard acted more consciously on principle than had his pragmatic predecessor. When compromise threatened to place him too close to what commentators called "accommodation democracy," he was even less willing to negotiate than usual. But Erhard was no ideologue, his critics notwithstanding. And when he did cite principle, it was grounded in his knowledge of economic interactions and their consequences. As long as the social market economy functioned without friction within its international context, and as long as economic growth continued each year to increase the gross national product undisturbed by state intervention or wrongheaded decisions, Erhard was willing to tolerate partisan interests, though not without complaint about "pardonable sins."

This approach was one way of keeping certain groups quiet, or, more precisely, of keeping their votes. But such short-term advantages were not to be gained without long-term damage. And because Erhard was capable of foreseeing this damage, and could well interpret the first disquieting signs of an affluent society applying the brakes to itself, he turned directly to the people with his calls for "moderation." It became grist for the propaganda mill of the short-sighted opposition, but also created conflict within his own party, which rightfully saw in these appeals a threat to the spurious ways in which certain groups were being placated.

Erhard's relationship with the CDU was also characterized by the fact that, after more than fifteen years of Adenauer's authoritarian rule, the party had a pent-up need to exercise its own autonomy. Nor could it be denied that following the retirement of the almost eighty-eight-year-old chancellor, the younger generation waiting in the wings was becoming restive.

But the period between Erhard's assumption of the office and the next *Bundestag* elections was too short to form a new cabinet and introduce a set of fresh faces. This popular signal to the public of self-regeneration would have had to be linked to a cut in the size of the cabinet, which would have blunted the effects of later negative events. But it was less than two years before the next election campaign. To disturb a structure held together by links between internal party factions and organized special-interest groups, with each of the

three different parties—CDU, CSU, and FDP—as well as the two
Christian denominations anxious to preserve their public image,
would have threatened the outcome of the election.

Konrad Adenauer retained chairmanship of the CDU into
Erhard's last year as chancellor. While Erhard at first considered this
to be logical and proper, the relationship between the chancellor and
the party was not without some stress. As minister of economics,
Erhard had grown accustomed to a tacit understanding splitting up
certain duties between him and Adenauer. In addition to his many
political interests such as foreign policy, which he viewed as his own
special domain, Adenauer took care to maintain a consensus between
the federal government and the party. Erhard, for his part, concentrated on economic and social issues, and on creating the kind of
domestic stability, which allowed West Germany to rejoin the international political scene. With this in mind it made sense to Erhard to
have Konrad Adenauer continue as head of the CDU. It took some
time for him to realize that those areas once covered by his predecessor now demanded his own attention.

Two and a half years before Erhard took office as federal chancellor, Franz Josef Strauss was named chairman of the CSU, the
Bavarian sister party of the CDU. The former federal minister had
been the foil for a great number of the charges directed against Adenauer during the *"Spiegel* Affair," and had subsequently resigned
from the cabinet. When Erhard was forming his cabinets in 1963 and
1965, Strauss let it be known that he was not yet interested in being
named to a cabinet post. This was a relief to Erhard in terms of his
negotiating position with the FDP, which was uncompromisingly
anti-Strauss. But it also meant that neither chair of the two Union
parties belonged to the federal administration. In the face of the
growing self-interest of each party, the seriousness of the situation
soon became apparent.

Another factor Erhard was forced to contend with was the
increasing emancipation of the CDU/CSU *Bundestag* caucus. Following the death of Heinrich von Brentano, the caucus on December 1
elected Rainer Barzel chairman. Two years before, Konrad Adenauer
had appointed Barzel to his final cabinet as minister for all-German
affairs. As Erhard was forming his first cabinet, however, the FDP
insisted that he appoint their chairman, Erich Mende, to that position. Erhard then offered Barzel the post of minister of expelled persons. But Barzel preferred to retain his position in the caucus, with a

view to becoming party chairman. The CDU, however, elected Erhard to that position at the convention in Bonn on March 23, 1966, and Erhard's predecessor, Konrad Adenauer, as honorary chairman.

From 1949 to 1956, and again from 1961 to 1966, the FDP was the coalition partner in Bonn of the two Union parties. But the FDP was always more influenced by the immediate demands of current events than was the CDU/CSU. That the FDP was seated on the right side of the *Bundestag* did not do justice to the diversity within the party, though it did reflect the national-liberal position held by the FDP as a whole until the early sixties. During Erhard's chancellorship the party could more fairly have been seated in the middle position, and later, after the founding of the social-liberal coalition, to the left of the CDU/CSU caucus. The greater personal skills, and perhaps the stronger ambitions, of their top politicians kept the party from being reduced to an irrelevant splinter group, as were the German Democratic Party and the German People's Party in the years preceding 1933.

With the exception of the CDU/CSU in the fall of 1957, neither of the large parties attained the absolute majority in parliament that would have entitled them to govern alone. To many voters, the FDP represented the reassuring option of not having to make a straightforward decision in one direction or the other, or of tempering the basic policies of the CDU/CSU or SPD, a position that can only be explained in view of Germany's particular history. Especially since the introduction of television, the FDP, whether benefiting from its coalition partnership or by playing its opposition role to the hilt, has always managed to maintain its share of the vote well above the five-percent mark required to be seated in the *Bundestag*.

No matter how sincerely each Free Democratic minister intended to adhere to the letter and spirit of the coalition agreement of Erhard's second cabinet, the difficulties which eventually led to the FDP's withdrawal from the coalition on October 27, 1966, were already programmed into the election results of September 19, 1965. In the final campaign waged by the CDU/CSU under Adenauer four years before, the FDP had received 12.8 percent of the vote, which translated into sixty-seven seats in the *Bundestag* and five ministerial positions. In the first elections under Erhard this number dropped to 9.5 percent of the vote, with forty-nine seats in the *Bundestag* and four ministries.

The willingness of the FDP to enter into a coalition did not depend on the liberalism of its potential partner. No one can seriously argue that federal chancellors Brandt or Schmidt espoused more liberal positions than did Erhard. But the professed liberalism of the FDP did serve a dual tactical purpose: on the one hand it bolstered the FDP's own political credibility, on the other it encouraged any potential FDP coalition partner to abstain from attacking it in public debate.

Ludwig Erhard was objective enough to respect the important liberal impulses generated by the FDP in German postwar politics. He never forgot the decisive role liberals played in implementing his social market economy. Nor did he contradict the FDP's claim that their mere existence strengthened the liberal elements of both major parties. Accordingly, he viewed the FDP not only as a coalition partner necessary to obtaining a governing majority, but also as an ally in maintaining a balance to the left wing of the CDU.

A dilemma every coalition partner of the FDP faced sooner or later was the occasional attempt by the minority to impose its views on the majority, like the tail wagging the dog. Yet no coalition between a larger and a smaller partner can endure if the smaller party must always bow to the opinion of the larger. A compromise must be found which realistically takes into account the balance of power; minor gains for the smaller partner must not be allowed to lead to a major loss of voting support for the larger partner, which in turn would endanger the entire coalition.

Cooperation between the coalition parties of Erhard's two cabinets was relatively smooth until the summer of 1966. Then more voices within the FDP, at first only in debate, called for what would eventually lead to a breakup of the coalition with the CDU/CSU. In August the FDP treasurer, Hans Wolfgang Rubin, who later would author a "progressive" paper on Germany that would signal the left turn of the FDP, demanded nothing less than the removal of Erhard as chancellor and the formation of a new FDP/SPD coalition. Leaders of the FDP modified and partly rejected this demand, but doubtless it had its effect within the FDP.

By the time SPD leader Kurt Schumacher died, Herbert Wehner[29] had worked his way to the top of the SPD through a combination of ruthlessness, tenacity, and an arsenal of subversive practices from his communist past. He was Ludwig Erhard's opponent and opposite. It was Wehner who determined the Social Democrat strategy, of which the Godesberg Program was an essential part. With this program the

SPD publicly distanced itself from Marxism, embraced democracy both as a form of government and of life, pledged its cooperation with religious institutions, rejected the notion of an ideological party, and stated its support of national defense, private ownership of the means of production, competition, and entrepreneurial initiative.

The Social Democrats had Wehner's sure political instincts to thank for this document. The Godesberg Program reflected majority opinion within the party and also took a major step toward establishing the SPD's ability to govern the country. And it was Erhard's intuition, grounded in his experience with mass psychology, that prompted his prescient declaration at the thirteenth national CDU party congress in Düsseldorf on March 31, 1965: "The actions of the Social

German policy meeting at the office of the federal chancellor, April 1966.
From left: Herbert Wehner, Willy Brandt, Erhard, Rainer Barzel, Fritz Erler.

Democrats suggest that they would find it advantageous to divide power between the major parties. They are playing with the idea of a system of proportional coalition among the major parties—proportional representational democracy. Socialism wants a piece of the prosperity we have created. So the SPD periodically concocts a national emergency in order to justify proportional democracy."

Once the SPD saw this stage of its larger goal within reach and had initiated contact with politicians of both Union parties, it directed the full force of its political aggression against the chancellor, who vigorously resisted their bid for power. The time had passed when Ludwig Erhard was applauded by the SPD opposition; the time had also passed when, crossing swords with the SPD's Heinrich Deist, Erhard could express his magnanimity and conviction in a paraphrase of Goethe's *Faust*: "To dispute with you, Herr Doctor, is both honorable and rewarding."

The Social Democrats had no easy task in their opposition to Erhard, whose political-economic life's work had long since borne much fruit, and to whom the term "social" in social market economy was not an empty word. Indeed, he could provide manifest evidence of his policies in West Germany: a progressive pension plan—another notable step in West Germany's record as a world leader in social legislation; the equalization of burdens—a communal effort of historical dimensions to attain a fair redistribution of property and burdens; relief payments and pensions to war victims, a demonstration of solidarity by the entire nation; and the Cartel Act, a significant legal step toward securing economic competitiveness in the interests of all consumers.

If the SPD criticized his economic and social policies, he needed only remind them what their former speaker, Professor Erich Nölting, had said in 1951 concerning the economic recovery of the Federal Republic, by then evident everywhere: that it was "a paradise for the rich and hell for the poor." And Nölting, like Erhard, had been a student of Franz Oppenheimer, the man whose teachings in "liberal socialism" had inspired an entire generation of modern thinkers. Whereas Erhard transformed Oppenheimer's concept into "social liberalism," Nölting was trapped in the socialistic theories of the old school.

Long before the state elections in Northrhine-Westphalia in the summer of 1966, when support for the CDU seriously eroded because of the crisis in the area's crucial coal-mining industry, the SPD received an "open letter" from East Germany's Socialist Unity Party (SED) chief Walter Ulbricht. Dated February 11, 1966, it called for agreement "on the great responsibility shared by the two strongest German parties." He then suggested a meeting between representatives of the SPD and the SED.

The SPD responded on March 18 that there was no basis for cooperation between the two parties. Nevertheless, the SPD said it would welcome an open exchange of views about the German question by SPD *Bundestag* representatives and the GDR. *Neues Deutschland*, the official newspaper of the SED, which published both letters on March 26, advanced a new proposal, calling for meetings of SED with SPD representatives in Chemnitz (Karl-Marx-Stadt) and Essen and guaranteeing security and free speech if the SPD did the same for the communists.

The many months of pseudo-dialogue in the newspapers and letters, at party conferences, and in parliamentary group meetings were eventually brought to a brutal halt by East Germany's rulers. The SED had attained its goal—the Social Democrats had entered into correspondence with them, top SPD officials had offered to hold discussions with the SED and had initiated free-conduct procedures for the SED speakers. Most important, they had agreed to changes and delays that came from the communist side. It was a victory on points for the SED. But it also helped make West Germany's public more receptive to plans of Social Democratic strategists who would soon implement their ideas of "change through rapprochement" and a "policy of small steps" as an answer to what they claimed was the Union parties' sterile rigidity.

Erhard had no illusions about the Soviet Union's ruthless exploitation of the Western democracies' hunger for peace and their willingness to relax tensions to enlist these peaceful yearnings in its plans for expansion. Division had made Germany the nation most deeply interested in and profoundly affected by policies of peace and détente— but also most vulnerable to the consequences of miscalculation. West German accommodations and compromises on this issue therefore could not compare with whatever concessions other Western countries could offer the Soviets or their satellites. The West German government made great efforts between 1963 and 1966 to stay in harmony with France and the U.S., as well as with the other NATO members, the democracies outside the alliance, and many Third World countries.

The agreement to issue visitors' passes from West to East Berlin during Christmas 1963 was followed on September 9, 1964, by the East German government's permission to allow pensioners to visit West Germany. On October 1, 1964, the Pass Office for Urgent Hardship Cases opened in West Berlin. A second agreement for visitors' passes allowed 1.4 million West Berliners to visit their relatives in East Berlin between October 30, 1964, and January 3, 1965. On November 25, after lengthy negotiations, a third pass agreement was signed that enabled another 824,000 West Berliners to visit East Germany over Christmas and New Year's. And another one million West Berliners made use of a short-term pass agreement to visit the Eastern Sector over Easter and Whitsuntide 1966. At the signing of this last agreement on March 7, 1966, it was also decided to extend the operation of the Pass Office for Urgent Hardship Cases. Representatives of West Berlin agreed to this "without regard to the differing political and legal positions and differences in opinion concerning the names of places, agencies, and offices." This protective clause was accepted by GDR officials across the years without comment.

The fourth federal assembly met in West Berlin on July 1, 1964, to elect the federal president, with the U.S. and West German governments rejecting Soviet protests against the location of the meeting. On August 22, 1964, the United States, France, and Great Britain reaffirmed in notes to the USSR their right to free access to the air corridor between the Federal Republic of Germany and West Berlin. On April 7, 1965, the *Bundestag* met in West Berlin for its fifth plenary session. East German authorities attempted to disrupt this meeting by tying up traffic on the approaches to Berlin, and closed the autobahn for a short time, under the pretense of carrying out major troop maneuvers with the USSR. On April 29, 1966, the German Foreign Office published a white paper on "Efforts by the German Government and Their Allies to Unite Germany, 1955–1966," which included the following: "To achieve German unity in freedom remains the foremost goal of German policy." And: "As long as Germany remains divided, the Federal Government will continue its efforts to alleviate the consequences of division for those affected by it, above all for Germans in the Soviet occupation zone. The steps necessary to this end, which should not be allowed to lead to a weakening of the Federal Republic's legal and political right of present possession, are not to be understood as a substitute for an international reunification policy."

On November 22, 1963, thirty-seven days after Erhard's election as federal chancellor, President John F. Kennedy was assassinated. During his triumphant visit to West Berlin on June 26, 1963, Kennedy, from a flag-draped platform on the steps of City Hall, had proclaimed before a million roaring West Berliners: "Today in the world of freedom, the proudest boast is 'Ich bin ein Berliner.'" He had also pleased his hosts in his address on arrival at the Cologne/Bonn airport three days earlier with the declaration, "Your safety is our safety, your liberty is our liberty, any attack on your soil is an attack upon our own." These statements resolved all doubt on the German side concerning the reliability of its American partner, doubt that had arisen at the time of Kennedy's election and his "complicity in the Berlin Wall."[30] German suspicion had been encouraged by de Gaulle's increasingly pointed gestures at disengagement from the U.S. In the event, France continued its psychological and political separation from the United States during the administration of Kennedy's successor, Lyndon B. Johnson, as well. A NATO crisis was the direct, and an EEC crisis the indirect, result of this.

The Special Relationship

Around this time a chasm suddenly opened in the two Union parties between the "Atlanticists" and the "Gaullists," with sections of the FDP, SPD, and public opinion lining up on each side. The labels these two divergent paths of political thought assumed only partially explained their purpose. This was due in part to the fact that each group was defined in opposition to the other, and also that the leaders of the two groups, federal foreign minister Gerhard Schröder and CSU Bavarian heavyweight Franz Josef Strauss, were engaged in a heated personal rivalry at the time. Clearly, however, Schröder would not have sacrificed European unity to an exclusively bilateral alliance with the United States. Nor, of course, would Franz Josef Strauss have wanted to release America from its commitment to Europe, and especially to the Federal Republic and Berlin, in order to grant Gaullist France a dominant role in Western Europe.

The Federal Republic's bond with the United States—its importance made only too clear by West Germany's situation in the mid-sixties—must be seen in its proper context. All of West German foreign and domestic policy interests were affected by this alliance, and often decisively influenced by it. For the first time in its history Germany was allied with the strongest economic and military power in the world. The basis of this alliance was the generosity shown by the Americans toward a defeated and demoralized postwar Germany. And for Ludwig Erhard, gratitude was a political and moral imperative.

When Erhard became chancellor, he could look back on many years of positive and untroubled relations with the U.S. He had always been fascinated by America's boldness and strength. By the sixties events had tempered America's once uncomplicated vigor, and had curtailed its will to reach beyond it own borders—at least during a long period of internal adjustment. Publicly its sympathies always remained with the "underdog," the weak and downtrodden. The Germans had profited from this after the war. There was a time during the last years of the ill-fated war in Vietnam when the Viet Cong were more popular with some segments of the American population than its own soldiers.

On December 28 and 29, 1963, Erhard paid his first official visit to Lyndon B. Johnson at the president's Texas ranch. From the first moment the two men enjoyed a strong rapport. The publicity-savvy Johnson saw to it that their mutual empathy was captured by photographers and television crews alike in surroundings charged by the dramatic Texas landscape and its folklore. The ambitious and energetic Democrat would be facing a presidential election the following year; having become president when Kennedy was killed, he wanted to be elected on his own strengths.

Erhard, on the other hand, considered it in the best German interests to demonstrate to the world the close partnership between Bonn and Washington. During their talks, both men expressed their determination to defend the rights and interests of the free world, to improve East-West relations, and to further develop the Atlantic alliance. Johnson reiterated America's unwavering commitment to keep its troops in Germany to support the establishment of a NATO nuclear force. He call the chancellor "a man after his own heart," and Erhard termed his personal relationship with the president "a special one." This description was picked up by American journalists, who used it to describe the affinity between the Federal Republic and the United States.

Up to that time the "special relationship" tag had been reserved for the link between the U.S. and Great Britain. But the strength of the German bond with the U.S., acknowledged by this phrase, had already thrown its shadow over the chancellor's November visit to

France. The talks with de Gaulle had been less than cordial. Now Erhard was scheduled to visit London on January 15 and 16, 1964, to meet British prime minister Douglas-Home and opposition leader Harold Wilson. But if he was worried that the British would be displeased at this "special relationship," he soon learned otherwise. Both Douglas-Home and Harold Wilson were totally preoccupied with the coming House of Commons elections.

Erhard met with Johnson at least a dozen times, including several times after his tenure as chancellor. But the post-Christmas meeting of December 1963 was without a doubt their most intense and successful. Both men had occupied their offices for only a short time, but both had enjoyed long political careers. The weight of their experi-

With U.S. president Lyndon B. Johnson at the White House, Washington, June 1964.

ence lay in domestic policy, and both had inherited difficult and unresolved foreign policy problems from their predecessors. They not only
wished to understand one another, they indeed were able to do so.

Discussions between the two heads of government were excep-
tionally open; they talked about their particular concerns, about the
areas in which they expected help from the other, and about which
actions by the other were undesirable. Johnson was emphatic when
he stated, "We Americans have vouched for Germany and for Berlin.
We have intervened on your behalf wherever you have been threatened militarily or politically. Now we need a gesture of friendship
from you: No German-Chinese relations at this time."

In view of America's critical engagement in Vietnam, Erhard considered this request reasonable. He agreed, even though West Germany and the People's Republic of China had already made significant progress toward establishing relations. And he persisted even
after his ambiguous Vietnam-policy communique drew accusations
that Germany was "behaving like a satellite state" of the U.S. An
uncharacteristically reticent de Gaulle waited until his second subsequent meeting with Erhard, in Bonn on July 3 and 4, 1964, to
express his displeasure with the German position on China, which he
felt compromised his own Asia policy.

The People's Republic of China, which in later years demonstrated
great understanding of the European situation and much interest in
keeping the North Atlantic Treaty intact, did not begrudge the Federal
Republic honoring its allegiance to its ally. And the two politicians
whose names are always mentioned in connection with the eventual
establishment and impressive evolution of German-Chinese relations
are Schröder and Strauss. It is a sad page in the history of postwar
German politics, revealing the internal tensions in the Union parties
that Erhard's chancellorship inherited and never fully resolved, that
these two particularly talented politicians proved an obstacle to one
another for such a long time.

German-American relations in those years were not free of problems arising from the differing obligations and responsibilities of the
two nations. A multilateral nuclear strike force was proposed by the
U.S. and welcomed by the Federal Republic, but opposed by France
and finally left unrealized. The future of NATO itself was seriously
threatened when France announced its withdrawal on February 21,
1966. And the German-American foreign exchange settlement for
American troops stationed in West Germany, which the Federal

Republic could not fully cover with the purchase of U.S. arms, raised questions. The fact that these problems did not damage relations between the two countries, and were handled with sensitivity even when they could not be resolved, was due in large part to the relationship of trust between Johnson and Erhard.

The impetus generated by the founding fathers of European unity, Schuman, Adenauer, and de Gasperi—all members of the war generation—had diminished years before Erhard assumed office as chancellor. Erhard believed this was due to what he thought was an erroneous decision to take an institutional rather than a practical approach to European unity. During his chancellorship the federal government undertook numerous European initiatives, but aside from some positive psychological results, none was successful.

Among West Germany's postwar accomplishments, second in importance only to reestablishing sovereignty and returning to the community of free nations, was the end of the centuries-long enmity with France and its transformation into a strong friendship. This new foundation of trust, though only partially anchored in institutions, would doubtlessly form the core of a united Europe. The military presence of Soviet Russia on the Elbe River, however, necessitated strong ties with the United States. Erhard, to attain the attainable, had confirmed the path taken thus far, but he made no secret of his view that a free and equal Europe must expand its borders beyond those of Charlemagne, "King of the Franks and Emperor of the West." He had also warned of the danger of the EEC isolating itself from the rest of the world through external tariff barriers.

With the election of General Charles de Gaulle as president of the Fifth French Republic and the rise of Gaullism, developments in Europe and Franco-German relations entered a new phase. Konrad Adenauer no doubt appreciated the General's grandeur, his authoritativeness and tactical political skills. Nevertheless, de Gaulle represented ideas many elements of which were more suited to Erhard than to Adenauer. One example of this was de Gaulle's rejection of a supranational EEC that would spawn a sovereign European nation state, as expounded by Adenauer's Foreign Office undersecretary Walter Hallstein. Hallstein was the man who first had translated Adenauer's foreign policy ideas into the language of bureaucratic legality, the same man who, in the words of EEC Commission president George W. Ball, had been struck by "thunder and lightning from the summit of Elysium." Hallstein's knowledge and strength of conviction often had impressed de Gaulle, but had not affected his policies. Konrad Adenauer, paradoxically, in an apparent attempt to salvage what he could, often acquiesced to ideas of de Gaulle that Erhard found unacceptable.

Erhard's personal reservations about the EEC always derived from his concern that it could become protectionist and eventually interfere with the growth of free international trade. But he never advocated more modest or limited solutions, or a French, German, or Franco-German hegemony within the EEC. De Gaulle did not find Erhard a comfortable conversation partner; and the General's attempts to put pressure on Erhard, as he had on Adenauer and others, led to a stiffening of Erhard's resolve. For this de Gaulle publicly expressed his respect for Erhard in later years.

At no time, however, did Erhard pursue an anti-Gaullist policy. De Gaulle's concept was that of "a Europe of fatherlands," a Europe, that is, in which size and power were not the ultimate criteria, which merged its economic and social forces and would be in the position to shoulder international responsibility decisively and with a common political will. None of this differed greatly from Erhard's own ideas. But de Gaulle, statesman of towering stature, also pursued a series of short-term, shortsighted goals, some of them in direct opposition to German interests. The German head of state clearly could not compromise on such issues. It was not difficult for Erhard to acknowledge France's spiritual authority, little affected as it was by the psychological and political turmoil of the war and postwar years.

What he found unacceptable was de Gaulle's proposal to assume joint responsibility—moral, political, and, above all, financial—for France's relatively tiny nuclear force, the Force de frappe, without a clear say in its employment and at the possible fatal danger of cutting off its ties with the United States. The hope entertained by many—of eventually obtaining a common nuclear force in this way—was too vague for Erhard, nor was he sure it was a desirable goal. At any rate, in view of de Gaulle's overtures toward the East bloc, the risk was too high. But the French president was very keen to pacify the left in his country by trying very hard to establish political and economic contacts with the communist East.

In the spring of 1966 France notified NATO that all command posts were to be off French soil by April 1, and that French troops would cease participation by July 1. President de Gaulle justified this by saying that the danger of a European war had been reduced. Konrad Adenauer took up the argument and declared at a CDU party convention in Bonn that Soviet mediation between India and Pakistan had proved that the USSR had joined the circle of peaceloving nations.

Erhard himself did not believe there was a real danger of war in Europe. But in the face of a feverish arms build-up by the Soviets, however, he saw NATO as the first line of defense and the sole dependable guarantee of freedom. Seen against this backdrop there is no real explanation for the behavior of the German Gaullists. It was an open secret that the very group within the CDU/CSU that supported de Gaulle was expressing doubt about the firmness of Erhard's policies in confronting the communist East.

It was a time when East-bloc strategists were frantically seeking ways to eviscerate the Hallstein Doctrine. This principle of foreign policy had been developed by a diplomat and eminent specialist in international law, Dr. Wilhelm Grewe, and named for Walter Hallstein. It stated that the Federal Republic of Germany could not maintain diplomatic relations with any country that recognized the German Democratic Republic. Taking their cue from the game of chess its opponents were trying to stalemate Bonn's foreign policy. Walter Ulbricht's visit to Egypt exemplified this strategy.

But it was also a time when East German propagandists, with the help of some West German sympathizers, succeeded in starting serious discussion among Bonn's political parties about the purpose of the Federal Republic's sole right of representation. Language was consciously used as a weapon, and the population became more lax in other matters—both served as psychological underpinning. It is true that East German jargon began to manifest itself in the Federal Republic only after Erhard's term as chancellor. The sole right of representation became a "claim" to sole representation, and finally an "arrogation."

And finally, these were also the years when the USSR held out the siren promise of détente, threatened an arms build-up, used its international capacity for subversion to influence public opinion, and exploited objective differences between NATO members to target some with diplomatic offensives designed to divide them.

But the Soviet Union and East Germany made no progress at all in this area between October 1963 and November 1966. To the contrary, during Erhard's administration not one member of the federal government committed to anything the GDR could view as upgrading its status, or that the Soviet Union and its Eastern European satellites could interpret as recognition of its European dominion. Instead, Erhard, in a series of internationally respected diplomatic steps, helped ease the communist camp's ideological lockjaw. In none of these initiatives was West Germany's own legal position jeopardized, much less put on the table as "political currency."

Yet because Erhard's foreign policy was guided by his knowledge of international economic interconnections, no one could persuade him that trade with East-bloc countries served the interests of West Germany's export industry. He resisted any quid pro quo on trade that would entail West German political concessions. All offers made to communist countries Erhard linked to the flat demand to respect West Germany's position in regard to international law. And this demand was met by the Soviet Union, as well as by those Eastern European countries who agreed to an exchange of trade representatives during Erhard's chancellorship.

On June 13, 1964, Ambassador Horst Kroepper delivered to Khrushchev a note with which the Federal Republic asserted its unequivocal opposition under international law to the recently signed "Friendship Agreement" between the USSR and the GDR. Kroepper told Khrushchev that should he consider a meeting useful, he could expect an invitation from Erhard.

This set in motion a process which in retrospect resembled the famous "ping-pong diplomacy" initiated by the People's Republic of China several years later when it normalized relations with the U.S. In this case, the ping-pong player was Alexei Adzhubei, editor-in-chief of Moscow's official newspaper, *Izvestia*, and Khrushchev's son-in-law. A number of West German publications had invited him to visit the Federal Republic.

Adzhubei came to Bonn on July 28, 1964, not for a political interview, but to convey greetings from Khrushchev to Erhard. Adzhubei asked Erhard if he would accept an invitation to Moscow, saying that Khrushchev wished to get to know him. Erhard made it very clear that according to diplomatic custom it was Khrushchev's turn to visit the Federal Republic, since Adenauer had visited Moscow as chancellor.

This began a dialogue of several weeks, which both sides pursued with great tenacity. The Soviets were represented by Adzhubei, at first, and then by the Soviet ambassador in Bonn, Andrei Smirnov. These men spoke for Khrushchev, but increasingly for his emergent enemies in the Kremlin, as well.

The fact that the Soviet premier would even consider a trip to Bonn was in itself a moderate sensation. The visit was clearly in the Soviet interest for a number of reasons, but, as always, Moscow tried to secure the most favorable conditions from the beginning. Erhard expressed his interest, but avoided giving the impression that the visit was more important to him than to Khrushchev, with the result that Khrushchev agreed to come to Bonn. But then Khrushchev set the next condition: the German question was not to be discussed. Erhard, however, let it be known that a meeting between the heads of state of the Federal Republic of Germany and the USSR would be unthinkable without broaching the topic most significant to their mutual relationship. And again Khrushchev agreed. The German question would be included in their discussions.

Adzhubei had returned to Moscow in the meantime, and his reports were remarkably free of the obligatory accusations made officially only weeks before that the Federal Republic was revanchist or militaristic. Adzhubei called his conversation with Erhard the "first constructive step toward improving relations." On September 3, 1964, Moscow announced that Khrushchev would visit the Federal Republic.

Later there was much speculation about whether Khrushchev's plan to come to Bonn contributed to his downfall on October 14, 1964, or perhaps even triggered it. Erhard had good reason not to take this speculation seriously. Several months before Khrushchev's fall the Soviet ambassador had asked him in extremely guarded fashion whether this invitation would apply to Khrushchev's successor as well.

The goal of Erhard's policy was the cautious easing of the Communist-bloc mentality in order to at least open discussion on the German question. This called for absolute determination in the face of all attempts to soften or cut back German positions and to keep on trying regardless of setbacks and the appearance of irreconcilability.

One example of Germany's constructive peace policy was Erhard's Peace Note of March 25, 1966, which helped ease tensions and gained international support for German interests. It was sent to all foreign governments with which the Federal Republic maintained diplomatic relations, as well as to the governments of Eastern Europe and the Arab states. In it, Erhard addressed West Germany's neighbors to the east individually about specific bilateral problems. "If at the proper time Poles and Germans can talk about their borders in the same spirit that led to accord between Germany and its neighbors to the west, then Poles and Germans will reach an agreement as well," it stated, adding that until a peace treaty was signed with all of Germany settling the border question, Germany, according to international law, would continue to exist within its 1937 borders.

The note addressed to the Soviet Union used clear but reserved language: "The government of the USSR has declared repeatedly that it does not desire war. The Federal Republic presumes this wish to be serious. Soviet reassurances, however, are undermined by the unambiguous and massive threats not infrequently directed at the German federal government." On the issues of disarmament and security the federal government stated its position emphatically and in terms universally understood. It was prepared to exchange formal nonaggression declarations with the countries of Eastern Europe, as well as to work together with them on comprehensive plans to prevent the risk of nuclear war, declaring "that all efforts toward security, disarmament, and arms control will enjoy decisive and lasting success only if step-by-step action is taken toward the elimination of international tensions. In Europe, this means, above all, that the German question be resolved in a just manner, by giving the entire German people the right to freely determine their political way of life and their fate."

The Peace Note drew a uniformly negative reaction from the East-bloc governments. But it was positively received by the East-bloc populations, insofar as Western radio broadcasts let them know what it said. The West and the Third World met Erhard's initiative with wide approval. The U.S. Government called it "constructive and trend-setting."

The impact of the Peace Note was due in part to its balance, but also, as Erhard acknowledged publicly, to its consummate form. This was largely the work of diplomat and author Erwin Wickert. Karl Carstens, at that time undersecretary of state, and a future president of the Federal Republic, said: "His exquisite expressiveness and the beauty of the language, distinctive to his novels, are evident in the Note as well."

Erhard's most precarious foreign-policy dilemma arose when it was revealed that the Federal Republic was secretly shipping arms to Israel. The chancellor suddenly faced opposition from all sides. It was never discovered who leaked the story about this arrangement, which had been initiated by Adenauer and Ben-Gurion.

Ultimately Erhard resolved the problem by going on the attack—

on March 7, 1965, he would announce the establishment of diplomatic relations with Israel. In retrospect this seems a normal albeit tardy step to take. At the time, it called for great courage, and led to a new relation between two peoples with a background in tragedy. Bonn ultimately gained much greater freedom of movement as a result of this diplomatic initiative—its sovereignty was strengthened and its foreign policy freed from the threat of extortion. But with the Arab world, the Federal Republic—a state without a colonial past in the Near East, a former enemy of the Allies (whom the Arabs still referred to as "imperialists"), and a major trade partner with important cultural ties to the Arabs—saw its influence wane as that of the communists increased.

As the Arab-Israeli situation had heated up during the 1950s, diplomatic relations with Bonn had grown in importance for the Israelis. But the Federal Republic had drifted into a relationship with the Arab states that made recognition of Israel awkward. This despite the fact that eighty-nine other countries—one of them the Soviet Union—had established ties with Israel without the least remonstration on the part of the Arabs. So when, in March 1960, Adenauer had offered Ben-Gurion an American-supported, 300-million–Deutsche Mark arms deal, it had been done in secret. Defense Minister Franz Josef Strauss, and later his successor, Kai-Uwe von Hassel, worked out the complicated technical provisions of the agreement with their Israeli counterpart, Shimon Peres. At home, the Social Democratic opposition was informed of the agreement in confidence, and raised no objections. The policy persisted unpublicized through the remainder of Adenauer's tenure and Erhard's first year as chancellor.

Then a furor arose when the *Frankfurter Rundschau*, a daily paper with SPD leanings, broke the story on October 26, 1964. This was followed five days later by a report in the *New York Times*. The Egyptian press covered the story extensively on November 12, and Cairo demanded to be officially informed by the federal government on "alleged German military aid to Israel." On November 23, the president of the *Bundestag*, Eugen Gerstenmaier, met with Egyptian president Gamal Abdel Nasser in Cairo. He proposed that the Federal Republic would cease military aid to Israel if the United Arab Republic would accept normalized relations between the Federal Republic and Israel.

What neither Konrad Adenauer nor the Americans had originally anticipated was the Soviet-instigated Arab threat to recognize the

German Democratic Republic. This weakened Bonn's position to an almost intolerable degree. Meanwhile, the publication of more details of the arms sale put strong domestic pressure on Bonn, in part for a commitment not to sell arms in any world trouble spots.

On January 27, 1965, Nasser announced he had invited Walter Ulbricht, chairman of the GDR's Council of State, to the United Arab Republic because of West German military support of Israel. Many years later it was made public how fine a net the GDR and the USSR had spun to entrap a number of the Arab governments. Ulbricht, in fact, had invited himself, under the pretense of taking a cure in Upper Egypt. But all of this was unknown at the time, nor would it have proved relevant.

Erhard publicly asked Nasser to withdraw the invitation, holding out the hope of replacing arms with the sale of other supplies to Israel, threatening serious repercussions should his offer be refused. Syria almost simultaneously attempted to blackmail the Federal Republic by demanding major financial support for the Euphrates Dam project. Failing that, Damascus would recognize the GDR.

An Arab summit conference of February 22, 1965, demanded an immediate halt to German arms deliveries to Israel. All attending states threatened to break off diplomatic relations with the Federal Republic, some threatening to recognize the GDR. Indeed, Nasser's invitation to Ulbricht had already constituted de facto recognition in the eyes of most observers.

Now was the time to act. Erhard, with Western support, quickly rejected any suggestions to break off diplomatic ties with Cairo. The official reason was that the United Arab Republic had stopped short of a formal recognition of the German Democratic Republic. But Bonn cut off economic aid to Cairo.

The Federal Republic used Spanish intermediaries in dealing with the Arabs. But despite the high degree of trust the Arabs had for Spain and the great diplomatic skills of the respected negotiator, the Marqués de Nerva, the attempt to reach an understanding failed.

Still, Erhard's preferred solution—introducing diplomatic relations with Israel while at the same time replacing arms with other aid— met with great resistance. Israeli prime minister Levi Eshkol issued a sharply worded statement declaring it odd that Germany, itself located in an area of major international tensions, should find in Israel's similar predicament a reason for no longer contributing to its security. Germany did not have the right, he continued, to consider Israel an area of conflict. Israel, rather, was all that remained to the Jewish people following the most terrible suffering ever to be visited upon a member of the family of nations.

The ambassadors of the three Western powers warned Erhard against taking a step that might lead to a break with the Arabs, in particular with the United Arab Republic. In a cabinet meeting of March 4, 1965, German foreign minister Schröder expressly opposed gambling with the German presence in the Arab states. On March 5 Erhard asked Kurt Birrenbach, CDU *Bundestag* member and seasoned foreign policy expert, to conduct negotiations to establish diplomatic relations with the Israeli government. The following thirty-six hours were taken up with discussions and conferences attended by ministers, leading members of the federal chancellery and the Foreign Office, and—on the morning of March 6—by Rainer Barzel, head of the CDU/CSU *Bundestag* caucus.

Three negotiating options were up for discussion: the establishment of full diplomatic relations; the establishment of a German consulate-general in Israel, which could, if negotiations with the Arabs failed, become an embassy; or the establishment of a German mission in Israel, similar to the Israeli mission in Cologne, an idea that had been under consideration for years.

Agreement was reached that West Germany's sale of arms to Israel must be terminated, and compensated for. In light of the talks he had held with American government officials only a few days earlier, Birrenbach tended toward the second model. Barzel, who had also just returned from a trip to America, where he had met with members of numerous Jewish organizations, supported an immediate establishment of full diplomatic relations.

Erhard also advocated full recognition, strengthened in his conviction by the expert advice of his closest circle of associates. One such expert, who was intimately acquainted with the Near East and who enjoyed excellent ties to the Arab world, expressed the tenable opinion that the Arabs would lose all trace of their traditional respect for the Germans should the Federal Republic give in to their current blackmail attempt and thus open the door to further coercion by coming up with a half-hearted solution. But the overriding reasons for Erhard's final decision were based on morality and history, and in this he found himself in total agreement with the leaders of the CDU/CSU in the *Bundestag*.

The Arab states reacted vehemently to Erhard's decision. On

March 8 King Hassan of Morocco canceled his scheduled visit to Bonn. On March 15 representatives of the Arab states held a two-day meeting in Cairo, after which they announced they would break off diplomatic relations with the Federal Republic should the latter recognize Israel. On May 5 the West German government agreed to establish diplomatic relations with Israel. On May 13 the Arab states, with the exceptions of Tunisia, Morocco, and Libya, broke off diplomatic relations with Bonn.

The Formed Society

It was no accident that at the beginning of the sixties strongly liberal democratic models of society emerged almost simultaneously in the two most advanced Western industrial nations, the United States and the Federal Republic of Germany. John F. Kennedy proclaimed the "new frontier," Lyndon B. Johnson the "great society," and Erhard introduced the concept of the *formierte Gesellschaft* (the "shaped" or "fully formed" society).[31] None of these models came out of the blue. They integrated ideas that were long in the making and goals that were necessary; and indirectly they were an answer to the more subtle challenges of socialism.

Erhard first used the expression *formierte Gesellschaft* on March 31, 1965, at a CDU conference in Düsseldorf; it originated with eighteenth-century poet and playwright Friedrich Schiller. This visionary concept was developed by Erhard together with a group of young intellectuals—political economists, historians, jurists, social psychologists, and publicists—brought together as a sort of unofficial advisory staff by Erhard's associate Karl Hohmann. Rüdiger Altmann and Johannes Gross[32] played a particularly large role in working out the concept's programmatic details.

Using the guidelines for a *formierte Gesellschaft* Erhard provided answers to questions that were just beginning to be articulated. With his sure sense of social currents he offered solutions to problems that more than twenty-five years later would prove a threat to the democracies of the industrialized world, as well as to the states of the now-defunct communist system and those of the Third World.

"Ludwig Erhard himself," Rüdiger Altmann wrote more than ten years later, "applying the provocative formula of a *formierte Gesellschaft*, attempted to plumb the idea of a more autonomous and expanded political potential for society in the face of state authority. It was a liberal formula deriving from Erhard's character and religious faith, displaying more rationality than the power and organizational apparatuses of the state are capable of."[33]

If, in later years, it was individualism degenerating ever more into naked egotism that eventually degraded the community spirit into empty words, the Union parties' response to Erhard's *formierte Gesellschaft* was a simple pragmatism with little patience for theoretical ideas.

In the meantime, the social vacuum was filled more rapidly than the bourgeois camp was able to grasp. These were the years when students, children of prosperous parents, costumed themselves as proletarians and played "class struggle" in the streets and at the universities. An elderly group of long-forgotten Marxist theoreticians, leftovers of the "Frankfurt School,"[34] provided the pseudo-philosophical basis with seductively convincing theories. The absence of economic conditions needed to realize their utopias proved their true intellectual worth soon enough, but even the most insipid neo-revolutionaries espoused them for years to come.

Erhard saw the *formierte Gesellschaft* as the logical next step in a social market economy. But whereas during the immediate postwar years Germans had followed him almost blindly because he led them out of their economic misery, he now encountered widespread indifference among a prosperous middle class. Clearly, as chancellor, Ludwig Erhard could not devote himself as intensively to propagating ideas as he had as director of the economy and, later, as minister of economics. After two decades of battling for a social market economy, Erhard, soon to turn seventy, may have lacked the strength to do so.

The concept of a *formierte Gesellschaft* was that of a dynamically balanced society, with well thought-out guidelines for overcoming the problems of that era and of crises yet to come. It rejected the collectivist welfare state, stressing individual responsibility while at the same time calling for solidarity with the underprivileged. It advocated linking productivity to a non-ideological social policy, and saw mutual international dependencies in relation to national progress. It cautioned against mindless consumerism achieved at the cost of a propitious future, and above all it tried to reconcile antagonistic group interests for the sake of the whole.

The reaction from the left was particularly revealing. The Social Democrats, on the one hand, had no sound argument against the concept, for which reason they employed cynical puns like *"die deformierte Gesellschaft"* (the deformed society) to oppose it. On the other hand, the political lethargy and indifference to theory of the CDU and CSU gave unwitting support to the SPD in their rather confused tactics.

The press of the East bloc attacked this proposed social model with catchphrases and slogans that later would be taken up by the "new left," both within and outside the SPD. The international left also could not resist ridiculing the *deformierte Gesellschaft* as half-baked, untenable, and insignificant nonsense while in the same breath warning against the danger of the idea.

Leo Leontiev, for example, a member of the USSR Academy of Sciences, devoted several pages of the *Literaturnaia Gazeta* of March 15, 1966, to the *deformierte Gesellschaft*, reporting that it was being "passionately welcomed" by the "emissaries of monopoly capitalism." The idea, he wrote, had been conceived "to serve as a weapon of Bonn's expansionist and revanchist policies."

For the *Bundestag* elections of 1965 Ludwig Erhard undertook his last massive political campaign, and it ended with an impressive victory. He interrupted his campaign, which lasted from August 8 through September 17, with only a few official duties: the seventy-fifth annual celebration of the German Reich's acquisition of the island of Helgoland, for example, and the opening of the Frankfurt Automobile Exposition. During the forty-one days of the election campaign he delivered close to seven hundred speeches, including short addresses to small communities he was passing through. In the end, he had spoken directly to roughly one and a half million people.

The campaign was organized down to the last detail, employing all available means of modern technology so that Erhard could make appearances in opposite parts of the Federal Republic within a few hours' time. Each event was timed to achieve a maximum of national and international coverage, and to provide local Union party *Bundestag* candidates with strong campaign support. The campaign trail covered land, water, and air—there were special trains, cars, planes, helicopters, vessels for river and sea, and even horse-drawn carriages. On each of his thirteen campaign trips Erhard was accompanied by an entourage of fifteen to twenty national and foreign journalists, joined by local reporters from newspapers, radio, and television. During this entire period Erhard spent only two nights in his own bed; on the other thirty-nine nights he slept in a special campaign rail car as it traveled back and forth across Germany.

Unless special dates or local events forced a change in his schedule, the days of the campaign followed a specific plan: breakfast on the train with government officials from the chancellor's office or press office, who kept him apprised of the latest domestic and international developments. The schedule allowed for time to keep in touch by phone or telex with Bonn, issue instructions, or arrange urgent meetings, so that there was no interruption in the business of government. Mid- or late mornings were taken up with campaign appearances, visits, or inspections. Meals were reserved either for meetings with representatives of Erhard's own party, local political dignitaries or other local people of note, or they provided a brief opportunity to relax.

Erhard spent afternoons traveling by car through fifteen to thirty towns and communities. Most of his visits were announced ahead of time, and German citizens greeted him in front of city halls or in marketplaces, at sports facilities or assembly halls. One, and sometimes two, major appearances were planned for each evening, followed either by a conversation with local CDU *Bundestag* candidates and other party representatives, or a talk with journalists following the campaign in the campaign train's parlor car. Every two or three days the train stopped in Bonn and Erhard spent several hours in his office, taking care of government matters that required his presence. But by afternoon he was back on the campaign trail, accompanied by a new contingent of journalists.

At a special party meeting on February 16, 1964, the SPD had chosen Willy Brandt, the mayor of Berlin, to succeed Erich Ollenhauer as head of the party and as their candidate for chancellor. The almost total adoption of Union policies expressed in the SPD's statements was a reflection of Brandt's campaign organization. Though still a political lightweight who employed a mobile staff of ghostwriters, Brandt's charisma was already being noticed, above all by the younger generation.

In this election campaign the Union parties could point to sixteen years of uninterrupted progress. The standard of living in West Germany had doubled since 1950, and the Federal Republic had become the world's third-largest industrial power, ranking second in trade, and first in social spending as a percentage of gross national product. The gross national product of this campaign year was 452.7 billion

Deutsche Mark (about $250 billion at the time), with an average per capita income of 5,884 Deutsche Mark (about $3,250). Roughly 90,000 people were unemployed, but at the same time there were approximately 1.2 million foreign workers in the Federal Republic.

All of this left the opposition little room for argument, criticism, or alternatives. The relatively low inflation rate at that time—a fraction of what Chancellor Brandt and Finance Minister Helmut Schmidt would later be responsible for—nevertheless led the SPD candidate to repeat in public a dubious joke his ghostwriters had come up with: "A soft chancellor can't make the mark hard again."

This remark enraged Erhard, and it happened that Brandt used it in a city in which both men were speaking at the same time at different events. When Erhard heard of Brandt's remark from a colleague during his own speech, he spontaneously retaliated, saying that he was already concerning himself with the German currency before some others had even set foot on German soil again.[35] Based on his own political past, Erhard did not feel it necessary to qualify this statement by adding that he did not mean to step on the toes of those emigrants who had turned their backs on the Third Reich out of political conviction. He simply did not intend to allow a candidate with no experience in economic matters to "deceive citizens with such simplistic demagoguery," as he put it.

The SPD and its followers, however, were furious. Using a tried and true method, they attempted to tar Erhard with the brush of National Socialism. It was the same ploy Herbert Wehner used throughout his entire political life—loudly accusing of maliciousness any political opponent who dared not to suffer a Social Democratic attack in patience, or even went so far as to fight back.

But there was a fact that the SPD truly could exploit, and it cost the CDU/CSU a percentage of the vote in 1965: leading Union politicians were publicly distancing themselves from Erhard and his policies. Right in the middle of the campaign Adenauer dropped one such bomb in rebuttal to a U.S. plan for a nuclear non-proliferation treaty advanced at the Geneva Conference on Disarmament: "The American disarmament plan is so abominable, so horrible, that with it Europe would be delivered into the hands of the Russians." Erhard was not informed of this statement in advance, to say nothing of agreeing with it.

The question of a non-proliferation agreement was of vital importance to the future of German sovereignty, the development of Europe, and to world military balance. But such a public overreaction carried the risk of seriously bedeviling relations with the United States. Erhard immediately declared that the Federal Republic had to be defended with the same type of weapons turned against it. But from that time on, the SPD could peddle the idea of a "dissension within the Union."

During this period Ulrich Frank-Planitz, who was then editor of *Civis*,[36] informed the chancellor that leading CDU/CSU politicians— several of them former members of his administration—were secretly meeting to talk about forming a Great Coalition with the SPD. This issue had refused to go away since November 1962, when Adenauer, who only a short time before had equated the SPD with the "decline of Germany," joined negotiations on forming a coalition government with the Social Democrats. Herbert Wehner had characterized "a time-limited coalition with the Christian Democrats" as a "guarantee for the continuation of the democratic order," and declared: "We will not tire of reminding voters that Adenauer himself recognized us as a party that can govern."

Erhard was unimpressed by the information he received concerning these secret talks. He knew support for a Union-SPD coalition existed, and believed it was prompted, in his own party, by a fear that the election results would be close. He also knew that such a coalition was the only way for the SPD to assume governmental responsibility. But despite Erhard's reputation as overly sensitive and thin-skinned, he believed that all of this was like counting the chickens before they are hatched. The final decision was up to the German voters. He felt secure in this, and the election results proved him right. With the exception of the 1957 election, the Union parties enjoyed their greatest success ever at the polls.

The CDU/CSU garnered 47.6 percent of the electoral vote, the SPD 39.3 percent, and the FDP 9.5 percent—a Union victory that should have relegated plans for a Great Coalition to the realm of dreams. But the stuff these dreams were made of proved more lasting than Erhard believed in those September days. The Union parties, which in the past had courageously and decisively tackled much greater problems with a much smaller majority, now shied away from assuming full responsibility. And their Free Democratic coalition partner had already prepared plans for Erhard's departure.

On September 20, 1965, the CDU again nominated Erhard for federal chancellor. But at the first meeting of the CDU party caucus, without the least consideration for the embarrassment it would cause himself or the federal president, Heinrich Lübke, Konrad Adenauer unabashedly read a prematurely penned memorandum from Lübke, counseling negotiations toward the founding of a Great Coalition, based on his expectation of a poor showing of the Union parties at the polls. However, nothing came of this.

The formation of Erhard's cabinet lasted five and a half weeks. During those weeks a light flu, and the cumulative effects of his campaign exertions, took a serious toll on Erhard's energy. As a result, all of the groups and individuals active in forming the cabinet presented their positions to the public more forcefully than the head of government himself was able to do.

Ludger Westrick, minister of the chancellery and Erhard's loyal and devoted friend of many years, had increasingly viewed his role as one of protection and conciliation. Acting from the best of intentions he occasionally intervened in such a way that the public effects of Erhard's actions were quite the opposite of what was intended. Westrick, without Erhard's approval, wanted to stop Undersecretary Karl-Günther von Hase, head of the government's Press and Information Office, and Undersecretary Karl Hohmann, head of the chancellor's office, from informing the public about the negotiations to form a cabinet. Spokesmen of the CDU/CSU caucus and other involved politicians, of course, were little concerned in their public statements with the chancellor's views.

Despite the prestige conferred upon those chosen for the cabinet, the majority of FDP members returning to the government had a harder time with their own party than with the CDU/CSU. This was particularly true of Finance Minister Rolf Dahlgrün and Vice-Chancellor Erich Mende, as in the debate about the statute of limitations it had already been true of Ewald Bucher. Bucher, who took over the Ministry of Post and Telecommunications in Erhard's second cabinet, had prematurely resigned as federal minister of justice in Erhard's first cabinet.

On November 5, 1964, the cabinet had dealt with the issue of the expiration of the statute of limitations on Nazi war crimes, which was scheduled in the former British and French zones for May 8, and in the former American zone for July 1, 1965. Based on Minister of Justice Bucher's legal arguments and the extensive data he presented, the cabinet, deciding against the opinion of Erhard, Ernst Lemmer,

Federal President Heinrich Lübke receives Erhard's second cabinet on October 26, 1965. First row, from left: Erich Mende, Lübke, Erhard, Gerhard Schröder. Second row, from left: Kurt Schmücker, Hermann Höcherl, Richard Stücklen, Werner Dollinger, Walter Scheel, Ludger Westrick. Third row, from left: Johann Baptist Gradl, Kai-Uwe von Hassel, Gerhard Stoltenberg, Rolf Dahlgrün, Alois Niederalt, Bruno Heck, Hans Katzer. Fourth row, from left: Ewald Bucher, Paul Lücke, Heinrich Krone, Hans-Christoph Seebohm, Elisabeth Schwarzhaupt, Richard Jäger.

Theodore Blank, and Paul Lücke, had rejected an extension of the statute of limitations on Nazi war crimes with retroactive effect, as specified in Article 103 of the Basic Law. But on March 25, 1965, following long, tortuous, and for the most part bitter debates which were joined in by parties abroad, the *Bundestag* passed by overwhelming majority a law extending the twenty-year statute of limitations on Nazi war crimes, the mandatory punishment for which was life imprisonment, to December 31, 1969. The next day Bucher had resigned.

If at the beginning of his chancellorship Erhard had been surprised by the degree of authority, influence, and information commanded by this highest office of government, by the end of his term he was no less astounded by how quickly all of this dissolved, despite his splendid showing at the polls.

But it was not Federal Chancellor Erhard who failed in November 1966. It is true that he was unable to balance a budget deficit insignificant according to today's standards, that he did not discipline opponents within his own party harshly enough, that despite his better judgment he did not have the political toughness to rebuff the interest groups of various organizations, his own party, and the media. He refused to employ the instruments of political power to shore up his chancellorship; it was against his nature. What this meant in November of 1966 was the end of a modern concept of gov-

In conversation with Ludger Westrick, February 1965.

ernment which had carried a profound study of democratic principles to its logical conclusion.

The political catchphrase "Great Coalition," which Adenauer used as well, became embedded in the consciousness of the Union parties like a tumor, and, astoundingly, it was the politicians with a right-wing reputation who made strong advances to the SPD.

There followed the phase of "is-and-shall-remain," as in, "Ludwig Erhard is and shall remain federal chancellor," which the CDU/CSU reformulated in ever new variations. The more often they did so, the less convincing it sounded. At the same time that the FDP was meeting in Stuttgart on Epiphany Day, January 6, 1966, to discuss the dismantling of the "Erhard myth," CSU *Bundestag* member Karl Theodor Freiherr von und zu Guttenberg was publicly supporting the formation of a Great Coalition.

Soon thereafter, elections for state parliament were held in Northrhine-Westphalia, Germany's largest and most populous state. Unemployment had been on the increase for some time along the Rhine and Ruhr rivers—though it was less than a quarter of what it would be under the coming SPD/FDP government. Only ten percent of the unemployed were miners, but the SPD blatantly exploited the crisis in the coal mining industry to its own advantage. Industry leaders were demanding hundreds of millions of Deutsche Mark in government subsidies, something that had become routine under Konrad Adenauer's administration. Now the miners were sent into the streets by their unions and the SPD.

On September 15, 1966, the *Bundestag* debated the Act to Promote Economic Stability and Growth at the first reading. On the same day Ludger Westrick, minister of the chancellor's office, tendered his resignation, explaining that he wanted to clear the way for a possible restructuring of the cabinet, an idea that Erhard had categorically rejected two days before. The carefully framed debate on the Stability Act was pushed into the background by Westrick's announcement, and this angered the CDU/CSU faction. Erhard accepted Westrick's resignation.

Erhard's final talks as chancellor were held with President Lyndon B. Johnson from September 24 to 28, 1966, and they ended in failure. Erhard was unable to get Johnson to extend credit for payment in American currency for the U.S. troops stationed in West Germany. Johnson greatly regretted this, but the domestic situation in the United States left him no alternative.

On October 3 the CDU/CSU caucus issued its last "is-and-shall-remain-so" declaration, joined on October 7 by the CDU party leadership. "We want to help you," Franz Josef Strauss declared at a Bavarian CSU assembly on October 9. Two days earlier Strauss had managed only with great effort to stop the party's executive committee from withdrawing all CSU ministers from Erhard's cabinet.

With the resignation of the FDP cabinet ministers there was no stopping the rush to a Great Coalition with the SPD. The SPD demand for new elections was rejected by Rainer Barzel, head of the CDU/CSU *Bundestag* caucus, who argued that voters had elected the Union parties for four years of political leadership, a popular decision the Union would abide by. On November 4, 1966, the *Bundestag's* Council of Elders joined the SPD and FDP in voting to put the SPD motion on the agenda of the next plenary meeting, a move designed to force Erhard to call for a vote of confidence. The CDU/CSU representative on the council, Will Rasner, termed the motion unconstitutional, because only the chancellor could call for a vote of confidence. And Erhard curtly rejected the idea, having no intention of subjecting himself to a "show trial."

It is unclear whether the budget deficit served the FDP as a pretext for a subjective decision, or whether for these liberals a deficit was truly seen as the writing on the wall about the "distribution state."

A constant war of attrition was waged against Erhard in interviews and newspaper articles, of which those that appeared in the *Bild*[37] were particularly harsh. Almost nothing happened in the Federal Republic that Erhard was not held responsible for, from the allegedly poor pay of civil servants to the crashes of Starfighter air force jets. Whenever the best of experts and the soundest judgment failed, blame was placed at the top. And long before the chase was over, the struggle began to divide up the lion's share.

Nevertheless, the CDU/CSU *Bundestag* caucus once again asked Erhard to put together a coalition with a workable majority for his cabinet. The FDP as well as the SPD was to be included in the negotiations. Erhard left no doubt about his refusal to head a Great Coalition. He did not have to face this event, for initial talks with Herbert Wehner were well under way.

On November 8 the executive board of the CDU decided to present the names of Rainer Barzel, Eugen Gerstenmaier, Kurt Georg Kiesinger, and Gerhard Schröder to the CDU/CSU *Bundestag* caucus as possible successors to Erhard. The next day the CSU executive board chose Kiesinger as its candidate. Gerstenmaier promptly withdrew his name that very same evening, and Kiesinger was elected. Coalition talks were begun with the SPD, though not without the Social Democrats intermittently attacking the CDU/CSU in order to improve their negotiating position. On December 1, 1966, the CDU/CSU-SPD coalition cabinet was sworn in.

Erhard was, of course, bitterly disappointed, deeply insulted, and profoundly hurt at being forced to resign, but even more so due to the attendant circumstances. It was some time before he could come to grips with his emotions. The confident and unabashed manner with which he had once applauded his own achievements—standing off to one side, so to speak, while observing Ludwig Erhard the institution—was something he never regained. More painful than his reflections on his own fate—on the ingratitude of politics and the merci-

Disappointment at the chancellor's bungalow on the evening of his forced resignation from office, December 1, 1966. From left: Ludwig Erhard and his wife, Luise, a security agent of the ex-chancellor, and Press Secretary Hans Klein.

lessness of "Christian" politicians—was the realization that parliamentarians of all stripes were departing from the path of the social market economy. A process had begun that threatened to reopen the sterile conflict between economic and social policy, and to reduce the state to a powerless appeaser of interest groups.

At the first session of the eighth *Bundestag* on December 14, 1976, which Erhard opened as chairman emeritus, he admonished the members with the full pathos of his conviction: "Remember that almost thirty years ago all [our] parliamentary parties, even while engaged in partisan strife, knew they faced the common task of [creating from] tragedy a new and better economic and social order that would allow genuine democracy to thrive with a credibility to persuade the world."

On February 4, 1977, Erhard was honored both by friends and former adversaries on the occasion of his eightieth birthday. On May 5, 1977, almost exactly two years after the death of his wife, Ludwig Erhard died of a heart attack.

Notes

1. *Die Zeit*. Influential weekly published in Hamburg.

2. *"Otto Normalverbraucher*," the name of a character played by actor Gert Froebe in the 1948 movie *Berliner Ballade*. Otto is a penniless, shabbilydressed man who became a popular symbol of the struggles to survive the hardships of the postwar years.

3. *Spielvereinigung Fürth*. A famous soccer club with a long and legendary tradition.

4. Jacob Burckhardt (1818–1897). Swiss art historian.

5. Martin Niemöller (1892–1985). Berlin pastor and World War I submarine veteran who during the Third Reich organized a group of anti-Nazi clergymen that formed the core of what later became the *Bekennende Kirche* (Confessing Church). Most of its leaders, including Niemöller himself, spent time in prison or concentration camps and some, like Dietrich Bonhoeffer, were executed. Others, like Gustav Heinemann, played leading roles in West Germany's postwar politics.

6. Jakob Wassermann (1873–1934). German-Jewish novelist of international bestsellers, of which *Der Fall Maurizius* and *Kaspar Hauser* were among the most successful. *The Jews of Zirndorf*, his first novel, was informed by a subject to which he was to return in his later writings—the conflicting tensions of a Jew deeply rooted in German culture.

7. Eugen Richter (1838–1906). Foe of Chancellor Bismarck, member of *Reichstag* (German parliament), and leader of *Freisinnige Volkspartei*.

8. Baron Franz August von Stauffenberg (1834–1901). Leading politician of the National Liberal Party, member of the *Reichstag* from 1871 to 1893, and ancestor of Hitler's would-be assassin.

9. Friedrich Naumann (1907–1918). Co-founder of *Deutsche Demokratische Partei* in 1919.

10. Horace Greely Hjalmar Schacht (1877–1970). German financier and leading banker in pre-Nazi Germany who headed the *Reichsbank* from 1923 to 1930 and again, under Hitler, from 1933 to 1939, when he was dismissed. He served as Hitler's minister of economy from 1934 to 1937. He was later a member of the anti-Hitler conspiracy. He was tried at Nuremberg in 1946 as a major war criminal, but acquitted.

11. Hitler quickly developed Germany's economy into what might be described as state capitalism. The Nazis gave greater power to the 1,500 cartels they inherited from the Weimar period, such as the "steel circle." All producers in an industry had to join the cartel for that industry. Cartels were virtually free to organize and operate as they pleased, as long as they did not conflict with the Nazi regime. Hjalmar Schacht as minister of economy was the general controller.

12. In a "revolt of conscience," Colonel Claus Count von Stauffenberg, a staff officer at reserve army headquarters in Berlin, managed to plant a bomb in Hitler's headquarters in East Prussia on July 20, 1944, which exploded at Hitler's feet without killing him. Stauffenberg, a field marshal, eight generals, and some 200 eminent Germans were hanged as a result.

13. *Die Erinnerungen von Theodor Eschenburg* (The Memoirs of Theodor Eschenburg), unpublished manuscript in the author's estate.

14. Wilhelm Hoegner, Social Democrat, formed the first postwar Bavarian state government in 1945, remaining as its head until 1946. He served again as minister-president of Bavaria from 1954 to 1957.

15. Joseph Dodge, a Detroit banker, and U.S. Treasury economists Dr. Raymond M. Goldsmith and Dr. Gerhard Cohn drafted the plans for the creation of the new Deutsche Mark, which eventually was to become one of the hardest currencies on the world exchange.

16. Though the economic health of the Bizone was the official goal of the Economic Council, it was in fact the first real step toward the creation of a West German state. In effect a provisional government, its fifty-two members were chosen by the parliaments of the states.

17. Theodor Blank, a Catholic trade union leader, had been chairman of the CDU in Westphalia since 1946. He became the Federal Republic's first defense minister in 1955–1956, and from 1957 to 1965 served as minister of labor and social affairs.

18. Josef Müller, from 1946 chairman of the CSU in Bavaria. He was minister of justice from 1947 to 1952.

19. In his historic radio address on June 21, 1948, Erhard, in refuting the charge, used the phrase "dominion of the capitalistic occupation powers" ironically.

20. Michael K. Caro, *Der Volkskanzler Ludwig Erhard* (Berlin: Kiepenheuer & Witsch, 1965), p. 124. Historians tell several anecdotes about Erhard's meeting

with General Clay. One such version has Clay saying, "Herr Erhard, my advisors tell me that what you have done is a terrible mistake. What do you say to that?" The German's reply came swiftly and without hesitation. "Herr General, pay no attention to them! My own advisers tell me the same thing." From: Edwin Hartrich, *The Fourth and Richest Reich* (New York: Macmillan, 1980).

21. Alfred Müller-Armack was one of the most influential thinkers who developed the famous concept of the social market economy. He was Erhard's respected state secretary in the Ministry of Economics during the "economic miracle" years until 1963.

22. Christian socialism, which grew out of the resistance to Hitler, was the basis of the Ahlener Program adopted by the CDU in February 1947. It called for workers' and employees' control of their workplace, and of economic decisions in general, as well as nationalization of heavy industry and some financial institutions. But what seemed like Adenauer's compromise with his party's left wing soon turned into a tactical ploy when, with the adoption of Erhard's economic program, the Ahlen principles became little more than a statement of ideals.

23. The *Kartel* (cartel), a nineteenth-century German invention, was originally regarded as beneficial to the economy as a means of survival during hard times. With 1,500 cartels in existence when the Nazis took over in 1933, the *Kartel* proliferated under Hitler as an instrument of state control over the economy (see note 11). The Allies in their occupation zones were determined to break up cartels, trusts, and syndicates which had become giant concentrations of economic power with interlocking directorates. Erhard's Cartel Act, designed toward the same end, ran headlong into a violent storm of opposition not only of industry and business interests, but, ironically, of the German Federation of Trade Unions as well. Erhard's draft law, submitted in 1952, had to battle it out for ten years on the floor of the *Bundestag* and in committee before an acceptable version was finally passed in April 1962.

24. *Lach-und-Schiessgesellschaft.* A popular satirical literary cabaret.

25. Rolf Hochhuth, prominent German playwright and author whose drama *The Deputy* became a worldwide success.

26. Friedrich Ebert, SPD leader, was elected chancellor in 1918 and became the first president of post–World War I Germany in 1919, remaining in this post until his death in 1925; Otto Braun, prime minister of Prussia from 1920 to 1932, went into exile in 1933; Gustav Stresemann was founder of the *Deutsche Volkspartei* (People's Party) in 1918, German chancellor from August to November 1918, and secretary for foreign affairs from 1923 to 1929.

27. Franz Böhm, Friedrich August von Hayek, Walter Eucken, Wilhelm Röpke, and Alexander Rüstow comprised the most important of a circle of economists who developed the neo-liberal ideas that later became Erhard's social market economy. Hayek, an Austrian, was awarded the Nobel Prize together with Gunnar Myrdal of Sweden in 1974. Eucken, who remained in Germany during the war, worked with Alfred Müller-Armack to elaborate the details of the social market economy. Both Röpke and Rüstow were exiled.

28. Eugen Gerstenmaier (1906–1986). CDU deputy chairman and *Bundestag* president (speaker) from 1954 to 1969. During the war he was part of the resistance group of von Stauffenberg and Carl Goerdeler. As a Lutheran, he worked

hard to turn the CDU into a genuine interdenominational party. Erhard's remark is quoted from: Hermann Kunst (ed.). *Für Freiheit und Recht: Eugen Gerstenmaier zum 60. Geburtstag* (Stuttgart, 1966).

29. Herbert Wehner (1906–1990). Principal SPD strategist and ideologue. Began his political career at age twenty-one as a communist, was imprisoned by the Nazis and eventually escaped to Prague and Moscow, where he served as assistant to the head of the Comintern, Georgi Dimitrov. Sent by Moscow to Stockholm in 1942, he was arrested as a spy. He joined the SPD on his return to Germany after the war, was elected to the *Bundestag* in 1949, and served as minister for all-German affairs from 1966 to 1969.

30. Michael Beschloss, *The Crisis Years* (New York: Harper Collins, 1991).

31. *Die formierte Gesellschaft* is a phrase hard to translate or to define even in German, denoting a modern society more fully and more rationally developed than present-day democracies. It assumes that the old society's major problems stem from organized interest groups and their lobbies—unions, industrial associations, professional groups, bureaucracies of all kinds. They were endangering the economic system, the social order, and the constructive operation of parliamentary democracy at a time when traditional state authority had become too weak to deal effectively with the conflict between disparate interests and the national interest. Erhard believed the *formierte Gesellschaft* was a strategy to save society as a whole from this growing anarchy of interest groups fighting each other for a bigger share of political power and economic wealth.

32. Rüdiger Altmann and Johannes Gross. Close advisors of Erhard: Altmann was a radio and television journalist and author; Gross was also an author and a representative of industry and trade.

33. Rüdiger Altmann, *Wirtschaftspolitik und Staatskunst: Wirkung Ludwig Erhards* (Stuttgart: Seewald-Verlag, 1977), p. 248.

34. The "Frankfurt School" was a group of internationally know social scientists and philosophers, most of them from the prewar era, who had come to the U.S., where they spent the war years. Among them were Herbert Marcuse, Theodor Adorno, and Max Horkheimer.

35. Erhard referred to the fact that Willy Brandt, as an anti-Nazi, had fled Hitler's Germany for Norway and later Sweden, returning to West Germany in 1947.

36. *Civis*: Journal for Christian-Democratic Politics. Published from 1954 to 1969 by a Christian Democratic student organization.

37. *Bild*, daily tabloid with circulation of five million.

[Top] *With his father and his son Peter, 1967 — Delivering an address before the Berlin* Reichstag, *1967 — With Bavarian minister-president Alfons Goppel and Goppel's wife at the Munich Crafts Fair, 1967.*
[Center] *With Helmut Kohl and Rainer Barzel at the eightieth birthday party for Ludwig Erhard, 1977 — Speaking at a session of the* Bundestag, *1968.*

[Bottom] *Cabinet meeting of the Great Coalition in the park of Palais Schaumburg, July 1967 — With his wife while visiting the ruins of Ephesus, 1968 — With his grandchild "Fröschle," 1969 — At the memorial of the unknown soldier in Paris, 1967.*

Chronology

1904	Born on April 6 in Ebingen, Württemberg.
1924–1930	Studies law in Tübingen and Berlin.
1932	Marries Marie Luise Schneider (with whom he will have two children).
1935	After scoring high marks on his first and second state examinations, serves as "referendar" and then "assessor" to become a lawyer at the Berlin Superior Court of Justice.
1940–1945	Member of the Foreign Ministry, first as research assistant, then, as of 1942, as deputy department head of the political division of radio broadcasting.
1945–1947	Interned by the Allies.
1948	Following full exoneration by a denazification tribunal, practices law in Tübingen and Würzburg. Honorary executive manager of the CDU in South Württemberg–Hohenzollern.
1949–1959	Member of the *Bundestag*.
1950–1957	Chairman of the *Bundestag* mediation committee. As of 1954 serves simultaneously as chairman of the Foreign Affairs Committee.
1950–1960	Member of the CDU executive committee.
1958–1966	Minister-president of Baden-Württemberg.
1966–1969	Federal chancellor of the Great Coalition.
1967–1971	Chairman of the CDU, thereafter honorary chairman.
1969–1980	Member of the *Bundestag*.
1988	Dies on March 9 in Tübingen.

3

Kurt Georg Kiesinger

by Günter Diehl

By the time Kurt Georg Kiesinger entered public life in postwar Germany as a *Bundestag* member, he was a man with a fully formed personality, both in the way he was perceived by others and in his own inner development. All the essential traits were there, and so were the more trivial ones, those that filled in the whole. The office of the federal chancellor, with all its importance, did not shape him, much less change him. This may have been a major reason Kiesinger was equal to the office. It was not to prove his undoing, as it did for Ludwig Erhard and Willy Brandt, for instance.

So I think we must first focus on the beginning half of Kiesinger's life, on his background and personal development. Always useful as a way of approaching a man's life, in the case of Kiesinger it is indispensable. His imposing figure and elegant gestures, his uncommonly broad erudition and cultural grasp, his gifts as a speaker—anyone who heard him speak as *Bundestag* member, minister-president of Baden-Württemberg, or as federal chancellor is sure to remember—can all too easily wipe from memory "the dark years," as Kiesinger called them. He himself can be blamed for some of this impression, for in his short book entitled *Schwäbische Kindheit*[1] (*Swabian Childhood*), a jewel among German memoirs, Kiesinger described his serene, happy, and secure early life and his childhood reveries so poignantly, so movingly, that it overshadowed the work's other leitmotif. And that was the bitter poverty and unbelievable hardship of lower middle-class life during and after the First World War.

It is characteristic of Kiesinger's style that the impressions of mood he creates are balanced by prosaic details. Though after the first few pages the reader might guess what is to come, it is hard to say just what creates the atmosphere in the quietly paced sentences narrating the story. There is certainly no lack of romanticism or nature worship, for the author does not shy away from them, and why should he? But descriptions such as "spring days awhirr with the sound of larks," and "tucked into a valley swept by rivers and guarded by cliffs," are balanced by the down-to-earth "sugar was considered a precious commodity and kept under lock and key." His description of his school days includes in detail how he ". . . fell into the hands of a few accomplished masters of the cane." But he then again takes the overview: "Perhaps it is the small things that memory preserves, because what is most important is concealed in the ordinary."

Everything has its price. Because politics later placed such great demands on his gifts for writing and speaking, and because in going into politics these talents took another direction altogether, there was little time left for Kiesinger to allow the writer and artist in himself free rein.

But the little time he did have was well spent. If Kurt Georg Kiesinger needed to earn a living and chose to go into politics after the war, then his other persona, the artist, was nevertheless to find ways to emerge from hiding. So it was the connection between language and politics that lent Kiesinger, even as chancellor, an extra degree of prominence and distinction beyond the circle of confidantes familiar with his work.

Yet it must be reiterated that the Swabian idyll his small oeuvre seemingly created concealed a bitter reality. Ragged, hungry, literally without anything to call his own, young Kiesinger entered the public arena driven by the desire for the great and the beautiful that was characteristic of Swabia,[2] land of Schiller, and by the need to speak out passionately on those things that were important to him.

The young Kiesinger exhibited great tenacity and imagination in clearing what seemed to be insurmountable hurdles, wresting privileges from uncompromising authorities. He succeeded, for example, in convincing the Stuttgart cultural ministry to extend his vacation period so that he could earn the money he needed to go to school, or in boldly approaching Prussian minister of culture Karl Heinrich Becker to personally request permission to enter Berlin University, a Prussian school, a request that Becker, to his credit, promptly granted.

But all of this could have ended in failure had Kiesinger not found a paternal friend who took an interest in the talented young man. Friedrich Haux, director of a Württemberg-Hohenzollern Knitwear Factory, supported Kiesinger so that he could continue his studies. Haux, who died in a plane crash in 1928, had a sure sense of Kiesinger's talent and played a major, and perhaps even decisive, role in his life. Kiesinger never forgot Haux's generosity. Ironically, Haux had invited him to come along on the plane trip that ended his life, but Kiesinger, tempted as he was to go on what would have been his first airplane ride, turned down the invitation because of other plans.

In this phase of his life, as a secondary-school and university student, another character trait was beginning to become evident. Kiesinger was driven by iron perseverance as a young man, and studied day and night. When preparing for his supplementary final secondary-school examinations, he chose English and Latin as his test subjects. He forewent a private tutor for lack of funds, and instead worked through a correspondence course in Latin, following the instructions page by page. "I supplemented this work with a refresher course in Roman history and daily readings in the works of the great Roman writers, Caesar, Livius, Cicero, and Tacitus above all. I formed a first and lasting impression of the Roman poets, of whom Horace, and then, increasingly over the years, Virgil, became my constant companions."

Kiesinger passed his exams, as he said, in order not to disappoint Haux, among other reasons. The thought of having to tell his mentor that he had failed would have been unbearable to him. He exhibited the same determination as a university student in Berlin, studying deep into the night and earning high scores on his examinations.

Though such achievement is nearly always appreciated and admired, it rarely brings the person striving for it any particular sympathy. But Kiesinger's personality was made up of many things. He burned the candle at both ends, leading a second, bohemian life in addition to his work. If this sounds overstated, it nevertheless best describes what happened. As a young man, Kiesinger enjoyed conviviality, always sharing the company of a great variety of people, spending time in pubs and back rooms and conversing with clever, amusing men. It is known that he was considered somewhat of a star in these circles and clubs, scintillating in his knowledge and memory and ability to express himself. It is no wonder that he believed he could "become a poet." But this plan soon waned. Once Kiesinger realized his ambition to study in Berlin he decided, having started out in philosophy and philology, to switch to law.

The most important elements, the major cornerstones, of

Kiesinger's personality now became manifest. One was the strong test that his difficult life had put him to, paired with the certainty that he would meet this challenge. Another was his ability to work constantly and with discipline, and to reach his goals by way of his own accomplishments. And finally, there was his flair for using his highly developed intuitive powers to grasp life at its fullest, to recognize talent, beauty, and harmony in art and in life. What was exuberant or ebullient in himself Kiesinger curbed, even fettered, with discipline, that cognitive, systematic force found also in jurisprudence, and the importance of which he increasingly recognized.

His choice of the law deserves a closer look. One might think jurisprudence did not at all suit Kiesinger's nature and character. It was philosophy and literature that nourished the creativity of this young aesthete and bon vivant. Why would he choose to don the austere robes of the legal profession? To understand this unusual and even unsuitable choice it helps to keep in mind that no one, not the German public and certainly not the international public, understood Kiesinger to be the eminent jurist that he was. In the opinion of his critics he remained "King Silvertongue," the high-flying, cultivated, somewhat high-strung poet-prince.

I am certain that Kiesinger chose the study of law because he knew that throughout his life his inclinations would lean toward philosophy, literature, and history, that he would always be wedded to them. He did not need to study them, his own interest in them was strong enough.

Kiesinger must have gone through a major phase of self-examination and recognized that as someone with his head in the clouds, a *brasseur de nuages*, he had to learn to keep both feet on the ground; if he was to master life and lead a "bourgeois existence," he would need to discover what it was that motivated modern society, politics, and economics. He already had the necessary ability, but it had to be fostered. Kiesinger believed he would succeed, he had put himself to the test in being accepted to university, and had met the challenge. He could be confident.

I hesitate to employ the expression "bourgeois existence" in connection with Kiesinger. I am not referring to a philistine life, but to an ordered existence with some security. In fact, Kiesinger had fallen in love and wanted to marry. Next to his grandmother and stepmother, eighteen-year-old Marie Luise Schneider had become the important woman in Kiesinger's life. I met Marie Luise Kiesinger briefly when she was a young woman, and later got to know her as the wife of the minister-president and chancellor. She had a beautiful face, well-proportioned features, a classical profile. She was a gentle and reserved woman who was comfortable with herself, and felt no need to present herself as extroverted. She was quiet rather than talkative, affectionate, most surely kind hearted, and very reserved. She never acted the statesman's or "boss's" wife. She was exactly what the young imaginative man was seeking and needed—a helm to stay the course of his emotions in turbulent waters. And now the sense of reality that Kiesinger had developed in his childhood and youth asserted itself. Anyone who wished to establish a family had to consider how he was going to earn his daily bread.

Kiesinger was just twenty-two years old when he went to Berlin in 1926. What induced him to move to what was then Germany's capital? He was familiar with politics, having debated the major issues with his Swabian compatriots, but it is believable when he says he did not go to Berlin because that is where the political decisions were being made, and certainly not because he wanted to get involved in them. It was his fascination with the metropolis—that intersection of power and intellect, wealth and impoverishment, art and life, the past and the present—that drew him. Kiesinger and his friends enjoyed the lights and energy, the bustle of Berlin in the twenties. At first he was blinded by this fascination; only later did he see the harsh side of city life.

Kiesinger was well received in the city and its intellectual-artistic circles, and after a short time he once again found himself in the center of a well-established circle. For all of his individuality he no longer was a loner. He joined the Catholic students' fraternity, "Askania," for its group of friendly and supportive, like-minded young men, as did many others who preceded and would follow him. Through the fraternity he gained access to those experienced "older gentlemen" who already had attained office and honor, and so the doors of Berlin society were opened to him. Kiesinger, in his student days, fully enjoyed the atmosphere that prevailed in Berlin at the end of the 1920s.

Ever alert, he made the acquaintance of Dr. Carl Sonnenschein, the Catholic social reformer who had attempted to reduce the gap between the working and the educated classes. Sonnenschein was an activist, not a theoretician. Kiesinger has mentioned the two card files that Sonnenschein maintained, one with the names of the rich, the other with the names of the poor, which he constantly kept up to date in order to be able to help.

Kiesinger neither wanted to nor could forget the experiences of his early years; he knew what it meant to work hard, and his sense of social justice never left him. But in contrast to many others who had first-hand knowledge of poverty, especially the poverty of the industrial working class, he did not choose a public life characterized by social envy and class hatred. He remained convinced that a democratically organized society would ensure anyone with the talent and the will a place suited to the individual's achievement and merit. He himself was a living example of this belief.

Kiesinger's personality, as we have noted, was formed by the time he entered politics after the war and became a member of parliament in the young Federal Republic. This is true as well of his attitude toward personal property, prosperity, and wealth. As a Swabian, Kiesinger was thrifty but not miserly. He aspired to a certain amount of security for himself and his family. It may seem incongruent that his first move from Bonn—to the office of minister-president of Baden-Württemberg—was also prompted by the consideration that the new office would guarantee a life of material security to himself and his family. It was surprising that this would be the determining factor for such a high-minded individual as he. I myself found it strange, felt it wasn't consistent with Kiesinger's character, but I was wrong. His Swabian temperament and the poverty of his youth played an important role here.

The positive and totally charming side of this was that Kiesinger was not a greedy man and did not seek high office for his own personal gain. He was satisfied to have a roof over his head he could call his own, and to be able to dress well and not have to deny himself a decent vintage. I never saw any sign that he was enticed by wealth. He could recognize its vulgar side and he judged his truly well-off friends and acquaintances by their good taste and their unpretentiousness.

Life in Berlin got off to a good start. All in all, these were wonderful and fulfilling years. Following a six-year courtship Kiesinger and Marie Luise Schneider were married at Christmas, 1932. In the November 6 election of that year the Nazis lost two million votes. Kiesinger, who had no intention of becoming active politically, viewed the fall of the Weimar Republic as disturbing, but remained a passive onlooker. He had few illusions, but saw no cause to become overly alarmed. The election results were encouraging.

It turned out otherwise. Hitler came to power when von Hindenburg and Papen defied the constitution and all established rules to name him chancellor. What Kiesinger has to say about this period is believable simply because his attitude was typical of countless young Germans who were not dedicated National Socialists but believed they should participate in order to keep the National Socialists from going to extremes. Kiesinger joined the Nazi Party in 1933,[3] feeling that what was good about the movement should be encouraged, and what was bad should be controlled. He recalls Hitler's peace slogans and the professions of Christianity. Based on public statements made by the National Socialists in 1933, many would later claim that their goals seemed not totally unrealistic.

Kiesinger quickly realized that he had greatly deceived himself, but his mistake was irreparable, for to correct it would have had dangerous, even life-threatening consequences. Kiesinger was not a "Nazi." Even those who did not know him during the twelve years of the Hitler dictatorship would know or feel this to be true when they met Kiesinger and became acquainted with what he said and wrote and did. The many young men and the few young women who attended Kiesinger's refresher courses in law in Berlin during this period all were of the opinion that he equipped his students with the mental tools necessary to recognize the National Socialist regime for what it was—totalitarian. In choosing to teach this course the young jurist had sought a niche for himself at the cost of a career better suited to his gifts. He did not go into judicial administration, but became an attorney instead, and in this way avoided membership in the National Socialist *Rechtswahrerbund*, the professional organization of German jurists.

Kiesinger had only a weak cover protecting him from the National Socialists, and that was his passive membership in the NSDAP. It served him now and then in succeeding to free some individuals from the claws of the Nazi regime.[4] He did not resist the government openly. He would have preferred to be left alone, but this was not to be the case, for neither his bearing nor his intellect allowed him to remain inconspicuous. He drew the attention of all those he encountered.

Until the end of his life Kiesinger continued to ask himself whether it was right for him to have conformed during the Third Reich, whether he wasn't living a double standard. His uncertainty always caused him to argue from a defensive position, which supplied ammunition to opponents who wished to defame him. He was deeply hurt by this, for he felt he was being treated unjustly; he had nothing to reproach himself for, particularly in comparison to other politicians of his generation on both the left and the right, not to mention those in the middle. This was no doubt true, and the issue shall be addressed further below, but Kiesinger himself was never free of the agonizing doubt that he had not lived up to his own standards. And that caused him to react to confrontations on the topic more forcefully than was necessary.[5]

Too Close for Comfort

The young lawyer initially hoped for an academic career, to become a professor, perhaps, were the regime to return even to a halfway civilized form of constitutional government. This hope bordered on self-delusion and when it passed Kiesinger for a short time even considered leaving Germany for South America, to begin a new life. But then the war came, and with one stroke the coordinates that had marked Kiesinger's life totally changed.

Germans generally applauded the occupation of the Rhineland, the annexation of Austria, and the incorporation of the Sudetenland—a result of the Munich Agreement—as more than right. Why shouldn't all Germans live together in one land? France, England, Italy, and Germany seemed all to be of the same opinion in Munich, with slogans like "Peace in Our Time" and *"le directoire européen."* Was one to believe that Daladier and Bonnet, Chamberlain and Eden totally failed to understand who their German partner really was or what goals Germany was pursuing? "It was acceptable to believe that Hitler was a German nationalist," Henry Kissinger has noted aptly, in describing the West's evaluation of the German dictator at that time. But with the march on Prague the Second World War became an inevitability.

Gnashing their teeth, the Western powers once again, and for the last time, submitted to Hitler's will. But an arms build-up began, and it was clear that the next time German troops so much as lifted a foot to march, it would signal the onset of a new world war. Kiesinger followed events with alarm, conscious of the issues at stake. The Hitler-Stalin Pact was signed and Hitler invaded Poland, after which that country was torn apart by Germany and Russia. The Western Allies could not prevent this, but contrary to Hitler's expectations they took up arms and began a war that would end in the total defeat of Germany.

To many Germans it appeared as if it were Germany that had been attacked, and National Socialist propaganda answered in a vocabulary of defense, making it seem as if the Nazis were fighting the good fight. Right or wrong, could one leave one's country in the lurch in the midst of war? It was a difficult issue to decide, and for most people the decision was made for them by the state. Those men who were able bodied were drafted into military service, and those who weren't were assigned to conscripted labor, usually at their old jobs.

It was a period of mixed emotions, and Kiesinger, too, was swayed by Germany's military successes. One doesn't topple a victorious military leader, Ernst Jünger later was to say in explanation of the general conduct of the time. And that may well be true. Kiesinger, who presumed he would be assigned to the second replacement reserves due to his poor health,[6] received an induction order. He was less than enthusiastic, fatalistic in fact. He later said that he wasn't going to let himself be killed for the Nazi regime, nor had he wished to kill others. Which sounds rather theoretical; it may be assumed his actual conduct was guided by other thoughts.

And here we come upon a universally accepted type of behavior. Any soldier who has killed another human being "in the line of duty" is not condemned for having done so if he has put his own life on the line. On the contrary, a soldier who returns highly decorated from battle is respected by friend and foe alike. No one would infer that he was not politically viable or was unfit to take his place in a newly formed, democratic society. Perhaps by putting our own lives at stake we become authorized to take the life of another. This seems to be universally accepted, so perhaps there is something to it.

Not to wish to kill another human being as an argument for refusing military service is not held to be particularly convincing. Such people are usually called "shirkers." Had Kiesinger returned from the war with the Iron Cross, he surely would not have left himself open to political attack.

But this is where providence stepped in to long-lasting effect. Among Kiesinger's students was Karl-Heinz Gerstner, whose father was Ambassador Ritter, the Foreign Ministry's negotiator for international economic issues. At the beginning of the war Gerstner, a fellow member of Kiesinger's fraternity, worked as a research assistant in the Foreign Ministry, and following the capitulation of France he served in the embassy in Paris in economic affairs. Gerstner told Kiesinger the Cultural Department was looking for people to work in a new branch responsible for radio broadcasts abroad. This branch was called "*Kult. R*" (for Cultural Department, Radio) and run by acting legation counselor Günther Rühle, a man with a golden party badge.[7] Head of the department was envoy Fritz von Twardowski. Kiesinger was receptive, and met with the deputy head of the radio division, Dr. Hans Schirmer, on April 5, 1940. He was immediately hired, and so released without further ado from military service, which was to have commenced on April 7.

Kiesinger's account of that first meeting—Schirmer describing the chief duty of the *Kult. R* as working together with the army high command to keep foreign broadcasting out of the hands of Goebbels—is correct only in part. But it did reflect the truth, something Kiesinger was to discover plainly within a few weeks. Hans Schirmer might express his opinion, overtly and covertly, to anyone he talked to, whether German or foreign, but he was too smart to make that kind of incendiary statement to someone he did not know well, so this could hardly have been the reason Kiesinger decided to join the Foreign Ministry. Much more important is the fact that Schirmer and Kiesinger understood each other and felt, without expressing it in so many words, that they were of like mind.

Kiesinger was correct in his impression that the Foreign Ministry was not, nor could be, a stronghold of the NSDAP. The ministry was staffed by those whose professional choice it was to conduct Germany's relations with other countries. Their knowledge of the world had been gained from years of personal experience abroad, and on the whole had a realistic picture of other nations' interests. This almost unavoidably led to a critical stance toward National Socialism as a political movement, and toward its Führer as well.

Part and parcel of their knowledge of foreign relations was an assessment of the relationships of power. There were many people at the beginning of the war, both young and old, who were convinced that the war could not be won. Gustav Adolf Sonnenhol[8] succinctly and correctly stated that this war would last longer than the preceding one, and would also be lost.

Those who lived and worked abroad soon came to the unpleasant realization that the anti–National Socialist sentiment prevailing everywhere was accompanied by anti-German sentiment as well. Eugen Gerstenmaier once described this well in his account of the policies of the Protestant World Church toward the Third Reich. Every patriotically inclined German familiar with the Church's position thus felt compelled to defend his homeland as a whole, despite the doubts lodged in his heart.

Cultural Department head Fritz von Twardowski was actually a naval officer forced out of duty in 1918 who went on to earn a university degree. He was interested in politics and, atypically for a naval officer, stood to the left of center. At thirty years of age he was assigned to the embassy in Moscow. In March 1932 Twardowski, obviously mistaken for the ambassador, was seriously wounded in an assassination attempt, which left him with a maimed hand. He then took over the Cultural Department, an appointment that spoke for the imagination of personnel decision making. (In 1950 he would surface in Bonn, where, among other things, he served as acting head of the Press and Information Office until 1952.) In those days the heads of the traditional departments of the Foreign Ministry were legendary demigods pointed out to young civil servants only from afar. "Twardo," as he was called, exhibited only moderate interest in the radio broadcasting operation newly assigned his department. If radio propaganda could somehow help Germany's combat forces, then perhaps it had its place. The entire enterprise—the war—was doomed at any rate, he felt.

The man who was really in charge of *Kult. R* was Günther Rühle, one of the very early members of the Nazi party, as evidenced by the number on his golden party badge, which was under one hundred. He was a man of medium height, with a wry manner, and in no way unsympathetic. He took personal pride in being loyal to and carrying out the wishes of Foreign Minister von Ribbentrop, assuming as he did the minister's wishes were Hitler's as well. Grotesque as it sounds, Kiesinger's assessment that *Kult. R* was less concerned with the war against the external enemy than it was with the war of influence between Ribbentrop and Propaganda Minister Goebbels was by no means preposterous.

One of the difficulties Kiesinger encountered as a young lawyer was that his intelligence and bearing made him stand out among the other employees and officials of the foreign service. His unique negotiating skills repeatedly led to his being assigned to mediate internal disputes. Rühle eventually appointed him deputy department head, an important title even if one questions the purpose of the department as a whole. Hans Schirmer, Kiesinger's predecessor in the position, had asked for a combat assignment because he no longer wanted to participate in the Berlin tug-of-war. According to Kiesinger, it was Schirmer who first told him of rumors of the mass murder of civilians in the east.

The victorious outcome of the western campaign in early summer of 1940 enabled the Foreign Office to extend its activities. Branches of the office were set up in the occupied territories, and an embassy was even established in France. Despite all kinds of shady occurrences, the cultural departments, including broadcasting and press, managed to attain a standard abroad that often was above that in Germany. The Ministry of Propaganda had only very limited authority abroad, which allowed Kiesinger to observe the Second World War from a European perspective, and to form his own impressions. These later would prove useful.

At the end of the war Kiesinger was interned by the Americans for sixteen months.[9] During this time he revealed an ability to endure adverse circumstances, to summon his strength when needed and take calculated risks. Even the various American officers and officials who encountered him realized that he was different. One U.S. officer who interrogated him predicted that he would play a major role in the new Germany.

On returning to his homeland, Kiesinger saw that Germany's defeat had brought about the desired destruction of the Nazi dictatorship, but had also plunged the country into disaster. It was something the Germans would have to surmount.

Following a second hearing in August 1948, Kiesinger received his clearance from the denazification tribunal of the district of Schönfeld. In its statement the tribunal declared:

> ■ On the basis of the evidence, the reliability of which cannot be questioned in terms of the witnesses offering it and the weight of their statements, it is herewith attested that from the beginning to the end of the Third Reich the subject in question offered active and effective resistance to the National Socialist dictatorship in whatever positions he held and whenever the opportunities arose, according to the extent of his powers. Through his resistance he proved not only to be a courageous and steadfast opponent of the National Socialist regime, but at the danger of being discovered at any moment also risked his property, freedom, and life. In doing so he incontestably fulfilled the condition set out by Article 13 of the *Befreiungsgesetz* (Law of

Exoneration) of September 5, 1946 and therewith to be
exonerated. ■

Kiesinger of his own volition has always stated, both in person
and in print, that he did not openly resist the National Socialist
regime. That was an honest self-assessment.

Barely had he been released from captivity when Kiesinger made an
optimistic attempt to establish an independent private practice, but
to no avail. Gebhard Müller, a fraternity brother, then suggested
Kiesinger as executive manager of the newly-founded CDU in Württemberg-Hohenzollern. Kiesinger, who in the interim was again
teaching a refresher course in law in the city of Würzburg, accepted
on condition that he could continue to teach, an activity he planned
to subsidize through a law practice. From that point on things happened quickly. Politics became Kiesinger's chief occupation and the
focus of his future life, though not its all-consuming impulse.

Kiesinger was exonerated by the tribunal in August 1948; in
August 1949 he was elected to the *Bundestag* with 75.2 percent of
his district's vote, nationwide the third-highest count in this first
Bundestag election. It was also Kiesinger's first election campaign in
which he addressed meetings. Perhaps voters appreciated the fact
that Kiesinger was an outsider to politics. He was no Weimar parlia-
mentarian familiar with the tricks of the trade; he symbolized a new
beginning. His fate and his life experience were like those of most of
his fellow citizens, and he could talk to them about the mistakes of
the past. This time things would have to be done differently.

Nevertheless, in the *Bundestag* Kiesinger was a newcomer, a
greenhorn in comparison to those great political figures who had survived from the Weimar era. But he remained unruffled by them, only
moderately impressed, for he knew who had supported the 1933 Act
of Enablement that had brought Hitler to power.

To his astonishment he was immediately elected to his party caucus's executive committee. He was probably right in assuming he was
chosen for the sake of regional balance. Joining the Committees for
the Protection of the Constitution,[10] for Law and Constitutional Law,
and for Rules of Procedure and Immunity, he also became a substitute member of the Committee on Occupation Statutes and Foreign
Affairs. As a new member of parliament he apparently proved himself quite capable of handling legislative and judicial questions. It

was Konrad Adenauer who encouraged Kiesinger's interest in foreign-policy issues and used it to his own advantage.

Adenauer's relationship to Kiesinger, if I see it correctly, was complex and ambivalent. They had not known each other before, but Adenauer soon realized that Kiesinger was not to be bullied and that, when their views clashed, Kiesinger often won. This increased Adenauer's respect for Kiesinger and his character, but it limited his plans for Kiesinger's role in German politics. The Swabian was suspiciously skillful, Adenauer noted soon enough, but perhaps that was the very reason he remained a loner who did not succeed in establishing a power base or even a foothold for himself within the party's caucus. What was troubling about this was that Kiesinger didn't even attempt to build alliances based on quid pro quo. If he initiated a resolution then it was carried, as often as not, by a majority of members across party lines. Kiesinger never forgot the terrible lessons of the Weimar period, when the democratic parties had failed to find an ideological common ground that allowed them to survive, when relatively insignificant feuds so weakened the republic that they all fell prey to Hitler. He never ceased to seek consent, or at least tolerance, whenever possible, even if it meant reaching beyond CDU/CSU party lines. This quality earned him the respect of opposition leaders, but it was precisely what made Adenauer, the partisan politician, suspicious. In the first months and years of the young Federal Republic, Kiesinger best applied his beliefs and views in the mediation committee,[11] which he headed from 1950 to 1957.

Perhaps the best example of Kiesinger's political skills was the establishment of the *Land* Baden-Württemberg. The people of southern Baden wanted to preserve a distinct state of Baden, but it appeared that the rest of the Baden region, by a slim majority at least, wished to merge with Württemberg, whose population favored merger as well. Since no agreement could be reached, the federal government was called in to mediate. A large majority of the SPD and the FDP voted for the merger, but Kiesinger's own party was almost unanimously opposed to it. Kiesinger put his total support behind the merger, and landed in serious trouble as a result. His own party rallied against him. In the debates preceding the vote, Kiesinger was the only member of the Union parties who spoke for consolidation, and for the establishment of a new strong state in southwestern Germany. Kiesinger did gain a few friends within his own party, and they succeeded in securing a majority vote. He had prevailed against all the odds. On May 4, 1951, the *Neuordnungsgesetz* (Reorganization Law) formally went into effect, but then was challenged in constitutional court. Against the express objections of his own party, a majority of the *Bundestag* named Kiesinger to argue the case in court, and he was ultimately successful.

Kiesinger's role in this debate, now largely forgotten, shows his true mettle. He very much identified with his home state of Swabia and could not imagine being without a homeland, a condition he considered appalling. As a Swabian he recognized as no other political leader the desire of his fellow citizens in southwest Germany to preserve their heritage and safeguard their independence. He understood their aversion to government leadership located far from its home base. But he also saw the need to combine resources in a way that made sense. And, not least, he knew that the economic structures of Baden and Württemberg were in need of consolidation to balance their strengths and weaknesses. Kiesinger recognized the dangers of particularism, and felt it made no sense to give the rivalries between Swabians and the rest of the population institutional sanction. Adenauer pointed to the weakening of the CDU position in the *Bundesrat* (lower house) as a result of the merger (instead of two CDU-controlled states there would be only one).

But party politics played little role in Kiesinger's thinking. Following the new state's election of a constitutional assembly on March 9, 1952, a coalition was formed consisting of the SPD, FDP, and the *Bund der Heimatvertriebenen* (BHV, the Federation of Expellees from former east German and Sudeten territories). The CDU, although the strongest party, was forced into opposition. Needless to say, Kiesinger's fellow party members held him responsible for this debacle. His stalwart defense and execution of an independent policy was obviously a risk. Kiesinger received belated but reassuring satisfaction when in 1958 he was elected minister-president of the state he had fathered.

In 1954 Kiesinger assumed the chairmanship of the *Bundestag*'s Foreign Affairs Committee, reflecting his growing influence in planning and executing German foreign policy. He had become his party's spokesman in parliamentary foreign-affairs debates, and several of the speeches he gave lingered on in the memories of *Bundestag* members, regardless of party affiliation.

Kiesinger had increasingly occupied himself with matters of foreign policy. In July of 1950 the Federal Republic became an associate member of the European Council, then one year old. Kiesinger was one of the members of the *Bundestag* assigned to the council's consultative assembly, often ridiculed as a debating club and considered insignificant, much as the European Parliament is today. This was an unfair assessment, for though the assembly's influence on the shaping of European policy was indisputably very weak, it nevertheless produced one result which was perhaps unintended and considered a byproduct. Many politicians and statesmen from various countries came to know each other personally and to talk about important matters of mutual concern. This led to a network of personal connections of inestimable value.

Most members of the consultative assembly, which was made up of fifteen different countries, already held high positions at home, or sooner or later rose to high office. When they met at some later date they knew with whom they were dealing. Kiesinger spoke of the "number of illustrious personalities" who belonged to the assembly, among them Winston Churchill. None of them yet had become "MDEPs," members of the European Parliament, who, according to a later regulation, were not permitted to join their national assemblies; but all were well-regarded members of their respective parliaments. Kiesinger noted that this seemed the best method of bringing the resolutions of the assembly into the debates back home, as Churchill had vowed to do and recommended to others as well.

The German representatives, among whom numbered Heinrich von Brentano and Carlo Schmid, faced an assembly that at the time of the Korean War openly and urgently demanded that West Germany contribute to the defense of Europe. Churchill himself brought a draft resolution to the table that envisioned the formation of a united European army. When the vote was taken, German members of the SPD abstained, as did representatives of British Labour and the Swedes. The motion nevertheless was carried by a large majority.

Kiesinger's network of personal connections with foreign politicians grew larger and stronger with time, and soon led to a number of specific foreign-policy missions. He frequently was chosen to negotiate delicate conflicts between parties that were frozen into rigid positions, and to find new approaches for their resolution. Kiesinger's command of foreign languages[12] served him well, as did his fairness toward opposing points of view, something that also characterized his dealings in the *Bundestag*.

The fact that he held a conspicuous position and attracted attention as a foreign-policy spokesman and negotiator led to Kiesinger being named chairman of the CDU/CSU working group in the

Bundestag on foreign policy, security, and all-German policy, winning election over Otto Lenz by a narrow margin of ninety-eight to ninety-four votes. In 1954 Kiesinger assumed chairmanship of the Foreign Affairs Committee and handed the working group over to Lenz. Following Lenz's premature death, Kiesinger chaired both simultaneously.

Kiesinger became inexpendable in the area of foreign policy. He was considered useful, but also a burdensome reminder to others of their own mediocrity and inadequacy. Despite assuming so many important functions, he did not succeed in building a power base. This was one reason he failed in his various attempts to secure high office within his own party and thereby gain political influence. Following the resignation of Erich Köhler,[13] Kiesinger, without effort on his own, was suggested for the office of president of the *Bundestag*. He complied with this decision but ultimately retracted his candidacy. Nevertheless he received fifty-five of the final votes cast.

Immediately following this he suffered a second setback, which once again landed him in an awkward situation. Adenauer wanted Kiesinger to be elected to the CDU executive board at the party convention, and Kiesinger consented. When the votes were counted, thirty-nine were cast for him, and fifteen against, with sixteen abstentions. Kiesinger found this margin too narrow and did not accept the post, a fact attesting to the man's sensitivity. In this respect he was much less tough than Adenauer, for example, who had been elected federal chancellor by one vote, namely his own, and who then used the weakest of all possible voting support to remain in power.

It may be that Kiesinger considered himself vulnerable because his opponents not so discreetly implied that his Foreign Office activities during the war made him appear unsuitable for high position. In any case, from the time of the CDU board election he reined in his ambition, became more circumspect, and had to be persuaded to run for office.

The suggestion, more than likely made by Adenauer, to establish a European Ministry in addition to the Foreign Ministry, and to put Kiesinger in charge, foundered on the objections of Foreign Minister von Brentano. Kiesinger agreed in part with Brentano, and did not pursue the plan, Adenauer probably liked the idea not least because it would have allowed him to play off Kiesinger against Brentano in the jurisdictional rivalry that would result.

When Adenauer went to Moscow in 1955 he had the excellent idea of taking Kiesinger and Carlo Schmid along as part of his delegation, as well as Karl Arnold[14] representing the *Bundesrat*. While there was no formal basis for this the chancellor must have felt from the beginning that hard decisions would be called for during the negotiations. He wanted to cover himself by including not only the foreign minister and high officials, but also the two proven foreign-policy makers from the major party caucuses.

The preponderance of professors of jurisprudence in the Foreign Office at that time weakened that office's political instincts. This led to West Germany making the mistake of assuring its Western allies that it would not enter into immediate diplomatic relations with the Soviet Union during the Moscow negotiations, but rather would seek to establish a commission to discuss the conditions for establishing diplomatic relations. (The basic German condition would be the return of all prisoners of war still in Russia.)

What hadn't been sufficiently thought out was the need of the Soviet Union to score a diplomatic success. The world's attention was focused on this major event, and the Russians were not going to be satisfied with the visit ending merely in the establishment of a commission. An excellent jurist, Kiesinger also possessed superior instincts as a politician. He soon realized that commitment to a limited objective would render his efforts pointless, unaware that Adenauer had already privately abandoned it.[15]

The open distrust the Allies exhibited toward the West German leadership following this visit was due, not least, to the pledge the Federal Republic had broken. Kiesinger was soon made to feel this in the European Assembly, as was Brentano when he visited the United States following the Moscow talks. The specter of Rapallo[16] haunted the governmental and editorial offices of Bonn, but the fearsome apparition was gradually contained, at least for the time being.

It would have been futile to treat our allies' concern over a German-Russian alliance as totally unfounded. Yet overcompensation carried risks of its own. Under the long shadow cast by the Treaty of Versailles, Gustav Stresemann's understandable decision to add Locarno to Rapallo in a system of accords strengthening Germany's position between East and West severely hampered the Weimar Republic's integration into the community of democratic nations, and was one of the more fundamental causes of the Second World War.

Even when dealing with the Soviet leadership in the Moscow of 1955 the old affinity between Germans and Russians could be felt. It is by no means certain what Adenauer would have done had the Russians offered German unification as a reward to Bonn for withdrawing from the West's defense system. The anxious expressions on Hall-stein's and Wilhelm Grewe's faces suggested they thought *der Alte* was capable of anything. Brentano, too, was alarmed. Everything turned out well in the end, but the West's chilly reaction and West Germany's own vacillation led to a neglect of German-Soviet relations for a decade to come, a neglect that fostered the illusion that tensions could be relieved without addressing their causes. But Kiesinger did not make this mistake, for he never forgot the lessons of that visit to Moscow.

Shortly after his return from the Soviet Union he published an article in the *Süddeutsche Zeitung*, which ended with the assessment: ". . . it seems certain to me that in the long run the Soviet Union will not close its eyes to the fact that a constructive relationship between a free, independent, and reunited German state and the Soviet Union is more valuable than the preservation of a status quo that is quite problematic, for Russia as well."[17]

Early on, Kiesinger had formed an accurate opinion on the grow-ing significance of the United States through the writings of Alexis de Toqueville. His first trips to the U.S. not only gave him a lasting impression of American life, but also acquainted him with America's political institutions. His characteristic blend of great sensitivity, sen-suousness, and a sharp, trained legal mind helped him to form a rela-tively deep and broad understanding of American policy as a mix of lofty ideals espoused with missionary zeal, and two-fisted struggle. It was a spirit Kiesinger found infectious, and when his daughter Viola married an American, Volkmar Wentzel,[18] Kiesinger felt at home on his visits to rural West Virginia, far from the mournful self-doubt of the German intellectual milieu.

In 1956 Kiesinger was part of a *Bundestag* delegation that toured Asia, and visited Iraq, Iran, Afghanistan, Pakistan, and India. He was forced to break off his trip, which was scheduled to end in Bangkok, by two bloody international crises. In Hungary, Soviet troops had crushed an anti-Soviet uprising and massacred its leaders. Mean-while, Egyptian nationalization of the Suez Canal had provoked an Israeli attack on the Sinai Peninsula. The Kremlin was threatening to deploy nuclear weapons; France and England were preparing for major battle.

In the end, the Americans were successful in dissuading their allies from a war the scope and outcome of which no one could fore-see. The German public little grasped the gravity of the situation, but Kiesinger understood the Federal Republic's vulnerability. It was a time for caution and vigilance. The next year he again traveled to the United States, and returned strongly convinced that West Germany could not stand alone in the world.

And that was precisely the issue when on January 3, 1958, Gustav Heinemann and Thomas Dehler[19] staged a massive attack on Adenauer during a *Bundestag* debate, charging him with deliberately obstructing German unification. Heinemann resorted to pseudo-theological language in representing Adenauer as a traitor to the German cause. The chancellor was nonplussed by such vague vitriol, and this was perhaps fortunate. In the heat of the debate his temper might have run away with him. The CDU caucus did not know how to defend Adenauer, and Heinemann's and Dehler's recriminations went unanswered for the moment. But on March 20 Kiesinger, in a well-prepared and well-documented speech, forced Dehler and Heinemann into a corner and released Adenauer from his.

As chairman of the Foreign Affairs Committee, Kiesinger paid a formal visit to Latin America in the summer of 1958, which took him to Chile, Bolivia, Brazil, Peru, and Mexico. I was in charge of the embassy in Chile at the time and organized his visit. It had been more than two years since Kiesinger and I had seen each other and I found that experience had changed him, in style if not in substance. Now his great poise, with its effective blend of decorum and discretion, dignity, and self-confidence, was evidence, in the eyes of his Chilean host, that he was a major politician, a statesman.

The German colony in Chile was still struggling toward unity, made up as it was of old-established immigrants from the German revolution of 1848, monarchists, emigrants who had escaped the Nazi dictatorship, and a number of National Socialists who had left Europe after the war. In their midst, Kiesinger exhibited sympathy for their motivations and feelings while remaining unswayed in his convictions. It is worth noting here the greeting Kiesinger was given by the chairman of the German Club in Valparaiso: "We have always held the flagpole aloft, no matter what flag was flying."

At the end of 1958, when his fellow citizens and party allies elected him minister-president of Baden-Württemberg, Kiesinger left the national spotlight for a provincial one. When Adenauer expressed his regret at this decision, Kiesinger responded by saying that he finally wanted the chance to govern, if not in Bonn then in Stuttgart.

In October of 1966 the Free Democratic Party toppled the Erhard government, aided by the acrimonious internal disputes taking place within the CDU/CSU. Yet even among Erhard's opponents in the Union parties there was no one who placed the least amount of trust in the FDP. The FDP could have formed a coalition with the SPD, going strictly by the numbers, but only by a majority of six votes, and that seemed too few to a number of pragmatists among the SPD. Still, it was already clear by that time that Willy Brandt favored a socialist-liberal coalition, a preference for West Germany that he shared with the East German Communists, led by Walter Ulbricht.

Both the CDU and the SPD felt great scruples forming a coalition together. This was more than understandable, for the long years of constant dispute, which had begun with the founding of the Federal Republic, had taken their toll. On the other hand, even Adenauer had played with the thought of the two major political parties joining forces in an emergency. Adenauer, of course, always had his own tactical reasons for considering such a move: he wanted to make the FDP more tractable and he succeeded in doing so, temporarily. But a number of those in the CDU's second ranks, concerned about the stability of the Federal Republic, took a different approach to the idea of a major coalition between CDU and SPD, and cautiously began to promote the idea. Had the moment arrived in the final months of 1966 to send the distress signal and clear the way for a coalition? All objective factors pointed in this direction. Dieter Oberndörfer speaks of a

> period of the most profound crisis that the Federal Republic had experienced since its founding: there was the structural crisis in the coal and steel industry; the onset of recession as the result of irresponsible concessions made to voters and an unbridled policy of public assistance, with its attending inflation, rise in unemployment, and ebb in the public coffers; the political strength of the new radical right; and the unprecedented low-point in the Federal Republic's relations with its most important allies—France and the United States—as well as the initial danger of an internationalization of policy on Germany[20]

As more and more leading members of the CDU decided, after lengthy soul-searching, to risk the experiment, a heated discussion arose about who would lead the Great Coalition and who the chancellor should be. All opponents who had faced off against each other in Bonn over the course of the last years had sustained serious battle scars, or damaged their own personal reputations in various intrigues.

A new balance would require as chancellor someone who had remained outside this "civil war." The minister-president of Baden-Württemberg came to be included in that group of candidates being considered.

A further major factor spoke for Kiesinger's candidacy: in his years as a member of the *Bundestag* and as chairman of the Foreign Affairs Committee he had developed his own inimitable style of dealing with political opponents, which was respectful and fair. This elevated him above the routine squabbling, a fact attested to (once Kiesinger had departed for Stuttgart) even by prominent leaders of the SPD such as Fritz Erler and Herbert Wehner.[21]

So it was the aesthete Kiesinger who prevailed, transcending the tangle of intrigues and conspiracies that unavoidably seem to accompany such major decisions. He stymied adversaries and competitors such as Franz Josef Strauss, Eugen Gerstenmaier, or Gerhard Schröder, without resorting to political tricks. During his eight years as minister-president, from 1958 to 1966, Kiesinger had not even attempted what he had failed to accomplish during his years in the *Bundestag*—to organize a circle of supporters. Nevertheless, he did have a number of influential friends ready to support him at the right moment. This could come as a surprise to his opponents, as Strauss, who underestimated Kiesinger's backing in the CDU, was to experience personally.

Kiesinger knew that, were he to become a candidate for chancellor, he could win a majority of the vote. He also felt certain that he was qualified for the office. In the two decades he had spent in political office since the war, he had formed an accurate and realistic idea of the importance of the chancellorship, and was confident he could serve with distinction.

He did not put himself forward as a candidate, but now that the office was offered him he was eager to head the government, to lead the country, and to put into effect policies he had long believed in.

Nevertheless, Kiesinger hesitated, torn between concern and confidence. During the war he had been a deputy department head in the Foreign Office under Ribbentrop. He had been a National Socialist, and even CDU colleagues had brought up his activities during the Third Reich in order to disparage him. The communist propaganda machine was already running as well, in the Federal Republic and all over the world, ready to accelerate the moment Kiesinger declared. Should he expose himself to this, and to the nerve-wracking and energy-consuming campaign he would have to face? Wasn't he happy enough in Baden-Württemberg? Didn't he have a totally fulfilling life that satisfied both his interests and his qualifications? Duty called, and self-consideration hardly seemed grounds for refusal. Yet what if a well-organized campaign against him rendered him ineffectual as chancellor and did harm to the country? Could he face that responsibility, take the risk?

Kiesinger struggled with this for days, suffering awfully as self-doubt and self-confidence, bad and good conscience, duelled with each other. He finally came to a decision, but these were the questions that stood at the center of his deliberation. During this period Kiesinger met with former associates and old friends from the Foreign Office during the war: Hans Schirmer, Adolf Sonnenhol, Erwin Wickert, and myself, both to ask for advice and to weigh the pros and cons. He needed approval and the reassurance that we would not abandon him. We had no illusions, professionally familiar as we were with the aims and methods of communist propaganda. We did not underestimate this propaganda, but we also knew how highly vulnerable its promulgators were. As for Kiesinger's opposition within the Federal Republic, and above all in his own camp, we reminded him of who among them had voted (in the *Reichstag*) for the Act of Enablement that had brought Hitler to power; of the misjudgment of Hitler made by Heuss and Adenauer, among others, that was difficult to understand even in retrospect; and of the deplorable attempts of others to pose as resistance fighters even though they had continued to draw full pensions during the entire twelve years of the Third Reich.

We believed that Kiesinger could ride out the storm, an opinion that was strengthened when unimpeachable documents came to light attesting to Kiesinger's actions and conduct in the Foreign Office. Conrad Ahlers and Claus Jacoby of *Spiegel* magazine had always enjoyed a good relationship with the CIA, probably based on mutual collaboration. Now their American friends did them a favor: they made available a document that had come from the files of the head of the SS. One of Kiesinger's colleagues in the Reich broadcasting department had penned a lengthy denouncement of him, asserting that certain men in important posts were systematically impeding the dissemination of anti-Semitic material. "It can be proven that it is current deputy department head Kiesinger who is obstructing anti-Jewish operations." Examples of this sabotage were then cited. Highly explosive in terms of the wartime situation was the statement that Kiesinger, with the agreement of Undersecretary Hans Fritzsche, planned to exert direct influence on German radio broadcasts abroad, because "it is very important to have control over this instrument at the decisive hour." What could "the decisive hour" be? Those at the Reich security headquarters correctly assumed that Kiesinger was not referring to the hour of final victory.

This document, which *Spiegel* published, could not have come at a better time. We all advised Kiesinger not to assume a defensive position. He agreed, but added that we, too, might have to step onto the scene if necessary. We told him he could depend on us.

The document at issue above is representative of the way in which conspiracies and intrigues were carried out in the shadows of the Nazi dictatorship. It is a useful example for those who wish to understand what transpires in a regime on its way to ruin.

It was characteristic of Kiesinger that when the topic of this denunciation was raised, even years later, he did not speak of it in terms of how important it was to the rehabilitation of his reputation, but rather of the fact that he had been betrayed by two men close to him.

Chancellor of the Great Coalition

Kurt Georg Kiesinger was elected chancellor of the Federal Republic on December 1, 1966, by a *Bundestag* vote of 340 to 109, with twenty-three abstentions.

The cabinet of the Great Coalition was an impressive one, which was no surprise given that two great parties had sent their best representatives to head the government. Anyone with an appreciation of the wealth of history's imagination got his money's worth. If twelve months before the Great Coalition I had been offered a bet that by the beginning of 1967 two such powerful and antagonistic figures as Franz Josef Strauss and Herbert Wehner would be members of one and the same cabinet, I would have taken ten-to-one odds against it. And now both were cabinet ministers. An arabesque of minor interest took place when *Spiegel* editor Conrad Ahlers became deputy chief of the Press and Information Office—the man whom Franz Josef Strauss had imprisoned on charges of high treason. It was said that Wehner had convinced his colleagues to vote for Ahlers, remarking that Strauss would just have to swallow it.[22]

The CDU surrendered the office of foreign minister, and it was filled by Willy Brandt, head of the SPD. We understood how Brandt and his friends must have felt when he became foreign minister. It had been forty-six years since a socialist had occupied the office. The CDU also gave up the ministry of economics, to be filled by Professor Karl Schiller of the SPD. The CDU has not held either ministry since.

The cabinet was, in many ways, a master stroke. Each of the two parties secured influence in all of the major spheres. Foreign, all-German policy, and economic development were in the hands of very powerful members of the SPD. On the other side were the chancellor, who was involved in foreign policy and had authority over policy guidelines, the minister of defense, Gerhard Schröder (CDU), in charge of security, and to a certain extent, Kai Uwe von Hassel, the head of the Ministry for Expellees and Refugees. Minister of Economics Schiller was counterbalanced by Strauss as head of finance, and Kurt Schmücker (CDU) as head of the treasury. It was a well-balanced cabinet all in all. Normally the formation of a government is a long and often agonizing process, the balance of personal interests and opposing areas of expertise achieved only through great effort, or not at all. Kiesinger formed his cabinet within ten days.

This was barely to be believed and people slowly began to appreciate the qualities the new federal chancellor brought to the office, recalling circumstances under which Kiesinger had even stood up to Adenauer. The civility and decorum of Kiesinger's management style led many mistakenly to assume that he would be easy to handle. There was no doubt that a mood of high spirits prevailed, despite all the predictions and the undercurrent of resistance in both factions.

Kiesinger attached great importance to the spoken and written word. To him, writing and speaking were means of mastering the world and its problems. As a result, he neither wrote nor said anything that he had not formulated himself. It is an exaggeration, of course, to maintain that he personally "wrote every line." That would have been nonproductive, not to say impossible. The various ministries delivered the material, the large and small building blocks that went into the construction of the whole. But Kiesinger did not simply incorporate these texts as delivered; he reworked them himself, adapting them to his own style. Essential statements, especially in the areas of all-German and foreign policy, he wrote himself. He expended a great deal of concentration and effort to craft texts and declarations in which form matched the content. No other West German politician ever spoke or wrote so well, though others have excelled (Eugen Gerstenmaier and Carlo Schmid being two examples).

Kiesinger's work method was time-consuming. It takes clear

Taking the oath as federal chancellor administered by Bundestag *president Eugen Gerstenmaier, December 1, 1966.*

Federal President Heinrich Lübke receives Kiesinger's cabinet on December 1, 1966. First row, from left: Paul Lücke, Hermann Höcherl, Käte Strobel, Lübke, Kiesinger, Willy Brandt, Georg Leber; second row, from left: Bruno Heck, Carlo Schmid, Werner Dollinger, Kurt Schmücker, Kai-Uwe von Hassel, Karl Schiller, Hans Katzer, Gerhard Schröder; third row, from left: Herbert Wehner, Gustav Heinemann, Hans-Jürgen Wischnewski, Lauritz Lauritzen, Franz Josef Strauss, Gerhard Stoltenberg.

Kiesinger delivers his statement of government policy to the German Bundestag, *December 13, 1966.*

thinking to write a clear sentence, and producing these clear thoughts took time. And in this area the new chancellor brought a great wealth of resources with him. He had already spent a good deal of time forming an opinion on the problems he would face, and had developed a method for resolving them. Now that it was necessary to act, he could call on what he had already worked out in his mind. Which was the secret of how he could come to quick decisions, despite his apparently characteristic deliberation, and take decisive action.

As head of the planning staff I occasionally performed some preliminary work for Kiesinger, and later I did a good deal of writing for him, much of which he accepted and used, several major statements on foreign policy and all-German policy included. It would be a grave error to assume that Kurt Georg Kiesinger was the sort of man who could be fed ideas foreign to him. Any attempt to use him for a specific purpose was doomed to failure. But the chancellor often consulted close aides and accepted their advice. We knew fairly precisely what he was thinking and planning, and the fact that we were of one mind assured productive cooperation on most issues.

The new chancellor spent a great deal of time reflecting on issues in private, but he was not a "lone decision maker." He always presented his ideas and plans for discussion. Kiesinger was the boss, the "Meister," as we called him, but in discussions he judged the quality of an argument without regard to the person offering it. He gave these talks an institutional form, reviewing the status of "small" and "large" events, an idea he had introduced. The "small" normally involved the daily discussion of reports and information gathered from all areas of governmental activity. Where necessary, directives prescribed how an issue should be handled, what should be done right away and what could wait until later. Many topics of discussion carried a great deal of weight and were of major significance to state and country, and these detailed talks often yielded results which then became the basis for executive action.

To those who were not involved in them, these meetings appeared far too lengthy. In truth they were extraordinarily time saving, and an excellent means of dealing with complex issues. One major advantage was that all of the major ministries were kept informed of, and could agree on, questions without a great deal of paperwork. All of the chancellors who followed Kiesinger took over this system of status discussions, which served them well.

The federal chancellery under Kiesinger did not mushroom into a shadow government, as it did as soon as he left office. Each ministry had a contact person in the chancellery, and in almost all cases, one office, with a staff of two or three, covered several ministries. Kiesinger, prudent as he was, resisted all attempts to hire more personnel. In Karl Carstens and Hans Neusel[23] and their assistants Kiesinger had a first-rate staff, even by international standards.

His own household was run in an equally modest and efficient manner. The bungalow constructed for Ludwig Erhard, an enthusiast of modern architecture, was built in a style not to Kiesinger's liking, and appeared unsuitable as a federal chancellor's working residence. The house, with its flat roof and modern design and furnishings, had a certain quiet elegance, and was admired because of its location among the beautiful old trees of the surrounding park. But proportionately everything was somewhat too small, starting with the bed in which Kiesinger could not fully stretch out. There was also a swimming pond too small to swim in, and so on.

Most meetings were held at the Palais Schaumburg, in the chancellor's room, which had been kept exactly as Adenauer had left it; or in the so-called "small cabinet room," also located on the second floor, where breakfast meetings were held occasionally. Meetings also took place in the Hallstein Room, which was furnished as a salon, as were other former anterooms.

The cabinet met in the large garden room, or cabinet room, where most of the ministers had a view of the park. We were still quite frugal then, so that the cabinet room was cleared and transformed into a dining room when high foreign officials were visiting. The room was not big enough to accommodate large seatings, so on occasions of any size the French doors were opened and the table extended into the next room, and then angled at the other end. To my great regret the chancellor's office still did not possess its own silverware. We used the silver and place settings from a Bonn hotel. It was rather bad, a sign not of unpretentiousness or frugality, but simply uncertain taste and a lack of style. We urged the chancellor to do something about this, for we knew that in Stuttgart he had placed great importance on representation, in the best sense, and that he possessed a sense of style. Kiesinger himself was quite modest, but he felt that the office of chancellor profited from good taste and decorum.

The chancellor's official duties dictated keeping to a strict daily schedule. Kiesinger understood it was necessary to follow the appointment calendar, something he basically detested. He felt he was always on duty, constantly dealing with public affairs, and therefore did not divide up his day, did not attempt to live partly as a public official and partly as a private citizen, as Heinemann later did, unsuccessfully, as federal president. Whoever took part in Kiesinger's professional life could count on being summoned to meetings or discussions at any hour of the day, and on weekends and holidays as well.

These meetings were often informal. We gathered in the bungalow in casual dress to discuss a particular matter. Some brought files and papers, others did not, and had to be provided with pen and paper. The "Meister" would sit leaning back in a comfortable armchair, his dachshund on his lap. He would serve us a glass of wine and start the meeting. Karl Carstens, Baron Karl Theodor von und zu

Guttenberg,[24] Neusel, and I would join them, and often Ahlers as well, and sometimes one or another official from the chancellor's office who was working on the issue in question. Mixed groups occasionally convened, joined by cabinet members and caucus leaders, and there were meetings to which we officials were not invited, of course, when the issue was one of party and coalition politics, of which we understood nothing anyway. And finally, to Kiesinger's arsenal also belonged nocturnal discussions with one or two others, Herbert Wehner, for example. A few bottles were always emptied at these night "skirmishes," and the most recent events gone over.

It soon became apparent that the chancellor did not consider Bonn, its hustle and bustle, or its atmosphere, a place where he could best apply his gifts in dealing with people. Even when there was no reason not to receive an important guest in Bonn, Soviet Ambassador Zemyon Zarapkin, for example, Kiesinger would arrange for the meeting to take place in Stuttgart. He was always drawn back to Swabia; he somehow felt more secure and stronger there in the familiar surroundings of his home state.

This practice caused several logistical problems. Luckily, the federal government had begun to make use of the helicopters that belonged to the federal border police. The chancellor used the landing field in the park of the Palais Schaumburg. We departed from there as well, and so there developed a relay service of couriers and files flown to the quiet meadow tucked in the valley where the "Meister" set up quarters in the comfortable hunting lodge of a Swabian friend.

Significantly, Kiesinger also began moving major coalition policy meetings out of Bonn. The so-called "Kressbronner circle" is a good example. In 1967 Kiesinger felt many of the media kept saying the Great Coalition only pretended to agree on all-German and Eastern policy. There were major disagreements, they claimed, between the chancellor and the foreign minister, between the CDU and the SPD. Kiesinger chose not to stand idly by while these rumors were circulating. He summoned the major players from both camps to Kressbronn, on Lake Constance. The success of that meeting caused the chancellor to repeat this more than once, but less frequently later on, as the election of 1969 approached.

There was justified criticism, both from the party caucuses and the membership of both camps, that the Kressbronner circle was attempting to settle their differences behind closed doors. It smelled

The captivating speaker at a convention of the Rhineland CDU in Oberhausen, February 1967.

Campaigning in Gundelsheim, Baden-Württemberg, March 1968.

to some of a conspiratorial technique designed to cut off open debate, and this was not entirely untrue. Kiesinger saw the situation differently, however. "The chancellor," he said, "must keep to himself much of what he would like to say aloud—there are many things he must decide behind closed doors." And then he uttered a sentence that was quite revealing of how he saw his own role: "The chancellor is a sort of head of family to the German people, and if he cannot maintain order among his own then he is not worth much. That is how the people feel about it."

"Maintaining order among his own" was the leitmotiv of Kiesinger's leadership style. Not an easy thing to accomplish in a coalition bringing together two such opposing political groups, but he succeeded in creating an atmosphere and mood within the cabinet similar to that of a large family—warm-hearted and comradely, with even the most irascible and nervous personalities getting along with each other. The cabinet was often in good spirits, and this was at times plainly visible to any observer.

On one such occasion the chancellor was celebrating his birthday, and the army military band arrived to serenade him. The uniformed musicians, wanting to show off their skills, launched into their version of Gershwin's "Rhapsody in Blue," as the party stood on the terrace drinking a toast to the guest of honor. There was polite applause, and then Georg Leber[25] went over to the chancellor and said, "Mr. Chancellor, would you mind my asking them to play 'Old Comrades'?"[26] Kiesinger, as expected, had no objection and soon the band was playing "Old Comrades," which immediately perked up the party. Everyone was beaming, and Carlo Schmid began regaling others with stories of his time in the military, when, as a young lieutenant stationed in Cannstadt, he would lead his men from drill through the city back to the barracks and, he related with sparkling eyes, salute with his sword the young ladies standing by the roadside. Thus inspired, he went over to the bandmaster and asked him to play the "Hohenfriedberger March."[27] The bandmaster regretfully declined, it wasn't in the band's repertory. The entire cabinet was deeply disappointed: what good was the army when the military band couldn't even play the "Hohenfriedberger March" by heart?

It was said that Kiesinger and Brandt evidently did not get along. Brandt was often ill tempered and sullen at cabinet meetings and spoke with Kiesinger only when necessary. While it is true that the foreign minister did wear a sullen expression and seemed generally dissatisfied with himself and the world, it had nothing to do with

Kiesinger or with the coalition government. Brandt was always unbearable before noon. His mood improved over the course of the day, and by evening he sparkled with joie de vivre, a roguish expression on his face as he entertained us all with marvelous stories and jokes. Willy Brandt had the best store of trade union and "buddy" jokes. Kiesinger could enjoy these stories, but expressed his disapproval if things became offensive. He himself was a great storyteller, and his stories were warm hearted and humorous, but without an especially sharp wit.

The chancellor had a great appreciation for the comic side of some rituals and traditions. Students on the Iberian peninsula of Portugal have a lovely custom of spreading out their capes on the path of dignitaries visiting the university. Nor can the recipient of an honorary degree protest when the university's rector, deans, and professors embrace and kiss him on both cheeks, just as at the award ceremony of the French Legion of Honor. In Coimbra those of us accompanying the chancellor were standing in a semicircle next to a group of Portuguese professors. Kiesinger, after he had embraced and kissed the last Portuguese, suddenly found himself face to face with us. Was he, in full view of the Portuguese, now to refuse to embrace us, or risk appearing silly if he kissed Neusel and me on the cheeks? He quickly asked, "Should I kiss you too?" to which I answered valiantly, "We would be delighted." So he did, and Kiesinger was always amused by the memory of this.

The chancellor was not only extremely well read, he integrated the great works of literature into his own conception of humanity and its history. As a result, not only in personal conversations but also in conferences and meetings, he would raise his eyes from his papers and make some general observation citing the great authors or historical events to underscore his opinion on the subject at hand. This was when the tutor, the pedagogue in him, emerged. He wanted to enlighten and persuade us. Whether the people he talked to were receptive to this or impatient greatly depended on their disposition and intellectual inclination.

I enjoyed sitting next to the chancellor on long plane rides. We would spread out our papers in front of us, compare proposals, draw each other's attention to details, and enjoy an amusing turn of phrase, whether our own or someone else's. There would be pauses when we would sit quietly, preferring to read or to think. By the time we arrived we usually had decided on what it was we wanted and how we would try to achieve it.

The role of chancellor in the Great Coalition involved difficulties unknown before. The two political partners had announced in their declaration of purpose the intention to disband soon, never to form a government together again. The institutional pressure to form a Great Coalition was to be eliminated by electoral reform. This program was highly unusual, for normally if parties work together successfully for a legislative session they attempt to continue their alliance. Their common denominator is cultivated to encourage cooperation.

This time it was different. The coalition partners would work together to accomplish specific and limited objectives and then, at the next elections, stand against each other. Even at the moment the cabinet was being sworn in and the members were shaking each other's hands without guile, they did not forget that at the beginning of 1969 at the latest, enormous electoral tensions would quickly dissolve what they shared in common. Then their differences, rather than being bridged, would have to be heralded.

Kiesinger clearly saw that it was more important to his coalition partners than it was to him to exhibit a strong personality—even by keeping conflicts alive. Where was the SPD to find these conflicts? This in itself was absurd, for the coalition parties had demonstrated to the German public time and again that they were quite capable of resolving difficult issues. Could either partner claim to have resolved any issue without the votes of the other?

One of the areas in which the SPD hoped it could distinguish itself was that of all-German policy and *Ostpolitik* (Eastern policy). The semantics used by both coalition partners revealed their differences to be minimal. With respect to the GDR, Kiesinger spoke of a "phenomenon," whereas Brandt used the word "entity." Since as foreign minister Brandt was jointly responsible for policy, he could only have criticized it now by saying that with the SPD alone in power, a bolder and more sweeping *Ostpolitik* would be possible. But the dilemma was that Brandt's joint responsibility extended to all decisions—including the refusal to recognize the GDR or the Oder-Neisse line.[28] The Federal Republic, with Brandt as foreign minister, remained free and secure during a very stormy phase of East-West relations, even after the troops of the Warsaw Pact had marched into Czechoslovakia.

The SPD believed it could find a way out of its predicament by devious means. Brandt and Wehner as well were quite familiar with conspiratorial techniques, and Brandt's closest aid, Egon Bahr, if not already familiar with them, soon became an expert. On the other side, the communists in East Berlin and in Moscow could not have failed to notice that the SPD was prepared to relinquish the basic positions of German postwar policy. The contacts between them became more intense, and the Free Democrats joined the fray from the moment the two parties decided to form a socialist-liberal coalition after the elections (a coalition Ulbricht had long dreamed of). When the SPD voted against electoral reform announced in Kiesinger's government policy statement, and the FDP voted for the socialist Heinemann for federal president the message was clear. In the SPD camp it was Wehner, of all people, who decided not to keep the chancellor in the dark. Kiesinger thought highly of him for this, correctly deducing from Wehner's conduct that he supported the idea of continuing the Great Coalition, if that became necessary.

Kiesinger accurately assessed the relationship among Brandt, Wehner, and Helmut Schmidt over the broad stretch of the coalition government. Though the SPD had originated as a workers' party and highly valued its solidarity with the working class, the entry of intellectuals and academics into the party leadership changed this somewhat. Brandt could not depend on Wehner and Schmidt, particularly when he was in trouble, as was made clear later when he resigned. Kiesinger sensed this, but it was a long time before it became obvious. As chancellor he didn't see, or didn't want to see, the new constellation that was forming. He wasn't totally blind to this development—he certainly was the man in Bonn who, all in all, had the best information at his disposal. But he overestimated the forces within the FDP who rejected a coalition with the SPD, as well as those in the SPD who were considering a continuation of the Great Coalition. Still, it would not have been possible for him to head the cabinet, successfully handle the long list of legislative projects, and take care of the foreign and security interests of the Federal Republic as efficiently as he did had he not believed that he could keep his cabinet functioning until the very last moment of its existence.

Kiesinger made use of private meetings primarily as a means of discipline and coordination, but he did not shy from publicly disclosing violations of cabinet discipline, nor from reprimands appropriate to these violations. I was often assigned that responsibility, for which I later came under fire, sometimes not from Brandt himself, but from assistants twice or three times removed.

In the final phase of the Great Coalition Kiesinger's determination to "maintain order among his own"—because he believed this was the precondition of bringing the coalition to a positive end—led to a type of self-deception. I was unable to figure out whether his optimism was pretense or whether he truly believed the game could still be won. His patriarchal tone was ridiculed by the "extraparliamentary opposition."[29] Kiesinger himself did not avoid confrontation with those of divergent opinions, and always took part in arguments within the cabinet and the coalition. He did not see this as in any way injurious to personal relationships. Just as once he had deplored his betrayal by former Foreign Office colleagues more than the political disagreements between them, so he refused to believe for a long time and was therefore more hurt to discover that during the second half of the Great Coalition he could not rely on his coalition partner to keep him informed of its goals and intentions.

From Paralysis to Action

To Kiesinger's lasting credit, the Great Coalition made no errors in foreign policy. This was due to the chancellor's profound understanding of international political developments and his ability to safeguard German interests by accurately assessing his country's significance, and to rank freedom, peace, unity, security, and prosperity as the basic priorities, in that order. No government was better able to do this than a government made up of the two major people's parties. That is why my SPD colleague, Friedrich Schäfer, was correct when he told me years later that the Great Coalition had not lasted long enough.

The achievements of the Kiesinger/Brandt government in foreign and all-German policy deserve all the more acclaim because they came at a time of great international tensions when the world stood at the brink of a major new war.

The challenge in 1967 was, first of all, to create a degree of understanding and order. The Federal Republic had a poor relationship with the U.S., Franco-German relations were going badly, and West Germany's dealings with Great Britain were troublesome. Discord between France and England was holding up the development of the European Community, and France's ambivalent position on the North Atlantic Alliance was creating problems for the defense of Europe. The larger situation was overshadowed by "nuclear complicity," as Kiesinger pointedly remarked to an attentive foreign press at the beginning of his term. It was a complicity, he said, between the U.S. and the Soviet Union designed to impose upon the community of nations a non-proliferation treaty, which would preserve the nuclear monopoly of those who were in possession, and would hinder civilian use of nuclear energy.

Meanwhile, the Soviet Union once again went on the attack to grab complete control of Berlin, to have both German states recognized, and to keep the other members of the Warsaw Pact in line. It was no secret to the men in the Kremlin, led by Brezhnev, that tiny cracks in the wall of the Warsaw Pact were heralding its demise. One cause of the initial erosion, though not the major one, was the successful effort by the Great Coalition to follow up Erhard's Peace Memorandum and improve relations with Moscow's satellite states. The Kremlin, and therefore the GDR, were determined to get Bonn to formally recognize the GDR as a second German state subject to international law in exchange for normalizing relations. But interest in activating relations with the Federal Republic was so strong in Rumania, Yugoslavia, Poland, and Czechoslovakia that they agreed to the solution we worked out: we would separate our claim to be the sole representative of all of Germany from having sole presence in the country. In future we would claim exclusive rights to represent Germany in countries where the GDR was recognized as well, in communist-ruled states, that is, that maintained full diplomatic relations with the GDR. Previously, we had used this formula only with the Soviet Union, when we established full diplomatic relations in 1955 despite the fact that full relations already existed between Moscow and the GDR. We based this exception on the fact that the Soviet Union was one of the four victorious Allies and carried a particular responsibility for the regulation of German policy.

Kiesinger—who had supported this decision in Moscow in 1955—along with Brandt and all the leading members of the cabinet agreed we should proceed along these lines as long as our claim to be the exclusive representative remained intact. Which was to say we would never recognize the "phenomenon" or the "entity" of the GDR according to international law. It is to Kiesinger's credit that he made the SPD stick by this. Despite all attempts by leading members of the SPD, who were supported by the majority of the leading left-liberal press, to get us to recognize the GDR, write off the idea of unification, and leave East Germans in a continuing state of subjugation, Bonn stood firm. And it continued to do so right up to the collapse of the East German regime. The consensus on all-German policy in the Great Coalition, which Kiesinger had secured and partially coerced, remained one of the great tools used to bring down the Wall.

This aggressive approach in dealing with the states of the Warsaw Pact was not something spontaneously planned or executed. Kiesinger was well aware of the risks involved. Astute observers long since had warned against any attempt to take the Soviet stronghold from the periphery. Moscow would not risk a reduction in its repressive methods on the edge of its sphere of influence, or allow democratic concessions there that might radiate toward the center. The Soviet suppression of the East Berlin workers' uprising in 1953 and of the Hungarian uprising in 1956 argued for this analysis. Only when the Soviet Union itself began a process of democratization would the Kremlin allow its satellites to do the same. The chancellor was convinced of the veracity of this thesis.

On the other hand, though we could not provoke the Soviets, neither did we wish to pursue any policy simply to please Moscow. There were all too many people prepared to ingratiate themselves to the Soviets and agree to anything they said. The chancellor believed the Soviet Union already was experiencing difficulties holding the communist empire together, especially with a second red sun blazing in the sky—the People's Republic of China. Presumably, the Soviet leadership could no longer massacre people outside the Soviet Union before the eyes of the entire world, as it did in Hungary. We began cautiously establishing diplomatic relations with Rumania and Yugoslavia, two communist countries that did not belong to the Warsaw Pact. To members of the Warsaw Pact we offered to establish commercial missions.

Kiesinger had sent his confidant, Hans Schirmer, to Moscow in 1968 as scout to find out if the Soviet leadership was reviewing its policy on Germany, and to see if they might be willing to negotiate. He hoped a political course could be mapped out if talks were held outside the public spotlight, and so did not involve questions of prestige. Those major members of the Soviet leadership who had been informed of the chancellor's initiative showed an interest in keeping up this sort of contact.

In the time that followed, Moscow came under pressure from reform movements in the Eastern bloc, and in order to prevent their spread again felt it necessary to employ repression. The "Prague Spring" blossomed in 1968, and after a period of indecision that Kiesinger anxiously followed, the Soviet leadership decided to invade Czechoslovakia. But it made sure troops from other Warsaw Pact states, among them the German Democratic Republic, would participate. Moscow didn't want to carry the responsibility for the assault alone, at least in the eyes of the outside world. Following the invasion into Czechoslovakia, secret German-Soviet contacts were broken off. They had become meaningless for the foreseeable future.

The chancellor himself exercised extreme caution in this critical situation. No one knew if the Soviets would use the opportunity to attack Rumania and Yugoslavia as well, two countries with whom the Federal Republic had only recently established diplomatic relations. The Soviets had accused West Germany of massive intervention in the internal affairs of Czechoslovakia. According to Moscow propaganda, it was the Germans who had initiated the "Prague Spring" and supplied the Czechs with weapons. What would happen if the Red Army decided to retaliate—in Berlin, say, or the Bavarian Forest?

Kiesinger, with the support of the Western allies, immediately took charge. In direct talks with Soviet ambassador Zemyon Zarapkin he dealt so deftly with the critical and delicate problems at hand that no grave threat to West German security arose. A maneuver that long had been planned for the vicinity of the Czech border was postponed, so that the Soviets could not use it as an excuse to apply further threats and pressure.

This was a characteristic example of Kiesinger's style. In critical situations his reflective, meticulous side yielded to decisive and purposeful action.

In the spring of 1969 the Soviet leadership, in league with East Berlin, tried to prevent the Federal Assembly from convening in Berlin to elect a new federal president. Once again it was Kiesinger himself who held the decisive talks with the Soviet ambassador. Zarapkin held out a vague offer if the Federal Assembly moved its meeting to a city in West Germany, but Kiesinger nevertheless saw to it that the assembly met in Berlin as planned, though at the last minute Willy Brandt, following direct contact with East Berlin, wanted to postpone the assembly and have it moved. Kiesinger was able to get the cabinet to act unanimously to resist Soviet pressure. It should be mentioned that the government that succeeded Kiesinger's believed it had to assuage the Russians, and so the Federal Assembly did not meet again in Berlin. Here, too, Kiesinger has been vindicated by history.

Events in the East bloc brought the Western allies closer together, making Kiesinger's work easier. He had been harshly critical of America at the beginning of his term, complaining Bonn had been kept in the dark about U.S. foreign and defense policies. Washington pricked up its ears at this and decided to take the new chancellor seriously, and to show him more respect than Ludwig Erhard. Nevertheless, the two major nuclear powers pressured the Germans to sign the non-proliferation treaty. The Federal Republic, as a state, could not have countered with a revisionist program, nor have hoped to realize this revision—the restoration of unity and self-determination— had it attempted to arm itself with nuclear weapons. The treaty, however, was unbalanced, and Kiesinger's vote to support it was linked to a demand for major changes.

A number of SPD voices called for the immediate signing of the treaty, while leading representatives of the CDU/CSU, among them Strauss and Adenauer, opposed the signing, believing that in the face of growing Soviet threats the Federal Republic should keep a nuclear option open. But Kiesinger's conditional policy won out. During his chancellorship the Federal Republic did not sign the treaty, and when the socialist-liberal government did, the treaty they signed was a better one, owing to Kiesinger's obstinacy. An accompanying note also was attached which expressly guaranteed the Federal Republic civilian use of nuclear energy. The Federal Republic also protected itself against the misuse of the hostile-nations clause in the United Nations covenant and were supported in this by the Western allies. The Soviet Union knew what it was up against.

Bonn soon established a good relationship with recently elected President Richard Nixon, nothing like the undeservedly frosty treatment Ludwig Erhard was shown by President Lyndon Johnson. [30] Nixon informed the chancellor fully and promptly of decisions to be made concerning American foreign and security policy. Noteworthy was Nixon's briefing of Kiesinger, conducted at the White House in the presence of Henry Kissinger, on the decision to end the Vietnam War.

Kiesinger was not afraid of contact with the American media, and thanks to the assistance of Jewish friends also established a more relaxed relationship with the American Jewish community. The chancellor even enjoyed a degree of popularity in the U.S. When he visited his daughter and her family in Washington, the photos the press released of Kiesinger holding his granddaughter in his arms or carrying her on his shoulders made a better impression on the American public than did all the diplomatic speeches delivered to the various distinguished committees.

With U.S. president Richard Nixon at the White House, August 1969.

The preamble to the Franco-German Treaty, insisted on by supporters of the Atlantic Alliance in the *Bundestag* and acquiesced to by Adenauer near the end of his tenure in office left cool relations between France and West Germany that lasted through Erhard's chancellorship. De Gaulle's remark, "We married but we didn't consummate the relationship," expressed the situation succinctly, but at the beginning of the Great Coalition, German "Michael" and French "Marianne" obediently headed for their conjugal bed.

De Gaulle and Kiesinger appeared to be well matched. Both were highly skilled at expressing their ideas, and both were superb speakers. Kiesinger clearly delineated West Germany's position on German and Eastern policy, on the Atlantic Alliance, and on British membership in the European Community. As the Federal Republic's representative in cultural affairs, Kiesinger was able to foster mutual cultural projects within the framework of the Franco-German Treaty. He established a common ground where de Gaulle was willing to meet him.

Anyone who paid careful attention could recognize the subtlety of de Gaulle's language, which only rarely closed off future possibilities. France's allies and friends benefited from the trustworthiness of the French leadership, which, regardless of its independent stance, always made clear that whoever attacked an ally of France would

have the French to deal with as well. The West might have had questions about this, but those in Moscow knew it to be true, and acted
accordingly.

Kiesinger and Brandt's counterparts in Great Britain were Labour
Party leaders Harold Wilson and George Brown. The Labour Party
had an advantage over German Social Democrats in that it had ruled
the United Kingdom long and often. But neither socialist nor Marxist
ideas played any great role in English everyday life, and London soon
recognized that under the prevailing circumstances Kiesinger was
better suited than Brandt to change France's negative position on
England joining the European Community. Kiesinger wanted Great

With British prime minister Harold Wilson in
London, October 1967.

Britain to join because it would have been very difficult to integrate a future united Germany into the European Community without England's support. A united Germany would be a "critical mass," acceptable to all only within a framework larger than that of a "little" Europe. Kiesinger succeeded in keeping the complicated three-way relationship between France, England, and the FRG relatively conflict-free, and certainly was more successful in this than his two predecessors and two successors.

Kiesinger pursued a similar course on his visits to Portugal and Spain, and was able to guide these two countries, which had played such a grand and significant role in European history, back to the path of the European democracies, in preparation for their later entry into the European Community. This was not only far-sighted, it was also courageous, given the times. The SPD, for good reason, had strong objections to these two countries, led as they were by two despots, Salazar and Franco, respectively. No chancellor of the postwar era, not even Adenauer, had visited either Portugal or Spain. Kiesinger convinced his foreign minister and the SPD cabinet members that the attempt was a worthy one, and would bear fruit in the future.

His visit to the Iberian peninsula provided Europe with a powerful reminder of the importance of including Spain and Portugal—where European civilization and history were evident at every turn—in the building of a new and democratic Europe. One result of the visit was that both governments began thinking and planning in European terms. Beyond any doubt, the Soviet advance into Czechoslovakia had changed the security situation, not only of Czechoslovakia's nearest neighbors, but of all of Europe as well.

What was the best way to deal with the Soviet Union? What was Moscow's opinion of the Great Coalition? Considering the circumstances, the Soviet leadership could not have been pleased with Kiesinger's government. The Great Coalition was in the position to gain the broad support of the West German population, even for major policy initiatives on the East. But a consensus on these issues in the cabinet and the *Bundestag* would have called for basic changes in Moscow's policy. The Kremlin would have had to state that it had no objections to the unification of Germany, would even support it if, in the process, Soviet interests would be guaranteed as well. But it was precisely this that the Soviet government no longer could, or would, state.

Kiesinger had attempted to find out if there was a margin of possible understanding that would allow talks with the Soviet leadership. There was not. The chancellor had not forgotten his experience in Moscow in 1955. He knew that any attempt to engage in exclusive negotiations with the Russians carried very high risks. The size and energy of the Soviet Union were clearly superior to those of West Germany. In addition, the Kremlin had its East German pawn with which to maneuver. Successful German policy would require alliance.

Kiesinger was convinced that Russia would not be able to hold its position. He repeated this often in public. Reading it now in the perspective of history, it appears, as does his opinion on *Ostpolitik*, as a beacon.

Moscow, however, believed it was nearing its goal, because it was counting on a change in German politics. The end of the Great Coalition was to signal this change. Indeed, the Kremlin had done everything in its power to support the emergence of a socialist-liberal coalition, believing it would be easy prey. First Walter Scheel, Wolfgang Mischnick, and Hans-Dietrich Genscher of the FDP were invited for a visit, followed one month later by Helmut Schmidt, Alex Möller, and Egon Franke of the SPD. During the election campaign, and in certain sections of the German press sympathetic to the Soviets, these visits were represented as if Kiesinger himself, along with all of the CDU, was a stumbling block on the path to agreement with the Soviet Union, one that should be cleared away as soon as possible.

It was rumored that Kiesinger was annoyed not to have received an invitation, and had tried to wrangle one to no avail. The situation in fact was otherwise. Had the Great Coalition continued to exist, Kiesinger would have met the Soviet leadership either in Moscow or in Bonn. But Moscow hoped to avoid this and to meet with more acceptable partners following the election. Henry Kissinger noted in his memoirs that Brandt had relieved the Allies of responsibility for Germany's reunification. That is how the whole world saw it.

The dramatic events in international politics the Kiesinger/Brandt administration was faced with led many observers to focus their attention on its foreign-policy activities. Thus one of the coalition's most amazing accomplishments is relegated to the background—the quick vigorous recovery of the German economy. In truth, what the Great Coalition accomplished in a short period of time—with Schiller and Strauss serving, respectively, as minister of economy and minister of finance—is close to incredible. It seems like a dream to recall that in 1968 the actual growth of the gross national product reached

7.3 percent, and in 1969 it even climbed to 8.2 percent. The budget was balanced on the spot, so to speak, and West Germany's debt was covered. At the end of the Kiesinger government the budget showed a surplus of 1.5 billion Deutsche Mark. Already at the halfway mark of the Great Coalition there was practically no unemployment, with only 247,000 people looking for work, 710,000 positions available, and 1.2 million foreign workers.

The Great Coalition majority of the *Bundestag* and the *Bundesrat* also enabled the chancellor to carry out a number of constitutional reforms and to enact emergency legislation. In view of its short time in office, the cabinet's domestic policy accomplishments have stood the test, and this applies as well to its financial and social policies, and to the relationship between federal and state governments.

Kiesinger made his personal contribution in the area of coordination, of balancing the conflicting interests of cabinet and society. His preferences for consensual government had its effect. Kiesinger's leadership style was exemplified by the "concentrated action," his integration of all relevant economic groups being one such example.

In the summer and fall of 1969, as the election neared, this atmosphere of consensus was perforce lost. There was contention concerning the revaluation of the Deutsche Mark. Kiesinger, on the advice of his old friend Othmar Emminger of the German *Bundesbank*, and others, was against revaluation. Minister of Economics Karl Schiller supported it, and his party along with him. The majority of the cabinet voted with the chancellor. Up to this day the delay in revaluation is viewed overwhelmingly as a mistake. Some even presume to say that this mistake determined the outcome of the election, an opinion that remains to be proven. More open to question is whether revaluation did not carry with it the seeds of the socialist-liberal coalition's later difficulties in financial and economic policies. Schiller, at any rate, soon abandoned ship.

With the election results on the evening of September 28, 1969,[31] the CDU, led by Kurt Georg Kiesinger, held its ground. Not least due to Kiesinger, the right-wing NPD (National Democratic Party of Germany) did not capture a seat in the *Bundestag*. But it was precisely this that had a fatal effect, for it enabled the Free Democratic Party to gain enough support to advance an SPD/FDP government. The SPD, having refused to support election reform, now reaped the reward for breaking the coalition agreement.

Kiesinger understood what had happened. The CDU was no longer a major part of the government; it wasn't even represented in the new constellation. It was a bitter fact, but was it his fault? Had he made a mistake? "It's up to the chancellor" had been his party's campaign slogan.

The chancellor had lost the majority. Kiesinger was convinced that democracy could thrive only if a changing of the guard was politically possible. But it was clear—from the way in which the Great Coalition dissolved to form the socialist-liberal coalition—that the wish to stay in power or to return to power at any cost rendered programmatic party goals secondary. The eagerness with which the socialist-liberal coalition set to work disguised for a long while the fact that political indifference had stolen onto the scene. Two decades later a deep doubt in the system's ability to function, and in the integrity of its players, would prove a threat to the existence of the major parties.

The Great Coalition did not endure for long, but the goals Kiesinger set out to achieve were realized twenty years later on the path he had marked out, while the plans of his direct successors were rejected by history.

Who knows, one day, were the situation to become critical enough, perhaps the Germans in recalling the Great Coalition will understand it in retrospect, and try it again. If so, they should not neglect election reform. That is a part of Kurt Georg Kiesinger's political legacy.

Notes

1. Kurt G. Kiesinger, *Schwäbische Kindheit* (Tübingen: Rainer Wunderlich, 1964).

2. Swabia (*Schwaben*). A region in the state of Baden-Württemberg in the southwest of Germany. Its capital is Stuttgart.

3. As many critics of West Germany were quick to comment, Kiesinger had joined the NSDAP at the very beginning of Nazi rule and therefore could not claim to have been coerced. Moreover, he had worked in the Reich Broadcasting Service and had been involved in radio propaganda for the Hitler regime. His defenders, however, could point out that Kiesinger, who had been a lawyer in private practice before the war, had put himself and his family at considerable risk to help Jews and others persecuted by the regime. The controversy over Kiesinger's past refused to die down, receiving national and international attention. Heinrich Böll called Kiesinger an "insult" to the German people, and Karl Jaspers referred to his election in similar terms. The furor culminated in the famous "slap" incident, when Beate Klarsfeld, a German woman living in Paris, publicly slapped Kiesinger's face at a CDU meeting in Berlin in 1968, shouting "Nazi! Nazi!" at the top of her voice. When she returned to her Paris apart-

ment she found a bunch of roses delivered with a card that read "Thanks— Heinrich Böll."

Dennis L. Bark and David R. Gress, *A History of West Germany*, Vol. 1: *Democracy and Its Discontent 1963–1988* (Cambridge: Basil Blackwell, 1989).

4. Among the individuals Kiesinger saved from the Nazis were Mathias Blasius, a financial officer of a Catholic congregation, who had been jailed in a concentration camp, and Ernst Wold, arrested by the Gestapo and released because of Kiesinger's intervention.

5. In his memoirs, *Erinnerungen* (Berlin: Propyläen Verlag, 1989) Willy Brandt said: "Kiesinger was too intelligent and cultured to have been a Nazi beyond carrying a membership card. He never disputed having at first succumbed, like so many others, to delusions, nor claimed to have been active in the resistance."

6. Kiesinger suffered from Römheld's disease, a gastrocardiac syndrome, probably because of malnutrition after World War I.

7. The golden party badge was awarded to the first very early Nazi party members with a membership number below 500. Later it also became an award for distinguished party service.

8. Gustav Adolf Sonnenhol (1912–1988). German diplomat, ambassador to South Africa and Turkey, who had joined the SS in 1939. As a student he was wounded in a street fight with communists and was consequently awarded the *Blutorden* (Blood Order) of the Nazi party, which is said to have given him some protection in his anti-Nazi activities. In his memoirs, *Untergang oder Übergang? Wider die deutsche Angst* (Stuttgart: Seewald, 1983), Sonnenhol described life in the Foreign Ministry during the war and argued that most service professionals were anti-Nazis who protected each other from investigation and arrest as long as possible.

See: Bark and Gress, op cit.

9. Kiesinger was interned in the U.S. Third Army Internment Camp 74, in Rheingönheim near Ludwigshafen, in Heilbronn, and in Ludwigsburg.

10. "Protection of the Constitution" (*Verfassungsschutz*) is a euphemism for intelligence and counterintelligence by agencies of the *Länder* and the federal government.

11. The *Bundestag*'s mediation committee attempts to reconcile the differences in proposed legislation between the upper and the lower house, the *Bundestag* and the *Bundesrat*.

12. Kiesinger spoke excellent English. He was fluent in French and had a basic knowledge of Italian. In addition, he knew Latin and classical Greek.

13. Erich Köhler (1892–1958). Economist and political scientist. Co-founder of the CDU in Hesse, chairman of the Bizone Economic Council, first president of the *Bundestag*.

14. Karl Arnold (1901–1958). Until 1933 a leader of the Christian trade-union movement and member of the Center Party. Co-founder of the CDU, long-serving minister-president of Nordrhein-Westfalen, the largest state of the Federal Republic.

15. Adenauer had failed to keep his promise to the other members of his delegation to inform them in advance of the negotiating objectives.

16. In April 1922, after secret negotiations, Germany and Russia signed an agreement at the Italian seaport of Rapallo, renouncing all claims to war indemnities of any sort, as well as those arising from Soviet expropriation of German property, and resuming diplomatic relations. It was the first important foreign-policy agreement signed by Germany since its defeat in 1918. Three years later, in October 1925, Germany, Belgium, France, Britain, and Italy met in Locarno to sign a security pact guaranteeing the borders as fixed by Versaille, ceding Alsace-Lorraine, formerly German, to France, and promising to come to each other's defense in case of attack by any of the signatories. Hitler abrogated the pact in 1936.

17. *Süddeutsche Zeitung*, September 17, 1955.

18. Volkmar Wenzel, who married Kiesinger's daughter Viola, is a photographer, author, and longtime editorial-board member of the *National Geographic* in Washington, D.C.

19. Gustav Heinemann, leading figure in the SPD, later minister of justice and president of Federal Republic. Thomas Dehler (FDP), formerly attorney general of the Federal Republic.

20. Dieter Oberndörfer, *Kurt Georg Kiesinger und die Grosse Koalition*, (Stuttgart: Deutsche Verlagsanstalt, 1979).

21. Fritz Erler, head of the SPD *Bundestag* caucus, died of leukemia on February 22, 1967, just before his long years of service to the cause of the Social Democrats could be crowned with a cabinet post in the Great Coalition.

22. See Note 41 on the *Spiegel* affair in Chapter 1, p.70.

23. Karl Carstens (CDU), state secretary of the Foreign Ministry (1960–1967), later became speaker of the *Bundestag* in 1976, and, in 1979, was elected president of the Federal Republic.

    Hans Neusel (1927–). State secretary of the Ministry of Interior (1985–1992), earlier official in Erhard's chancellery, personal aide to Kiesinger, and head of the federal president's office. Barely escaped an assassination attempt by the Red Army Faction in 1990.

24. Baron Karl Theodor von und zu Guttenberg (1921–1972). Leading CSU member of the *Bundestag*, parliamentary state secretary in Kiesinger's chancellery. The scion of a very old and distinguished aristocratic family, many of his relatives were executed or jailed after the 1944 assassination attempt on Hitler.

25. Georg Leber, prominent SPD and trade union leader, became minister of communications in Kiesinger's cabinet and later minister of defense under Willy Brandt and Helmut Schmidt (1972–1978).

26. "Old Comrades," a traditional Prussian march, one of Hitler's favorites.

27. "Hohenfriedberger March," an eighteenth-century Prussian military march.

28. See Note 29 in Chapter 1, pp. 69–70.

29. The "extraparliamentary opposition" began in the mid-sixties as a radical student movement that developed into several branches of the New Left by the end of the decade. It included among its leaders such internationally known figures as Rudi Dutschke, spilling over from university campuses to the streets of the major cities with its demonstrations against the war in Vietnam and U.S. installations in Germany. Later, a small but intense faction moved toward full-

fledged violence and terrorism (the Baader-Meinhof group and the Red Army Faction).

30. Two incidents were seen as harsh treatment of Erhard by Johnson. The first was in 1964, when the U.S. president first persuaded Bonn to support the multilateral force (MLF) at some political cost, and then suddenly canceled the project without prior notice. The second, in 1966, came during Erhard's visit to the U.S., when Johnson denied his requests for some degree of direct access to NATO nuclear weapons and for relief from payments for U.S. military supplies to Germany and for stationing U.S. troops there. Erhard returned empty-handed and some, like Helmut Schmidt, later argued that Johnson effectively caused Erhard's fall.

31. The election results in 1969 gave the SPD 42.7 percent of the vote, the CDU 36.6 percent, the CSU 9.5 percent, and the FDP 5.8 percent, thus adding up to a majority of 48.5 percent for the socialist-liberal bloc, as against 46.1 percent for the conservative sister parties CDU/CSU.

[Top] *During the first visit of a federal chancellor to Communist East Germany, looking out of the window of his hotel in Erfurt, March 1970 — Campaigning in Hessen as candidate for chancellor, 1966 — Addressing a* Bundestag *session, 1982.*
[Center] *With Olof Palme and Bruno Kreisky at a meeting of the Socialist International, 1975 — With Leonid Brezhnev and Egon Bahr*

on a Black Sea cruise, 1971.
[Bottom] *The historic moment when Brandt fell to his knees before the*
memorial for the victims of the Warsaw ghetto, December 1970 — As mayor
of Berlin with Marlene Dietrich and Mr. and Mrs. Herbert von Karajan,
1961 — With Foreign Minister Walter Scheel on the Bundestag's government
bench, 1973.

1913	Born Herbert Ernst Karl Frahm in Lübeck on December 18.
1930	Joins the Social Democratic Party (SPD), changing party membership in 1931 to the Socialist Workers' Party of Germany (*Sozialistische Arbeiterpartei Deutschlands*, SAP).
1933	The SAP goes underground. Karl Frahm assumes the name Willy Brandt. Emigrates to Norway in April.
1936	Enters Germany illegally to work with the SAP resistance group in Berlin.
1937	In Barcelona during the Spanish Civil War.
1938	Deprived of German citizenship by Nazis.
1940	Granted Norwegian citizenship. Flees to Sweden following the Wehrmacht's invasion of Norway. Political and journalistic work in Stockholm.
1945–1947	Returns to Oslo at the end of the war. Correspondent at the Nuremberg trials, and Norwegian press attaché in Berlin.
1948	Reassumes German citizenship. Heads SPD liaison office in Berlin.
1949–1957	Elected Berlin SPD representative to the *Bundestag*.
1955–1957	President of the Berlin City Assembly.
1957–1966	Governing mayor of Berlin. Runs unsuccessfully as SPD's candidate for federal chancellor in 1961 and 1965.
1964	Chairman of the SDP (honorary chairman in 1987).
1966–1969	Foreign minister and vice-chancellor of the Great Coalition.
1969	Elected federal chancellor.
1971	Receives Nobel Peace Prize.
1974	Resigns as chancellor in May after Günter Guillaume, his personal aide, is exposed as a GDR spy.
1976	President of the Socialist International.
1977	Chairman of the North-South Commission.
1992	Dies October 8 in Unkel am Rhein.

Willy Brandt

by Peter Zudeick

October 21, 1969, 10:00 A.M. In the German *Bundestag*, the president of parliament, Kai-Uwe von Hassel (CDU), reads a letter from Federal President Gustav Heinemann (SPD): "Following Article 63, Paragraph 1, of the Basic Law, I move that the German *Bundestag* elect Herr Willy Brandt as federal chancellor." Almost one and a half hours later von Hassel announces the results: "With 495 total votes cast, number of "yeas" 251, number of "nays" 235, with four invalid votes and five abstentions." Applause, hesitant at first, grows only slowly. Helmut Schmidt is the first to congratulate Brandt, followed by representatives of the Union parties—Kurt Georg Kiesinger, Rainer Barzel, and Richard Stücklen. They are followed by Walter Scheel, Hans-Dietrich Genscher, Wolfgang Mischnick, and Werner Mertes of the FDP and, finally, Herbert Wehner.

Wehner shakes Brandt's hand and then attempts a wooden and halting embrace, abruptly resting his head on Brandt's shoulder. Brandt, embarrassed and touched, pats him on the back, both men fighting back tears. Equally abruptly, Wehner breaks off his abortive embrace and turns away. Willy Brandt has become federal chancellor, a moving moment for both men. Brandt's path to the chancellorship had been long and rocky, and had started out as no other before it.

Herbert Ernst Karl Frahm was born on December 18, 1913, in a working-class suburb of Lübeck, a port on the Baltic Sea with an 850-year history. "His mother was very young, an industrious little sales clerk at the consumer cooperative," Willy Brandt wrote in 1960, in his book *Mein Weg nach Berlin* (My Path to Berlin),[1] referring to "the boy Herbert Ernst Karl Frahm" in an oddly distant, third-person voice. "He never met his father, he didn't even know who his father was. And never wanted to know. He bore his mother's name; his father was never spoken of at home."

Herbert Frahm stayed with a friend of his mother's during the day while she worked. In 1918 Herbert's grandfather, Ludwig Frahm, returned from the war, and the child grew up in his home. Grandfather Frahm was an active unionist and member of the Social Democratic Party. As a farm worker on a large Mecklenburg estate he had witnessed the practice of flogging. "His own father," Brandt later wrote of his grandfather, "had been treated like chattel and 'bent over the bench,'" and the boy had grown up in the tradition and atmosphere of the workers' movement. "Socialism meant much more to my grandfather than a political program, it was a kind of religion to him," Brandt related. "Socialism was to make all men brothers, eliminate all inequality, even eliminate money. Herbert never tired of listening to these predictions, and his heart would pound when his grandfather would sing the workers' songs of struggle—the 'Workers' Marseillaise,' and the 'Socialists' March'—along with the folk songs of the region."

There was no question that young Herbert Frahm would become active in the labor youth movement ("I was born into socialism, so to speak."): the Labor Sports Club, the Labor Mandolin Club, and the *Falken* (Falcons)—the organization of Socialist Youth Workers—of which Herbert became local chairman at fifteen, and later deputy regional chairman. In 1930, not yet seventeen, he became a member of the SPD. The age required for membership was eighteen, but an exception was made in his case because he already worked for the *Volksbote*, the Lübeck newspaper of the SPD.

The *Volksbote* editor-in-chief was Julius Leber, *Reichstag* representative and chairman of the Lübeck Social Democrats. Leber was an early mentor to Herbert Frahm, and many years later Willy Brandt still spoke of him with great respect and special emotion. On January 31, 1933, one day after the Nazis assumed power, Leber was attacked by the SA thugs and seriously injured. He was locked up in a concentration camp until 1937, then joined the resistance against Hitler, was arrested again and executed in January 1945. Whenever Willy Brandt discussed Leber—whether in public or in private—it was always with a lump in his throat.

As a young socialist, however, Herbert Frahm sharply opposed Julius Leber, who was a moderate Social Democrat. In 1931 a group of SPD activists protested the ineffectual opposition policies of the SPD members of the *Reichstag* by founding the Socialist Workers' Party (SAP), which Herbert Frahm immediately joined. He wrote in the *Socialist Workers' Journal*, the party newspaper: "Our transformation has reached the point where we stand no closer to the SPD ideologically than does any other proletarian party. To the contrary, we are perhaps the most distant of all." He became chairman of the Lübeck Socialist Youth Association (*Sozialistischer Jugendverband*— SJV), the youth organization of the SAP, and also a member of Lübeck's SAP executive committee.

The break with the SPD and, above all, with Julius Leber meant, among other things, that Frahm lost his modest income from contributing to the *Volksbote*. He had wanted to become a journalist, and Julius Leber had promised him that the party would help with a stipend.

Instead, after receiving his secondary-school certificate, Frahm took a job with a shipping brokerage in February 1932. Meanwhile, he continued his political work. "Evenings and Sundays were now entirely devoted to politics. I held small meetings—sometimes very small meetings, spoke in debates on many occasions, and discovered that public speaking came easily to me," Willy Brandt reported. "I could speak with facility on any subject at all. At eighteen, in my double existence and without the public taking much notice, I had become a party leader on a small scale."

But there was growing unrest in the SAP. Election results were disappointing, and one day after the *Reichstag* fire on February 27, 1933, SAP leaders dissolved the party, fearing communist infiltration. Those on the left of the party, Herbert Frahm among them, ignored this decision and called a convention of their now "illegal" party for March 11, 1933, in Dresden.

Most delegates to the convention assumed an alias, and Herbert Frahm did as well. He chose the name Willy Brandt because, as he later related, the advertising slogan of the Brandt silk store in Lübeck stuck in his mind: "If saving is what you wish to do, then Brandt is definitely the place for you."

At the Dresden underground party conference, the SAP "Reich leadership" chose to send several comrades abroad, to carry on what had now become "illegal" activity. Willy Brandt was given the assignment of making secret preparations for journalist Paul Frölich[2] to leave Germany for Norway by way of Denmark. But when Frölich was recognized and arrested on the island of Fehmarn, the SAP leadership in Berlin decided that it would be Willy Brandt (he used his Dresden alias from that time on) who would go to Norway. At night on April 1, 1933, Brandt, now nineteen years old, journeyed to Travemünde. He crossed the Baltic to Denmark in a fishing cutter and proceeded to Oslo, where his task was to establish an SAP office and to head the central foreign office of the Socialist Youth Organization.

From the beginning Brandt was interested in more than this. "I quickly decided that I did not want to live solely as an emigré." He didn't wish to be an outsider, he wanted to put down roots, to belong. Soon he was working for the *Arbeiterbladet*, the Norwegian Workers' Party (NAP) newspaper and writing for a number of other party and union papers. He worked in the refugee relief organization, and in the NAP's youth organization. He maintained contact with his SAP comrades in Germany, and when in the summer of 1936 the SAP leadership in Paris appointed him to assume political leadership in Berlin, he returned there in August by way of Paris, visiting Oslo again at Christmas. In February 1937 the order came from Paris that he was to act as the SAP's liaison in Barcelona and cover the Spanish Civil War as a correspondent for Scandinavian papers.

In September 1938 the Nazis stripped Willy Brandt of his German citizenship, and in 1939 he applied for Norwegian citizenship. At the German invasion of Norway in April 1940, Brandt did not yet have his Norwegian papers. As he was fleeing the Germans he sought the advice of his friends on what he should do, and whether he should try to hide. "Instead, it was decided to put me in Norwegian uniform. I hoped, as one of thousands of Norwegian soldiers, to be treated as a prisoner of war, and probably to be released soon thereafter. If I remained a civilian, I would face much worse were my true identity to be discovered."

The plan worked: Brandt was captured as a "Norwegian soldier" and interned for four weeks, after which he was allowed to return to Oslo. The danger of being discovered was great, however. So on the advice of his Oslo friends Brandt went to Sweden early in August of 1940. This was illegal, as he still had no papers. He stayed in a refugee camp at first, but with the help of a Swedish politician he soon was able to travel to Stockholm as a free man. By the end of August 1940 the London office of the Norwegian government in exile had forwarded Brandt his citizenship papers. He was now a Norwegian.

Settling in Stockholm, Brandt again found work as a journalist. At the beginning of 1941 his Norwegian girlfriend, Carlota, arrived in Stockholm bringing the couple's daughter, Ninja, who had been born in December. Brandt married Carlota in the spring. He continued his political activities, making contact with Norwegian and German refugees and with the German resistance. Willy Brandt soon became one of the principal political leaders in exile. At thirty-one he was still an SAP functionary, but his influence extended well beyond that.

Bruno Kreisky, who later was to become chancellor of Austria, recalls the period of exile in Stockholm: "Willy Brandt was the essence of political rationalism for that era, and also of political leadership. Willy Brandt became the representative figure of German-speaking emigration."

By July 1942 a broad circle of socialists from Scandinavia, Germany, France, Austria, Hungary, and Czechoslovakia were holding periodic meetings in Stockholm. They became known as the "little Socialist International." Brandt was secretary of the group, which intended to draw up a set of "democratic socialists' peace goals," and he played a substantive part in formulating these goals.

In late summer 1945, after the departure of the Nazis, Brandt returned to Norway. Living in Oslo, he continued to work as a journalist and traveled often to Stockholm, where he kept an apartment. In the fall he was offered the opportunity to go to Germany as a correspondent for several Scandinavian papers to cover the war crimes trials in Nuremberg.

"I agreed, because in this way I could form a picture of what was left of Germany following the Nazis and the war. I also wanted to find out what would happen, given such misery and confusion, and military occupation."

As the entire foreign contingent in Nuremberg was made up of military personnel, Brandt acquired a Norwegian uniform, with an armband that read "war correspondent." From Nuremberg he traveled through occupied West Germany, making contact with Social Democrats along the way. In February 1946 he met with Kurt Schumacher in Frankfurt. Brandt had rejoined the SPD in Stockholm in October 1944 and in May of 1946, as a newspaper correspondent and invited delegate for Sweden and Norway, he had attended the first convention of the reconstituted Social Democratic Party of Germany, held in Hanover. He considered the convention's re-establishment of social democracy in the Western zones a "momentous thing," but expressed concern about Kurt Schumacher's attempt to speed up developments, because "it could accelerate the process by which Germany (and Europe) might be divided." Brandt was skeptical as well of Schumacher as a person: "I respected Schumacher's importance, but I didn't like his dogmatic assertions and outbursts, or his absolute demand for obedience."

At any rate, Brandt appeared to have arrived at a dead end. "My first contacts with Schumacher and Ollenhauer did not give me the impression that my immediate cooperation was being sought." The party leadership inclined to the opinion that people like Brandt could accomplish more abroad. Brandt was undecided for a while about just what it was he should do. There were offers and possibilities—to head the English or American press service, to work as an editor on the *Hamburger Echo*, to serve as press attaché to the Norwegian Embassy in Paris. Finally, Halvard Lange, Norway's foreign minister, offered his friend Brandt a position in Berlin instead of Paris—as press attaché to the Norwegian Military Mission to the Allied Control Council—and Brandt accepted. "And so I became an officer [and a major at that] without having been a soldier. The left sleeve of my uniform jacket that I seldom wore in Berlin identified me as a 'civilian officer.'"

In spring 1947 Rut Hansen also arrived in Berlin. She had been a married Norwegian emigrant when Brandt met her in Stockholm in 1943. Her husband had died in the interim, and Carlota Brandt had settled in Oslo. "We separated without animosity, and divorced in 1947," according to Brandt. On September 4, 1948, Rut and Willy Brandt were married by a Norwegian army chaplain stationed in the Harz mountains, who volunteered to come to Berlin for the ceremony. A Norwegian pastor in Berlin had refused to marry the couple, as they had been living together before Brandt was granted a divorce from Carlota. One month after the wedding, Peter, the first of Rut and Willy Brandt's three sons, was born.

Brandt's job as press attaché was to write reports on Berlin and Germany. "Foreign Minister Lange asked me to devote special attention to political events. In the course of that year I wrote, on average, one report a day. Their political substance increasingly dealt with the beginning Cold War." The duties and the atmosphere of the position as a whole were tolerable, despite the many shortages suffered in postwar Berlin. But this was not the work Willy Brandt truly wished to do. "The Norwegian milieu in Berlin was friendly and pleasant. One met the Allies, and correspondents from many countries. I quickly expanded my German contacts." Willy Brandt had decided to enter politics.

His opportunity arrived in the fall of 1947. The Berlin representatives of the SPD executive committee (located in Hanover) were looking for a new leader. Erich Brost, who held the position, had received a license from the English military government to found a newspaper. (He started the *Westdeutsche Allgemeine Zeitung* in Essen.) "A sphere of activity opened up to me," Brandt wrote in retrospect, "in which I could help gain understanding and support for a rational policy on Germany, but it also gave me the opportunity to do party work in Berlin. The time had come for me when, as a German in Germany, I could accomplish more for democracy and peace than I could in the position I held at the time."

There were difficulties—former comrades from Norway plotted against him. But in the end the executive committee confirmed Brandt's appointment. On January 1, 1948, now thirty-four years old, Brandt assumed his new post. He gave up his Norwegian citizenship and applied to resume German nationality. On July 1, 1948, Brandt received his naturalization papers. "The certificate bore both my names—the one I received at birth, and the one I had used in my political work since I was nineteen. I had fled Hitler's Germany as Willy Brandt, I had been active in emigration as Willy Brandt, and as Willy Brandt I had returned to Berlin as a Norwegian official. It was to remain my name in Germany as well." (In August 1949 the Berlin police president approved the formal name change—a few days later, Willy Brandt went to Bonn as a Berlin representative to the first German *Bundestag*.)

Brandt's position within the Berlin SPD was difficult from the beginning. Chairman Franz Neumann was Kurt Schumacher's man, but the assured and ardently anti-communist group around Neumann did not intend to tolerate a "watchdog" from Hanover. As a result, Brandt soon joined Ernst Reuter's retinue.

Schumacher and Reuter both wanted to revitalize democracy—and social democracy—from the ground up. But their actions were informed by very different temperaments and impulses. Schumacher embodied the willful personality who tended toward the excessive—he devoted himself totally to a cause, and lost himself in it. Reuter was a humanist influenced by Quaker beliefs, who even in the midst of taking decisive action knew there were limits to what human beings could accomplish. The one barely countenanced contradiction, while the other tolerated even those opinions he considered to be false. Whereas Schumacher harshly castigated mistakes made by the occupation powers, Reuter warned his fellow citizens against holding grievances or having false expectations: "It is not the Allies, but Hitler, not today, but yesterday that defines the test the German people must undergo." Unlike Schumacher, Reuter favored closer contacts with the United States.

Party headquarters in Hanover watched developments in Berlin with distrust. Berlin, in Schumacher's opinion, was "making foreign policy on its own." Willy Brandt, as "Reuter's man," was included in this distrust and not unjustly, for Ernst Reuter was Willy Brandt's new mentor. "Just as, when younger, I did not feel that the twenty years that separated Julius Leber and myself were important, the moment Reuter and I met I felt that we understood one another."

In 1948 Reuter became governing mayor of Berlin, with Willy Brandt acting as his public disciple. Brandt no longer advocated a socialist unity party, so thoroughly had he been revolted by the auto-cratic party in the East. Instead he supported Reuter in advocating that social democracy follow an independent, distinctly anti-communist, and exclusively Western path. "The first thing needed today is that we create order in our part of Europe and the world, that we order our own ranks and not yield one step. Anyone who gets involved with the communist unity front will be destroyed by it," Brandt said in a speech to the Berlin SPD in March 1948.

Greatly affected by the Soviet blockade of Berlin, Willy Brandt became an outspoken cold warrior. "Berlin belongs to Europe, not to Siberia," he declared, proclaiming a "national responsibility to resist the unlawful system in the [Soviet] zone." Foreign papers such as the London *New Statesman* attributed to Brandt "an alarming tendency toward chauvinism." But in the December 1948 elections in West Berlin, the SPD received 64.5 percent of the vote, and Reuter was reelected as governing mayor of the city. Brandt later concluded: "In Berlin the Social Democrats took over the leadership of the struggle for freedom. In West Germany they were trounced, with their backs to the wall."

After the Berlin blockade was lifted on May 12, 1949, attention focused on the west, on Bonn. On May 23 the Basic Law (constitution) of the Federal Republic was enacted and Bonn was named the country's "provisional" capital. Berlin retained only the right to send eight nonvoting members to the *Bundestag*. Ernst Reuter offered Brandt a magistrate post, but, said Brandt, "I had decided to enter the soon-to-be-elected *Bundestag*." In his first plenary speech Brandt declared that: "Berlin's task, among other things, is to make as difficult as possible the stabilization of a Soviet order in the Soviet zone, and thereby to keep open the path leading to the reunification of West and East Germany."

Brandt went to the *Bundestag* for the first two legislative periods (1949 to 1957). During this time he attempted to establish a power base within the Berlin SPD. But as "Reuter's man" he was in the minority position. The majority position belonged to Franz Neumann, chairman of the Berlin SPD. Neumann had prevented the Berlin SPD from uniting with the communists, and since then had been revered as a champion of freedom. Neumann and his followers, the *Keulenriege* (truncheon squad), were traditionalists who understood the SPD to be a classic workers' party. Brandt and the Reuter wing of the Berlin SPD, the "American faction," supported opening the SPD to the center, to middle-class voters.

During the early fifties Willy Brandt, following his convictions, worked tenaciously, step by step, local chapter by local chapter, to slowly win over the Berlin SPD to his side. In 1952 he ran for the chairmanship of the Berlin SPD for the first time, and suffered a bad defeat. In 1954, a year after Reuter's death, he campaigned again and this time drew only two votes less than Franz Neumann. Neumann appointed Brandt as his deputy. In December of that same year the SPD again was voted the strongest party in the City Assembly, and Otto Suhr became governing mayor in a Great Coalition. Willy Brandt succeeded Suhr as president of the Berlin City Assembly—against the will of Franz Neumann.

Mr. Berlin

Brandt's next big opportunity, the chance to become governing mayor, arose with the death of Otto Suhr in August 1957. Following trips to the U.S., Italy, and Yugoslavia, Brandt's popularity had grown considerably, and the role he played during the Hungarian uprising endeared him to the public once and for all. He became a kind of folk hero. On the evening of November 5, 1956, at reports of the bloody suppression of the Budapest uprising, tens of thousands of Berliners demonstrated before the city hall in the Schöneberg section of the city. "To the Brandenburg Gate," they chanted. Some wanted to arm themselves. Willy Brandt climbed into a police vehicle mounted with loudspeakers and persuaded the demonstrators to march instead to Steinplatz, where he calmed the crowd. Meanwhile, at the Brandenburg Gate, police clashed with those demonstrators who wanted to march into the eastern sector. Once again Brandt appeared at the scene of the crisis, and succeeded in quieting the crowd. He did so a third time, that same evening, at the same location. "This story," said Klaus Schütz, who later served as governing mayor of Berlin, "stands at the center of Willy Brandt's Berlin experience. He was the new hero."

On October 3, 1957, Willy Brandt became governing mayor of Berlin, and in January 1958, party chairman of the Berlin SPD. The "truncheon squad" around Franz Neumann was then mercilessly forced from power. Annemarie Renger[3] recalls, "Quick as a flash, friends of Franz Neumann lost their positions. There wasn't a dry eye in the house. Everything considered 'left' at the time had to go."

In December 1958 Brandt regained an absolute majority for the Berlin SPD, with 52 percent of the vote, but nevertheless continued to head the Great Coalition. He was now at the height of his power in Berlin—governing mayor and head of the state SPD, with his people running the party in the city. Abroad he was known as "Mr. Berlin." But in federal party politics his career had not yet taken off.

Both in 1954 in Berlin and in 1956 in Munich Brandt had failed to be elected to the SPD executive committee, among other reasons because he supported party reform. From early on the impetus toward the SPD becoming a people's party came from Berlin, supported by Ernst Reuter, Willy Brandt, and Klaus Schütz. On the federal level it was Fritz Erler and Carlo Schmid who strongly promoted party reform. Superficially, the issues may have seemed mere formalities to some: the address of "comrade," the established use of the second-person familiar pronoun "Du" instead of the more formal "Sie," the red carnation worn on May Day, the closing salutation, "with socialist regards," used in correspondence. But all of these and more were to be thrown overboard as ballast left over from the nineteenth century. A decisive step in this direction was taken in 1958 at the party convention in Stuttgart. Organizational reform was adopted when, after two false starts, both Willy Brandt and Fritz Erler were elected to the executive committee. (Brandt said, "My experience

The governing mayor with Axel Springer at the 1959 ground-breaking ceremony for a new Berlin publishing house. At left: Ernst Lemmer, minister for all-German affairs.

attests to the fact that, on the path to assuming exceptional political responsibility, it does one no harm to encounter difficulty and resistance.")

Following this organizational reform, which greatly limited the influence of the party's full-time officers, the public image of the party was essentially determined by the SPD faction in the *Bundestag*—by Fritz Erler and Herbert Wehner—and by the mayor of Berlin, Willy Brandt. The second principal impetus toward modernizing the SPD was the Godesberg Program of 1959, with which, contrary to popular belief, neither Willy Brandt nor Herbert Wehner was involved in any major capacity. But the program's departure from Marxism as the sole ideological foundation of social democracy, as well as its renunciation of an avowed anti-capitalism and its shift to a market economy were exactly what Brandt wanted. "In its totality and essence, it is a timely statement, for it will make it more difficult for our opponents to contend with the distorted image of German social democracy, rather than its reality," he said in Godesberg. And then he stated his goal: "We want to assume political leadership of the country, and we shall assume it."

In the *Bundestag* elections of 1961 Willy Brandt, aged forty-seven, for the first time opposed Konrad Adenauer for the chancellorship. At first Carlo Schmid was also considered by the SPD as a candidate, but at a closed meeting of the party presidium in May of 1959 the decision went to Brandt. Carlo Schmid, as he recalled it, turned down the nomination and spoke in favor of Brandt, who was initially hesitant. Schmid wrote, "Willy Brandt was of the opinion that he was needed in Berlin, that the city's recurring problems could be overcome only through his personal intervention. He didn't want to admit that as federal chancellor he perhaps could do more for Berlin than was possible as governing mayor." Others remember it differently. By some accounts, in July 1960 the Brandt team organized a virtual "putsch" against party chair Erich Ollenhauer, who wanted Carlo Schmid to be nominated.

The 1961 SPD campaign was personality based, American style. Willy Brandt was popular, photogenic, and had a "presentable" wife. Brandt was packaged as both Berlin warrior *and* private citizen, statesman *and* youthful hero—it was a formula that had already been successful in Berlin. The opposition joined the fray with an equally personal smear campaign against Brandt. Brandt's penchant for alcohol was given great emphasis. One opposition slogan, "Willy Brandy," had been coined ten years earlier by his Berlin adversary Franz Neumann.

But most importantly, Brandt's political opponents exploited openly and disparagingly his illegitimate birth and his emigration. Kai-Uwe von Hassel (CDU), minister-president of Schleswig-Holstein, declared, "I do not disavow my ethnic or national citizenship for personal or any other advantage. I cannot abandon the community that fate has chosen for me just because I feel threatened by it, and then show up again when the risk has passed." Richard Jäger, CSU representative and vice-president of the *Bundestag*, mentioned Brandt in the same breath with Hitler: "If he wishes, as did Adolf Hitler—whose family name actually was Schicklgruber—to enter history under an assumed name, then that is the one aim of his that disturbs us least." Franz Josef Strauss, not wanting to be left out, remarked, "There's one thing we surely shall be allowed to ask Herr Brandt: 'What did you do out there for twelve long years?' We know what we did here." And Konrad Adenauer struck the crowning blow, saying, "If anyone has been treated with the greatest possible consideration by his political opponents, then it is Herr Brandt, alias Frahm."

That was on August 14, 1961, and Adenauer's nervousness was only too understandable. Construction on the Berlin Wall had begun the day before, and it was Willy Brandt who talked with the Allies, trying to avert the worst, whereas Adenauer did not find it necessary to interrupt his election campaign to go to Berlin. True, Brandt did not reach an agreement with the Allies, but once again the population of Berlin saw him in the role of freedom fighter.

Brandt's next move was to write a dramatic letter to President Kennedy in Washington. The letter demanded, among other things, that the Western Allies proclaim a three-power status for West Berlin. The American reaction was cool, and Adenauer took the opportunity to make Brandt look foolish by releasing Kennedy's answer out of context in the press. In fact, Kennedy did agree to strengthen U.S. military force in Berlin and to send Vice-President Lyndon Johnson to the city. When Brandt found out that the chancellor wanted to accompany Johnson to Berlin, he told an American diplomat that if Adenauer showed up, "the rocks will fly." The U.S. embassy in Bonn politely advised Adenauer to stay home.

Johnson's visit proved a total success for Willy Brandt. The *Bundestag* election campaign long since had become a Berlin campaign, and Brandt declared. "In Berlin there was war in the streets. We salvaged the peace, securely, coolly, calmly. Otherwise the Federal Republic would look very different today."

But all his success mattered little in the end. It is true that in the election of September 17, 1961, the SPD gained 4.5 percentage points over four years earlier, and the CDU lost the absolute majority. But with 45.3 percent of the vote the CDU was still far ahead of the SPD's 36.2 percent. Adenauer could continue his coalition with the FDP.

Brandt was disappointed. He vacated his seat in the *Bundestag* and returned to Berlin. He became deputy chairman of the party in 1962 but as he was seldom in Bonn he was criticized more and more frequently within the SPD caucus and at party headquarters for neglecting his office. When Erich Ollenhauer, party and caucus leader, fell ill and it became apparent that he did not have long to live, Brandt was in no way the undisputed candidate for the post. Fritz Erler, deputy caucus leader, was making his own claims clear behind the scenes. It was Herbert Wehner who stood up for Brandt, publicly declaring on December 14, 1963, the day of Ollenhauer's death: "For the duration of Erich Ollenhauer's illness Willy Brandt is acting party chairman." (It was rumored that Ollenhauer had already died when Wehner made this statement, and that Wehner knew it.) This order of rank prevailed. In February 1964 Brandt was elected party chairman and simultaneously nominated as candidate for the chancellorship in the *Bundestag* elections to be held in 1965.

Konrad Adenauer resigned in 1963. Ludwig Erhard was viewed as a transition candidate, even within his own Union parties, and the SPD leadership believed they would have an easy time of it with

Meeting with former First Lady Jacqueline Kennedy on one of many trips to the U.S. as governing mayor of Berlin, May 1964.

With civil rights leader Dr. Martin Luther King.

Erhard. But public opinion polls soon revealed that Brandt did not have strong support, even less than he had had in 1961. The Union campaign again made much of Brandt's emigration, the Springer newspapers[4] abandoned their "Berlin hero," and the SPD conducted an unimaginative and lackluster campaign. Brandt's suggestions were not followed, and he was unmoved by the strategies party headquarters had come up with. He preferred the company of a circle of intellectuals who campaigned for him in Berlin. But his convictions remained unchanged: "I am assuming the SPD will become the strongest party. It will not only be part of the government, it will lead the next administration."

The initiative for forming this circle had come from the novelist Günter Grass, who in July of 1965, together with Hans Werner Richter, had founded the "Election Office of German Writers," or "Willy's Election Office" as it soon came to be known. The idea was that the writers would give the SPD's *Bundestag* campaign a little verbal polish. Karl Schiller[5] supported the idea, as did Herbert Wehner, who actually thought little of writers and later disparagingly referred to the Berlin group as a "melange." The Berlin SPD made office space available to the group not far from the Gedächtniskirche and put them on the payroll. Günter Grass himself did not work there, but went on the road to beat his drum for the "Ess-Pee-Dee," most often accompanied by fellow writers Paul Schallück and Max von der Grün. But not everyone in the SPD was enthusiastic about Grass's participation. Many found his writings pornographic, and he was not considered the ideal publicist.

A number of young writers worked in "Willy's Office" in Berlin, among them Peter Härtling, Hubert Fichte, Nicolas Born, Günter Herburger, Hans Christoph Buch, and Peter Schneider. Publisher Klaus Wagenbach kept the books. Essentially, they did preliminary work for Willy Brandt, Karl Schiller, Helmut Schmidt, and Fritz Erler, but much of what they wrote was never used: "Keep your wife, change your party—SPD," or, in support of a new German policy, "It's no use dozing in the waiting room. Once a day at least ask about the train."

Toward the end of the election campaign the office came up with a proclamation that was used equally as often as the official slogan of the SPD headquarters. It called for a "policy that prepares for the future," for "objectivity and a willingness to negotiate," and for a "government of Social Democrats." It was signed by sixty-two intellectuals, among them Ilse Aichinger, Ernst Bloch, Max Born, Tilla Durieux, Günter Eich, Axel Eggebrecht, Rudolf Hagelstange, Marie-Luise Kaschnitz, Fritz Kortner, Siegfried Lenz, Erwin Piscator, Marcel Reich-Ranicki, and Wolfgang Staudte. Heinrich Böll did not sign, and roundly criticized his colleagues' engagement: "It is either ridiculous or suicidal to pick a bouquet of flowers for a party that, when it comes to the 'Emergency Powers Act,'[6] is clearly willing to endorse it later, and when it comes to 'rearmament' is more papal than the Pope; a party that waves banners at its convention that read 'The borders of 1937,' that out of opportunism squandered the first and only real chance for an antinuclear movement in the Federal Republic; that makes no secret of the fact that it is a Great Coalition it is really after—a Great Coalition, that's all we need, absolute political promiscuity."

But then things turned out quite differently. The SPD had neither the opportunity to lead the new government, as Brandt had hoped, nor to form a Great Coalition, as Böll had feared. While Brandt gained three percentage points over the 1961 election, with 39.3 percent of the vote he still did not have enough votes to even appear to pose a threat to Ludwig Erhard. The Union parties, with 47.6 percent of the vote, had their second-best year at the polls since 1949.

Willy Brandt was deeply hurt, even shocked, by these results, which to him meant a personal defeat. "The German people did not vote against the SPD, they voted against me." Totally depressed on the evening of the election, and without first conferring with the heads of the SPD, he then declared, "I shall not be a candidate for the office of chancellor in 1969." Herbert Wehner tried to save the situation by suggesting that Brandt serve in the *Bundestag* as opposition leader. But Erler, head of the SPD's *Bundestag* caucus, wouldn't hear of making room for the failed candidate. Willy Brandt returned to Berlin in defeat—for the second time.

As he had following his defeat in 1961, Brandt fell into one of the depressions his Berlin friends had long been familiar with. At such times he would withdraw into himself for days, barely available for comment, especially during the autumn rainy season. "We always said, 'He's got his flu,'" Klaus Schütz recalls. Rut Brandt put it this way: "His depressions as a rule came in the late fall. It was hard not only for him, it was hard for me and the children and his staff. One day he suddenly wouldn't feel well, and his office then had to be notified and all his appointments canceled. He wasn't available to anyone, not even to his own family. I usually called Egon Bahr, who wasn't afraid to visit him. The newspapers would report that Willy was suffering from a 'cold and fever.'"

But contrary to rumors circulating at the time Brandt did not consider resigning as party chairman. He did, however, suffer greatly from this new defeat. "During my vacation in October with my sons Peter and Lars," Brandt recalled, "I was able to recover from my setback only slowly. Phases of my depression may also be explained by the exhaustion a politician in our time suffers due to the exertions of an election campaign or the crises of responsibility. I sometimes ask myself if we aren't the victims of a merciless exploitation that we ourselves practice and allow to be practiced upon us."

It was at this point that the Erhard government arrived at a crisis.

The writer Klaus Harpprecht, who for many years was Brandt's advisor and confidant, writes, "As almost always when he just didn't want to go on, everything happened at once: there was no other way out of the crisis of Erhard's government than the Great Coalition." The coalition clearly was not Brandt's achievement but Herbert Wehner's and—at the crucial point—also Helmut Schmidt's. As early as December 1962, during the government crisis known as the "*Spiegel* Affair," Wehner had held talks with Union politicians such as Paul Lücke and Baron von und zu Guttenberg, and those talks were now reestablished.

Erhard's administration was encountering critical difficulties. The budget proposals for 1967 showed a deficit of four billion Deutsche Mark, and on October 27, 1966, the FDP cabinet members resigned because no way of eliminating this deficit could be agreed upon. The SPD persuaded the FDP to vote for a *Bundestag* motion that would force Erhard to call for a vote of confidence. This was the equivalent of an indirect motion of no-confidence, without direct consequences. By this point, in the fall of 1966, Willy Brandt was already in favor of forming a coalition with the FDP. "My experience in Berlin with the SPD/FDP model had been positive. I already had been in contact with leaders of the Free Democrats for a long time." But the vote count was uncertain. The SPD and FDP together anticipated 251 votes in the election for chancellor. This was two more than the 249 votes needed for a "chancellor majority." But Brandt was not sure: "A trustworthy colleague from the FDP came to inform me that in a secret ballot I could not count on all the votes of his caucus." In addition, as Brandt recorded in 1974, the FDP was not the right partner for the SPD on economic and social issues.

But what may have decided it was the fact that more and more of the Union was in favor of choosing Kurt Georg Kiesinger as Erhard's successor, and Kiesinger, who also had the support of the CSU, wanted a Great Coalition. "Which Brandt actually didn't want," recalls Helmut Schmidt. "He was in Berlin, and viewed what we were doing in Bonn from a distance and with skepticism"—"we" being Schmidt and Wehner.

Only after Fritz Erler joined the discussion from his sickbed and vehemently argued for a Great Coalition could a hesitant Brandt be persuaded on November 25, 1966, to agree to a joint meeting of party and caucus executive leaders.

The SPD caucus was against a Great Coalition, and a conference of SPD district secretaries and department heads also announced their opposition. But the persuasive powers of Brandt, Schmidt, and Wehner combined, by the evening of November 27, to convince the caucus to support a Great Coalition.

This still didn't solve Brandt's problem. "I did not object in principle to a temporary association with the CDU/CSU, but I did raise the question of whether I myself, as party chairman, would have to be part of such a government." At first he preferred to remain entirely outside it, then he flirted with the idea of becoming minister of research or transportation, and ultimately Schmidt and Wehner convinced him to become foreign minister. Helmut Schmidt remembers that Brandt was suddenly cheered by the suggestion: "I was quite surprised. In the end Brandt reached for the Foreign Ministry with great determination."

The Great Coalition

The new government was sworn in on December 1, 1966. Herbert Wehner was named minister of all-German affairs, Helmut Schmidt, acting chairman of the caucus executive committee, formally assumed the position following Fritz Erler's death. Kurt Georg Kiesinger became federal chancellor, and Willy Brandt vice-chancellor and foreign minister. "Anyone with a sense of history," Brandt said on taking office, "will not find it easy to ignore that a man of my convictions has become German foreign minister."

The importance of the event was not lost on the intellectuals who had supported Brandt, but they interpreted it differently. The members of the Berlin writers' office sent a telegram of protest, and on the day before the government was sworn in Günter Grass wrote to Kiesinger, who had joined the NSDAP in 1933: "How are we to commemorate those resistance fighters who were tortured and murdered, how are we to commemorate the dead of Auschwitz and Treblinka if today it is you, a 'fellow traveler,' who dares to set the political standards? What will history instruction look like in our schools from now on? Hasn't Herr Globke wreaked enough damage already?[7] Is the old Stalinist Ulbricht going to be able to point a finger at us for this reason?"

Later, Brandt himself pointed rather laconically to Erich Ollenhauer's statement, according to which Kiesinger's Nazi-party membership and service in Ribbentrop's Foreign Office could not be held against him. "Once we accept this, then Kiesinger, the former 'fellow traveler,' and Brandt, the anti-Nazi emigrant, could be seen to represent the true German reality." Did Brandt *agree* with Ollenhauer's comment? Alfred Grosser[8] characterized the precarious relationship between Brandt and Kiesinger as follows: "The veteran fighter of the Nazi regime gave the chancellor of the Great Coalition absolution, as it were, for his years in the Ribbentrop ministry, whereas the CDU chancellor gave the lie to the campaigns waged by many of his party friends against the 'Reds' and the man who had 'denied his fatherland.' Each magnified the respectability of the other, so to speak."

Brandt approached his new position with joy and an eagerness to get to work. First, the discord between the Federal Republic and its partners to the west had to be cleared up. France had withdrawn from NATO's military arrangements, which had led to fierce feuding between Gaullists and those in the Union who supported the Atlantic alliance. The French had to be assured of German amity and the Americans, who feared that a strong Europe under French and German leadership could work against U.S. interests, had to be assuaged.

Brandt's main area of concern was policy toward the East. It was here that he saw his true mission. The foreign-affairs portion of

The federal foreign minister receives Indian prime minister Indira Gandhi in Bonn, September 1968.

Kiesinger's official speech upon assuming office was dominated by a statement of the "new" *Ostpolitik* that Brandt's foreign office formulated. This policy did not, of course, come out of the blue.

Konrad Adenauer had set the direction of West German foreign policy: "Germany belongs to the West in its traditions and in its convictions. All of Germany belongs to the West. In this partnership alone our future lies." It was Adenauer's goal to seize the reins of action and achieve sovereignty for the Federal Republic by integrating with the West. The consequences this had for "Eastern policy" were demarcation, isolation, and confrontation. The Social Democrats under Kurt Schumacher, in contrast, furiously held to the idea of a unified, centralized German state, and denounced all other objectives on the part of the Allies and Adenauer.

In this matter, Willy Brandt differed with the SPD leadership from the beginning. During the first years of the Federal Republic his position was much closer to Adenauer's than to Schumacher's, with all its implications. Especially during his Berlin years, Willy Brandt was a classic cold warrior, not to be outdone in confrontational policies and separatist rhetoric by anyone from the Union. "To ask us to agree to the division of Germany is to ask us to be dishonorable. Anyone who agrees to this is not one of us" (June 1961). "Breslau, Oppeln, Gleiwitz, Hirschberg, Glogau, Grünberg:[9] These are not merely names, they are living memories rooted in the souls of generations, and constantly rapping at our conscience. To relinquish is to betray, who would deny this? The right to a homeland cannot be bartered away for a mess of pottage" (June 1963).

But it was precisely in Berlin that Brandt had seen just how vital a "policy of small steps" could be. It had become clear to Brandt, during the course of informal contacts with the Soviets, talks with the GDR (that had led to some four million Berliners visiting each other across the Wall), and, in 1962, with the settlement of the "Cuban Crisis," that the two superpowers were settling on the status quo in Europe.

One ramification of the Godesberg program was the SPD decision to back Adenauer's policy of integration into the West. Herbert Wehner had signaled this SPD foreign policy turn in a speech to the *Bundestag* of April 1960. The other logical consequence was a new policy on the East. In October 1962 Brandt gave a lecture at Harvard University in which he stated: "We have to seek ways to surmount and to permeate the blocs of today. We should concentrate on supporting developments promising us more than mere survival; that can help advance peaceful and dynamic transformation." Brandt published his Harvard lectures in book form under the revealing title *Coexistence—The Obligation to Dare.*[10]

In a speech to his fellow party members delivered in 1963 he stated: "The solution to the German question can only be *with* the Soviet Union, not *against* it. We cannot give up our rights, but we must realize that, in order to attain them, a new relationship is required between East and West, and with it a new relationship between Germany and the Soviet Union." Egon Bahr, Brandt's press spokesman in Berlin, at a lecture at the Protestant Academy in Tutzing in July 1963, for the first time used the phrase "change through rapprochement."

According to Bahr, German foreign policy up to that point was frozen in status-quo thinking, and had failed because it was a "policy of all or nothing." The Soviets were not going to let the GDR simply be snatched away from their grip, the idea that the regime in East Berlin would be toppled was illusory, and, moreover, the GDR would have to be "transformed with the agreement of the Soviet Union." And that was why—short of granting actual recognition—concessions might be considered for the GDR government, so "it becomes feasible to relax the borders and the Wall and thus make the risks more tolerable." An initial test set for the beginning of 1966 with an exchange of speakers between the SPD and the SED failed to come about. But not only Social Democrats were looking for ways to unfreeze the "victory or defeat" policy toward the Soviets. Beginning in 1963, first under Adenauer and then under Erhard, Foreign Minister Gerhard Schröder had moved cautiously toward an opening to the East under the slogan "a politics of motion." Bonn established commercial missions in Poland, Rumania, and Hungary in 1963, in Bulgaria in 1964, and in Czechoslovakia in 1967. Erhard's Peace Note of March 1966 contained the offer of a nonaggression pact with Eastern Europe.

The Great Coalition partners consequently agreed to address the issues of normalizing relations with the Federal Republic's neighbors to the east and of exchanging nonaggression accords. Foreign Minister Brandt sent an emissary to Rumania, arranged in advance by Brandt's predecessor, Gerhard Schröder. Diplomatic relations with Yugoslavia—severed in 1957 when Belgrade recognized the German Democratic Republic—were resumed. The restrictions of the Hallstein Doctrine generally were relaxed, but not abandoned.

Even the chancellor's office now officially acknowledged the existence of the GDR. Chancellor Kiesinger received a representative of the GDR, who delivered a letter from GDR minister-president Willi Stoph, and the chancellor even responded to it. Kiesinger said at the time, "We recognize, of course, that something has been established over there, a phenomenon, and I have entered into correspondence with it." That was the utmost concession of which Kiesinger was capable; he never would have recognized the GDR, or even the Oder-Neisse Line.

This was one reason why the Great Coalition's *Ostpolitik* soon stagnated. Another was the reaction of the GDR, which now made new demands and tried to turn the Hallstein Doctrine on its head. SED chief Walter Ulbricht instructed the countries of the East bloc to take up diplomatic relations with Bonn only if the Federal Republic recognized the GDR.

Foreign Minister Brandt spoke increasingly of a "policy of détente with staying power." He sent Egon Bahr, now the Foreign Office's chief of planning, to East Berlin to quietly sound out the possibilities for mutual rapprochement. The SED members Bahr spoke with signaled that Bonn's recognition of the Oder-Neisse Line would be a reasonable precondition of resuming efforts at détente.

At the SPD party convention in Nuremberg in March 1968 Brandt spoke of the SPD's willingness to "recognize or, respectively, honor the Oder-Neisse line, until such time as a settlement can be arrived at by means of a peace treaty." And for the first time he formulated publicly and without legal jargon the guidelines for his policy on the East that later were to make history under his name: German unity was not on the political agenda; self-determination was not to be achieved in the foreseeable future; the GDR would exist into the foreseeable future. The goal of a new and realistic German policy therefore must be "to organize the two parts of Germany in such a way that they can live next to and with one another." Obviously this was not the policy of the Great Coalition; Willy Brandt was striving for something else.

The prospect that the 1969 *Bundestag* elections would bring about a change in leadership did not look particularly good in March 1968. The absolute majority rule Brandt was striving for seemed impossible. Five weeks after the party convention in Nuremberg the SPD received less than 30 percent of the votes cast in the *Landtag* state elections in Baden-Württemberg. Polls confirmed that this result was indicative of a general trend: the SPD had lost face in the Great Coalition and had been repudiated, above all by younger voters. The government's response to the actions of the rebellious student movement had been attributed in part to the ruling SPD. The brutal side of the state revealed in 1967 and 1968, primarily during the demonstrations against the Shah of Iran and the war in Vietnam, was, at least in Berlin, Social Democratic.

It belongs to the generally accepted myths of that era that the SPD, and Willy Brandt in particular, bonded with the APO (extra-parliamentary opposition) generation. At an SPD party convention in Hamburg in 1977 Brandt posed the question of what would have happened to society, and to the state, had the SPD "not had the courage to admit the restive '68 generation into its ranks and its debates." But the truth is that the SPD under Brandt's leadership fiercely tried to distance itself from anything resembling a student revolt. Helmut Schmidt was one of the *Bundestag's* most outspoken opponents of the student generation, and even following the assassination attempt on student leader Rudi Dutschke, Willy Brandt criticized the "dreamers and radicals who believe they should espouse the ideals of a national communist leader in Southeast Asia or follow the slogans of a South American ultra-revolutionary." It was SPD chairman Brandt, talking of "law and order," who tolerated expulsion proceedings against members of the party who participated in demonstrations against the war in Vietnam carrying signs that proclaimed, "I am a member of the SPD."

"The students fought for elementary freedom for those countries that do not possess it. But in those countries that do, democratic freedoms are dismissed as existing in name only. In Germany at present they prefer to march under the flags of Eastern Asian or South American revolutions," Brandt stated at the Nuremberg convention in March 1968. It cannot be said of Willy Brandt that he had any special sensitivity or understanding for what motivated those who took part in the student revolt.

The policies that this generation opposed—the emergency powers amendments, the war in Vietnam, the exploitation of Third-World countries—were not seen as problems by Willy Brandt. "To me '1968' means the year of those difficult young people," Brandt was to say twenty years later, acknowledging that he had not been concerned with Vietnam. The ideological line according to which the free West had to be defended against the communists in Vietnam was only too self-evident to mainstream politicians, and at that point Willy Brandt *was* mainstream.

Nor did rebellious students in any way look to Willy Brandt as their new idol. "Break Brandt's bones, all power to the [soviet] councils," was one slogan the students chanted in the streets while Brandt was chancellor. So it is necessary to take a closer look when addressing the issue of Willy Brandt's relation to the student generation of the late sixties.

The majority of the students who rebelled, and not only a radical minority as SPD and Willy Brandt hagiography would have it, considered the SPD to be a revisionist party, and the Great Coalition to be a betrayal of the concept of parliamentary democracy and the constitutional guarantees of the Basic Law. The radical democrats—the leaders of the student movement like Rudi Dutschke, Hans-Jürgen Krahl, Bernd Rabehl, and others—certainly put no great hope in Willy Brandt. But an immense circle of sympathizers was not that far removed from the mainstream parties. A survey taken in February 1968 revealed that the great majority of young people polled did not want the "revolution in Germany" that Rudi Dutschke was calling for, and were at best mere observers of the APO rebellion. But they did want extensive reforms of politics, the economy, and society—a basic democratization of German society. And two out of three youths questioned, and three out of four students, said that demonstrations held for the purpose of propagating this goal were a good thing. And they, surely, were the future following of Willy Brandt and the SPD.

What may have contributed to the myth of Brandt's proximity to the APO generation was his own family situation. To the horror of many of his friends in the SPD, Brandt allowed his sons Lars and Peter to accept parts in the film of Günter Grass's novella, *Cat and Mouse*, which showed them playing around with an Iron Cross. And Peter Brandt was placed under youth arrest for two weeks for taking part in a demonstration protesting against the war in Vietnam. The SPD leadership went so far as to fear for the party's chances in the elections because of what was going on in the Brandt family, and demanded that Brandt lay down the law at home. Brandt, however, forbade the party to involve itself in his family affairs, which undoubtedly won him a great deal of sympathy from young people. "It was important for me," Brandt later wrote, "that I be confronted within my own family with the ideas and emotions of this generation."

But he certainly was not its advocate. That role was taken by Gustav Heinemann. On Easter Monday 1968, Heinemann delivered a self-critical talk on the radio following the assassination attempt on Rudi Dutschke, in which he signaled his understanding of the youthful rebels. For conservatives and for broad circles within the SPD, however, events such as the assassination attempt on Dutschke were nothing more than the curse that followed the evil deed. But according to Heinemann, "Anyone who points a finger of blame at those considered to be instigators or string-pullers should realize that the rest of the fingers of that hand are pointing back at himself." Gustav Heinemann's dry, unpretentious manner, far removed from the pathos of the statesman—and as such, quite different from Willy Brandt's—spoke to many of the young. The writer Horst Krüger wrote of him, "Should I use the word 'sincerity'? Should I say 'credibility'? Among the many representatives on the Bonn scene his effect is astonishingly sincere, and his life reflects this." The fact that Gustav Heinemann became federal president in March of 1969 was the supreme test of a socialist-liberal federal government.

As early as 1967, when it became apparent that serious illness would ultimately force Federal President Heinrich Lübke to resign from his second term, Willy Brandt staked the SPD's claim to the highest federal office. "I thought it right, in terms of national policy, that, following a Free Democrat and a Christian Democrat, a Social Democrat should become the next federal president." But that would be possible only with the help of the FDP. When Heinemann was elected president on March 5, 1969, with the help of the liberals—though only on the third vote—this served as a signal for a socialist-liberal coalition in Bonn. Heinemann himself spoke of a "partial change of power."

But not everyone saw it that way. FDP chairman Walter Scheel interpreted Heinemann's election as "an isolated act" designed primarily to block the election of opposing candidate Gerhard Schröder. "We wanted the election of this man to prove to young people that democracy has not ossified." Those Social Democrats who wished the Great Coalition to continue—Herbert Wehner and Helmut Schmidt, above all—considered Heinemann's judgment of a power change to be overstatement. Nevertheless, in the spring of 1969 SPD chairman Brandt and FDP chairman Scheel agreed to seek a socialist-liberal coalition, or at least not to rule one out through other agreements. This was not done publicly, but sufficient signals and hints pointed that way.

On July 28 Walter Scheel stated in an interview with *Spiegel* magazine, when asked how large a majority vote would be necessary to consider forming an SPD/FDP coalition: "I personally would be prepared to represent the better platform with the lowest possible majority, regardless of which partner was required to attain it." In an internal meeting of the party in August, Willy Brandt maintained that he would join in a coalition with the FDP even with a mere two-vote majority. But he didn't pin himself down publicly, though in a *Spiegel* interview of September 14 he revealed that "I cannot imagine a coalition in which there would be room for a Foreign Minister Brandt. Even in a Great Coalition it is highly improbable that there would be a Foreign Minister Brandt." Only Walter Scheel was completely candid. On ZDF (Second German Television) three days before the election he responded to the question of whether he would wish to form a socialist-liberal coalition if the majority were for it with, "I am of that opinion." When it actually came down to it, however, it was Scheel who hesitated and Brandt who acted.

On the evening of September 28, 1969, chances for a socialist-liberal marriage looked rather bleak. At 9:00 P.M. the computer forecast predicted that the Union would gain the absolute majority with 47.6 percent of the vote, the SPD 41 percent, and the FDP around 5 percent. "It is clear that the claim to leadership lies with the CDU/CSU," Barzel, the party caucus leader in the *Bundestag*, declared on television. Celebrations began at the Palais Schaumburg and at CDU headquarters, and in the park outside the chancellor's office Union youth staged a torchlight procession. At FDP headquarters the mood was somber, and at the Ollenhauer Haus SPD supporters of a second Great Coalition were in top form.

But over the course of the evening the computer numbers moved in another direction, signaling majority support for a socialist-liberal coalition. Karl Schiller urged his colleagues to show their colors, but they preferred to confer while Schiller stated to the television cameras: "I personally lean toward a coalition with the FDP. But the SPD is not committed, of course."

The SPD leadership met in the executive committee office. At 10:30 P.M. Willy Brandt took the decisive step. "From my office I called Scheel and told him that I publicly would point out that the SPD and the FDP had more votes and mandates than the CDU and CSU, and that I therefore would attempt to form a new federal government together with the Free Democrats." Scheel recalls that he responded to Brandt's suggestion with a blunt, "Yes, do that!" Brandt had the impression that Scheel was greatly distressed by the FDP's poor showing. "Scheel reacted cautiously. He didn't discourage me from making my announcement, but neither did he accept my offer."

Shortly before midnight Brandt went on radio and television. "The SPD is the strongest party, followed by the CDU. The FDP suffered a great loss and the CDU a lesser one. One who loses greatly and one who loses less greatly, even if combined, are still losers. A coalition of losers would not be an appropriate outcome of this election. On top of which, those former FDP voters who wanted a coalition with the CDU voted for the CDU. The FDP followers of Scheel, who wanted something else, voted for Scheel. After all, before the election it was said that whoever voted for the FDP was voting for the FDP and the SPD. The SPD and the FDP together have more votes than the CDU and CSU. That is the result."

The Union had campaigned under the slogan, "It all comes down to the chancellor." The SPD countered with "We're creating a modern Germany," and "We have the right men." It was not a Brandt campaign; surveys in the summer of 1969 showed that only 19 percent of those polled were in favor of Willy Brandt. Karl Schiller, minister of economics in the Great Coalition, was the man of the hour; the SPD had geared its campaign to him. "The SPD had white-collar workers and the bureaucracy to thank for its mandate in 1969. It was they who were willing to take a chance on change, who looked to the Social Democrats for a higher measure of modernity, efficiency, competence, and intellectual substance, as well as for creativity and an affiliation with the middle class," was the analysis of the situation offered by Peter Lösche and Franz Walter. Their conclusion: "The election of 1969 was a Schiller, not a Brandt, election. It was the honorarium and commission for a successful economic policy."

According to the exact figures the Union, with 46.1 percent of the vote, remained the strongest party. The SPD followed with 42.7 percent and the FDP captured 5.8 percent. Brandt wrote in 1976: "I concluded, as did others, that together, the SPD and FDP could come up with twelve seats more than the Union parties. Clearly this was only five seats more than the absolute majority needed to elect the chancellor. I was determined to take the risk, even if the 'small' coalition made up of SPD and FDP wouldn't survive for the entire legislative term."

The phrases Brandt used when recalling this situation are plain:

"I was certain of the path I was taking," and, "I left no question in anyone's mind that I wanted to become federal chancellor." And in fact, Willy Brandt seized the initiative on election night, as the Union leadership was still formulating offers to the FDP and members of his own party still believed that their coalition with the CDU/CSU would continue. Arnulf Baring[11] has written about this evening: "Brandt was quite different than usual. No one, before or after, ever saw him as dynamic as he was on the evening of September 28; he had never been so resolute or energetic. No longer was he playing Hamlet, or Parzival; he was a man of determined and vigorous action. It was as if Brandt, 'this oversized boy,' (as Herbert Blankenhorn[12] always called him) had been waiting for this precise moment, as if suddenly all the floodgates of his energy had been opened and Brandt was grown-up and free."

Hans Ulrich Kempski reported in the *Süddeutsche Zeitung*, "When Brandt set out for home afterwards he acted as relaxed as if he had already been elected chancellor. He had lost his pensive, apprehensive air. During the last two decades I have never before seen him in a comparable mood of such profound confidence. So I was compelled to ask him if he wasn't afraid he was deluding himself. But he answered—with the same decisiveness that had lent him so much authority in the circle of the party presidium just hours before—that no one dared object to his analyses and judgment, that any skepticism was insignificant. 'We'll do it,' he said."

The formation of the government proved of little difficulty, there were scarcely any essential differences. Even the election campaign was strangely lacking in substance. There was no question that Karl Schiller would be reappointed minister of economics. Herbert Wehner, who opposed this coalition, left the cabinet to become parliamentary caucus leader of the SPD. Helmut Schmidt was named minister of defense, Walter Scheel vice-chancellor and foreign minister, and Hans-Dietrich Genscher was appointed minister of the interior. Josef Ertl was named minister of agriculture, the only true surprise, for Ertl, who had never disguised the fact that he belonged to the right wing of the FDP, had highly disparaging things to say about Willy Brandt on the evening of the elections and in the days that followed. Brandt later said that it was Karl Hermann Flach, at that time correspondent for the *Frankfurter Rundschau* and later general secretary of the FDP, who suggested that Ertl be brought into the socialist-liberal cabinet. What Brandt did not mention was that the effect of this was to neutralize the potential for considerable damage emanating from within the FDP.

"The coalition discussions were harmonious," Brandt wrote in 1976 in retrospect. "After they were concluded I took a brief 'working vacation' to the Eifel. The *Bundestag* election of chancellor was set for October 21." Egon Bahr, Herbert Wehner, Leo Bauer, and Conrad Ahlers accompanied Brandt to the Eifel to draw up the statement of government policy that was to serve as the basis for the work of the coalition. The coalition agreement itself was drawn up in rather general terms.

Brandt later depicted his election as chancellor on October 21 as problem-free. He never had any doubt that he would be elected, he said, and before noon he was already signing chancellor autograph cards. But in truth not everyone involved in planning the coalition was so confident. One week before, parliamentary leader Helmut Schmidt had called for "iron discipline" from party members and strictly forbade SPD *Bundestag* representatives to travel home the day before the vote: Willy Brandt's election was not going to fail because of delayed trains or flights canceled due to fog, or to any other imponderables. Schmidt wanted to avoid any possibility of mishap, so he called a meeting of all of his party's *Bundestag* members for the morning of October 21. SPD representatives had to state where they were staying and "in which bed they were sleeping," according to Schmidt's orders.

The narrow vote justified Schmidt's concerns: Brandt was elected by a smaller margin than he expected. Only 251 members voted for him, three less than the coalition majority, but nevertheless two more than the requisite absolute majority. Four voting cards were disqualified. They read: "Poor Germany," "No thank you," "No to Frahm," and "Amos 5:20," referring to the Bible verse that reads, "Is not the day of the Lord darkness, and not light, and gloom with no brightness in it?" The quality of opposition to Brandt promised to remain constantly at a low level.

The Brandt Era

It was nevertheless clear that this was an historic occasion. For the first time in thirty-nine years a Social Democrat again headed the government. The last SPD chancellor had been Hermann Müller, who

had served during the Weimar Republic. But Willy Brandt projected
the arc of the historical significance of his chancellorship even further
back, invoking August Bebel, the legendary SPD chairman who died
in 1913, the year Willy Brandt was born. "My point of reference, with
all due respect to Hermann Müller, is Bebel. I now see an excellent
opportunity to achieve what unfortunately was not to be achieved in

Taking the oath as federal chancellor, administered by Bundestag
President Kai-Uwe von Hassel, October 21, 1969.

the Weimar Republic—the great balance Bebel spoke of: 'It is important to create a Fatherland of love and justice—insofar as this can be accomplished on earth.'" With noticeable self-confidence, and in the presence of foreign journalists, Brandt stated: "Now Hitler has lost the war once and for all. I see myself as chancellor not of a vanquished, but of a liberated, Germany." He would venture a new beginning—this was the message of such statements, and it was exactly what voters expected of a socialist-liberal coalition.

"The policies of this administration shall stand under the sign of renewal," was the keynote sentence of the greatly anticipated statement of government policy of October 28, 1969. With his first appearance as chancellor before the German *Bundestag*, Willy Brandt opened what later was to be known as the "Brandt Era." And he spoke quite consciously to the generation of restless youth: "In these last years many in this country have feared that the second German democracy would go the way of the first. I have never believed this. I believe it less today than ever. No, we are not standing at the end of our democracy, we are only just beginning."

Brandt pledged internal reform and the democratization of society; he promised to take seriously the desire of the young to have their say, to participate. "Such a democratic system calls for extraordinary patience in listening to others, and extraordinary effort toward mutual understanding. We cannot create the perfect democracy. We want a society that offers more freedom and that demands more responsibility." The relationship of citizen to state and government fundamentally was to be changed. "Government can function successfully in a democracy only if it is held aloft by the democratic engagement of its citizens. We in government are in as little need of blind consensus from our people as our people are in need of arrogant self-importance and stately distance from us. We are not seeking admirers, we need people who will think with us, make decisions with us, and share responsibility with us, critically." And further, "We have not been 'chosen,' we have been elected. Therefore we seek to communicate with everyone who is striving for this democracy."

With utterances such as these Brandt won the hearts and minds of those young voters who long had considered the SPD to be the "lesser evil." He was quoted repeatedly in the days to come by both friends and enemies, especially his words, "We want to take a chance on more democracy." With this campaign slogan Brandt became a figure with whom people could identify, above all many younger Social Democrats and liberals who had taken flight into a revolution-

Federal President Gustav Heinemann receives Brandt's first cabinet, October 22, 1969. First row, from left: Gerhard Jahn, Käte Strobel, Heinemann, Brandt, Walter Scheel, Karl Schiller, Georg Leber. Second row, from left: Helmut Schmidt, Alex Möller, Erhard Eppler, Hans-Dietrich Genscher, Walter Arendt. Third row, from left: Egon Franke, Lauritz Lauritzen, Hans Leussing, Horst Ehmke, Josef Ertl.

ary dream world, and who now were returning to the reform fold. The promises of October 28, 1969 were the starting point of Willy Brandt's unprecedented popularity, which was to reach its zenith in the elections of 1972.

Brandt's list of reform proposals was extensive—land reform, a profit-sharing employees' fund, lowering the voting age to eighteen, new marriage and divorce laws, university reform, more construction of new universities, equal rights for women—it was a department store catalogue of reform promises.

What later was to become the chief concern of the Brandt Era, a new *Ostpolitik*, did not play a major role in the government statement of 1969. Brandt wished to become the "chancellor of domestic reforms," as he had announced to the *Bundestag* caucus on October 3—a source of some concern to his coalition partner. Ralf Dahrendorf, who had helped draft the FDP's government policy statement, wrote to his party chairman, Walter Scheel: "A certain difficulty for us, primarily in the area of publicity, but perhaps a substantial difficulty, lies in the fact that the chancellor has met with widespread response to his 'government of domestic reforms.' It would certainly be a good thing if somewhere in the statement of government policy the idea of domestic reform could be tied to the necessities of foreign policy." Historical developments prove Dahrendorf's fears to have been unfounded.

But in October 1969 foreign affairs still played a rather subordinate role. "Our country needs cooperation and agreement with the West, and understanding with the East," Brandt said, and a first step toward this understanding was the offer of "mutual renunciation of the use and threat of force." The GDR must be a party to this renouncing of force. The basic principle of socialist-liberal policy on all-German affairs was as follows: "Twenty years after the establishment of the Federal Republic of Germany and the GDR, we must prevent further drifting apart in the lives of the German nation; therefore, we must seek to arrive at a life 'with one another' through an agreed-upon life 'next to one another.'" Furthermore: "Recognition in accordance with international law of the GDR by the Federal Government is beyond consideration. Even if two states exist in Germany they are not foreign countries to one another: their relations can only be of a special kind."

This formula went much further, to be sure, than what had been the consensus on all-German policy up to that point. In commenting on Brandt's statement of government policy opposition CDU/CSU caucus leader Barzel argued: "How do you intend to bring your assertion on the 'two states of Germany' into line with the preamble of the Basic Law, or with your demand for the right of self-determination for all Germans?" Brandt answered, "A realistic policy must start out from the realities."

What had been referred to only timidly in the government statement was turned into practical policy with breathtaking speed. Newly named foreign minister Walter Scheel replaced the Hallstein Doctrine with new marching orders: "Contractual agreements with the GDR should help overcome the division of our people. For this reason, our position on GDR foreign relations will be determined by the degree to which East Berlin meets our efforts to arrive at a 'life with one another through a regulated life next to one another.'" In practical terms the "Scheel Doctrine" was saying that Bonn was prepared to recognize the borders of the GDR proportionate to the degree that the GDR opened up these borders.

On January 30, 1970, Egon Bahr, state secretary in the chancellor's office, flew to Moscow for his first talks with Soviet foreign minister Andrei Gromyko. In three rounds lasting until May the two men negotiated the basic elements of the Moscow Treaty. The final negotiations on the German side were handled by Foreign Minister Walter Scheel. On August 12 the treaty between the Federal Republic of Germany and the Soviet Union was signed by Chancellor Brandt and Premier Alexei Kosygin, and the foreign ministers of both countries. The core was an agreement that both states would "resolve their issues of conflict solely through peaceful means," and would "commit themselves to honoring absolutely the territorial integrity of all the states of Europe within their present boundaries; they declare that they will make no territorial claims; that they consider the borders of all states of Europe inviolable, today and for the future, as they are defined on the day of the signing of this treaty, including the Oder-Neisse Line, which forms the western border of the People's Republic of Poland, and the border between the Federal Republic of Germany and the German Democratic Republic."

Another treaty between Bonn and Poland to normalize mutual relations was signed in Warsaw on December 7, 1970; on September 3, 1971, the three Western allies and the Soviet Union signed the Four-Power Agreement on Berlin; on December 21, 1972, the treaty between the Federal Republic and the German Democratic Republic was signed. In preparation for this latter treaty two spectacular meetings were held between the federal chancellor and GDR prime minister Willi Stoph, the first on March 19 in East Germany (Erfurt), and the second on May 21 in the West (Kassel).

In his January 14, 1970, "State of the Nation" address to the *Bundestag,* Brandt had declared: "The federal government is proposing to the government of the GDR negotiations on the exchange of non-aggression agreements, to be based on equality and non-discrimination. A contract cannot come at the beginning, but must come at

The signing of the treaty between the Federal Republic of Germany and the People's Republic of Poland in Warsaw, December 7, 1970. First row, from left: Foreign Minister Walter Scheel, Undersecretary Egon Bahr, Federal Chancellor Brandt, Polish Communist Party secretary general Wladyslaw Gomulka, Polish prime minister Josef Cyrankiewicz, and Polish foreign minister Stefan Jendrychowski.

the end of negotiations." This sentence refers to a GDR initiative in December 1969 submitting to the president of the FRG the draft of a state treaty between Bonn and East Berlin.

GDR prime minister Stoph suggested a meeting in East Berlin, but as Brandt insisted on entering the country through West Berlin, and refused to land at the East Berlin airport of Schönefeld, they agreed to meet in Erfurt. Brandt was met at the Erfurt train station by roughly two thousand excited GDR citizens. In front of the "Erfurter Hof," the hotel where the conference was to take place, the crowd broke through police barricades shouting, "Willy, Willy," then "Willy Brandt," and then "Willy Brandt to the window." Brandt recalls, "I hesitated and then went to the window and looked out at these enthusiastic and hopeful people. They had seized the right to hold a spontaneous rally. For a moment they felt free enough to show their feelings, and I was moved. But I had to consider the fate of these people, for I would return to Bonn the next day but they would not. So I gestured to them to show more restraint, and they understood me. The crowd fell silent. I turned around with a heavy heart. Many of my colleagues had tears in their eyes. I was afraid that hopes would be raised here that would be impossible to satisfy."

Though no agreement was reached in Erfurt, the meeting there was a great success for the federal government. The one held on May 21, 1970, in Kassel was a debacle. The right-wing NPD (National Democratic Party of Germany), which had failed to clear the five-percent hurdle in the 1969 election, the *Junge Union* (youth party of the Union), and the Association of Expellees staged anti-Stoph demonstrations and overshadowed the conference. The GDR flag hanging in front of the Schlosshotel was pulled down by a member of the NPD and ripped apart, the ribbons from the wreath that Stoph had laid at the Memorial for the Victims of Fascism were stolen. This second meeting resulted in a "pause" in communications between Bonn and East Berlin, but not in a "break-off of relations or, respectively, of efforts" between the two, as Brandt noted following his final talk with Stoph.

In spite of this setback, both sides negotiated roughly thirty separate treaties, agreements, protocols, and exchanges of letters at the state level before the Treaty on the Basis of Relations was signed. Among them were an entire series of accords complementing the Four-Power Agreement on Berlin: a transit traffic agreement, a visiting agreement, agreements on the post office, on telephone and telegraph commerce, and so forth. In addition, there were protocols on inland waterways, rail border-crossing traffic, transport of waste, and other matters of shared concern.

The apparent successes of the Brandt/Scheel government's *Ostpolitik* did not, of course, silence the opposition. While Rainer Barzel and other Union politicians such as Ernst Majonica and Richard von Weizsäcker were open to a policy of reconciliation with the East, Franz Josef Strauss, Bavaria's minister-president, steered the majority of the Union toward an opposite course. Strauss called Brandt the "chancellor of the sell-out," and spoke of the "Finlandization" of Germany, that is, of neutrality with Moscow's blessing. CSU representative Baron Karl Theodor von und zu Guttenberg thundered in the *Bundestag* on May 27, 1970: "You, Mr. Chancellor, are in the process of surrendering Germany's Western identity to join that of the Soviet Union."

The policies of the new government stirred controversy among the public as well. The furor came to a peak with Brandt's visit to Warsaw to sign the treaty normalizing relations between the Federal Republic and Poland on December 7, 1970. Two wreath-laying ceremonies were planned for that morning, the first at the grave of the unknown soldier, and the second at the memorial for the victims of the Warsaw ghetto. At the second ceremony wreaths were laid in place and Brandt, according to protocol, arranged the ribbons, bowed his head, took one step back, and folded his hands in front of him. Suddenly he sank down onto his knees, remaining frozen in this position for half a minute, then stood up and turned away. It was an unprecedented gesture. Was it rehearsed?

Brandt later emphasized that it was not. "Early that morning I had considered, of course, the need to find an appropriate way to express the special commemorative quality of the monument to the Warsaw ghetto. Under the burden of recent German history I did what people do when words fail them, and in this way commemorated the millions who were murdered." He said also, "I was not ashamed of my action, despite the malicious commentaries about it in the Federal Republic. Those who wanted to understand me could understand me, and many in Germany and elsewhere did understand." But there weren't terribly many in Germany who did. A poll taken by *Spiegel* magazine reported that 48 percent of those surveyed considered Brandt's gesture to be excessive, and only 41 percent thought it appropriate.

But international appreciation of Brandt's policy of reconciliation contrasted sharply with sentiment in Germany. In 1971 Brandt was awarded the Nobel Peace Prize, the citation stating that "Federal Chancellor Willy Brandt, as head of the West German government and in the name of the German people, has extended his hand in a policy of reconciliation between old enemies. In a spirit of goodwill he has performed a magnificent service in laying the groundwork for peace in Europe." And this time the reaction at home was as positive as that abroad. "Herr Brandt is the right choice," wrote the London *Times*. The *New York Times* agreed: "Willy Brandt has done more than any other German to wipe out the image of a Germany tending toward neo-Nazism and thirsting for revenge." The report on the vote of the Nobel committee arrived in Bonn on October 20. Brandt recalled that "the reaction was overwhelming. The *Bundestag* congratulated me. My friends in the party were a little happier than others, of course. That evening a group of young people organized a torchlight procession in front of my house—it was not the first, nor the last." There was also a small private celebration at Brandt's villa on the Venusberg in Bonn. Hermann Höcherl of the CSU was the only guest to attend from the opposition. "In doing so he displayed a more open attitude than those of his colleagues who spread the absurd rumor that the Nobel Prize had been decided upon by a committee of the Socialist International," Brandt wrote.

A few days later he spoke before a group of unionists. "If I achieve nothing else, I will still be proud of what we have done so far. Our serious intent to help alleviate tensions has been recognized, the international press no longer reports on Germany and war, but on Germany and peace; and there is confidence in our ability to contribute in a constructive way to the necessary establishment of peace in Europe." In his response to the laudatio delivered on December 10 in Oslo, he stated that, to him, receiving the prize above all meant that in the eyes of the world, "Germany has been reconciled with itself; it has found its way back to itself, just as the exile could rediscover the peaceful and human features of his fatherland."

Despite all of its successes and honors, Brandt's government encountered ever greater difficulties. This was due above all to its coalition partner, the FDP, which suffered three stinging defeats in state elections in 1970. In Lower Saxony and in Saarland the liberals failed even to be seated in parliament, and in Northrhine-Westphalia they barely cleared the five percent necessary to be seated. It was said the FDP was in an irreversible process of disintegration, and fears that

FDP *Bundestag* members were deserting the party made the rounds. Erich Mende, Siegfried Zoglmann, and Heinz Starke were considered unreliable; it was well known that they had not voted for Willy Brandt. And there were at least three other critics of Brandt's *Ostpolitik* on the right wing of the FDP: Ernst Achenbach, Gerhard Kienbaum, and Knut von Kühlmann-Stumm. If they, too, deserted, the situation would be critical for the Brandt/Scheel administration. But the government cheered itself with an optimistic statement addressing the rumor of the possibility of new elections: "Indications that the government would not shy away from new elections should serve to remind the opposition that support for the policies of the federal government, particularly concerning concrete issues of foreign policy, is much greater among the general population than among the present majority coalition in the *Bundestag*." But the erosion of this majority seemed inexorable.

At the instigation of Erich Mende and Siegfried Zoglmann, a "National-Liberal Action" was founded. Both men anticipated being expelled by the FDP, and crossed over to the Union at the beginning of October 1970. They were followed by Heinz Starke, and with his defection the government majority shrunk to the 251 representatives who had elected Willy Brandt chancellor. When one of Berlin's representatives, Klaus-Peter Schulz, went over to the CDU in October 1971, and his colleague Franz Seume joined him in March 1972, the majority was sustained, since votes cast by Berlin representatives were not counted. But things became problematic when, also in March 1972, SPD representative Herbert Hupka switched to the CDU, and FDP representative Wilhelm Helms did the same one month later. The government then had only 249 representative votes, the opposition had 247, and further desertions were to be expected. At this point opposition leader Barzel, prodded by Franz Josef Strauss, head of the CSU, decided to risk a "constructive vote of no-confidence" against Brandt. It was on April 23, 1972, the day for state elections in Baden-Württemberg, that Helms announced he was joining the CDU. On April 24, Barzel moved to topple Brandt. A vote was scheduled for three days later in the *Bundestag* to decide the following motion: "The *Bundestag* expresses no confidence in Federal Chancellor Willy Brandt, and elects Representative Dr. Rainer Barzel as his successor to the office of federal chancellor of the Federal Republic of Germany. The federal president is requested to release Chancellor Willy Brandt from office." Several of the CDU/CSU executive committee—Hans Katzer, Gerhard Stoltenberg, and Richard von Weizsäcker—opposed the motion, but Barzel was quite sure of himself. And the majority of the coalition representatives was also convinced of Willy Brandt's imminent fall.

On Thursday, April 27, 1972, at 1:22 P.M. Barzel sat in his first-row parliamentary bench seat with his head in his hands, staring straight ahead as if paralyzed. All around him Social Democrats and Free Democrats were embracing each other and crowding around Brandt with tears of joy in their eyes. Rainer Barzel could not believe it. Two-hundred-sixty representatives had cast their votes; Herbert Wehner had advised the SPD not to take part. And *Bundestag* President von Hassel had just announced: "Of 260 votes cast, 247 representatives have voted for the motion, and ten have voted against it, with three abstentions. The absolute majority of eligible votes is 249. I declare

Rainer Barzel congratulates the chancellor following the CDU/CSU's failed motion of no-confidence in the Bundestag, *April 27, 1972.*

that Dr. Barzel, the candidate proposed by the CDU/CSU parliamentary caucus, has not attained the majority vote of the members of the German *Bundestag*."

And Barzel had prepared his coup so well, was so sure he had assembled enough troops to become chancellor! "Three votes from my own party were lacking. But there was no mistake that everyone in the party had agreed on the motion beforehand!" Barzel later wrote. "This was no accident or spontaneous change of mind. On any side. There was another will at work here."

This "other will" was almost certainly money. Baron Knut von Kühlmann-Stumm and Gerhard Kienbaum, both FDP, stated they had voted for Barzel, which meant he should have received at least 250 votes. Barzel himself was anticipating five coalition votes, for a total of 252. But Karl Weinand, SPD caucus secretary, insisted he had restored one of the coalition renegades. This would mean that four Union members had simply not voted for Barzel. One Union member, Julius Steiner, stated in 1973 that Karl Wienand had bribed him with fifty thousand Deutsche Mark. But there were contradictions in Steiner's statement, and even a *Bundestag* investigatory committee could not clear things up. Over the years the names of potential "betrayers" kept cropping up—luminaries such as Erich Mende and Hermann Höcherl among them, but the true circumstances have never been clarified. Karl Wienand, whose political career ended due to other affairs, retired and refuses to break his silence on the matter.[13]

Herbert Wehner, Wienand's superior at the time of the vote, when asked in January of 1980 whether everything had been above board in the failure of the no-confidence vote, answered,

> ■ What is above board? That people get paid off? How was it done? There are people today, I could list them, but I wouldn't even consider it, because that would reveal the strange side of our democracy, and I would continually be hauled into court. I can't even use what people connected to those people told me at the time. A great many things. No, no, this was dirty, people must have known that. A caucus leader must know what is going on, what attempts are being made to pull the rug out from under a government. The government itself doesn't have to know everything. ■

But this interpretation should be viewed with caution, for it is of a piece with Wehner's usual self-portrayal as the valiant page who had to carry out the dirty work of the Sun King, Willy Brandt. "I always knew things would get difficult. Someone has to be the patsy and that someone was me. I know two people who actually brought if off. I am one of them, and the other is no longer in parliament." And that person can only be Karl Wienand.

For the socialist-liberal coalition and its chancellor, Willy Brandt, April 27, 1972, was a joyous day. On the day before and the morning of the vote in the *Bundestag* there was a swell of public endorsements, demonstrations, spontaneous work stoppages, and protests in support of Brandt. Following the victory over Barzel the government received a flood of letters and telegrams, most of which interpreted the motion of no-confidence as a dirty trick by the opposition, and viewed Willy Brandt as the conquering hero.

But at first the opposition retained the upper hand, and Barzel launched a second attack. On April 28 the *Bundestag* rejected by a 247-to-247 tie vote the budget submitted by the chancellor's office. With this the leader of the opposition demonstrated that the government no longer carried the majority, and therefore was incapable of governing in the long run. "I personally would have been glad had this paralysis of parliament caused new elections to be held that spring," Brandt wrote. "But in terms of national policy, it was imperative that the treaties with the East not be allowed to languish, and that the chances for the Four-Power Agreement not be gambled away." So the government sought ways to get the opposition to agree to the ratification of the treaties with the Eastern bloc. An inter-party commission worked out a resolution to interpret the treaties, employing, for example, such wording as: "The inalienable right to self-determination shall not be affected by these treaties. The policy of the Federal Republic of Germany, which strives for the peaceful re-establishment of national unity within a European framework, does not contradict the treaties, which do not prejudice the solution of the German question."

For the government, the test of this resolution represented a considerable concession to the opposition. "The wording pushed to the limit what I could answer for responsibly and avoid deception," Brandt said. When the treaties were passed in the *Bundestag* on May 17, 1972, only 248 representatives voted in favor of the Moscow and the Warsaw Treaties—Union representatives abstained from voting. The government had made major concessions, but gained no opposition votes. On June 3 the documents were ratified, and the four powers signed the concluding protocol on the Four-Power Agreement on Berlin. With this the East bloc treaties went into effect.

After passage of the treaties the coalition partners agreed, after some hesitation, on a conceivable, constitutional way to call new elections: that fall the chancellor would ask for a vote of confidence, and the coalition would not pass it. As a result, the *Bundestag* would be dissolved and there would be new elections.

The *Bundestag* election, held November 19, 1972, was to be the SPD's greatest postwar victory at the polls, and would impressively reaffirm the socialist-liberal coalition, even though the Brandt/Scheel government—with the exception of its foreign-policy successes—was having serious difficulties. On the one hand, many voters were disappointed that the major reform promises had brought very little in real gains. Despite the fact that the government had proclaimed a willingness to enter into a dialogue with the young, rebellious generation, the socialist-liberal and, above all, the SPD leadership had in fact tried to clamp down on activities that appeared too radically democratic.

By November 1970 the SPD presidium had passed a resolution stating that any cooperation between the Social Democrats and the communists was detrimental to the party. In January 1972 Brandt issued the so-called *Radikalenerlass*, or decree on radicals, constituting an agreement with the minister-presidents of the individual *Länder* to prevent so-called "enemies of the constitution" from entering public service. Minister of Justice Hans Maihofer justifiably referred to this decree as a "judicial nullity," for it simply reiterated what long since had been set down in the Basic Law and Civil Service Law: Only those loyal to state and constitution could be "civil servants." However, the terrorist activities of the Baader-Meinhof group had created a climate in which the state was hypersensitive to everything that came from the "left." This resolution, which entered history as the *Berufsverbot*, or professional ban, led to a practice of poking and prying into people's lives that was difficult to reverse. The government's reputation suffered greatly, both in the eyes of the young, who had taken seriously Brandt's promises of renewal, and of those abroad.

On the other hand, such actions appeased those critics who had accused Brandt's administration of a general destabilization of both domestic and foreign policy. With his announcement of extensive domestic reforms, Brandt had raised not only hopes, but fears. Many citizens actually were afraid that Willy Brandt would destroy German society, the very same goal the rebellious students were striving for. The age structure and social profile of the SPD had changed radically since 1968–1969. Many young dissidents had joined the party, and the Young Socialists played a large role in intraparty discussions. Traditional SPD voters, and middle-class Germans in general, were most disconcerted by debates on nationalization, the control of investments, and the overthrow of capitalism.

In addition, the country was experiencing significant problems with the economy. The inflation rate was up and discussions on the federal budget for 1972 were strained. As early as March 1971 Brandt had asked his ministers to come up with a reasonable spending policy. Finance Minister Möller desperately tried to curb the demands of the other ministers, particularly of Defense Minister Helmut Schmidt, who was the most obstinate opponent of Möller's cost-cutting policies. Finally Möller gave up; he resigned on May 13, 1971, and Minister of Economics Karl Schiller assumed his post. But he too was forced to endure wearying debates, above all with Schmidt, who resisted any cuts in defense spending. Following an argument on monetary policy in which Schiller was opposed by the president of the *Bundesbank*, Karl Klasen, the "super minister" resigned on July 7, 1972. His successor to both ministries was Helmut Schmidt, who was replaced by Georg Leber as minister of defense.

As a result of all this, the socialist-liberal coalition presented a strange image in the fall of 1972. It had achieved the historical breakthrough of a new *Ostpolitik* with breathtaking speed, but was struggling with monumental difficulties in domestic and financial policy, and dealing with the bloody ending to the Palestinian hostage-taking at the Olympic Games in Munich. There were conflicting signals about prospects for the election campaign just under way. Nevertheless, this campaign became one long victory march for the administration, or, more precisely, for Willy Brandt.

Under the slogan, "Willy Brandt must remain chancellor," the Federal Republic experienced a "Willy" campaign. "Elect Willy" initiatives sprung up everywhere—the chancellor's popularity reached a level experienced neither before nor since. A "loyalty campaign" of unprecedented dimensions was staged. It seemed that half the population was sporting "Willy" stickers. Hundreds of leading cultural, scientific, and sports figures called for the election of the SPD. By 1969 the writers' initiative founded in 1965 to support Brandt had grown into a broad celebrity movement. Stage and television actors took out newspaper ads announcing they were voting for Brandt (they included Siegfried Lowitz, Horst Tappert, Martin Benrath, Claus Biederstaedt, Gila von Weitershausen, Inge Meysel, Hans Söhnker, Michael Verhoeven, Hans-Joachim Kulenkampff, and Peter Frankenfeld). The "Social Democratic Voter Initiative" had established an office in Bonn in 1969, with a full-time staff paid by the SPD and the Friedrich Ebert Foundation. Günter Grass was again one of the most active campaigners for Brandt, and he was joined by Siegfried Lenz, Luise Rinser, and Heinrich Böll, who in 1965 had refused to sign the election proclamation of the Berlin Writers' Office.

In the summer of 1972 a book appeared in the stores with thirty-five scientists, artists, and writers setting down their "thoughts on a politician." Heinrich Böll wrote, "It speaks for Willy Brandt that he is the first German chancellor to depart from the tradition of the master race; he is neither master nor ruler who clicks his spurs and flashes his whip. . . . Willy Brandt's life is the stuff of legend, almost that of a fairy tale come true. It was not the legitimate, pugnacious Catholic from Munich who became federal chancellor, but the illegitimate Herbert Frahm from Lübeck, who underscored this 'ur-flaw,' this idiotic dowry of bourgeois original sin, by being, in addition, not only a socialist, but an emigrant." What Willy Brandt had been reviled for in election campaigns from 1961 to 1969, what the SPD had preferred to hush up, now became an overwhelmingly positive argument: Brandt as the symbolic figure of the "other Germany." Brandt himself formulated it this way: "My path truly did diverge from that of most of my countrymen. That was not their fault, nor was it my disgrace." Georg Picht[14] wrote: "The fact that Willy Brandt went to Moscow and knelt at Auschwitz [*sic*] lent the word 'freedom' a new meaning in the eyes of an international public. It is intolerable to Brandt's adversaries that he broke through the circle of distrust that surrounded and continues to surround Germany, and that through the acknowledgment of German guilt he restored the honor of the citizens of our country." And Alexander Mitscherlich,[15] writing in the same vein: "The feelings of sympathy Willy Brandt aroused were based on the view that historical events in Germany from 1914 to 1945 represented an entire whole, and that no one is entitled to cut a piece from this whole simply because it displeases him. That section of the public sympathetic to being represented by Brandt were those who avoided trying to make the Nazi era disappear." Tübingen law professor Jürgen Baumann, with a nod toward ex-chancellor Kiesinger, said, "I feel at home in a republic led not by a former National Socialist, but

by a former emigrant. National Socialism perverted the legal standard of the German people to such an extent that the restoration of a
healthy legal standard and a healthy self-perception was to be
achieved only in this way. The destruction of a legal standard was
worse for the German people than all the material damages they sustained. Willy Brandt, as federal chancellor, contributed greatly to
healing this wound. It is not merely a matter of the improved image
of the West German state abroad. It is primarily a matter of our
image of ourselves, of the dignity of our nation."

In this brief historical moment everything came together. On the one
hand was Willy Brandt's *popularity*, a function of personal charisma
and that mysterious quality—"closeness to the people." Long before
he entered the national political stage Brandt was an uncommonly
beloved man, both in Berlin and abroad, above all in the United
States. On the other hand was the quality of *statesmanship*, which he
refined more and more—the stage direction of his person, a bearing,
and pathos, all of which seemed to symbolize a dignity derived not
merely from his office ("dignity of our nation" and "honor of our citizens" were the phrases used by Jürgen Baumann and Georg Picht).
And, finally, there was the *moral authority* that Brandt increasingly
commanded. In the 1972 campaign he systematically introduced the
English word "compassion" as a guiding political concept. "For John
F. Kennedy and his brother Robert there was a key word that encom-
passed their political passion, and that word is 'compassion.' It trans-
lates not simply as *Mitleid* (pity), rather, the correct translation is the
willingness to suffer with someone, the ability to be charitable, to feel
for someone else. Have the courage for this kind of charity! Have the
courage to be merciful! Have courage for those around you! Remember these oft-forgotten values! Find the way back to yourselves!"
This was an appeal that reached many ears—and hearts. "Willy
Brandt's politics emerged from his person," writer Peter Härtling has
said. "When he spoke of having compassion for the weak of society, I
took it seriously. And it moved me immensely."

Brandt moved many diverse elements of society simultaneously,
not just the young, women, or intellectuals. Above all, the success of
the "Willy" campaign owed a great deal to the enormous mobilization
of workers. Almost two-thirds of the working class cast their votes for
Brandt (even among traditionally more conservative Catholic workers, the figure was over fifty percent).

At the same time, the anti-Brandt campaign reached unprecedented dimensions. Many employers entered into the campaign warning of the abolition of the free market system and of a socialist state of the Eastern variety. A series of ads for the "Association for the Advancement of Political Objectives" was nothing more than a thinly disguised anti-Brandt campaign waged by industry. One ad read, "For years Willy Brandt has proved that he is not a strong leader, but merely a Marxist paper tiger! We love peace, and therefore wish for a reconciliation with the East. But we must avoid one day becoming a satellite of Moscow."

This was but one example of how the 1972 election campaign escalated the kind of vilification Brandt's person had invited from the start. He polarized people as no other politician before him; he was either loved or hated, there was little in between. His followers were often devout admirers, his detractors often his bitter enemies.

On November 19, 1972, over ninety-one percent of eligible voters went to the polls, a record in the electoral history of the Federal Republic. For the first time the SPD had the strongest showing, with 45.8 percent of the vote. The FDP increased its voter base to 8.4 percent, and the Union received only 44.9 percent. This meant that the socialist-liberal coalition had an absolute majority in the *Bundestag*, with 271 representatives to the opposition's 225—a triumph.

But despite this comfortable margin the government did not have an easier time of it. It appeared, rather, that it was running out of steam. Brandt has written: "But after the great success of November 19, 1972, it proved difficult to fall back into step; it was more difficult than I had expected." Exhaustion set in everywhere. Brandt himself had to be hospitalized "to set my vocal cords in order." The negotiations to form the cabinet were carried out largely in the absence of the chancellor, who communicated from his hospital bed. It appears that the SPD reacted to its major victory almost euphorically. Brandt warned his own people "not to overdraw the account." In retrospect he noted: "Within the circle of my party and the cabinet, especially among friends from the intellectual sphere, many of whom had taken part in the voter initiatives, one saw signs of disappointment. I could not avoid the suspicion that they expected more from us than a humane, progressive, and well-balanced program. They expected, if possible, a miracle, or at least a purification of our society, preferably overnight. People who otherwise were quite critical, who distrusted the concept of a perfect world, and rightfully so, now appeared to expect us to perfect the world. They were—necessarily—to be disappointed."

Both Peter Lösche and Franz Walter agree with this analysis, and speak of a growing detachment from the SPD of those who elected it: "Many in the SPD confused the popular vote in favor of the government's foreign and all-Germany policy, which had been at the center of the *Bundestag* election, with support for radical, experimental reform in all areas of social policy."[16] That, without question, was *one* element of the rapid decline of the Brandt/Scheel administration. But only one.

Federal President Gustav Heinemann receives Brandt's second cabinet, December 15, 1972. First row, from left: Brandt, Heinemann, Walter Scheel. Second row, from left: Josef Ertl, Gerhard Jahn, Erhard Eppler, Georg Leber, Egon Franke, Walter Arendt, Katharina Focke, Horst Ehmke. Third row, from left: Helmut Schmidt, Egon Bahr, Klaus von Dohnany, Werner Maihofer, Hans-Dietrich Genscher, Hans Friederichs, Hans-Jochen Vogel.

Willy in the Clouds

The problems of the socialist-liberal coalition—dissent among its cabinet members, the resignations of Möller and Schiller, Helmut Schmidt's immense increase in power—were only temporarily disguised by the overwhelming victory at the polls in the 1972 election. In addition, there was now growing dissatisfaction over stagnating reform policies and the *Ostpolitik*, growing problems concerning budgetary and financial policies—the passage of the federal budget was repeatedly postponed—the oil crisis, air traffic controllers' strike, and the civil servants' strike with the government's devastating defeat at the hands of Union of Public Service Employees (ÖTV) chief Heinz Kluncker. Within a very short period of time the government's reputation was at an all-time low.

It was rumored that Brandt would resign at the beginning of 1974 at the latest. In the summer of 1973 *Die Zeit* forecast a "fall of discontent" for the Federal Republic: "Once again discontent is ignited by the leaders of the Federal Republic. They have not given the impression lately that they have events firmly in hand. Rather, it seems that they have abdicated to the apolitical mediocrity of the ministerial bureaucracy. And this applies to the federal chancellor as well. Not a few among his own party have intimated that he has found himself a pedestal in the clouds, far from the intrigues of the dirty world of domestic policy." The phrase "Willy Wolke" (Willy in the clouds) was soon making the rounds.

In the end it was Herbert Wehner who used the general discontent with Willy Brandt to stage a public revolt against the head of his party and government. In particular the *Ostpolitik*, which always had been close to Wehner's heart, was not going as the caucus leader had thought it would. Instead of bringing in the harvest, Wehner felt the chancellor was resting on his laurels and letting things take their own course. A number of situations contributed to Wehner's assessment. Klaus Schütz, governing mayor of Berlin, was, with *Bundestag* president Renger's support, demanding that Berlin's *Bundestag* representatives be granted full voting rights, thus subjecting the Four-Power Agreement on Berlin to an unnecessary test. Minister of the Interior Genscher was putting a strain on relations with East Berlin and Moscow by locating the Federal Office of the Environment in West Berlin. And negotiations with Czechoslovakia, which Wehner believed

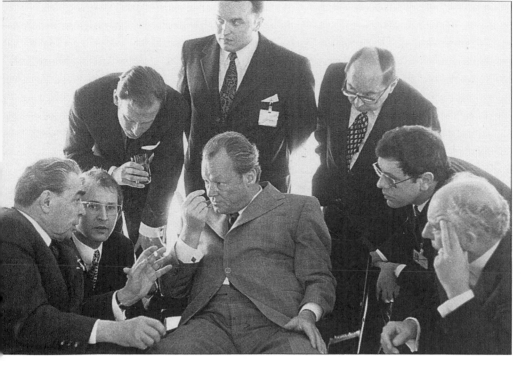

In conversation at the chancellor's bungalow with Soviet premier and party chief Leonid Brezhnev, during Brezhnev's official visit to the Federal Republic in May 1973. To the right is Foreign Minister Walter Scheel.

Brandt was not pursuing energetically enough, ended in a postponement of the signing of the Prague Agreement until December 1973.

Wehner was particularly upset by the fact that, following the signing of the treaty with the GDR, the old practice of ransoming prisoners from East Germany and of reuniting families was stopped, because normal relations were supposed to introduce a quota system. The actual result, however, was that for the time being, nothing was moving. Wehner, with the intercession of East German attorney Wolfgang Vogel, arranged to meet SED chief Erich Honecker at Honecker's weekend home in Schorfheide, near Berlin, on May 31, 1973. They were also joined by FDP caucus leader Wolfgang Mischnick. Honecker agreed during this meeting to continue the old practice despite the treaty.

Wehner unleashed his fury at his perception that Brandt was dragging his feet on Eastern policy at the end of September and beginning of October 1973. In Moscow as part of a *Bundestag* delegation, he used this trip to take aim at the Bonn government. There were several men within the government trying "to undercut and damage" the Four-Power Agreement, particularly Berlin policy, something, Wehner stated, he would have nothing to do with. Diverging from his usual custom, Wehner willingly granted interviews, and gathered journalists around him on several occasions for background talks. There was a definite message he wanted to convey, and he expressed it with the sentence: "The gentleman prefers his bathwater lukewarm—as in a bubble bath." "The gentleman" was Willy Brandt, the "Number One," whom Wehner characterized as "removed" and "lethargic." *Spiegel* magazine did attribute one quote to Wehner, however, that was not accurate: "What the government is lacking is a head." What Wehner actually said was that in order for the Warsaw Pact treaties to work the Federal Republic needed to appoint to the East a highly placed contact man, whose responsibility it would be to sound out the potential for further developments. What the government is lacking, he said, was a head that could pursue this matter.

Brandt received word of Wehner's attacks during a trip to the United States. He had delivered a speech in New York to the United Nations, and then had gone on to Chicago and to the Aspen Institute in Colorado Springs, where he was to receive an award. It was here that he heard of Wehner's attacks. He broke off his trip to return to Bonn the next day. "The man's got to go," was his first reaction, but then he decided against taking strong measures against Wehner, and merely summoned him to his villa on Venusberg for a talk. "I received a reprimand," Wehner later said. "It was not a pleasant exchange."

Brandt reports that Wehner immediately expressed his regret and said, "Tell me what I should do." And at the end of the meeting Wehner implored Brandt "to give him another chance." But the relationship between the two was never the same, and talk of Brandt's weakness in decision making once again made the rounds.

The situation in the government was growing increasingly uncomfortable. Vice Chancellor Scheel philosophized in public that any alliance had only a limited reserve of solidarity, and in the fall of 1973 decided that he would become a candidate to succeed Federal President Gustav Heinemann. Brandt semi-officially referred to Scheel as a "miserable soul for sale." *Spiegel* ran a cover story entitled "Chancellor in Crisis," and polls revealed that only 38 percent of the population expressed satisfaction with Brandt's policies. Not even one year earlier the number had been 57 percent. Günter Grass, who only four months after the *Bundestag* election had said, "Fat and all too sure of itself, the SPD is loafing in the shadow of a majority," now struck a major blow. On November 26, 1973, on the television news magazine *Panorama*, he read a text published three days later in *Vorwärts*, the SPD newspaper:

> ■ The SPD and the FDP have fallen into a sluggish rut. It seems the sure victory at the polls last fall has lured the Social Democrats and the liberals into crippling self-complacency. Peevishly Willy Brandt has withdrawn once more into foreign policy. The speeches he delivers—whether to the United Nations or to the European Parliament—are notable, but he falls strangely silent on domestic policy, making barely an effort to clear up the confusion, both in language and in concept, that surrounds areas of reform such as co-determination, education, environmental protection, land.
>
> It often appears that the successes and the surfeit of honors Brandt has enjoyed have served to isolate him, removing him to a sphere caricaturists like to locate above the clouds. It is true that he allows overeager advisors to shield him from reality. Blessed with the gift of radiating strong charisma, he now radiates listlessness rather than energy. ■

Brandt suffered a serious political defeat with the round of talks on civil service tariffs. The ÖTV[17] had demanded a fifteen-percent raise in earnings and wages. Meanwhile, the country experienced the immense economic problems brought on by the oil crisis at the end of 1973. Brandt tried and failed to persuade the ÖTV to scale down its demands. There were countrywide strikes across the board. The chancellor had lost his battle with union chief Kluncker.

There were losses at the polls. In March 1974 the SPD lost 10 percent of their constituency in the Hamburg state election, and did little better in local elections in Hesse, Rhineland-Palatinate, and Schleswig-Holstein. Finance Minister Helmut Schmidt more and more openly undermined the chancellor. He publicly criticized Brandt's slack handling of rebellious Young Socialists and all sorts of new party members, especially those from the academic sphere who acted as if they *were* "the SPD." The image of the SPD, according to Schmidt, "is determined by a few people at the head of the party, by the many individuals and majorities at the delegates' conventions, and by the many interviews held across the broad spectrum of the party. And one of the main impressions formed by the people of this country, from Regensburg to Flensburg, is that the SPD devotes a great part, too great a part, of its energy and activities to internal debate. And I can only say that the overall effect is not attractive. Nor do people understand the half-baked gibberish of the academics who are drowning our resolutions in their phraseology."

On March 6, 1974, Schmidt openly criticized Brandt on television, not bothering to disguise his own claims to the top position. He advised Brandt over the air to "replace three ministers with five others, or seven, or two," but added that mere replacement was not enough. "A change in government personnel alone might merely prove to be a trick. It has to go a bit deeper than that, than merely replacing a few people."

Brandt appeared to be resigned. At a meeting of the executive committee of the SPD on March 8, 1974, he offered only a weak defense against Schmidt's attacks. But the very next day he invited Herbert Wehner, his other major adversary, to meet with him. On March 12 the two men talked at the chancellor's bungalow, and after this, for the first time in a long time, they sat next to each other in caucus meetings. Wehner apparently was shocked at Helmut Schmidt's efforts to unseat Brandt. The thought that the chancellor would be toppled by someone within his own ranks seemed to Wehner a terrible thing. It was evident that he—and others—clearly thought that Brandt represented the center of the party as it saw itself. "We must not abandon the middle of the spectrum of our fellow citizens," Wehner declared at the Bremen party convention on March 17, 1974. "He who would accomplish so much, historically, must not restrict himself to one wing of the party, but must cover the center. Anyone who allows himself to be forced from the center soon will find out how quickly the vacuum is filled."

In 1972 Willy Brandt had rediscovered the center and been buoyed to victory by it. On the occasion of the Dortmund party elections in October of that year, he had proclaimed the "New Center," the shift of the majority from the political "right" to the political "left," that is to say, to a socialist and liberal center. "There, where the need for conservation and change—more accurately, conservation through change—is understood, there is the new political center." Brandt saw this as a rejection of political extremism, but not of radical democrats. "A party like the SPD must continually challenge and test itself. Even those groups with more radical ideas, insofar as these ideas are based on principles of freedom and democracy, should be able to bring their suggestions to the table—either to have them accepted, if only partially, or to experience for themselves why they are not acceptable."

It was the meaning of this center that Brandt now sought to define. In the final days of March 1974 Brandt penned a ten-point declaration approved by the executive committee on April 1. "Without a center no democracy would have a majority. He who abandons the center sacrifices his ability to govern. Social Democratic determination means to lead the center," he stated in his "April theses." And further: "Those who are dissatisfied among the SPD sympathizers, or former sympathizers, can be divided into two camps: those who feel that things are moving too slowly, and those who believe that the SPD is too radical. The SPD cannot possibly please both groups at the same time, at least not in the phase in which it is working indefatigably to have its governmental programs passed."

The party leadership was jolted by these April theses and the coalition expressed new confidence as well. Willy Brandt flung himself into the Lower Saxony election campaign with enthusiasm, Herbert Wehner was happy, and Helmut Schmidt adapted to the new situation and held to Brandt's line. The chancellor had ushered in a breath of fresh air; he was confident that he had everything under control again. It was at this moment that his personal aide, Günter Guillaume, was arrested.

On April 24, 1974, Brandt recorded the memo: "Return from Cairo midday. While still at the airport I was instructed by State Secretary Grabert that Guillaume had been arrested this morning and admitted that he was an 'officer of the NVA'" (*Nationale Volksarmee*, East German army). Brandt had known since May 1973 that Guillaume was under suspicion. At that time Minister of the Interior Genscher had informed the chancellor that the Office for the Protection of the Constitution was in possession of information according to which Guillaume was an agent of the GDR. But Genscher conveyed the wish of the president of the office, Günther Nollau, to allow Guillaume to

*Brandt with his
personal aide, Günter
Guillaume, in 1972.*

remain at his post so that he could be observed. In the summer of
1973 Guillaume even accompanied Brandt on his vacation to Norway, with Genscher's full knowledge.

Brandt informed only State Secretary Horst Grabert, head of the
chancellor's office, of the suspicions surrounding Guillaume, and in
June 1973 Nollau took Herbert Wehner into his confidence. On April
24, Brandt also noted: "For a long time it appeared to me that this
was based on unfounded evidence. Then two months ago I was told
that there was just cause to bring in the Federal Prosecutor's Office. I
assumed, of course, that the intelligence agencies would do what was
required."

Even after Guillaume was arrested, Brandt was not at first unduly
concerned. On April 26 he commented on the Guillaume affair dur-

ing a radio broadcast from the *Bundestag*: "There are moments when one believes that one is to be spared nothing." Brandt went on to specify that Guillaume had never been entrusted with secret documents, a grave error, as it later turned out. "I was thinking at the time of his routine work in the chancellor's office. The exception—that secret documents had, in fact, passed through his hands during the 1974 summer vacation in Norway—was something I was unaware of at the time of my *Bundestag* statement."

On April 29, though, the prospect of Brandt's resignation was first discussed in the chancellor's office. "It is becoming clear to me that I have to take responsibility for matters that extend far beyond the actual duties of my office." Brandt reckoned with the "most vehement campaign since we entered office," above all in terms of the Springer press. "The damage done is great enough as it is, but a mood of public hysteria is being created. *Bild*[18] is outdoing itself." The turning point arrived, however, when officials of the BKA, or Federal Criminal Investigation Office, in questioning Brandt's bodyguards about Guillaume's activities, began eliciting stories about Brandt's "women." Guillaume, it seemed, was privy to secrets of this sort as well. "They weren't competent enough to expose a spy, but they were competent enough to spy and embroider on my private life," Brandt later complained.

On May 3 Nollau was updated by BKA chief Horst Herold on the progress of the case. Nollau feared that the government "would be made to look ridiculous" were Guillaume to testify in court on the details of Brandt's private life. When Nollau passed on the news of this to Herbert Wehner, "Wehner was shaken to the core," Nollau wrote. "He literally caved in and then blurted out, 'That will break our back.'" Wehner informed Holger Börner, SPD parliamentary caucus secretary, who called Brandt. But Brandt had already been apprised of the news by Genscher's aide, Klaus Kinkel.

The next day leading Social Democrats and Union party members met at the Friedrich Ebert Foundation in Münstereifel to discuss the situation. That evening Brandt spoke with Wehner, who confronted him with the details of Nollau's investigation. Brandt declared the accusations laughable, but Wehner repeated Nollau's opinion that a public airing of the entire affair would be deadly. And then Wehner uttered a sentence wholly typical of him: "I will stand by you, you know that, but it will be hard." Brandt, he said, must decide what he was going to do within the next twenty-four hours.

Brandt then spoke to Holger Börner and Karl Ravens. "Late that night I told them that I was about to decide to resign. My two friends tried to dissuade me, saying that the issue of responsibility had to be dealt with separately. They argued that the adversity I had faced since the beginning of last year had worn me down. Nor would I deny that."

On the afternoon of the following day, May 5, Willy Brandt, Helmut Schmidt, Herbert Wehner, Holger Börner, and SPD treasurer Alfred Nau sat down together for a meeting in Münstereifel. Brandt relates: "I made my decision known, established the reasons for it, and nominated Helmut Schmidt to become my successor. Schmidt in particular tried to dissuade me." Schmidt himself reports that he yelled at Brandt for wanting to throw in the towel due to ridiclous accounts of his affairs with women. He would be happy to become federal chancellor, Schmidt said, but not due to such a senseless reason.

Back in Bonn, Brandt penned a letter of resignation to Federal President Gustav Heinemann. That same evening he showed the letter to Walter Scheel, who was visiting his home. Scheel tried hard to change Brandt's mind, but on May 6 the letter of resignation was submitted to Heinemann. The next day, as Brandt arrived at a meeting of the party caucus, SPD representatives stood to applaud him. Herbert Wehner interrupted his talk to greet Brandt with the words, "We feel pain at what has happened, respect for your decision, and love for the person and policies of Willy Brandt." Egon Bahr buried his face in his hands and wept.

On the television news program *"Tagesschau,"* Brandt issued the statement: "On the evening of May 6 I submitted my resignation to the federal president, therewith assuming full responsibility for negligence in connection with the secret-agent affair. It was a decision no one but I could make. There is evidence that my private life would be dragged into the speculations surrounding the spy case. Regardless of what is written on this matter, it is and remains grotesque that a German federal chancellor should be considered vulnerable to blackmail. I, at any rate, am not."

But he *was* vulnerable to blackmail. He had already been blackmailed by Herbert Wehner, who had barely concealed his threat that Brandt would not survive another smear campaign. And Brandt had taken too heavy a blow, and was in no condition mentally or physically to wage a battle, or brave an ordeal. "I would have been hunted, my life made unbearable. Was I in good enough form to endure additional burdens?" he asked rhetorically in a *Spiegel* interview in 1984.

He then answered his own question: "A few of my best friends doubted that I was, and so did I."

There is much to Klaus Harpprecht's interpretation of events: "During that period Brandt must have registered the fact that in this day and age no politician can succeed in wrestling into existence more than one or two great ideas before his dividend is used up." Brandt, according to his former advisor, never considered the office of German chancellor to be "the fulfillment of his most passionate hopes and private desires." This cannot be entirely correct—after all, Brandt ran for the office four times without coercion. Nevertheless, there is something to Harpprecht's statement that, "only after his fall did he establish himself as what he may have wanted to become almost since childhood: the latter-day successor to August Bebel, the leading figure of his youth, the political-moral 'super-father,' whose image occasionally merged in his memory with that of his own grandfather, the angular, warmhearted worker who offered the boy Herbert Frahm the protection he so needed."

Following his fall it took quite a while for Willy Brandt to create the new role for himself that was to stamp his image on the public consciousness for some time to come—that of the unifying figure respected by all sectors of the party, by young and old, left and right. At first Brandt stood in the background. Continuing as SPD party chairman, he covered the rear of Helmut Schmidt's administration, shared responsibility for the government's economic cost cutting, and helped to pass anti-terrorist legislation. He supported Schmidt's energy policies and even his rearmament policies—at least in the beginning. But his sphere remained the international stage. In 1976 Brandt became president of the Socialist International, and in 1977 chairman of the North-South Commission, both of which positions he assumed with great enthusiasm. He continued to concern himself greatly with policies on peace, disarmament, and development, and thus increasingly clashed with the government's policies.

After 1980 Brandt's position on rearmament stood at cross purposes with the position taken by Helmut Schmidt. Brandt stated that, "We do not want to isolate ourselves from what calls itself the peace movement." He had "experienced much worse things than young people demonstrating on German soil against arms and for peace." Suddenly Willy Brandt once again was the standard-bearer of hope, recalling the promises of his first administration: "I also feel pledged to those who came to us back then. They certainly didn't make the party more boring."

In the fall of 1981 the debate about the identity of the Social Democratic Party—with the alternative movement on one side and the governing party on the other—reached its pinnacle. Brandt defended a course of integration and criticized those attempting to "play off the core constituency against the new stratum." He insisted a party like the SPD must not stick to its traditional moorings but "craft alliances," as a party seeking the majority. Brandt spoke increasingly of a "majority this side of the Union," of the possibility, that is to say, of a Red-Green alliance, and he encouraged then–state governor Holger Börner in forming a Red-Green coalition government in the state of Hesse.[19]

But Brandt was unable, either as party chairman or advisor, to set his house in order, prepare the way for his successors. After the end of the socialist-liberal coalition he did nothing to relieve fundamental oppositions heightened by personal quarrels within the SPD. On the contrary, he exacerbated the situation through his own irritating activities and statements, an example being his public attack before the 1987 *Bundestag* elections on SPD candidate for chancellor Johannes Rau. In the face of growing criticism, Brandt decided not to seek reelection as chairman of the party, and in 1987 resigned voluntarily and was succeeded by Hans-Jochen Vogel. Brandt then was named honorary chairman of the party, and went on to become a legend in his own time, a myth. Which does not change the fact that he occasionally reacted to German unification in patriotic tones that made many of his followers uneasy.

The "Willy" myth is based less on political substance than on political style. Brandt gave credence to the belief that "listening to a democracy" meant listening to, accepting, and incorporating the opinions of others, but that participation in politics was not determined by the four-year election cycle. He was a sophisticated partner in debate, a brilliant and erudite speaker, someone who weighed the issues and gave every argument its due before he came to a decision. It was a process he was able to introduce successfully to public discourse—to the point of self-stylization.

Willy Brandt, with all his flaws, stands for a chapter in Germany's political culture, for a piece of federal German civility. He stood and stands for the "other Germany," the Germany that did not collaborate with the Nazis, but took up resistance and went into emigration. This above all marked his reputation abroad (he was rebuked for it at home, maligned as "Willy Brandt, alias Frahm," or as a "traitor to the fatherland"). And this above all was decisive in giving Brandt the credibility he enjoyed as a symbolic figure for the young generation of the seventies.

In the final years of his life Brandt withdrew more and more from the public eye. He separated from his wife Rut in 1979. A press announcement stated, "Willy Brandt and his wife have amicably agreed to take the step toward legally dissolving their marriage." The two were divorced in December 1980, after thirty-two years of marriage. In 1983 Brandt married Brigitte Seebacher, who worked for the SPD.

When Willy Brandt died on October 8, 1992, at the age of seventy-eight, he had already ascended in the eyes of most of his contemporaries to an eternal Olympus, illumined only by the mild evening light of "history" that obscures criticism and melts differences. Indeed, most of the appreciations of him written after his death read that way. Nevertheless, it is true—viewed either from a critical distance or from a critical proximity—that in Germany's history after 1945 there were two chancellors who permanently altered the profile and direction of German politics—each in his own way. One was Konrad Adenauer, and the other was Willy Brandt. With the understated serenity to which he inclined later in life, Willy Brandt himself once summed it up in these words: "Man hat sich bemüht." I tried.

Notes

1. Leo Lania (Lazar Herrmann), *Willy Brandt, Mein Weg Nach Berlin* [My Road to Berlin] (Munich: Kindler, 1960).

2. Paul Frölich, author of a biography of Rosa Luxemburg.

3. Annemarie Renger, private secretary of SPD chairman Kurt Schumacher, *Bundestag* member beginning 1953, *Bundestag* president from 1972 to 1976.

4. Axel Springer, media baron of a powerful newspaper empire with almost total control of markets in Berlin and Hamburg, Germany's two most populous cities, thus dominating public opinion with his large-circulation nationwide dailies. An uncompromising anti-communist, he steered an anti-Soviet, anti-GDR course after unsuccessfully trying to convince Khrushchev in Moscow to support German unification.

5. Karl Schiller, SPD economist, economics minister in Kiesinger's coalition government, when he was credited with stabilizing the country's troubled economy in 1967. Remaining economics minister in Brandt's first cabinet in 1970, and becoming "superminister" of finance and economics in 1971, he resigned from both a year later.

6. Provoked by the student revolt of the sixties, the *Bundestag* in May 1968 passed a series of amendments to the constitution which allowed parliament to declare a state of emergency. Determined SPD opposition in effect limited the government's emergency powers under the amendments to an actual foreign invasion rather than civil unrest. Also, in reaction to student radicalism, the Brandt government issued a *Radikalenerlass* (extremist directive), which provoked an uproar among large sections of Brandt's own party and the FDP.

7. Hans Globke (1898–1973). As a member in the Third Reich's Interior Ministry drafted the detailed regulations of the Nuremberg racial laws which became the "legal" basis for the Nazi acts of terror against Jews. From 1953 to 1963, as state secretary, he ran the chancellor's office for Adenauer under unceasing attack both in Germany and abroad as a classic example of the *Schreibtisch-täter*—the administrator who did his criminal work at a desk.

8. Alfred Grosser, French political scientist and author of *Germany in Our Time*, among other books. Born in Germany, he fled to Paris along with his parents in 1935, joining the resistance in 1941.

9. Breslau, Oppeln, Gleiwitz, etc., are the German names of towns formerly belonging to Germany, but now part of Poland.

10. Willy Brandt, *Koexistenz—Zwang zum Wagnis* (Stuttgart: Deutsche Verlagsanstalt, 1963).

11. Arnulf Baring, *Machtwechsel: Die Ära Brandt-Scheel* (Change of Power: The Brandt-Scheel Era). Stuttgart: Deutsche Verlagsanstalt, 1982.

12. Herbert Blankenhorn, career foreign-service officer closely involved with the anti-Nazi conspirators in the 1944 plot to kill Hitler. He was Adenauer's chief aide in laying the foundation of West Germany's foreign policy who later enjoyed a distinguished career as Bonn's ambassador to NATO, Great Britain, and France.

13. Karl Wienand, former secretary of the SPD's *Bundestag* caucus, has been charged with spying for the East German communists from 1970 to 1989. A trial date set for January 1995 had to be postponed indefinitely because of Wienand's poor health.

14. Georg Picht, theologian and education specialist, whose book *Die Deutsche Bildungskatastrophe* (The German Education Catastrophe) first warned of a coming crisis in the German educational system.

15. Alexander Mitscherlich, leading German psychoanalyst whose *The Inability to Mourn* (New York: Grove Press, 1975) became a bestseller when it was first published in Germany under the title *Die Unfähigkeit zu Trauern*.

16. Peter Lösche and Franz Walter, *Die SPD: Klassenpartei—Volkpartei—Quotenpartei. Zur Entwicklung der Sozialdemokratie von Weimar bis zur deutschen Vereinigung* (The SPD: Class Party—Peoples Party—Quota Party. On the Development of Social Democracy from Weimar to German Reunification) (Darmstadt: Wissenschaftliche Buchgesellschaft, 1992).

17. Interior Minister Genscher, negotiating with public employees, found himself having to surrender in the face of a series of strikes throughout the public sector, when the states and municipalities caved in and granted virtually all the benefits and pay raises demanded by the ÖTV (Union of Public Service Employees). The stage was set for an 8 percent inflation rate and high unemployment.

18. *Bild*, tabloid daily with a circulation of five million readers at that time.

19. The Greens, so named because of the emphasis on the environment, coalesced from groups organizing anti-nuclear citizens' initiatives in the early seventies into a political party, which for the first time entered the *Bundestag* in 1983 with a vote of 5.6 percent—only slightly fewer than the FDP. In 1985 the Greens agreed to enter a coalition with the minority SPD to form a government in the state of Hesse, where Holger Börner, formerly the SPD caucus secretary in the *Bundestag*, had become minister-president (governor) of Germany's most populous state. The coalition broke apart two years later.

[Top] *With Ronald Reagan and Richard von Weizsäcker at Checkpoint Charlie in Berlin, 1982 — With Henry Kissinger in Munich, 1974 — Addressing May Day celebrations of the German Trade Union Federation in Saarbrücken, 1979.* [Center] *With Count Otto Lambsdorff, 1982 — With Hans-Jürgen*

Wischnewski, 1982 — At a Bundestag *session, 1982.*
[Bottom] *The former chancellor interviewing Leonard Bernstein for TV station SAT 1, 1985 — In the studio of TV station ZDF with Reinhard Appel, 1976 — With Herbert Wehner, 1976.*

Chronology

1918	Born December 23 in Hamburg.
1937	Graduates from Lichtwark School in Hamburg.
1937–1945	National Labor Service, military service, first lieutenant in anti-aircraft battery. Prisoner of war.
1942	Marries Hannelore Glaser. Son dies in infancy in 1943, daughter born in 1947.
1946–1949	Studies political science and economy in Hamburg; degree in political economy.
1946	Joins Social Democratic Party.
1947–1948	Chairman of federal executive of the Socialist Students Federation (SDS).
1949–1953	Member of municipal economic and transportation office in Hamburg. Becomes head of transportation in 1952.
1953–1961	Member of the *Bundestag*.
1961–1965	Senator for interior affairs in Hamburg.
1965–1987	Re-elected to the *Bundestag*.
1967–1969	Chairman of SPD *Bundestag* caucus.
1968	Deputy chairman of SPD.
1969–1972	Federal defense minister.
1972–1974	Federal "superminister" of economics and finance, then federal minister of finance.
1974–1982	Federal chancellor.
1983–present	Co-publisher of the weekly *Die Zeit*.

Helmut Schmidt

by Reinhard Appel

Biographical Note: *Helmut Schmidt was born on December 23, 1918, barely a month after World War I had ended and Kaiser Wilhelm had abdicated. His father Gustav was a teacher who, in the Prussian tradition, placed great emphasis on self-discipline, toughness, and hard work—character traits he sought to imbue in Helmut and his younger brother Wolfgang from early age. Neither boy is said to have talked back to his father, who died in 1982 at the age of 92, nor was there much show of paternal sympathy for the cuts and bruises from the usual rough child play. Helmut's mother, Ludovica, on the other hand, was a woman with more tender inclinations who loved the arts and took the children to concerts and museums.*

Hamburg-Barmbek, where Helmut was born, was known in those days as "red Barmbek"—a Hamburg district with a reputation as a working-class stronghold in a city famed for its socialist leanings. There was a cosmopolitan air in Hamburg early in the century. As a member of the Hanseatic league, which for centuries dominated trade with the Scandinavian countries and Russia, Hamburg is Germany's biggest port, a virtual "city-state" in its own right. Helmut Schmidt's life has been deeply marked by his relationship to the city of his birth. It was here that he grew up, went to school, and got married, and here that he found his first job and eventually entered politics after returning from the army and attending university. When he left public life after being voted from office as federal chancellor, he returned to Hamburg to take the helm of one of Germany's most respected newspapers. In prose hardly characteristic of him he once declared his love for Hamburg—"this city with its scarcely hidden

*Anglicisms; its pride in tradition; its mercantile pragmatism com-
bined with an endearing provincialism. . . . I love her with sadness
for she sleeps, my beauty, she dreams. She is vain about her virtues
without really using them. . . ."[1]*

*Helmut Schmidt was sent to a Hamburg school regarded as
experimental in its day. The Lichtwark Schule (named after a former
head of a Hamburg art gallery) was liberal, co-educational, and as
much focused on artistic as on academic achievement, while stressing
independence, self-reliance, and a sense of critical judgment. Here he
began to "prepare mentally for a career as urban planner or archi-
tect," but after graduating in 1937 he was conscripted. First assigned
to an anti-aircraft battery, he was ultimately promoted to lieutenant,
attached to the anti-aircraft unit of a tank division, and sent to the
Russian front. Near the end of the war he was transferred to the
western front where, in April 1945, he was captured by the British.*

*Schmidt lived through the Hitler years under the cloud of a family
secret that might have had calamitous consequences. As he told his
biographer, Jonathan Carr,[2] he first learned in 1935 that his real
paternal grandfather had been Jewish—a serious blemish under the
Nuremberg racial laws. While Schmidt was in the Wehrmacht he
decided to marry his high-school sweetheart, Hannelore (Loki)
Glaser, at which time he was fortunate in having his unit commander
approve the marriage and testify to Schmidt's "pure Aryan" origins.
While still in the service, the Schmidts had their first child, Helmut,
who died when only a few months old. They had a second child,
Susanne, who was born after the war in 1947, while Schmidt was
studying political economy at Hamburg University.*

*Schmidt joined the Social Democrats in 1946 during his time at
university, where he also met a young professor of economics, Karl
Schiller, who was to play an important part in Schmidt's life.
Schiller, also a member of the SPD, quickly rose in the ranks of the
party during the fifties, becoming economics minister in 1966 in the
coalition government headed by Kurt Georg Kiesinger. When Schmidt
graduated in 1949, Schiller, who was then head of the Hamburg
municipal office for economics and transportation, offered him his
first steady job. In the next four years Schmidt worked his way up in
the Hamburg administration, finally heading the transportation section, and, in 1953 he was elected to the* Bundestag *in Bonn. A speaker
of prodigious talents, Schmidt soon took a leading part in the SPD
debate on a number of issues, especially in the area of defense,
becoming known as the SPD "shadow minister of defense" as he*

argued against the introduction of nuclear weapons in the German defense forces. In 1958 he was elected to the national executive committee of the SPD.

After eight years in Bonn, Schmidt returned to Hamburg in 1961 to assume the position of senator for interior affairs. Less than two months later, a hurricane struck much of northern Europe, causing the waters of the River Elbe to burst over the dikes in Hamburg. Caught unawares in the early-morning hours of February 17, 1962, more than 300 people were drowned. Power lines were ripped down and parts of the city were cut off from the outside world as the floods engulfed about one-fifth of Hamburg. Schmidt took command of the situation with an energy that brought him national fame overnight as a "crisis manager" without peer. He mobilized an army of more than 40,000 rescuers, including Bundeswehr *and Western Allied troops, police, Red Cross, and deploying about 100 helicopters.*

In 1965 Schmidt was again elected to the Bundestag, *becoming SPD party caucus leader in 1967 and, a year later, deputy chairman of the SPD. At the end of October 1969, Schmidt became defense minister in the first Great Coalition cabinet formed by Chancellor Willy Brandt. While in office he firmly supported the presence of nuclear missiles in the Federal Republic and opposed a policy of détente without preserving the existing balance of defense forces in Europe and the continued presence of U.S. troops.*

When Karl Schiller resigned as minister of economics and finance in 1972, Schmidt took over the "superministry" of these two portfolios, which, after the election later that year, was split into its two constituent parts, making Schmidt minister of finance.

Chancellor Brandt announced his resignation on May 6, 1974, after an East German spy, Günter Guillaume, had been uncovered in the chancellery and Brandt accepted "responsibility for negligence." Schmidt, the obvious choice to replace Brandt, then became chancellor in a series of events of which many versions exist; Helmut Schmidt tells his own in the interview that follows. When the Bundestag *elected him, by 267 votes to 225, Schmidt was fifty-five years and four months old, the youngest chancellor to hold the position in the history of the Federal Republic.*

In the following eight years in office, Schmidt imposed his own sober and pragmatic style on a government that sought to consolidate the gains of previous administrations during a period of greater economic turmoil. He steered his country through the troubles caused by the oil crisis with an economic and fiscal policy many regarded as

270 The German Chancellors

a model of restraint. He confronted the rise of worldwide terrorism with determined action in Mogadishu when a Lufthansa jet with eighty-six passengers and five crew members was hijacked by four Arab terrorists. A German crack anti-terrorist squad he dispatched succeeded in killing or wounding the terrorists and freeing the hostages without serious casualties. A number of domestic terrorist actions, among them the kidnapping and killing of industrialist Hanns Martin Schleyer, posed a new and dangerous challenge to his administration.

In foreign policy, Schmidt held fast to the Western Alliance as the cornerstone of German security, despite initial tensions with U.S. president Jimmy Carter over such issues as human rights, the "neutron bomb," and the build-up of Soviet SS-20 missile deployment without an adequate NATO response. At a meeting of the U.S., Britain, and France in Guadeloupe in January 1979, where Germany joined the Big Three wartime victors for the first time to discuss European defense, Schmidt put forth what later became known as the NATO double-track decision, adopted by NATO's foreign and defense ministers in December 1979. Taking an important step in extending the gains made by his predecessors in building a stronger European community, Schmidt joined French president Giscard d'Estaing in developing the idea of a European monetary system with a single European currency.

Schmidt also continued to pursue a policy of détente toward the GDR, even though a "summit meeting" with East German leader Erich Honecker in 1981 failed to yield much in the way of tangible results.

By the fall of 1982, internal differences and rivalries within the SPD coincided with the growing restlessness of the FDP, Schmidt's coalition partner, with whom tensions, especially over budget matters, finally came to a head, leading to a collapse of the government coalition on September 12, 1982. Parliamentary maneuvering between the FDP and their old coalition partner, the CDU/CSU, brought about a "constructive vote of no-confidence" in the Bundestag, which Schmidt lost, 256 to 235, on October 1, 1982. That same day Helmut Kohl took over as the sixth chancellor of the Federal Republic.

Helmut Schmidt had been in office as chancellor for eight and a half years and, though relatively young at 64 years of age, the strains of office had clearly left their mark on his health. After his defeat he declined to run again as chancellor in the elections set for

March 6, 1983, but he remained politically active and, until 1987, continued to represent his Hamburg constituency in the Bundestag. *In May 1983, he joined the distinguished Hamburg weekly* Die Zeit *as co-publisher, a role he continues to fulfill with his customary zest.*
—Eds.

Helmut Schmidt is the Federal Republic's only surviving former chancellor. More time will have to pass before history can make its judgment and a biography, still to be written, can do justice to his political achievements and shortcomings. Meanwhile, there have been dozens of books, mostly on specialized subjects, written by and about Schmidt. I was interested, however, in his current views on his predecessors in office—from Adenauer to Erhardt to Kiesinger to Brandt—as well as his opinion of his successor, Helmut Kohl. His views are much more differentiated and subtle than many might expect of a member of the Social Democratic Party. Even when he is not holding office as a loyal party member of the SPD Helmut Schmidt clearly enjoys a candid discussion and, happily, rarely minces words, whether talking about a political ally or an enemy. So a hint of the famous "Schmidt the Lip"[3] remains, though his wide-ranging global sweep, his acute political reasoning, and his precise language never descend to the level of cheap sensationalism.

For this interview I first sat down with Schmidt for several hours on July 1, 1993, in his office on the ground floor of the Parliament Building in Bonn and, several weeks later, at his vacation home on the Brahmsee, a tranquil lake near Hamburg. It was the same Bonn office where I had visited Kurt Schumacher at the beginning of the fifties. The portrait of August Bebel that hangs in the office perhaps stems from that time, but the portrait of Immanuel Kant more than likely was chosen by Schmidt, for he constantly uses the Königsberg philosopher as a reference point when discussing morality and politics. He, who always rejected any state-inspired moral code, now complains about the decline of moral values in German society, blaming, among others, television, the public's unwillingness to assume sacrifices, its lack of patience, responsibility, and solidarity, and the failure of politicians as a group. He does not deny his own and his generation's share of responsibility for this development, but to reverse it he appeals for a renewed commitment to the values of the past, urging at the same time more self-restraint and deploring the "what-can-I-get-for-nothing" mentality.

Of course, I also questioned Helmut Schmidt about the events that led to his becoming chancellor in May 1947, and about his famous talk with Willy Brandt and Herbert Wehner in Münstereifel. His answers supplied a more subtly articulated version of what happened than is commonly known. He confesses, though he claims no one believes him, that he got "cold feet" in the face of assuming the chancellorship. And his observations about the behind-the-scenes details of his resignation as chancellor in October 1982 make valuable reading for historians, his contemporaries, and interested parties alike. Schmidt speaks quite openly about the difficulties within his own party, to which he still feels loyal and for which he did menial grass-roots work, "even to the point of painting posters with 'Loki'" (his wife's name), for much longer than his raucous Marxist-oriented leftist colleagues. He concedes a major mistake of his chancellorship was not to have assumed the leadership of the party along with the chancellor's office.

Schmidt recalls suffering nights of depression following the murder of industrialist Hanns Martin Schleyer by members of the leftist RAF (Red Army Faction), and remembers the "round table" he formed with other political leaders, including those of the opposition, to protect the state from harm, something he misses in today's government in terms of the threat Germany now faces from the right. He considers the Human Rights Act he signed in the Finnish capital along with GDR chief Erich Honecker ("a man of insignificant intellect") to have been crucial in advancing the movement for human rights, for instance in Walesa's Poland and Havel's former Czechoslovakia.

As in the past, Schmidt continues to believe the NATO double-track decision,[4] where he won his way against the initial resistance of the U.S. president, was decisive in the eventual success of détente and German unification. He makes a point of giving credit to Helmut Kohl and Ronald Reagan for sticking to this policy after Schmidt left office. He recalls with satisfaction how Mikhail Gorbachev, the last Soviet premier, in effect directly confirmed this view. Gorbachev told Schmidt he had realized after the NATO double-track decision that the ideological struggle and the arms race begun earlier by the Kremlin leaders "was bound to fail." Helmut Schmidt gave us permission to quote from a memo about this meeting with Gorbachev in Bonn in 1992.

Schmidt is convinced Bonn's policy toward the East would have been impossible unless West Germany had persisted in its policy toward the West. One reason Willy Brandt brought Schmidt into his cabinet as minister of defense, he says, was because he was known and trusted in the West. But Brandt had insisted at the time that Herbert Wehner assume leadership of the SPD caucus in parliament. Wehner accepted, if somewhat reluctantly.

Schmidt acknowledges that initially he had extraordinary respect for the political gifts of Willy Brandt, an admiration later modified during the Great Coalition, not least due to Brandt's "wishy-washy" position on the Emergency Powers Act.[5] At one point he refers to policies proposed by Egon Bahr, whose advice Brandt constantly sought, as being too "goody-goody."

Nor is Helmut Schmidt loath to be forthright in the views he expresses about more current political affairs and the personalities now in charge, speaking with an acumen, political grasp, and precision of language that remain undiminished. His physical appearance, too, seems unchanged from that of his active days in Bonn. Referring to the Balkan conflict and the civil war in Somalia, for instance, he notes "an apparent lack of experience on the part of newcomers Kinkel[6] and Clinton." Helmut Kohl, whose policies he views critically at times, nevertheless receives a compliment. "Kohl is anything but a weak man. He knows how very well how to use power."

Schmidt terms the Maastricht Treaty[7] one of "the worst international treaties" he has ever read, a "mishmash," a "product of bureaucrats" with which Germans "did not exactly crown themselves in glory." He questions Bonn's monetary policies and the stability of the mark, and generally expresses fears that Europe is moving backward rather than forward.

He bitterly criticizes reunification policies, considering the restitution-of-property laws and the wage and income policies to be extreme errors by the government as well as the unions. He believes the *Solidarpakt* (solidarity pact)[8] to be totally inadequate, on top of having been arrived at too late. He is "glad" Honecker, the former communist head of the GDR, could "escape to Chile," and incensed that it was the "little guys, the lowest in the chain of command," who were the first to be hauled up before the judges. Schmidt had no sympathy for those Germans who "were in no danger," yet now presume to pass judgment on those who lived in the former GDR.

Even though one may not share Schmidt's views, they deserve discussion, for they reflect the experience of a former chancellor who firmly and confidently steered his country through a difficult time of global economic crisis and threats to domestic tranquillity, and who acted with resolution and sound judgment. He successfully defended his administration against the challenge of Helmut Kohl in 1976, and Franz Josef Strauss in 1980. When he left office in 1982, it was not due to a loss at the polls but to an about-face of his coalition partner (the FDP) and the failure of his own party to stick with him. But even today opinion polls confirm that many Germans beyond his own party continue to trust him. It is worth listening to what he has to say.

Appel: *Of the six postwar chancellors you are the only one living who was seated in the Bundestag as far back as the fifties and so had personal knowledge of Adenauer's chancellorship. How do you judge Adenauer and your other predecessors to the office today? Your party, the SPD, was, after all, bitterly opposed to Adenauer's policies in the beginning, accusing him, among other things, of reinforcing the division of Germany through his alliance with the West.*

Schmidt: The position of the Social Democrats on the Parliamentary Council, if I am correct, at first was relatively moderate toward Konrad Adenauer. There were the usual political differences normal between members of major political parties, each with its own intellectual, philosophical, and historical tenets. When the Federal Republic was established in 1949 the polemical friction increased between the Social Democrats and Adenauer, due largely to Kurt Schumacher. It was Adenauer and not Schumacher who became federal chancellor. And though Schumacher died three years later, in the summer of 1952, for a number of years to come the style of his parliamentary debates with Konrad Adenauer imposed its stamp on the relationship with this important German chancellor, at least for younger members like myself. I came to the *Bundestag* in 1953. In addition, as you suggested, Social Democrats suspected Adenauer of still having a mental attachment to the separatist tradition he was said to have pursued in the years following the First World War; that Adenauer was not so very interested in the reunification of the two German states created after the war, or in reuniting the German nation. I recall quite well the journalist Walter Henkel saying to me in the fifties: "*Der Alte* thinks the (Siberian) steppes begin in Magdeburg." Perhaps what Henkel said was correct, if a bit exaggerated. To me, as a young member of parliament, Adenauer represented Rhineland Catholicism, more inclined toward Rome or France than Berlin. Protestant Prussia begins not in Magdeburg but a little farther to the west, and Adenauer, regardless of his governmental positions in prewar Berlin, apparently had little in common spiritually with Prussia. Adenauer consciously concurred with the European integration

policy initiated by France—by Jean Monnet and Robert Schuman—
and to many Social Democrats this initially confirmed the secret
Rhineland separatism attributed to Adenauer for years.

A: *You said "initially."*

S: Yes, to me, as a young man—I arrived at the *Bundestag* when
I was all of thirty-five years old—and to Schumacher, whom you just
mentioned.

A: *You considered Schumacher a mentor?*

S: Yes, he once had been, for he had died by then. To me, Ernst
Reuter[9] was the mentor, but then he too died in 1953, unfortunately,
to my great distress. I myself had imagined Reuter, and not Erich
Ollenhauer,[10] to be the true heir of Schumacher's leadership. And I
was at first affected by Adenauer's approval of the Schuman Plan,
which, incidentally, I myself supported in newspaper articles I wrote
as a young man—earning me Schumacher's reproach, and a written
reproach at that.

A: *Did you approve of it because you saw in it the first signs of an
orientation to the West?*

S: Yes, and also of a reconciliation with France. Since 1948 I had
been fascinated by the ideas of Jean Monnet. I met him in Strasbourg
in 1948 and was fascinated by the Schuman Plan. Kurt Schumacher
wrote a letter to the head of the SPD in Hamburg to put a stop to
what this young man was doing.

A: *Schumacher went so far as to say that you should not only be
read the riot act, but . . . ?*

S: Yes, on top of which I was no longer permitted to publish anything in the party paper. So as of 1948 I was a European, in the way
the so-called "European" wing of the party was later referred to. But
I suspected Adenauer's European policy at first as more of the same
old separatism he was believed to favor. At the same time, however,
as *Bundestag* representative, but also later, as caucus leader, federal
minister, and then as chancellor, I, like Kurt Schumacher, always
held that Germany must be united again as one state, one nation. I
was not convinced that Adenauer saw it that way.

A: *You continued to hold to that opinion even when it appeared
hopeless?*

S: Oh yes, oh yes. I never imagined that I would live to see it, that
was something else. But I was always resolved that we in the West
must never do anything to complicate or make impossible an eventual
reunification. And then the Schuman Plan quickly led not only to the
European Coal and Steel Community, but also to the European

Defense Community (EDC), the ratification of which the French National Assembly rejected in Paris in 1954. But out of that quickly developed EURATOM, the European Atomic Energy Community, and other organizations, all of which then became the European Economic Community, or EEC, as it was called then.

A: *Did you yourself support the European Defense Community?*

S: I did, yes, but my party did not—at least not the majority of the party. Then in 1957 I was sent to the European Parliament and there I began to establish personal contact with leading Frenchmen, and influential Dutch and Italians as well, almost all dead now.

There was a decisive turning point in the Social Democratic position toward Adenauer's foreign policy, made public on June 30, 1960, in a major speech by Herbert Wehner, which, if my memory serves me, he did not clear at the time with the SPD leadership. I think Ollenhauer and other Social Democrats as well were surprised by it. But Wehner knew he could depend on people like Carlo Schmid, and above all on Fritz Erler, those who shared the ideas of Ernst Reuter. He knew they were on his side. Wehner was of the same mind as the greater part of the Social Democratic Party leadership at that time. He was confident that among the party leadership was an entire group of influential people who shared his opinion. My position was clear. In the fifties I had co-founded the London Institute for Strategic Studies, so I was already known as a *"Westler,"* as they said then.

But "Uncle Herbert's" speech came as a great surprise to the public, and the party caucus as well; yet at the same time, as was quickly established, it was also liberating. That is to say, his speech eliminated the last major opposition to Adenauer's foreign policy. Socialists had been pro-EC in the fifties already. What wasn't eliminated, however, was the distrust Social Democrats felt for Adenauer as a person.

A: *In the elections of 1961, after the Wall was built, Adenauer lost the absolute majority he had attained in the 1957 elections. In a famous letter to Heinrich Krone, he said that, in the event of a coalition with the FDP and should he be elected chancellor, he would serve for two years only. And then he governed with the FDP—the party that had failed at the polls after campaigning against him now governed with Adenauer, without, however, its chairman, Erich Mende. Adenauer left office in 1963, Erhard took over as chancellor, and Mende became his vice-chancellor. Do you believe that Adenauer's relationship with the SPD had changed before this?*

S: Yes, and the process probably advanced even further after Adenauer lost the absolute majority. That is something I cannot judge precisely, for I was not in Bonn at the time—from 1961 to 1965 I was serving as a senator in Hamburg. I only know that from the end of the fifties to 1961 I was among those who were of the opinion that, whatever the constellation, the man was too old and too rigid. He must have been in his late eighties by then.

A: *But Social Democratic policy was influenced by Adenauer's orientation toward the West, and later, of course, by Khrushchev's 1958 ultimatum on Berlin. The SPD first tried to sound out the chances for a German confederation with the "Germany Plan" of 1959, and with a visit to Moscow.*

S: The SPD's "Germany Plan" was the first public document of détente produced by German postwar politics. Franz Barsig[11] and Uncle Herbert had thrown it together overnight in a journalistically simplified, skewed fashion, based on a memorandum that represented the extended efforts of six or seven people. I recall that Wehner, Kurt Mattick,[12] and myself were involved, among others. It was actually a rather carefully worked-out document. I was responsible for the economic part of it. I still have my section of the work, which foresaw a gradual consolidation of the GDR's economy and the Federal Republic's economy, and also dealt with the currency problems that would arise, as well as with the differences in productivity and the problems this would cause in terms of competitiveness. I was aware of all of that at the time. The published version of the "Germany Plan" simplified all of that, fitted it to the tabloid reader's sensibility. And in retrospect, from a foreign-policy point of view, it truly should not have been published on the day it was, which was one, two, or three days after Carlo Schmid and Erler had returned from Moscow, the Soviets having given them the cold shoulder on the topic of reunification. But Herbert Wehner wanted to publish the document anyway. This was before his famous speech of June 30, 1960,[13] in which he announced the SPD's change of course.

A: *Another of your predecessors was Erhard, who held the office for three years even though his place in history is more tied to the currency reform of 1948 and his social market economy, from the time when he served as minister of economics. What is your recollection of Erhard?*

S: He deserves very special credit for two things about the currency reform. As economist he is due the highest praise for dismantling very quickly all conceivable economic controls and then turning over economic activity to the market. However, it didn't happen the way people who weren't there to experience it idealize it today, forty years later. For example, it wasn't true that anyone who had the money could build ships. You needed the permission of the Allies for that; it was a major investment, and was denied in part, and the ships, at any rate, only could be relatively small—today you would call them nutshells. Nor was it true that anyone could import or export whatever he wished. There was an agency, it was called the Joint Ex- and Import Agency (JEIA). When people today say that Erhard created a market economy from one day to the next, overnight, so to speak, well, your name would have to be Kohl to believe that. But over the course of the fifties Erhard gradually succeeded in establishing more and more of a market economy, even in the face of the Western Allied resistance, who were much more opposed to it than the public.

His second great service was to the West German people, in preaching to them a message of optimism, which he did successfully. Otherwise, he was not a particularly notable chancellor later on. But these two great services he performed in the fifties make him a historical figure in my eyes.

A: *You were in Bonn during Kurt Kiesinger's three years as chancellor of the Great Coalition of CDU/CSU and SPD, having succeeded Fritz Erler as head of the SPD caucus. You wrote in your book[14] that "the Great Coalition did a good job." Would you say the same of Kiesinger as chancellor?*

S: No, I wouldn't. Kiesinger was a highly gifted speaker, but he didn't exactly invent the concept of hard work. In addition, neither he nor Willy Brandt, his vice-chancellor, liked each other. Neither Brandt nor Kiesinger had the ability to overcome their personal animosity and govern jointly, at least in the final twelve months of the Great Coalition their animosity had reached the point where it seemed the only time they spoke to each other was during cabinet meetings. I got the feeling at the time, and still have it today, that in those last twelve months it was the two caucus leaders, Barzel and myself, who were governing the country, at least in terms of legislation. Initiatives no longer originated with the government. One of the most difficult legislative acts was the attempt to eliminate the Allied reserve powers,[15] part of the *Deutschlandvertrag*, or General Treaty, in what were known as the *Notstandsgesetze*, or "Emergency Powers Act." The emergency reserve powers of the Allies—they had reserved all conceivable rights of direct intervention—was what we wished to get rid of. They had been a special target of the left in Germany. The government wanted the revision, but did not present it to either faction with the necessary conviction, and was too cowardly to fight for it. Barzel and I knew each other well from the second half of the fifties, and it was we who put it through—pushed it through, as well as the many necessary compromises.

Here I would like to insert an addendum to the topic of Adenauer. Adenauer wanted, and rightfully so, for Germany to participate in the joint military defense of western Europe with the inclusion of German soldiers. He imagined we could do this with the stroke of a pen, which, coincidentally, would have led to his becoming commander in chief of the German troops which would be raised. He totally disregarded the entire discussion about *innere Führung* (inner leadership),[16] and about personnel selection from among the former colonels and generals of the Nazi-German army. In the fifties a large coalition formed within the defense committee of the *Bundestag*, made up of people like Erler, Adolf Arndt,[17] and myself on the Social Democratic side, and, on the CDU side, of people like Georg Kliesing[18]—he lived in nearby Königswinter—and Rainer Barzel, then a civil servant and *Bundesrat* (upper house of parliament) representative to Minister Spieker of the Northrhine-Westphalian state government. In this capacity Barzel had access to the defense committee, whose chairman was Richard Jäger of the CSU. Barzel's presence should not be overlooked here, for much credit is due him for hammering out the Military Service Act. Erich Mende, too, played a role, and other politicians as well, of course, but I cannot recall them all. Against Adenauer's opposition we then wrote the Military Service Act, which became part of the Basic Law. And from that time on Barzel and I knew that we could trust one another, even when we were of different minds on things, so that it was possible for us both—Barzel had meanwhile become a *Bundestag* representative, and I was head of the party caucus—to conceal from the outside world the inability of the Kiesinger/Brandt administration to function during the last twelve months of its existence. It was also possible for me to get the Emergency Powers Act through, which was, by the way, much more difficult to accomplish within the SPD caucus than within the CDU/CSU caucus. So we've already arrived at the time of Kiesinger's government, the Great Coalition.

A: *In your book you wrote that even now, in the first third of the nineties, you would still favor a Great Coalition in some situations, despite the fundamental reservations one might have. Of the Great Coalition of 1966 to 1969 you wrote that, all in all, it did a good job. Kiesinger's administration had, of course, yet another politically sym-*

bolic significance for postwar Germany: reconciliation, Kiesinger being a former member of the NSDAP and Willy Brandt a former emigrant. You, incidentally, remain up until today the only chancellor who belonged to the Second World War generation, the only postwar politician who served in the Wehrmacht.

S: In discussing the Kiesinger/Brandt administration, we must mention that Erhard left office when the German economy was in recession, after which began the brilliant teamwork of "Plisch" and "Plum,"[19] that is, Strauss and Schiller.[20] In terms of areas of responsibility the minister of economics was more powerful in those days than today, for he was responsible as well for the country's energy policy and trade policy, which today is handled in Brussels. In addition, he was also directing monetary and credit policy, long since transferred to the finance department. Karl Schiller and Franz Josef Strauss—two totally different personalities—knew how to cooperate with one another, turning the recession around in no time, and giving the German people the impression that everything was going quite well economically. It wasn't Kiesinger who accomplished this, but those two. They too, by the way, belonged to the Second World War generation.

The Brandt Legacy

A: *Willy Brandt's five years in office came to an abrupt end with the incident surrounding Günter Guillaume, a spy for the GDR, who testified in the Markus Wolf[21] trial that he, Guillaume, had been "turned into a tool against Brandt" for the purpose of toppling Brandt's administration. In those crucial days in May 1974 you urged Willy Brandt to remain chancellor. It has been said of your election as Brandt's successor that Herbert Wehner had planned Willy Brandt's fall for a long time. What is your comment on that version of events?*

S: First of all, I consider the myth of the "long-time plan" to be rubbish. Wehner did not invent Guillaume's existence in a long-time plan, and in my opinion it really was this spy affair that was the cause of Willy Brandt's resignation. Even today I do not believe that the events called for his resignation. Had Willy Brandt wanted to remain in office, he could have done so. And then it would have been necessary to investigate who was responsible for security, who had Guillaume under surveillance—he most certainly was—and had not kept Brandt well-informed in timely fashion. All of this would have had to be checked. But Brandt had had enough. Whether or not Wehner was the determining factor in Brandt's decision to call it quits, or played a major role in that decision, I don't know. I wasn't present at the talk between the two of them. But it is true that Wehner was dissatisfied with Willy Brandt's indecisiveness on many points.

A: *The same Brandt who had scored the greatest electoral victory in the history of the SPD.*

S: That's another story. This was due in great part to the attempt by the opposition to bring the government down with a constructive vote of no-confidence, which the German public saw as a stab in the back. That really incensed many people. And that's quite an important point, for otherwise we would never have enjoyed the triumph at the polls. But Wehner, regardless of the success at the polls, was dissatisfied with a certain indecisiveness on Brandt's part in several areas. I no longer recall exactly which. And then there was Wehner's statement—surely not apocryphal because it was confirmed by a number of journalists—he made while in Russia with a *Bundestag* delegation, that Herr Brandt "prefers his bathwater lukewarm." That hit Brandt particularly hard. I would guess, without knowing it for sure, that from then on the personal relationship of trust between the two was only maintained—just barely—for the sake of appearances, but it was never truly restored.

A: *Was that evident in party meetings at that time? You were, after all, part of the Brandt/Wehner/Schmidt troika.*

S: No, they both behaved well, particularly Wehner, who fit well into such meetings. Their views differed on many occasions, but the disagreements never became public. We never showed our differences, all three of us had great self-restraint.

A: *You didn't want to become federal chancellor, although you were always mentioned as the only possible Social Democratic candidate if an election for a new chancellor were to become necessary.*

S: I was familiar with the speculation and it wasn't so far off the mark, something which became quite clear in Münstereifel: "If Willy Brandt resigns, Schmidt must take over." That was clear to me as well, but I was afraid of the office, or, more precisely, I was afraid of the responsibility. I was terribly upset when I left Münstereifel and spent the whole trip home lamenting to my wife about what I was getting myself into.

A: *But you had never before been afraid of responsibility?*

S: Yes, of course, but this office was, to my way of thinking, a bit larger than the offices I had held until then. I can only tell you the truth, even though no one has ever believed me. But that's the way it was. Anyway, it was decided in Münstereifel that Willy Brandt would resign. It was I who then formulated the crucial sentence of his resignation announcement, the one that begins something like: "I assume the responsibility for neglecting . . ." etc., etc.

A: *Willy Brandt's major political achievement was his policy toward the East, which you have always applauded.*

S: Yes, but it wouldn't have been possible without the backing of a policy toward the West pursued with consistency and conspicuous determination. And for that, Brandt—because he couldn't appoint the foreign minister, that was left up to his FDP partner, Walter Scheel—needed Schmidt, who was well respected in England and in America as someone who not only supported the Western alliance, but also had given it a great deal of thought and had written books on it. He needed someone for his *Ostpolitik* he could depend on, someone who was well known in the West from I don't know how many international conferences. And that is why—from Brandt's point of view—I had to become minister of defense at the beginning of his chancellorship. I didn't want to.

A: *Why not?*

S: Two reasons: First I was very happy as head of the party caucus. A caucus head is powerful, and if the caucus head says, "I can get the caucus to agree to such-and-such," then the government can go ahead and do it, and if he says, "I can't get that through," then the government can't do it. It all had to do with his assessment and his judgment, much more so than anyone else's in close proximity to the chancellor, or who advised him. That was already true during Kiesinger's time in office, and I knew in principle that it would be true of Brandt's administration as well, only with a different coalition partner. I was quite comfortable as caucus leader, and I was respected in that role. When the Emergency Powers Act came up, for example, both the SPD's minority on the left and its majority on the right asked me to speak for them in the *Bundestag* in presenting the controversial views within the party. The minority had refused to appoint a spokesman to represent it, after weeks of harsh debate. Even in retrospect I like to think of that as a major indication of their trust in me. So I was well respected, why should I give up the position as head of the caucus? I wanted to keep it, I felt quite comfortable in the office. The other reason, of course, being that I was aware of—not least from the debates surrounding the emergency powers—the pacifist, count-me-out attitude held by many Social Democrats. Though largely concealed, it was becoming more public, and I was familiar as well with Willy Brandt's wishy-washy attitude toward this. I recall that, at least once, a number of representatives wanted to take a potshot at me as minister of defense, because of this. Right away some called me "Noske"[22] and tried to malign me as following in Noske's footsteps when I assumed office. Foreseeing more of the same I had no desire to become minister of defense. But they wore me down in the end, Willy Brandt and Herbert Wehner, that is. I set one condition, however, which had to be met and indeed it was. As defense minister I wanted my back to be covered, I wanted to be protected from attacks within my own ranks, and so I asked that Wehner not be named to Brandt's cabinet, but leave the administration and take over the party caucus. Uncle Herbert was not at all pleased with this at first. As a former communist, he was quite proud of holding a federal office as cabinet minister. To him this was the highest recognition of his long political journey. So to give up this position was something not at all to his liking. But then he understood my political motives and accepted them. And so Wehner became the head of the party caucus—and I became minister of defense.

But to return to Willy Brandt's *Ostpolitik*: Essentially I was the one who covered for it with the Western Allies. I was not opposed to Brandt's policy on the East, not in the least. I went to Moscow as early as 1966, on my own initiative as deputy caucus leader, and I worked on the Germany Plan drawn up by the SPD in 1958. I returned to Moscow in 1969, together with my deputies, Alex Möller and Egon Franke, in order to sound out the chances for German reunification. So, God knows, I was not in favor of tensions, but I did know that a policy of détente would work only if the East respected the West's, and West Germany's, determination to defend itself. And later, after May 1974—Brandt was chancellor for four and a half years, from fall 1969 to May 1974—later, I did nothing to alter his *Ostpolitik*. I did, however, put a brake on the enthusiasm—people were acting like we were proclaiming world peace, there was that degree of enthusiasm at the time. I put a quick end to the enthusiasm of people like Erhard Eppler—who thought of himself as the archangel of peace. I also was ruthless in putting a brake on Egon Bahr's exuberance—he thought he was the peace angel in person— though as chancellor I always sought his advice on issues where I thought his judgment was prudent. But this attitude, that it was the Germans alone who would set the world straight, was one I never

shared. That was the view of some of the group around Willy Brandt;
he himself didn't share it, he was realistic. But at times he didn't get
along at all with Pompidou and not so well with Nixon, though somewhat better with Ted Heath, who then was applying a second time for
England's membership in the European Economic Community. The
first EEC application had been made by Harold Macmillan ten years
earlier, but de Gaulle had crushed the motion and then Pompidou
acquiesced, and Brandt as well. I did not remain minister of defense
for a long time, barely three years, not even that. From the fall of
1969 to summer 1972.

A: *Today, do you still consider the concept of holding two ministries to be a good one?*

S: Yes, of course. The Ministry of Economics is totally superfluous today, we don't need it. It doesn't exist anywhere else in the Western world, except in Germany. There is no such thing in France, nor
in the United States. If it's anything we need, it's a ministry of industry. The Ministry of Economics today is a ministry of ideological drivel
and economic forecasting and not much else. On top of which, the
only area of responsibility it still claims is antitrust and fair-trade
legislation. Everything else is handled elsewhere, money and credit in
particular, which is under the Finance Ministry, as it is in every other
industrial democracy in the world.

A: *Your relationship with Willy Brandt was always marked by
civility and by your respect for his political achievement, but it never
came to a personal friendship between the two of you, or to total
political harmony. Did that change after both of you left office?*

S: Up until the time of the Great Coalition I would have walked
through fire for the man. Perhaps he wasn't aware of it, but then I'm
not the sort of person who wears his heart on his sleeve. So I became
disillusioned with Willy Brandt during the time of the Great Coalition. It upset me terribly to witness Kiesinger and Brandt's inability
to get along with each other in any appropriate fashion. It also upset
me when I saw that Brandt wasn't going to stand up to the party caucus for the Emergency Powers Act, which he had approved in the
cabinet. He didn't even show up, but left it instead to me, to little
Schmidt. I reacted very negatively to this. Two or three years earlier,
following the 1965 elections, I had encouraged him to become opposition leader, to no avail. At that time he didn't want to return to
Berlin. It's true that he hadn't won the '65 election, but the Social
Democrats' share of the vote had increased quite nicely, up to forty
percent, I think. Before that we had been teetering around the mid-

thirtieth percentile, perhaps a little less. He wanted to stay here in Bonn, but Fritz Erler wanted to remain caucus leader. There was a struggle, a contest between Brandt and Erler. I can remember as if it were today—that was 1965, when I returned to the *Bundestag* from Hamburg—that Brandt asked me: "What do you think?" and I answered: "We have you to thank for the success at the polls, so you should have the first choice at becoming caucus chair." I relate this only to characterize my relationship with Brandt. That's the way I felt at the time, though after Ernst Reuter's death it was Fritz Erler who became my political model. I didn't know Brandt well then. He had been president of the Berlin City Assembly, and then governing mayor of Berlin, so he was rather far away. I had encountered him in the fifties in the *Bundestag*, but we did not have any close contact. For my part, my relationship with Brandt was one of total trust until the years of the Great Coalition. That trust diminished in the second half of the coalition. We never developed a close personal friendship. I have no idea what he thought of me.

A: *There were also difficulties between you and Brandt during your chancellorship, when you were fighting for the NATO double-track decision. But when I read in his widow's book[23] that you were one of the few people to visit him I thought that perhaps the two of you had cleared up your differences.*

S: I recall going to see him.

A: *Would you call that visit a man-to-man discussion on earlier policies?*

S: No. We did talk about many things, of course, but "a man-to-man discussion" connotes clearing the air of old irritations. And that, I think, it was not.

A: *Your relationship to the SPD, which you continue to consider your political home, has been marked by differences of opinion at various points. What was it that brought about the change in administration eleven years ago, in 1982? Was it the partial loss of trust in the SPD under the leadership of Willy Brandt? Or the about-face of the FDP?*

S: The FDP would have it that they were totally blameless, and that differences of opinion within the SPD were the cause. I have been a member of the SPD for forty-eight years now; surely there are relatively few people still alive who have been members of this party for so long. And particularly the people who were the source of all conceivable kinds of difficulties during my time as chancellor had joined the party only a few years earlier. For eight years in Hamburg-

North I was the leader of a local party numbering ten thousand people, I know the party from the bottom up. As a young pup I not only pasted up posters but got down on the floor with my wife and painted them myself, because there weren't any printers then. For years I also traveled to various local party organizations as a speaker. I was invited to speak frequently, chiefly on economic issues. I didn't become a Social Democrat by attending academic seminars. Those people who came to the party from the '68 student movement were furious at the Great Coalition, which wasn't my doing, after all. They were furious not only at the Great Coalition, they were also furious at the so-called extremist decree,[24] issued during Brandt's chancellorship, against my explicit advice. But Wehner and Brandt agreed on it. As opposed to the two of them, I had a great deal of administrative experience; I had worked for the Hamburg city government for four years, and for four years was Hamburg's senator of the interior, so I had eight years' experience. I was familiar with public-service law and laws governing civil service, of course, and I argued that they were extensive enough, and therefore that the extremist decree should be dropped. But the gentlemen wanted it, and they wanted it as a defense against the CDU accusing the Social Democrats of tolerating communist infiltration. That was their motive at the time. But the academic leftists within the SPD ascribed it to me, as if I were the one who had come up with it. They didn't want to believe who really had come up with it. Nor did I correct them, there was no point to it. Then they tried to make me look ridiculous as a so-called *"Macher"* (doer) who had no theoretical knowledge, and gloated over the label of "sergeant" bestowed on me by *Humanité*, the French communist newspaper. They weren't pleased, of course, that Giscard d'Estaing and the German chancellor were working so closely together, and Moscow wasn't too happy about it either. They ridiculed me as *"der Macher."* We did have a knowledge of theory, of course, but it wasn't a neo-Marxist theory.

Then in 1973 and 1974 came the first explosion in oil prices, which led to an increase in the price of crude oil and heating oil and gasoline. Willy Brandt was still chancellor then. The situation became so serious at the time that, for example, we had to introduce a ban on driving on Sunday.

A: *Which was successful.*

S: Yes, yes—it had to be. It was the fall of 1973 and as finance minister I explained in a public address that the world had changed, and that we would have to tighten our belts for a few years in order to deal with the economic consequences. Unemployment was just beginning to rise at the time. And I was told by Ehmke, supposedly at the instruction of Brandt, not to give such defeatist speeches. Well, fine, six months later, as of May 1974, I was in charge of the government myself, and then we had to deal with the economic consequences—foreign trade, the foreign-currency situation, and inflation and unemployment. We were much better able to handle the economic consequences of this explosion in oil prices than our industrial neighbors in the democracies of Western Europe. We handled it relatively well. And I thought, "Now we can catch our breath and these academic Young Socialists will begin to show some restraint." But then at the end of the seventies came the second explosion in oil prices. We had just gotten over the first one, and now the situation was quite difficult in all of the Western world, and that was just what these young theoreticians were waiting for, to blame me for my totally wrong economic policies, which, moreover, were without any theoretical basis. That wasn't the SPD. The SPD has one million members, and nine hundred thousand of them were on my side, I'm sure of that, but those members didn't have the opportunity to be interviewed by *Spiegel*, or by Reinhard Appel. The only ones who could do that were the elected members in Bonn, who were on executive committees, or in an association that called itself the Young Socialists, or in the so-called "Frankfurt Circle," and so on.

Which is to say that my relationship to the SPD was still all right, I was still the man they trusted. If you look at the opinion polls from that time I did not do badly at all, quite the opposite. No, my relationship with the SPD and its members was all right, but my relationship was equivocal with the few of them who used the Bonn arena to sound off about the SPD in the media. It was also marked in part by maliciousness. I'll never forget what Lafontaine, for example, said about my "virtues." Why are you shaking your head?

A: *Because I found what he said—that someone with your second-rate virtues could also run a concentration camp—objectionable.*

S: Yes, I'll never forget that. That was the public expression of the way they talked about me among themselves. But the Saarlander (Lafontaine) was more of a smart-mouth than the others.

But to return to your question. In this economically difficult situation of rising unemployment, the need to support prosperity and growth with more borrowing, which the CDU found deplorable— since then, in the eleven years since 1982 the CDU has tripled the debt, and it soon will be up to four times what it had been—anyway, in this situation two things in the FDP came together. One was that people like Genscher, but certainly others as well, had become convinced that the influence of the FDP could be maintained in the long run only if, from time to time, it changed partners. That was also the conclusion they drew from the events of the summer of 1966, when they practically toppled Erhard. Therefore—a change of partners now and then! Today, in 1993, they are changing partners again. In my opinion that does not necessarily mean the FDP is unreliable by nature, it is the inherent reason for its existence, without which it would not be able to survive as a third party. If, in people's minds, the FDP is a party that is always riding on the coattails of the CDU, or the SPD, then it loses its meaning as a party. By the fall of 1982 we had had thirteen years of a socialist-liberal coalition, four and a half years under Brandt and eight and a half years under Schmidt. And so there was surely this underlying motivation on the part of the FDP—at some point there would have to be a change of partner. The vehicle for this was provided not so much by the academic socialists' opposition to my economic policies, but rather by the opposition of the pacifist sector of the Social Democratic Party to the NATO double-track decision, which the FDP, naturally, had helped to formulate and then later executed under Kohl. The FDP could claim this intraparty heckling proved the SPD was an unreliable partner.

The other motive was a personal one. Lambsdorff[25] was facing criminal proceedings, a tax-evasion case and a second criminal investigation. In the spring of 1982, the *Bundestag* tried twice indirectly to extend indemnity to Lambsdorff. The first attempt collapsed with the SPD caucus because Hans-Jürgen Wischnewski, who was secretary of the SPD's *Bundestag* group at the time, warned the SPD presidium, "not with me." And the second attempt failed because of me. I sent my undersecretary, Gunter Huonker, to the heads of the party and the caucuses of the socialist-liberal coalition with a memorandum which they had to initial to show they had read it. The memo was short, half a page, and it said: The bill you intend to propose won't get my countersignature, and without it the federal president cannot put it into effect. And this triggered Lambsdorff's enmity; this was the second time he failed. In the meantime he has been cleared in the criminal case—and rightfully so, I think—and he paid a penalty in the tax case.

Leadership

A: *When you think back on your eight years as chancellor, and recall the most important political issues, were there decisions you would make differently today, or judgments you would formulate differently?*

S: In retrospect, I probably made a mistake at the very beginning. I probably should have said to my friends in the party: "You know I am not especially eager to become federal chancellor. But if you consider it necessary, then the leadership of the party and the chancellor's office must be held by one and the same person." In retrospect it was probably a major mistake not to have done that. The many troubles I mentioned before—the leftist pacifist and leftist Marxist currents within the party—probably would have been easier to handle had to two offices been joined, but I'm not absolutely sure about this. Otherwise I had a clear view of the dilemma at the time, but I didn't want to embarrass Brandt too much—that was my motive. I also knew that leading these troublesome groups within the SPD would require an additional expenditure of energy. Brandt, after all, was head of the party and chancellor at the same time. I did not foresee that Brandt, as head of the party, would let all of those currents I had criticized before more or less go on undisturbed. That was something I hadn't expected.

As far as the eight and a half years that followed, I'm sure I made a fair number of minor mistakes. I'd have to think for a long time before I could enumerate them. I made some mistakes in personnel choices as well, but I'd prefer not to talk about that because those people are still alive. I don't believe I made any major mistakes. The close collaboration with France was absolutely correct, the relationship between France and Germany had never been closer except between Adenauer and de Gaulle in the later years. The fact that inept finance ministries in Paris and Bonn are endangering that relationship today is something I view with concern. We should not believe our economy can steer unscathed through the troubles of the next few decades to come without a close alliance with France. Fine. I consider the seven years that President Giscard d'Estaing was in office, if you examine them closely, to have been a very important and positive period. We were mutually successful; together we invented the European Currency System (EWS), and together we invented the world economic summit talks—and all sorts of other things. Nor

Taking the oath as federal chancellor administered by Bundestag *president Annemarie Renger, May 16, 1974.*

Federal President Gustav Heinemann receives Schmidt's first cabinet, May 16, 1974. First row, from left: Hans-Dietrich Genscher, Heinemann, Schmidt, Georg Leber, Egon Franke, Hans Apel, Hans Matthöfer. Second row, from left: Karl Ravens, Helmut Rohde, Kurt Gscheidle, Josef Ertl (concealed), Walter Arendt, Erhard Eppler, Katharina Focke, Hans Friderichs, Werner Maihofer, Hans-Jochen Vogel.

always to the delight of others, but we provided leadership to the European Community, which cannot be said today. The European Community is totally without leadership, because the gentlemen in Paris and the gentlemen in Bonn don't speak with each other every fourteen days, as we did at the time.

One great success, in my eyes, was the double-track decision, which the Americans did not want at all at first, but which introduced and made possible and more or less forced détente upon the successor to the successor to the successor to Brezhnev, namely Gorbachev, and Reagan, who was not at all in favor of the idea.

A: *Do you believe the NATO double-track decision was an essential prerequisite, so to speak, for developments that eventually led to the reunification of Germany?*

S: Yes, *one* of the essential prerequisites. And Gorbachev is of that opinion as well.

A: *You asked Gorbachev, who came to power in 1985, who it was in Moscow who had suggested the idea of total bilateral disarmament in the East and the West. Gorbachev explained that he himself had suggested it, after countless analyses had made clear to him that Moscow was defenseless against Pershing missiles, and had gotten itself into a "jam." He knew, he said, that it was you who had suggested the double-zero-arms control option. He also said he wanted to write a book on disarmament, on the "agony of the regime," for it also had become clear to him that the attempt to engage in a kind of battle with the entire world, both ideologically and in the arms arena, was doomed to failure. As the initiator of the NATO double-track decision, you must feel deep satisfaction when you read that.*

S: But that's not important to me today.

A: *Did Willy Brandt view this situation in the same light?*

S: No, no. I don't think Brandt saw it that way.

A: *There were many other moments of your chancellorship of major significance to German postwar politics. I am thinking of the murder of Hanns Martin Schleyer by the RAF (Red Army Faction), for example, and how you dealt with this threat to the state. This is an undisputed fact, or do you feel differently about it when you think back on Hanns Martin Schleyer's tragic end?*

S: No, it weighed on my mind for nights at a time, because I had to consider the possibility that things would turn out as they did. I wouldn't do anything differently, looking back on it. But I sought the advice of many people at the time, and also made these advisory meetings public. That is one mistake Kohl is making at the moment,

Federal President Walter Scheel receives Chancellor Schmidt's second cabinet, December 15, 1976. First row from left: Egon Franke, Georg Leber, Scheel, Schmidt, Hans-Dietrich Genscher, Hans Apel, Hans Matthöfer. Second row, from left: Helmut Rohde, Karl Ravens, Antje Huber, Kurt Gscheidle, Josef Ertl, Marie Schlei, Werner Maihofer, Herbert Ehrenberg, Hans Friedrichs, Hans-Jochen Vogel.

Federal President Karl Carstens with Chancellor Schmidt's third cabinet, November 5, 1980. From left: Carstens, Schmidt, Dieter Haack, Egon Franke, Count Otto Lambsdorff, Rainer Offergeld, Volker Hauff, Antje Huber, Jürgen Schmude, Hans-Jochen Vogel, Hans-Dietrich Genscher, Herbert Ehrenberg, Josef Ertl, Hans Matthöfer. (Not pictured: Gerhard Rudolf Baum, Hans Apel, Kurt Gscheidle, and Andreas von Bülow.)

in terms of these anti-foreigner sentiments. He is not showing the German people that the entire government apparatus is engaged in ending this outrage. We handled it differently then. We made our determination very visible. We also totally included the opposition, of course; Kohl and Strauss were involved from the beginning. And the suggestions they gave were followed, though not all of them, of course. We always were in agreement, and we agreed that the authority of the state should be made visible to the German people, and to the world as well, which was inclined at the time to believe that, once again, we were on the path to some sort of insanity, similar to the Nazi era.

A: *When you think back on those you met with and what you thought of them, of Gierek,*[26] *for example, or Kadar, or Honecker, has your opinion of them changed over time?*

S: Barely. I thought Erich Honecker to be a man of insignificant intellect. Kadar, the Hungarian, on the other hand, I did not consider insignificant. He was the head of a small country, who in 1956 had made a major human and political error, and spent the next thirty years trying to learn from it, to correct it and make amends, as much as possible. My most important and valuable encounters in the sphere of foreign policy were, starting at the top, with Giscard d'Estaing and, in second place, with U.S. president Gerald Ford—who unfortunately held the office only for a brief period—and with Henry Kissinger, his secretary of state (we had known each other for decades), and with my friend George P. Shultz, who later again served for years as secretary of state under President Reagan.

A: *He belonged to your circle of confidants during your time as chancellor?*

S: He did and still does today. When I wanted to know what was going on in America and how to judge some situation, George Shultz was my most important contact. I have friends in many countries whose judgment and overall view of things I trust, whose friendship has been tested and whose trustworthiness is unquestioned.

A: *But your meeting with Honecker at that time was unavoidable. Did you wish to meet with him?*

S: I did wish to meet with him, it was part of the policy of détente. Yes, I wanted to. After all, it is not true, as many of these self-styled leftists in the SPD like to suggest, that I put an end to the policy of détente with the East.

A: *About reunification, you write in your book that you are "sure that what belongs together will grow together." But you also write:*

The representatives of a divided Germany during the conference on security and cooperation in Europe, in Helsinki, July 1975. Helmut Schmidt and Foreign Minister Hans-Dietrich Genscher; Erich Honecker and SED Politburo member Hermann Axen.

"We imagined reunification would be different." Could reunification have gone better, and why did the SPD suffer such a drastic loss at the polls in the 1990 elections, especially in the new German states?

S: Those are two different questions. To answer the first: Indeed, we should have been better able to plan with less pain the political, economic, social, and legal processes of the reunification of the two German states, with fewer sacrifices involved. And one of the worst sacrifices—which still exists as we speak, in the summer of 1993—is that in the four years since 1989 some forty percent of all jobs that existed in the GDR then, and even in 1990, have been lost.[27] That was not entirely necessary or unavoidable. The reason for the difficulties endured by the sixteen million Germans of the former GDR, the new citizens of the Federal Republic, is not just one reason, but a multitude of reasons and political mistakes as well. One political error was the regulation for the privatization of communist or state property (*Vermögensregelung*) and the establishment, questionable in a parliamentary democracy, of a trusteeship, or *Treuhand*[28], which is beyond the control of, say, the *Landtag* of Thuringia or of Saxony or of Brandenburg, or the *Bundestag*. Today I know that in the former GDR, even in the former GDR under Lothar de Maizière,[29] there were people opposed to the return of property, under the *Vermögensregelung*, to the grandchildren or the children of the sons-in-law of those people whose property originally had been expropriated. Today I know that Wolfgang Schäuble,[30] the West German who conducted the negotiations, also had quite different ideas about it, ideas he was not able to realize. So there were a series of mistakes that could have been avoided.

A: *Might there not have been even greater migration (from East to West) without the actions taken at the time?*

S: One had to expect migration in principle. I expected it in 1958, when the SPD presented the aforementioned "Germany Plan," but not with a migration of such magnitude. The magnitude of the recent migration was directly tied to unemployment to the bleak prospects for the recently unemployed.

As to the other question you asked, I don't know the answer. I don't know why in 1990 the leaders of my party acted in a way that created the impression among so many East German voters that they were not terribly enthusiastic about the reunification of the German nation.

A: *Willy Brandt, too, was quite disappointed by the election results.*

S: Yes, and rightfully so. There was little imagination in the way the Social Democratic Party of Germany approached the problems of reunification in 1990, which was the main reason for its miserable showing at the polls, particularly in the five new eastern states.

A: *In view of your concern about the latest stage of German integration, are you afraid that the reunification process could still fail?*

S: The word "fail" could be interpreted in several different ways. Germany cannot be rent apart again. But if we continue along the path we are on, Germany could sink into a moral swamp, a swamp in our conduct toward foreigners who live here, and crime in general. We've never had such a high rate of crime in Germany. We could sink into a swamp of violence between Germans and foreigners. The present recession could certainly develop into depression, if we continue as we have been. But none of this has to happen, and even if it does, that doesn't mean that reunification has failed. What it really means is that the state is not achieving what our neighbors and we ourselves can demand of it. There is a crisis of trust. I am afraid we soon will experience the lowest voter turnout since 1949, because many people are saying that there's no point in voting. Nevertheless, I would not speak of a possible "failure" of reunification. But if our leadership continues to flounder, and cannot engage the people, then we will find ourselves in a considerably dangerous situation economically and politically.

A: *Reunification is not yet completed!*

S: No, no, of course not. And it will surely take a number of years before, for example, the eastern *Länder* will create enough jobs to match the number of those that existed before or create as many jobs as existed in 1989. But I would hesitate to use the word "fail."

A: *In your new book,* Handeln für Deutschland *(Action for Germany), you ask whether a "united Germany" will have "a limited life span." You have rejected the idea that reunification could fail, but isn't "a limited life span," as you formulated it, nevertheless an expression of skepticism?*

S: Yes, one should be skeptical, if one remembers how brief the life span of the first German democracy was. It lasted from 1919 to 1930, and after that it was no longer a democracy, but a state governed by a senile president by means of emergency decrees. And if you also remember that Bismarck's German Reich existed for only a little over a half-century. In developing the domestic, economic, and social policies in the decades to come, Germans should be aware of their history, never forgetting the policy errors made in Berlin and in Germany that were the cause of the hypertrophic foreign-policy illusions developed under Wilhelm II. This was one of the several reasons for the First World War, and one of the several reasons for the destruction of Bismarck's Reich. Germans should be aware that it was the insanity of people like Hitler and Goebbels—not to forget Himmler and Göring—an insanity a great number of Germans conformed to, that caused the Second World War—that was meant to cause it, war is what Hitler wanted—and brought about the total collapse of Germany. The causes that brought Hitler to power, however, lie in the domestic-policy failures of those who wanted to support the Weimar

Republic, but failed to resist energetically enough the onset of disintegration: the onset of violence in the streets, on the one side by the SA, and on the other the Red Front *Kämpferbund* (communist militia). Such an historical overview appears necessary to me today because the present era, beginning with the sixties, has seen too much violence on the streets, with people savagely exceeding the limits of the law. At first it is only called violence against property, but then quickly becomes violence against persons and a ruthless disregard of the respect for one's fellow human beings, for one's neighbor.

A: *Could Weimar happen again? Once again we have unemployment and political apathy, and maybe also the secret wish for "a strong man," because there is so much uncertainty.*

S: Helmut Kohl, the present chancellor, really is anything but a weak man. He is a man who knows very well how to use power. He is strong enough. But the other question is whether he uses the power of government to the extent necessary, and whether his comrades-in-arms do too. I was deeply displeased by the Bad Kleinen[31] affair, for example, where ineptitude, mixed with arrogance on the part of the federal authorities, recreated a situation similar to that of the "*Spiegel* affair" thirty years ago. At that time parliament was deceived, public opinion was deceived, the chancellor, Adenauer, was deceived, and today Chancellor Kohl is possibly being deceived. But I have been equally displeased over the past twenty-five years by the growing disposition toward violence among the young, by the way in which demonstrations almost routinely turn violent, and the way the police are routinely disparaged as "bulls," as "pigs." I am also displeased by the overall picture of our judicial system, including the occasional over-ambitious federal prosecutor on the one side, and on the other, the occasional over-solicitous judge. But to this picture also belongs the widespread extent to which teachers are abdicating their educational responsibilities. Teachers' training stresses how to impart knowledge to students, their training at the least should also give strong emphasis to the need of teachers to control discipline. The degree of violence teachers tolerate in today's schools is inconceivable to people of my generation.

A: *Shouldn't that be addressed to parents as well?*

S: Correct. There seems to have been a misunderstanding all around—beginning in the sixties and culminating after 1968—as if schools, if they have an educational role at all, are to teach students to disrespect authority.

*After the successful constructive vote of no-confidence by the
CDU/CSU and FDP in the* Bundestag *on October 1, 1982, the ousted
chancellor congratulates his successor, Helmut Kohl, immediately
following Kohl's election.*

A: *You and Willy Brandt were in charge of the government then.
Aren't we all partly responsible for this development?*

S: Without a doubt. The socialist-liberal coalition and its followers are also partly responsible. But in education, the main responsibility lies, above all, with the parliaments and governments of the
individual *Länder*, for according to the Basic Law, neither the federal
government nor the *Bundestag* has any great influence there.

Unification

A: *I would like to return to Germany's unification. We cannot reverse
decisions made and directions taken in 1989/90 and 1991, but isn't
what we are now seeing economically—a forty-percent rate of unem-*

ployment in various regions of the former GDR—a sort of dog-eat-dog competition between east and west?

S: This expression, "dog-eat-dog competition," is actually a tautology. Every economic competition strives to expand the market, and therefore production, and therefore profits, and therefore the operation of one's own enterprise, while forcing the competition from that market. That is the essence of economic competition. If it becomes clear in the process that individual competitors are being pushed aside, not just slowly, but very suddenly, and have to go bankrupt, then we call it dog-eat-dog competition. Fine, let's use the expression. At present there are two separate dog-eat-dog competitions going on simultaneously, each contrary to the other; one following the collapse of the former Soviet Union and of communist positions of power in the entire eastern half of Europe, and the other in the wake of the unification of the two German states. In one of them a number of East German manufacturers, who until 1989 or 1990 were part of a centralized, planned communist economy, were forced to close down, because up until then they were guaranteed a market for their products, just as they were guaranteed delivery of the raw materials they required. Those businesses today face competition from the open market, and they cannot keep up—and their products are no longer marketable. The outstanding example of this is the *Trabant*, the passenger car manufactured in the GDR. Once the new federal states in the east were introduced to the Deutsche Mark and to free trade, it soon became apparent that no one wanted to buy this antediluvian automobile. East Germans had to wait years for an allotment to buy a *Trabant*, and now no one wanted to buy one, it was eliminated from the market by used cars from the west. These used cars were already two, three, four years old, but they nevertheless were better than the *Trabant*, and cheaper to boot. "Trabi" production ceased, and those workers lost their jobs. One can take this as an outstanding example of the so-called dog-eat-dog competition which West German industries won at the cost of former East German industries.

At the same time there is something completely different going on: A sector of Czech industry, a sector of Polish industry, sectors of industry in other parts of Eastern Europe are in the process of undercutting the prices of Western European industry, and how are they doing that? They can do it because production costs, particularly wages and incidental labor costs, are much lower in Eastern Europe than in Western Europe. And that in turn causes a defensive reaction here in the West. What the West would like to do—which would be catastrophic for the Poles and the Czechs—is to strengthen the borders, the trade borders of the European Community, to turn them into a fortress. That would be bad, the totally wrong thing. But this dog-eat-dog competition from Eastern Europe, at a cost to Western European industry, provides at the same time the key to understanding the dog-eat-dog competition waged by German industry in the west at the cost of German industry in the east, i.e., production costs, in particular, wages and incidental labor costs. The fact that within a very brief period of time East German factory and office workers were given equal wages and the same social benefits as western workers required that they pay the same social contributions. And this is one of the primary reasons for the so-called dog-eat-dog competition that led to such high unemployment in East Germany.

A: *Aren't there any political or social reasons for controlling these devastating consequences?*

S: We've missed that chance. It was something the Bonn coalition under Helmut Kohl did not foresee, and they missed their chance. It was crucial that wages rise only gradually in eastern Germany. And the unions made a grave mistake in this context. Talking about the solidarity pact—this agreement should have been one of the major components of a solidarity pact. The so-called solidarity pact, first, came much too late, and second, was restricted to the sixteen *Länder* governments and the federal government. It is a caricature of what was actually needed, namely that West German employers and enterprises and West German unions act in solidarity with their East German brothers. Is that clear enough?

A: *Yes, very clear. Could reunification have come at an earlier date?*

S: I am convinced neither the Soviet leadership under Brezhnev nor under either of his successors, Andropov or Chernenko, would have permitted reunification of the two German states. Even had any of the Soviet general secretaries wanted it, he would not have been strong enough to win out over the Soviet power structure, for whom reunification was an anathema. It took the collapse of the Moscow power structure, in addition to Gorbachev's idealistic visions, for reunification actually to happen. And certainly before that it called for Warsaw, Budapest, Prague, and other capitals to arrive at the conviction that this communist power structure was evil. It called for the will to freedom, within Russia as well, as embodied, for example, by Sakharov. People like Sakharov and Havel and Walesa are symbols for what we attempted to set in motion in 1975—successfully, as we now know—with the Helsinki agreement, with the Conference

With Soviet state and party chief Leonid Brezhnev in the chancellor's office during Brezhnev's state visit to Bonn in November 1981.

on Security and Cooperation in Europe—a movement for the individual's right to freedom. Without this freedom movement, without the human rights movement or the peace movement or Charta 77—the names have changed—or the Solidarity movement in Eastern Europe, there would have been no chance for reunification, even in 1989. There were many factors in play. Anyone who maintains that reunification would have been possible ten years earlier is a wild dreamer.

A: *You didn't mention Stalin's note of March 1952.*[32] *Is it your opinion that the opportunity did not exist at that time for a reunification of divided Germany?*

S: This is a German discussion that will never end. You have to view Stalin's global policies through a global perspective. You have to

look at Stalin's strategy through his eyes. To him, everything was
global strategy. That was the time of the first war in Korea; it was the
beginning of the Cold War. To believe that Stalin was afraid of the
Cold War and therefore would have agreed to a development that
would have led to German reunification is, to me, an unlikely proposition. But this eternal German discussion about Stalin's note of
March 1952 is something I no longer want to pursue.

A: *Germans are also discussing how to deal with people who
worked in the past for SED (East German Communist) state agencies
or the secret police and for those who, for purely humanitarian reasons, kept up contacts (with the communists). I'm thinking, for
instance, of the Protestant Church, or of those lawyers who tried to
do the best they could to help people under conditions dictated by
the division of Germany. Even Manfred Stolpe, who was repeatedly in
the spotlight, had dealings with the state when the SED was in
power.[33] You call him a friend. What do you say about the public discussions on him and his behavior at the time?*

S: I have called Stolpe my friend and I stand by that. Next to
Bonn's permanent representatives in the GDR, Stolpe was, particularly
following my years in office, my most important source of information on the situation of Germans living in the GDR at that time. In
addition, after I left office in 1982, I regularly—almost every year—
lectured in the GDR, always organized and prepared by Stolpe. These
lectures were held in large churches or in church premises, they were
church events. I am sure the secret service and other GDR authorities
planted their spies there to report on what I had said, and what I said
was never particularly favorable toward the gentlemen in East Berlin.
But it would have been difficult for them to interfere with Helmut
Schmidt, and surely they knew it was Stolpe who had organized
everything. So to me, Stolpe is a man you can depend on. I feel only
disdain for those in the west who are attacking him; people who were
in no danger themselves shouldn't presume to judge the mote in his
eye. I can understand former East Germans who criticize him, just as
I can understand those in the anti-Nazi resistance movement who
criticized those of us who as soldiers at the time carried out the orders
we were given, and criticized our superiors for carrying out orders
they received from their superiors. Stolpe is a man I would compare
with those officer of the Second World War who obeyed their orders
by day while actively planning to overthrow Hitler. I don't mean to
elevate Stolpe here to an armed resistance fighter, and I don't want to
compare him to Stauffenberg,[34] but given the psychological and polit-

ical situation, he was an outstanding example of someone who did what he couldn't avoid doing in view of the power system at the time, and, on the other hand, had the courage to help many, many people suffering under that system, all the while keeping his commitment to freedom untarnished.

But to return to your question about people who worked for the power structure of the GDR authorities, in government, or in the politburo, on one of those two tracks, state or party. I have a very simple take on that. Anyone who broke the laws as they existed then belongs before a judge, but that person cannot be convicted by laws that did not apply to the GDR. He cannot be judged according to laws valid in the Federal Republic at the time. Nor do I believe he should be judged according to the principles that applied to the Nuremberg trials, as established by the Allies. I am, if you will, very conservative on this point. Basically, I was very glad that Erich Honecker was allowed to escape to Chile, regardless of how the details were arranged.

A: *But then it is difficult to prosecute those soldiers who shot people trying to escape over the Berlin Wall.*

S: I was outraged that one of the first things to happen was the criminal prosecution of those little guys, the lowest in the chain of command. I found that very unfortunate.

A: *"Action for Germany," you write in your book of the same title, "also means understanding Germany's role as a medium-sized power in global affairs, and carrying out that role in a rational manner." We now are experiencing a global increase in regional conflicts, right next door as it were, for instance the conflict in the Balkans. Because in this case Germany at an early stage supported the recognition of the Slovenes and Croats striving for independence and indeed managed to accomplish it. Americans such as Secretary of State Warren Christopher are accusing Germans of being partly responsible for the escalation in the war. What is your opinion on this?*

S: The Americans stumbled into the Balkans with the idea that they could clean up the situation—encouraged by their temporary success against Iraq in the Middle East. They thought they could set things straight in Somalia as well. I very much doubt they'll feel that way the next time things start up in Kosovo, or between Georgia and Russia. And now, in terms of the Balkans, they don't want to take full responsibility for the collapse of illusions concerning their ability to set things straight, and so they're looking around for someone to share the blame with. I found it most unfortunate at the time that

The former chancellor, after delivering a speech to the General Assembly as representative to the Bundestag, June 1983.

Genscher, while still foreign minister, prematurely pushed for the recognition of Croatia. Genscher must have known that if it came to a Serbo-Croatian conflict he would not have the troops to help Croatia.

A: *He was trying to defend the right of self-determination of the Croatian people by pushing for international recognition.*

S: Yes, but once the state of Croatia was recognized, and the state of Serbia attacked the state of Croatia, which had been recognized internationally, then he was helpless, then he didn't know what to do. He should have foreseen that. I found that most unfortunate at the time. Not to mention, of course, that it called up memories that others—and not only in the Balkans—had of the collaboration between Croatians and Germans in the time of "Adolf Nazi." The entire Western world, if it retained some bit of history in the back of its head, would realize that the only time there has been peace in the Balkans was when Turkey had a major part of it under its iron thumb, and the Austro-Hungarian monarchy had the other part under its thumb— not so severely perhaps, but under its thumb nevertheless. And that later there was peace only because Tito was holding the lid on with a huge army that had sworn its allegiance to him, and a secret police apparatus, and an iron thumb, and besides which, they were afraid they would be attacked by the Soviet Union.

Keeping all of that in mind, you come to the conclusion that of course one should employ diplomacy and everything else possible to keep the peace, but if that doesn't work and they start shooting at each other anyway, and you want to end the shooting, then you'll have to send in exactly as many soldiers as Tito had, let's say several hundred thousand, and you'll have to supply replacements for them as well, because they'll have to be given leave now and then, so that they can go home and see their wives and conceive children. And then you need appropriate logistical support for these troops, and if you don't think you have all of that—and the West doesn't have all of that, nor can it assume that public opinion would support it—then you should stay away from such ventures. The governments in London and Paris realize this, apparently they have a better knowledge of history than does our new Foreign Minister Kinkel, and much better than President Clinton. On top of which, just as a certain affinity exists between Germans and Croatia, the Second World War also created affinities between the French and the Serbs, the English and the Serbs, and, going much further back, there is the affinity between the Serbs and the Russians. And that is much more difficult than Herr Kinkel imagines. It seems that the new men in Bonn and in Washington lack experience, and in the next twelve months Secretary of State Christopher must either get others to accept his misgivings, or he'll have to go. I know Christopher quite well, he's essentially a very cautious man.

A: *Isn't it a sad sign that it required the kind of force that Tito exercised to hold together Yugoslavia, a state created by the victors of the First World War?*

S: It was an artificial state, an artificial construct that the victorious powers hammered out in their treaties on the outskirts of Paris in 1919. An artificial construct can be held together only with force. Bismarck was not able to create a lasting peace either at his Berlin Congress in 1878, and he knew it. I think his expression, that peace in the Balkans was "not worth the bones of one single Pomeranian grenadier," originated at that time. But I learned that at school, Herr

Appel, and who today learns history at school? Who of our many *Bundestag* representatives knows anything about the Berlin Balkan Congress of 1878? They don't learn history any more at school, and perhaps they themselves don't read enough. And those are important prerequisites for leading a country located, with its eighty million people, in the middle of Europe, a country now charged with joint accountability. The bad thing about it is that these eighty million Germans are causing a great deal of concern among their neighbors, not publicly, but in secret. We have twice the population of Poland, Poland has forty million people, five times that of the Netherlands, and I don't know how many times the number of Czechs, and probably one and a half times the number of French, or English, or Italians. That's why an alliance with France is of such major importance, more important now than before reunification, and that's also why the European Community is so important. But when I look at the Constitutional Court, which will soon hear a complaint that the Maastricht Treaty violates Germany's Basic Law. I realize how provincial many of those are who wish to have a say here in Germany.

A: *But developments in Europe—which, with the Maastricht Treaty, even after reunification, intended quite consciously to tie Germany into the European Community—appear more and more stalled. The home markets, for which we entertained such hopes for an economic upswing, isn't advancing.*

S: No, not "entertained," those hopes were awakened by government propaganda! In reality, the Common Market has continued to move ahead gradually since the time of the Schuman Plan; it would continue to develop even without the Maastricht Treaty. The Maastricht Treaty is one of the worst international instruments I have ever read. It contains important matters, with totally unimportant ones right next to them. It's total chaos, total confusion. The governments haven't paid sufficient attention, they've allowed the bureaucrats to throw in all kinds of things. Then, right at the end, they included even more lofty measures. Kohl deserves credit for proposing a single currency bank and a single currency. But in terms of a common foreign and defense policy, and political union and I don't know what all else, all of that was thrown into the treaty at the very end. No, it's not a good treaty. The Germans did not crown themselves with glory on that one.

A: *But the commitment to give up national sovereignty in favor of Europe, provided for in our constitution as far back as 1949, or to give up national currencies, that is to say the deliberate economic* and monetary unification of Europe—those were conscious goals of German policy. Should they be criticized?

S: No, to the contrary. I, together with Giscard d'Estaing, invented this system of European currency so we can create a monetary community later. But at the time I didn't advertise this future plan.

A: *Are things moving backward rather than forward in Europe?*

S: Yes, unfortunately.

A: *Might the Maastricht Treaty cause the Deutsch Mark to slip, and with that set off an anti-European sentiment? The German mark, after all, is viewed by many as the expression of our hard work and our competence. Which brings up the question: Could other members of the European Community, who perhaps aren't so hardworking, water down our currency?*

S: Of course, there are many who fall for these and other catch phrases which, incidentally, some people in top positions at the *Bundesbank* have been subtly suggesting. The Germans, now and for some years in the past, have been among the less hardworking nations of Europe. Things were going so well for us that we didn't need to work hard, believing that hard work was no longer necessary. Since reunification a good deal of hard work has once again become necessary for the years ahead of us. Nothing is just going to drop into our lap in the years to come. The Deutsche Mark was made into an artificial symbol of Germany; for some it took the place of the national anthem or the Kaiser. The Deutsche Mark is a sensitive instrument; it can be ruined by the wrong financial policies in Bonn, and that is what we are seeing at present. We now have an annual inflation rate of four percent; it has hovered around that for quite some time now. And that is worse for the Deutsche Mark than whatever financial-policy actions the governments of the European Community might jointly undertake or not undertake. The Deutsche Mark could be ruined by excessive demands on our social security system. Talk to the effect that areas of weaker economic development and areas of stronger economic development cannot be served by one and the same currency is false. The creation of a currency union is difficult nevertheless, and there are specific interests in some organizations, and specific people within these organizations, who are opposed to the idea. Not one of the eleven central-bank presidents of Europe has any interest in giving up his own bank, or in transforming it into a branch of the European Central Bank. And the same is true of the executive committee of each central bank, etc., and true of the individual governments, which, for their part, essentially control monetary policy. That is true in England, and it has always been the case in France up to the present time, though Prime Minister Balladur has announced that in the future there should be an autonomous French central bank. In actuality, monetary policy in France, in England, and in Italy as well is not in the hands of the central bank, but in the hands of the government, and that's why it's so bad. Our monetary policy over the last forty-five years has been so successful because politicians had no say in it. Because the *Bundesbank* was autonomous. The decisive point concerning a European currency union is that the European Central Bank should be autonomous, as autonomous as the *Bundesbank*!

A: *The Bonn government, heading a unified Germany with greater international and global responsibilities, is seeking a seat on the United Nations Security Council. Is this the right time?*

S: I view that as inflated ambition and an inflated need for prestige. So far a very limited number of countries have had a permanent seat on the Security Council, and those are the countries that possess their own nuclear weapons. If other major and important countries now wish to, or should, have a seat on the council, then the first country one should consider is the mammoth state of India, which is a bit larger and more important, for Asia at least, than is Germany. Then one should consider Nigeria, Brazil, Japan. If all of them are to be considered for permanent seats on the Security Council, then why not Germany too? But for Germany alone to be striving for a seat is something I find pompous, and not at all necessary at present. We have been able to represent our own security interests and our foreign-policy interests relatively well without being a member of the United Nations Security Council.

A: *Even though the United Nations expects us to contribute financially to the settling of world conflicts and even militarily?*

S: That is another matter entirely. Our financial contributions are totally separate, whether or not we are members of the Security Council, nor can others decide what we have to contribute, whether or not we should send troops to Somalia—that is our decision alone. The Japanese, for example, contribute a very large sum to the United Nations without being members of the Security Council. Any number of smaller states participate, or have participated, in the "blue-helmet operations" and they would never dream of laying claim to a permanent seat on the Security Council. German policy should not be allowed to dissipate itself, either in the direction of the United Nations or in the direction of Eastern Europe. It must not presume to act as the bridge to Russia; rather, it is most important that Germany anchor itself in the European Community. The most important thing is our relations with France and with Poland, our two most important immediate neighbors. And at the same time they are the nations with whom we have been most involved, in past generations and in past wars.

A: *You often return to the question of German identity. You have traced the restless quality of Germans, their abrupt mood swings and emotional eruptions, to a lack of identity, which also results from the division of Germany. Now that this division has ended, have we found our identity?*

S: No, we have not, because we are far from having overcome the division of Germany mentally or spiritually. Even were we to achieve full economic and social integration without additional suffering in the years to come, say in the next fifteen or twenty years, even if we succeed in that, I believe it will take two generations before the German people integrate spiritually and mentally. And that integration is desirable.

Corrupting Influence

A: *Isn't your concern about German identity and your call for greater solidarity among Germans also a political-moral issue?*

S: I recently heard former President Richard von Weizsäcker answer a similar query. A journalist commented to von Weizsäcker that as federal chancellor I had refused to exercise moral and intellectual leadership. Weizsäcker's response was that although it was true I had said that, I did in fact exercise both. I had simply declined to play the role of ideological pioneer. But I would like to believe that I hammered in quite a few moral and intellectual pegs in the many speeches I delivered to the *Bundestag* as well. And some of them brought results. When Kohl was opposition leader he was always set on the simplistic idea that the chancellor should be able to proclaim eternal truth, something he, as chancellor, hasn't been able to achieve either, of course.

A: *You lament a growing unwillingness to sacrifice, and a loss of patience, and you miss a sense of duty and solidarity.*

S: I have always attempted to make clear my fundamental moral beliefs in terms of the way people should behave toward one another and within a society—always, and certainly during the time I was federal chancellor.

A: *Who in our present society, in today's time, commands the authority to credibly pass on a sense of values?*

S: Of those in office recently, only one person, Richard von Weizsäcker.

A: *We live in a time of changing values.*

S: Yes, and television, in particular, brought that about. Television is one of the major factors in the decline of established Western moral traditions. There is no doubt about it.

A: *What do you base this on?*

S: Last night I again spent an entire hour flipping through the channels. I lost count of the number of murders and deaths and acts of violence I witnessed. There are twenty-five channels to view in Germany today, and by the end of the decade it will be two hundred, thanks to satellite technology. And what are they broadcasting? Murder, death, violence, corpses, conflagrations, catastrophes. Take a look at the evening news: crime and catastrophe. A fifteen-year-old today grows up accepting violent acts as a normal part of society. And in addition to TV, that fifteen-year-old can rent videos which confirm this, with sex thrown in to boot.

A: *You have always been very critical of television even when you were chancellor.*

S: I saw what was coming. I foresaw the deformation of European society through the medium of television. I spoke out against television, but to no avail. Now, suddenly, those in the CDU who once considered commercial television to be absolutely necessary, and who clamored for greater competition and variety and I don't know what else, are having second thoughts. It will certainly be some time yet before some degree of self-control is exercised by the networks themselves, and as for international self-control, it will never come to that. No, television is transforming all of European society.

A: *And now you yourself are the co-publisher of a newspaper, of a medium that . . .*

S: In my paper you will find no dissemination of violent acts, no pictures of women who have been violated or of children wandering the streets with an arm missing and blood pouring down their faces. You will not find that in my paper.

A: *But you do report on a world that is getting worse.*

S: Yes, true. But the danger occurs when these reports are transmitted as images, experienced by I don't know how many millions of young people as living images.

The ZDF broadcast, "Journalists Ask—Politicians Answer," April 1972. From left: Hans-Dietrich Genscher, head of the FDP; Franz Josef Strauss, head of the CSU; CDU/CSU caucus leader Rainer Barzel; SPD caucus leader Helmut Schmidt; Reinhard Appel (ZDF); Johannes Gross (Deutsche Welle); and Theo Sommer of Die Zeit.

A: *Do you believe this is one explanation for the apathy surrounding politics and politicians?*

S: No, that has nothing to do with television. That has to do with the present inadequate class of politicians. I was speaking of the moral decline of our society, which has to do with television. Television is not the only factor, but it is a major factor.

A: *A further factor being that churches no longer have the authority to transmit values and to offer direction?*

S: That the churches have lost authority was inevitable. This is the result of a gradual process going on for centuries now. It continues in the twentieth century and will probably continue into the twenty-first. It is an unfortunate fact, and it does play a role. But the churches are not entirely free of violence themselves; how many burnings at the stake, how many burnings of witches do we have behind us? You can't just ignore that. The Church's authority is waning, the authority of the schools has declined widely.

A: *And what do you see as the solution?*

S: The example that must be set by individuals, whether it be the head of a university or faculty, or the head of a school. But above all, the example that must be set by politicians, who play a leading role every day on television. I don't know how many talk shows they appear on each year.

A: *As chancellor, and as politician, you understood how to use television to your own advantage.*

S: I used television and I would do the same tomorrow. I'm not saying that television is a bad institution. I am criticizing the way it is used by some editors, producers, and owners in the industry—television and video industry—owners who are interested only in money and nothing else. If they could earn more money selling hamburgers, then they would be selling junk food. Those who exploit television irresponsibly as a business are, in my eyes, the people who should be attacked. The technology is here to stay, and will grow just like airplanes or automobiles.

A: *The dangerous growth in the number of nonvoters improves the chances for the success of the smaller parties. Could this cause the SPD to enter into further coalitions, or another Great Coalition?*

S: It could be that a Great Coalition is the only possibility left, even if it still will achieve nothing. A Great Coalition does not necessarily provide all the answers. The coalition partners could simply sink together.

A: *But all in all you gave good marks to the Great Coalition that governed from 1966 to 1969.*

S: Yes, and I would again today. It did all right in principle, but as a coalition of the two popular parties without any opposition, its existence also helped the student movement from America and France to come to Germany, where the "extra parliamentary opposition" became excessive. A Great Coalition is nothing particularly desirable. They have a Great Coalition in Switzerland, where things are easy to control. It's a small country, smaller than the state of Hesse, with Geneva and Zurich serving as the two poles. Germany isn't Switzerland, and a parliamentary democracy should have a clear ruling majority and a clear opposition minority. But if we allow ourselves the luxury of passing an election law that allows four or five or six parties into the *Bundestag*, then it could come to the point where a Great Coalition is unavoidable. That is why I was always in favor of the majority voting system.

A: *But there's no majority for that.*

S: No, of course not, otherwise a few people would be out of work. The FDP would say that majority vote would endanger all that is sacred to the Western world, which is false. The liberals in England have survived, despite a quite explicit majority voting system.

A: *The SPD, FDP, and the Greens would have to join to govern without the CDU. But you said that to govern with the Greens was an absolutely abominable thought. Count Lambsdorff, on the other hand, recently stated that the Greens had transformed themselves into a democratic party.*

S: My skepticism concerning the Greens is that their motivation concerns a single issue. They've now joined with the "Democratic Reconstruction Alliance 90," and in the meantime taken in the pacifists and a few leftist intellectuals as well. It could be that such a coalition will teach them to be more realistic, that there are other problems just as pressing as the conservation of the natural environment. Perhaps that will happen. But one thing I know for sure is that the motivation to conserve the natural environment, essentially a commendable goal, is not enough for a party that wants to govern. They need a few more goals than this one. They must also know what they intend to do about taxes, and the budget, and foreign policy and defense. They must also know what they want to do about the rise in crime in Germany. It's not enough to say at every opportunity, "But where are the women, where is the protection of the environment?" That is what concerns me. And there are certain types of politicians among the Greens who don't exactly arouse in me the feeling that they are capable of making dependable judgments in areas outside the protection of nature and the environment.

A: *If we were to hold a popular election for chancellor today, judging by the polls, you might win a great majority, far beyond the SPD constituency. What is the first thing you would do as chancellor, now, today?*

S: First, let's disregard the role I would play in this; I'm too old for any major role. But what our country needs now is a different government, different people, people who have not become imprisoned by their own actions, who cannot easily disown their own earlier statements, positions, and points of view. A new government would have a great many things to tend to. Once having conferred among themselves they would have to establish a roundtable on pressing economic and social issues, and come to a consensus on them. Nothing is more ridiculous than this spectacle with the pompous and misleading name "solidarity pact." Who is in solidarity with whom? The governments of sixteen *Länder* and the federal government were at the table, but management wasn't there and the unions weren't there, and their solidarity is necessary. The back-and-forth between the *Länder* and the federal government over a few percentage points had a negative effect. The banks, the employers' associations, and representatives of the trades weren't at the table, nor were representatives of the community, nor the *Bundesbank*. That wasn't a solidarity pact, that was self-deception.

And then a totally different task would be to stop the stream of foreigners pouring into Germany. That is something that cannot continue. No matter how idealistic you are, if every year three-quarters of a million foreigners stream into Germany, it can only lead to violence and murder, for there are neither living quarters for them, nor jobs.

Yet another task in another area would be to inform public opinion, and the thinking of employers and the unions, that, for the time being, instead of dividing up future gains in income and profits, we must now think about how to share our burdens fairly.

And then there is the task of making it clear to the above group that unemployment figures will not go down in the long run unless we totally reorient ourselves, unless we change the amount of money we allot for applied research and its application to industrial development, production, and world sales, and therewith create more jobs. Anyone now can produce steel, anyone now can build ships. German ships are too expensive because their price includes inflated wages and incidental labor costs. German steel is too expensive. Much of what Germans have manufactured in the past can be produced in many developing countries, in East Asia, for example, for much less than we produce it. And the Hungarians and the Czechs and the Poles, in the meantime, can manufacture these goods for much less than the East Asians. We're not going to succeed against this competition. We need new products that the others cannot yet produce themselves. If we are to maintain our very high standard of living, then we must be more open.

Another task is education. We just spoke of television, we could just as well have been talking about our schools or universities. The laxity with which German universities are run today will not bring progress. Anyone can study here for as long as he wishes; there are no interim examinations or qualifying examinations, anyone can just slack off at the taxpayers' expense. Young people's education is being grossly neglected. In many families television has taken over the role of educator. Parents and children can't talk to each other because one of them is sitting in the basement watching one station while the other is upstairs watching another. Who still reads books? How many representatives of the government are there who have read Kant or Bebel? Germany is in a deplorable state because necessary truths are not being voiced.

A: *Our economy also seems to be in a questionable state. People are talking about the severest challenge of the postwar period; on top of which the Deutsch Mark, which has never been encroached upon, is being tested. Germany's position seems threatened, the economic measures that the government came up with set off an incendiary domestic debate; and then there is the crisis of reunification, which could turn out to be the greatest challenge of the postwar era. Can we meet this challenge?*

S: Yes, certainly we can meet it. But for that we need decisive leaders, leaders who know how to separate the important problems from the unimportant and the totally unimportant, and who then turn their attention to the important problems and lead the German people to solving these important problems together. Without leadership nothing will happen. Germany at present is without leadership, but it is not the only country in Europe that lacks leadership. That, unfortunately, is true as well of England and of Italy. Perhaps France now has more of a leader in Balladur than it has had in the past few years, I don't know. But the lack of leadership in these three major countries—Italy, England, and Germany—is a calamity.

Notes

1. *Die Welt*, July 28, 1962.

2. Jonathan Carr, *Helmut Schmidt: Helmsman of Germany* (New York: St. Martin's Press, 1985).

3. Helmut Schmidt's reputation for his combativeness and pugnacious way of always telling people off earned him the name *Schmidt-"Schnauze"*—roughly "Schmidt the Lip"—since his early days in the SPD. Later, as chancellor, his style mellowed and he became known more as the *"Macher"* (doer) than the "Lip."

4. NATO in December 1979 decided to deploy 572 new intermediate-range nuclear warheads in West Germany, the United Kingdom, and at least one other continental NATO country (the first track), unless the Soviet Union agreed to remove its SS-20 missiles in negotiations (the Schmidt-inspired second track) to be begun simultaneously with U.S. deployment.

5. Emergency Powers Act, see Note 6 in Chapter 4, p. 260.

6.   Klaus Kinkel, federal foreign minister.

7.   The Maastricht Treaty was signed by the twelve member nations of the European Union in December 1991 with the aim of extending the Union's political and economic powers, and providing for a common European currency beginning in 1997. Despite some difficulties in several countries, the agreement has now been ratified by all member states.

8.   The *Solidarpakt* is an agreement reached in March 1993 by the government coalition partners (the CDU/CSU and the FDP), the individual states, and organizations representing industry and labor to finance economic reconstruction in the eastern states of what used to be the German Democratic Republic. The accord shifts the way federal funds are allotted in favor of the newly joined states and places a 7.5-percent surtax on all salaries and wages to be used for reconstruction in these eastern states.

9.   Ernst Reuter, mayor of Berlin from 1948 to 1953.

10. Erich Ollenhauer, SPD chairman from 1952 to 1953.

11. Franz Barsig, journalist, speaker of the SPD executive committee.

12. Kurt Mattick, local SPD chairman in Berlin.

13. Kurt Wehner in his speech signaled the SPD's readiness to find a bipartisan approach in foreign policy with Adenauer by acknowledging the Atlantic Alliance and NATO without reservations; by abandoning its demands for the departure of the Federal Republic from NATO; by accepting the need for defense financing; and by confirming the SPD's unwavering commitment to the right of the Germans to determine for themselves their destiny as a unified nation.

14. Helmut Schmidt, *Handeln für Deutschland* (Action for Germany) (Berlin: Rowohlt, 1993).

15. The Western Allies in the General Treaty reserved all emergency powers necessary to ensure the safety of their troops deployed in Germany—a significant limitation to domestic German sovereignty to which German negotiators in 1954 agreed only to achieve West Germany's equal status and the right to join NATO. Adenauer's political opponents argued these Allied powers could override German police authority and allow them to do virtually anything they wished in the name of ensuring their troops' safety. After much debate, the *Bundestag* in 1968 amended the Basic Law to turn responsibility for the safety of Allied troops over to German authorities.

16. *Innere Führung* (inner leadership) denotes a principle adopted by the *Bundeswehr* for its armed forces to act as "civilians in uniform" by basing military training on the democratic values enshrined in the Basic Law.

17. Adolf Arndt, manager of the SPD *Bundestag* caucus from 1949 to 1961. Municipal minister for science and the arts in Berlin from 1961 to 1963.

18. Georg Kliesing, prominent *Bundestag* member since 1953.

19. Plisch and Plum were two characters in the enormously popular Wilhelm Busch comic-strip story of the same name published in 1888.

20. Franz Josef Strauss, CSU, was minister of finance, and Karl Schiller, SPD, was economics minister in the Kiesinger-Brandt coalition cabinet.

21. Markus Wolf ran East Germany's foreign espionage network for thirty-three years, gaining the reputation of a spy master who infiltrated agents into the

highest echelons of Western power, including NATO headquarters and Brandt's office. In 1993 he was sentenced to a six-year jail term for treason by a Düsseldorf court, but the German Supreme Court ruled in 1995 that he cannot be held accountable under the West German law.

22. Gustav Noske, as Socialist minister in Germany's post–World War I cabinet from 1918 to 1920, was held responsible when government troops fired on rebellious workers in street clashes and was forced to resign.

23. Brigitte Seebacher-Brandt *Die Linke und die Einheit* (The Left and Unity) (Berlin: Siedler, 1991).

24. Extremist decree, see Note 6 in Chapter 4, p. 260.

25. Count Otto von Lambsdorff, FDP, federal minister of economics.

26. Edward Gierek, general secretary of the Polish Communist Party; Janos Kadar, secretary general of the communist Hungarian Socialist Workers party, from 1956 to 1988, after having been arrested in 1951 and rehabilitated two years later.

27. Two years after Schmidt cited these figures in his interview the labor statistics in eastern Germany had shown little improvement. The Statistical Office reported an unemployment rate of 15.5 percent for February 1995, compared with 15.8 percent two years earlier. In the western part of Germany, where unemployment had been 7.3 percent in 1993, the figure went up to 8.8 percent at the beginning of 1995.

28. The *Treuhand* (trustee administration) was established at the end of 1990 for a period of four years to privatize the planned economy of the former GDR and lay the foundation for the renewal and modernization of the eastern German economy. In the four years of its existence, the *Treuhand* privatized some 14,000 enterprises, about 98 percent of what it had inherited. About 190 large and medium-sized businesses were closed, and 3,340 liquidated.

29. Lothar de Maiziere, CDU, became the prime minister in the first free elections held in eastern Germany on April 9, 1990. After unification he became deputy chairman of the CDU. Since then, after charges surfaced that he collaborated with the communist secret police, he has left politics.

30. Wolfgang Schäuble, since 1991 chairman of the CDU/CSU caucus in the *Bundestag*.

31. The railroad station of Bad Kleinen, a small town in the state of Mecklenburg, was the scene of a spectacular shoot-out between Red Army Faction terrorists and police in June 1993, ending in the death of a policeman and a terrorist. Interior Minister Rudolf Seiters had to resign because of charges that the police had bungled the action.

32. On March 10, 1952, a Soviet note to the Western powers proposed a peace treaty with a reunified Germany from which all foreign forces have been withdrawn, and which would permit "free activity of domestic parties and organizations," grant amnesty to all former Nazis, keep Germany neutral, and allow Germany its own national armed forces. The note come in response to the decision of the Western Allies to sign the General Treaty with West Germany, which in effect made Bonn a partner in a common European security system. Adenauer, not believing reunification was possible on acceptable terms and fearing a complete U.S. withdrawal from Europe, was hostile to the proposal,

and the West declined to discuss it. Just what Stalin really meant by his "peace offensive" has remained a question over which historians have been puzzling ever since.

33.   Manfred Stolpe, SPD, minister-president of the formerly communist state of Brandenburg in October 1990, which is governed by the only coalition in Germany comprising the SPD, the FDP, and the Greens. Before unification, as an official of the Evangelical Church of Berlin-Brandenburg, he had been responsible for "humanitarian" questions—a euphemism for matters dealing with the legal emigration of GDR citizens to West Germany. Though his opponents acknowledge the need for Stolpe to have had contacts with the communist secret police to help people leave the country, they claim these had been unnecessarily friendly. An investigation by a parliamentary committee has since cleared Stolpe of all charges.

34.   Colonel Claus Count von Stauffenberg, would-be assassin of Hitler. See Note 12 in Chapter 2, page 138.

[Top] *At a CDU election campaign meeting in Bochum, 1983 — The chancellor during his state of the nation address on November 8, 1989 — In his study, 1989 — With chancellery chief of staff Rudolf Seiters, 1991.*
[Center] *Erich Honecker's state visit in Bonn, September 1987 — Celebrating on the evening of Germany's unity before the* Reichstag *in Berlin, with Willy Brandt, Hans-Dietrich Genscher, Kohl's wife Hannelore, Richard von*

Weizsäcker, and Lothar de Maiziere.
[Bottom] *With Ronald Reagan in Bitburg, May 1985 — At the breakthrough meeting of German unity in the Caucasus, July 1990, with Mikhail Gorbachev and Hans-Dietrich Genscher; behind them, Raisa Gorbachev, Theo Waigel, and Hans Klein, among others — With François Mitterand on the battlefield of Verdun, 1984.*

1930	Born April 3 in Ludwigshafen.
1946	Joins Christian Democratic Union.
1947	Co-founder of the *Junge Union* (CDU youth organization) while in high school.
1950–1956	Attends universities in Frankfurt and Heidelberg, studying history, law, and political science.
1954–1961	Deputy chairman of *Junge Union* of Rhineland-Palatinate.
1955–1966	Member of executive committee of the Rhineland-Palatinate CDU.
1956–1958	Research assistant at Alfred Weber Institute of University of Heidelberg.
1958	Awarded Ph.D.
	Assistant director of Mock foundry in Ludwigshafen.
1959–1969	Advisor to Federation of Chemical Industries, Ludwigshafen.
1959–1976	Elected member of Rhineland-Palatinate *Landtag* (state assembly) in Mainz.
1960	Marries Hannelore Renner, with whom he will have two sons.
1963–1969	CDU caucus leader in *Landtag* of Rhineland-Palatinate.
1966–1974	Minister-president of Rhineland-Palatinate.
1973–present	National chairman of Christian Democratic Union.
1975	As CDU chancellorial candidate, loses election to Helmut Schmidt.
1976–1982	Chairman of CDU/CSU caucus in the *Bundestag*.
1982–present	Federal chancellor.

6

Helmut Kohl

by Oskar Fehrenbach

Helmut Kohl, starting out in an era of change, arrived at the high point of his life just as that era came to an end and a new one began. Anyone attempting to define Kohl's political role must consider above all that he is the chancellor of two distinct epochs of world history. And because of this there is a fundamental difference between his biography and those of his predecessors. A line drawn in history in 1989/1990 divides his time in office, and signifies one of the most momentous fissures of our century, far and away the most significant since the end of the Second World War. Nothing remains as it was before. A more sober mood has followed the elation of reunification. A new phase of global confusion has followed the end of the Cold War. What first appeared simple has proven difficult.

At first it seemed that history had exhausted all its possibilities. There was talk that capitalism had "triumphed" over socialism. So it was not surprising that American author Francis Fukuyama stirred interest with his thesis that the end of history had arrived. Only liberal democracy would survive, he wrote; other alternatives, other political systems, were untenable. The only question remaining concerned that of the internal and self-generated weaknesses of our open society. But "history"—in one of its more bitter lessons—has in the meantime taken its revenge, as it were, for all of the unresolved problems obscured or repressed by the confrontations of the Cold War. This time history's message was that there is no end in sight. Let no one believe he knows what will occur after this new historical era.

The epoch marked by the Cold War is over. It now belongs to history, and therefore to the past. It returned to Germans the unity they lost together with the Second World War, and at the same time confronted them with the historical task of finding a new identity against the backdrop of an increasingly imponderable world order. But like many other European countries, Germany, too, has been overtaken by its own history. The crisis, in Kohl's words, is: "We have been living beyond our means." It is not only the burdens of reunification that are troublesome; problems long neglected in the former Federal Republic now clamor for attention. The blessings of the welfare state, recklessly enjoyed by the Germans—the world's highest-paid champion whiners with the longest paid vacations and the highest sick-day absences—must now be reclaimed one by one. The state must economize at every turn. But the economy must be revived at the same time, and innovative structures developed—a Sisyphean task with little chance of instant success.

This turning point has raised for all involved a plethora of old and new questions, new risks and problems of adjustment. No country—and Germany least of all—could simply go on from where its past history stopped. And no chancellor, Kohl included, could have prevented the crisis of adjustment that emerged from the pain of reunification and the fundamental changes occurring in all of Europe.

Any evaluation of Helmut Kohl's chancellorship must therefore be full of ambivalence: How serious is the crisis of confidence that holds the party state in its grip? Is there a crisis of democracy as well? How serious and long-lasting are the economic, financial, and psychological burdens with which the state has been encumbered? How is right-wing extremism to be overcome? How long is the path that leads back to normality, or are the social-structural deformations of Germany as it has evolved of an enduring nature? How much time will it take for the Federal Republic to clarify its foreign-policy role, secure it constitutionally, and position it on the solid ground of political consensus? Will Germany remain an incomplete, immature nation? Will Schiller's words from *Xenien* prove true of the German people: "The century has given birth to a great epoch. But the great moment finds a small people"?

No one can simply erase the doubt. How much time remains for the chancellor of reunification to complete his life's work? Kohl has accomplished the extraordinary, there can be no doubt about that. But what has been accomplished thus far needs time to mature, needs to overcome unanticipated obstacles and misjudgments and a lack of solidarity. Kohl was so brilliantly successful in setting the reunification process in motion that even his most hard-boiled critics like Rudolf Augstein, publisher of *Spiegel*, and *Zeit* co-publisher Theo Sommer have humbly acknowledged his statesmanship qualities. But it is yet too soon to deliver a final judgment.

There can be no doubt, however, that Kohl has contributed decisively in giving a new dimension to European integration, one that will extend far into the next century. And yet optimism about a common Europe has receded, if not for Kohl himself then for broad sections of German society. There is uncertainty that the growing reservations about, and resistance to, the process of European unification can be overcome without major loss of time and substance.

As long as such questions remain open, a comprehensive and conclusive appreciation of Kohl's entire term of office will be impossible. It might even be premature at this time to admit him to the gallery of honor of Germany's postwar chancellors. Yet the true qualities of the others in whose distinguished company he would find himself can hardly be understood without reference to the "Kohl era," for all the historical tracks of the German postwar period lead there. All that was accomplished or left undone in those years must now be measured against the achievement of German unification—an event which, like a concave mirror, has gathered in its focus all that happened under the general heading of "German postwar politics" and is reflecting them now with enhanced intensity. Without an appreciation of Helmut Kohl's chancellorship some questions cannot even be posed, much less answered. But already, despite the fact that Kohl himself is still being tested, certain conclusions seem unavoidable.

The sudden collapse of the Soviet empire and the end of the Cold War marked the end of forty-five years of continual East-West confrontation. There is no longer any doubt that Chancellor Kohl had a significant role in these events. Reunification and its ratification by the Two-plus-Four agreement with the World War II victors finally brought the war to a close with a pact that in moment and significance is equal to a peace treaty. This achievement, too, belongs largely to Helmut Kohl (along with Foreign Minister Hans-Dietrich Genscher). Ultimately, Kohl, more than any other Western leader, must be credited with liberating the Eastern bloc from the confines of the Warsaw Pact and ending the divisions of Europe. These accomplishments— regardless of the uncertainties that lie ahead—ensure Kohl a prominent place in history, right next to Konrad Adenauer. Whatever comes, his position is secure.

The end of that first epoch, which already can lay claim to the title "the Kohl Era," signals an end to German complaisance. The world's power relations, long defined and stabilized by the polarization of the two superpowers, have been shaken. Antiquated national conflicts, dating back to the early part of this century and long believed resolved, have recrudesced. Europe has been wracked by the eruption of diverse separatist movements. From the disintegration of the Soviet Union into the Commonwealth of Independent States, to the bloody civil war in former Yugoslavia, historical conflicts swept under the rug by totalitarian terror have re-erupted in nostalgic retrospection. The recent past appears well ordered and risk-free by comparison. Berlin historian Arnulf Baring[1] has spoken of the past as a "doll's house," in contrast to the difficulties encountered today. And events may yet justify his skepticism.

But the Cold War was anything but child's play, even if it appears in retrospect as an era of confidently calculated peace. While it is true that the "balance of terror" proved an effective and increasingly calculable instrument for the prevention of war, historical revision (in which the left is a curiously active participant) should not be allowed to absorb the shock waves of memory. The Korean War, the Berlin blockade, the East German workers' rebellion, the bloody suppression of the people's revolts in Hungary and Czechoslovakia, and the Cuban missile crisis—these were authentic crises, threats to the security of the world. Their successful resolutions were far from foregone conclusions at the time.

Hushed up and forgotten as well, of course, is the fact that the easing of political tensions was possible only because it was ensured by a policy of alliances. Only under the protection of the Western powers could West Germany develop freely and almost unimpeded into the near-perfect welfare state. Wars—and this was one of the ground rules of nuclear intimidation—were ruled out.

The apparent paradox is resolved when we take into account how reality has changed. Issues today discussed with passion, without leading to domestic-policy consensus on foreign or defense-policy, were never discussed in the era of nuclear threat. Which is to say that high risk ruled out all intervention—despite flagrant violations of international law, despite brutal violations of human rights. There was no dearth of moral justification for intervention. Today, in contrast, conflicts akin to civil wars are played out below the threshold of a nuclear threat, with the result that the thought of possible intervention to create or maintain peace can no longer be simply repressed.

Such actions suggest themselves because they appear tractable. Even the Green Party no longer rules out military intervention in principle.

This shift in foreign-policy focus from the avoidance of nuclear risk to the upholding of international law coincides with the emergence in the world of an ever-increasing number of local conflicts. While wars fought across national borders remain as unlikely as before, the probability of civil war has increased. However genuine its global threats, the Cold War gave coherence to global politics. Recent history has moved from bipolar order to multipolar disorder.

The second epoch does not yet have a name or a clear outlook for the future. Nevertheless, it is bound to the first epoch in all essential aspects. The Federal Republic must work out the problems that reunification has created, and not only define but practice its increased responsibilities. The link between epochs is obvious, primarily because Helmut Kohl, simultaneously with reunification, was able to design an architecture of European policy, which in all its essential elements continues the policy of Konrad Adenauer. This policy retains the essential tenet that all issues concerning Germany can only be resolved under one common European roof. Despite the many adjustments that reunification has dictated in foreign and domestic programs, Kohl's policy—in its political orientation—calls for sustaining and continuing the political course set by Adenauer: the Atlantic Alliance, the dominance of Germany's tie to the West, the resolute continuation of European integration, the primacy of Franco-German friendship, the social market economy, and the strict rejection of a separate national course for Germany. "We are not wanderers between East and West," Kohl emphasized in the *Bundestag*. That this is no small danger can be seen in the reaction of Green Party representative Antje Vollmer: "Too bad, definitely too bad!"

This continuity between the Federal Republic's first and present chancellors signifies anything but a repudiation of the past. Rather, it reflects the premise that Germany can overcome the false paths it has taken and the transgressions it has committed only if it learns their lessons for the future. Kohl's concept, like Adenauer's, is based on the idea that the commitment after World War II to a united Europe is irreversible. The new constellation brought by the recent years of change has not called this commitment into question; if anything it has confirmed it. This means that what has been achieved so far will be made more secure in an area that has become more unstable.

That was more than enough reason for the "chancellor of unity" to run for office again in 1994, to face the challenge of the ballot box again, and not to rest on his laurels. It was a battle for the continuation of the liberal-conservative alliance, while taking into account that an "election victory" as the strongest party would have left the CDU with alternative options. Only a liaison with the radical right was totally out of the question.

Reunification was one thing, a stroke of luck if you wish, but the consolidation of Germany's position within Europe, with irreversibility a given, is another. How long this will take is as difficult to calculate as how long it will take for the standard of living between the old and new states of the Federal Republic to equalize. The fixed point of European orientation is the Maastricht Treaty, which is part and parcel of reunification. It secures a supranational roof over German unity, a commitment Kohl expressly took on with the Two-plus-Four agreement. This was worked out in agreement with France, but it serves Germany's own interests as well. All of these "obligations" are closely connected to the credo of Kohl's foreign policy: Only a policy of political alliances entered into willingly will secure for Germany a peaceful future and the necessary protection from its own perpetually re-emerging temptation to go its own way as the central power of Europe. "The future architecture of Germany must fit in with the future architecture of Europe," the chancellor stated in a declaration to the *Bundesrat* at the end of 1989, and nothing has changed in the interim.

And this was one more reason for Kohl to run for office again, to challenge fate and to deal forcefully with speculation that he was weary of the office. This man is not weary in the least—he has proved this once more. There is evidence that his time has not run out.

Profile of a Man Born to Power

Political portraits always involve arguments with actual history. If the comforting thesis that "men" no longer make history is indeed true, then the individual becomes of secondary importance, though much can be said for the inverse: History reaches out, as it were, to all men and women competent to assume responsibility. There is hardly another politician's birth date that provides as much of a clue to the man as Kohl's does. His life can be read from the very beginning as political biography.

Kohl was born in Ludwigshafen-Friesenheim in 1930, the son of a mid-level revenue officer. He was a boy during the Nazi era and the war, and therefore did not run the risk of implicating himself. Perhaps his Catholic upbringing in a moderately nationalistic household protected him somewhat, but most important was his age. He was an anti-aircraft gunner's assistant of fifteen when the war ended. This serves as a kind of historical sound barrier, for at that age Kohl may well have comprehended the horror of Germany's national catastrophe, but did not have to ask himself, or be asked, if he had contributed to it personally. "My generation was too young to have become involved in guilt. But it was old enough to be conscious of the horrors of war." The mature Helmut Kohl speaks repeatedly and explicitly of the "blessing of a late birth." It is a typical sign of his determined nature that he expresses such unpleasant facts unabashedly when they can be of use to him, well aware of the ambiguous effect they will have. Such an example was his speech to the Jerusalem Knesset in 1984. He first reminded his audience of Germany's great humanistic tradition, and then added, as a representative of the younger generation: "I mention this as one who could not be touched by guilt in the Nazi era because of the blessing of having been born late, and of my fortunate circumstances at home." These much-quoted words have been criticized and reflected upon ever since, and have offended many people both inside and outside Germany. But the resultant political effect is clear: Kohl has remained personally unimpeachable. And what is more, he embodies a new generation that cannot be accused of any direct involvement in the past, even if it has never denied that it shares responsibility for overcoming the past. He never strays from this argument, though in the same breath he adds the remarkable comment that he himself was not "incapable of seduction." This is a constant in Kohl's mind: Youth "can be seduced."

The open and resolute manner in which Kohl pursued the leadership gifts that already were evident in his school days, and the decisiveness with which he approached politics—and the policies of a particular party—as a high school student are directly tied to his propitious birth date. He must have realized early on where the opportunities and challenges of "zero hour" at the end of World War II lay. Kohl grew up, and, as it were, into the period of political and economic recovery, itself a turning point in German history. This must have served to broaden and focus his view of the future, aware as he was of his own strength and drive. To those in his immediate sur-roundings, his schoolmates and peers, Kohl possessed the aura of a boy of action who always held his head high. Whether or not he actu-ally boasted as a young man that he wanted to become chancellor is irrelevant. Even if not true, it makes a good story, for it suits the image of the brash local boy, and he never tires of dispatching it to the realm of legend.

Kohl came to maturity in the years of the founding of the Federal Republic, in an era of great political debate on the country's future path. Conscious of the debacle of the war, he was filled with the yearning for national reconstruction, and was glad to lend a hand to any useful task like pasting up posters for it. He also enthusiastically attempted storming the barriers of the Franco-German border at Lauterburg, manifesting for the first time his dual identity as German and European, typical of the political consciousness of the "new" gen-eration during those first years of the Federal Republic.

He was inspired at first by the rather nationalistic slogans of SPD chairman Kurt Schumacher, but then Kohl adopted Adenauer's policy of alignment with the West, and at the same time became an eager student of Ludwig Erhard's social market economy. Anyone who fol-lows Kohl's biography—up to his negotiations with Mikhail Gor-bachev—repeatedly encounters his sense of timing which begins to appear as some fated personal timetable that always has him board-ing the history train at just the right moment.

Kohl graduated from high school in 1950 and immediately began his university studies in Frankfurt, then transferring to Heidelberg. During his academic years he always kept his sights on the realities and practice of politics. He dedicated his doctoral dissertation to a little-explored issue of local import: "The Political Development of the Palatinate and the Revival of Political Parties After 1945." It was clear to his dissertation advisor that Kohl wished to enter politics and was not considering an academic career. It comes as no surprise that the doctoral candidate's research resulted in his own increased know-ledge of regional events. He joined the CDU in 1946, and one year later the *Junge Union*, which counts him as one of its founding mem-bers. He advanced first in the local, then in the state, and finally in the national political arena. He was always the youngest and the tallest, who nevertheless carried with him, almost from the begin-ning, a good measure of practical experience and could look back on his youth as a decisive chapter in his development. The revolt against his "elders" was not long in coming.

For ten years Kohl worked for the trade association of the chemical industry, carrying out his political engagement in his free time.
These were the years when Germany was still governed by the
"grandfathers," who had gained their political experience during the
Weimar Republic and had then opposed National Socialism. Kohl
represented, as almost no one else did, the postwar generation, with
its fresh and unspent vitality, which felt called upon to succeed the
prewar old guard. The generation in between was virtually absent
from political life.

Kohl pursued his path resolutely and purposefully, not satisfied
with partial success. He preferred to bide his time, which explains his
decision to turn down an offer from Rhineland-Palatinate's minister-
president to join the state cabinet in Mainz. Kohl had set his sights
higher. But after fifteen years of setting the stage he showed no hesitation, at thirty-nine years of age, in taking the next step. In 1969,
robust, determined, and armed with reform slogans, he was elected
minister-president of Rhineland-Palatinate. He soon turned this
agrarian state upside down with local, social, and educational
reforms, earning marks for his progressive thinking. Kohl was seen as
a "rebel" who knew how to gather about him a group of independent
followers and who was unconventional and receptive to gifted colleagues, including those from other states. He was not a lone warrior,
but a group leader who sought and located new talent. One of his
mentors pointed out Kohl's "crushing straightforwardness," his quality
of not mincing words.

The key to Kohl's rise to the top, differentiating him from most
other successful politicians, has been his work for the party. Kohl
must have recognized early that this was to be the royal road in West
German politics. He anticipated and helped realize a significant shift
of power in the Federal Republic from the chancellor's office to the
political parties. And the party continues to be for Kohl the native
soil he must constantly till. He devotes to it, by his own account, one
quarter of his time and energy. "A party is a piece of homeland. One
isn't really at home in a party if, to paraphrase Rilke, one doesn't suffer with it. You suffer like a dog when things are going poorly, and
rejoice when things are going well."

Kohl has headed the Christian Democratic Union since 1973; he
made it into a modern popular party and has given it the appearance
of a platform party. He knows the inner life of the party better than
anyone; he knows what the party base thinks and feels. It could be
said that he is one of the great beneficiaries of the slowly developing

*The chairman of the CDU at a major party campaign event held in the
Westfalenhalle in Dortmund, January 1987. To his right, CSU chairman
Franz Josef Strauss, and to his left, CDU general secretary, Heiner Geissler.*

"party state," were it not for the fact that he is one of its main cre-
ators. Any attempt to topple Kohl would have to come from within
the party, but those attempts that have been made, from the office of
the general secretary, have proven counterproductive. Kohl has left
by the wayside such intellectuals as Biedenkopf and Geissler, general
secretaries who tried to become generals rather than secretaries,
wishing to shape the party to their own political tastes.

Kohl's loyalty toward those he trusts is often emphasized, but he
deals firmly with those who break this trust. He commented recently,
"It has been said of me that I am so out of touch with everyday life

that I don't notice those who are trying to saw off the legs from under my chair—we're talking about fellow combatants from decades past. Now I am not someone who lays aside old friendships like a book I finished reading yesterday, and that really got under my skin." Asked whether the "general" hadn't mutated into an "adjutant," Kohl replied, "I have never understood this discussion. I am chairman of the party. It is not a decorative post, nor must I apologize for being chairman of the party. It is true that I am a chairman who cares about the party, and the party appreciates that. And that is probably why it elected me."

Kohl has kept his finger on the pulse not only of power issues, but of policy issues as well. Former CDU general secretary Geissler's proclaimed opening up of the party to the left, and his progressive-sounding vision of a multicultural society not only were met by the majority of the party with (growing) resistance, but increasingly clashed with a political reality that more and more revolved around conservative issues. If it is a truism that power and majority are only to be gained from the center, then Kohl has never forgotten it, not even when the issues appeared to drift to the right. Experience has confirmed again and again that no national election in the Federal Republic can be won from a position on either the extreme right or the extreme left.

Despite all opposition to, and even hostility toward, Kohl, who often has been pronounced dead within the party, his position has grown increasingly unshakable. "Kohl is the CDU. The CDU is Kohl," wrote the *Stuttgarter Zeitung* in June 1993, on the twentieth anniversary of Kohl's chairmanship of the CDU, a record no one in the party has come even close to attaining. But the assertion that Kohl will not tolerate close rivals is unfair, or at least only partly true, for where in this world is the party leader who would grant declared rivals free rein? It was the critical party convention of September 1989, in which the faction led by Lothar Späth, Rita Süssmuth, and Heiner Geissler was defeated, that strengthened Kohl's position— in no sense unchallenged up until then—as never before. Seldom has a challenge to power been resolved in such an elegant, smooth, and effective manner (albeit with the help of the opposing camp's bungling).

Kohl's successful career has not, however, been without its defeats. The first major one came during the 1971 CDU convention in Saar-brücken, when Rainer "Candidus" Barzel was named party chairman. Kohl, as the newcomer from the Palatinate, knew he was risking defeat and did not shrink from it; his time would come. And there was the *Bundestag* election of 1980, when Franz Josef Stauss became the Union's candidate for chancellor, though Kohl was closer to majority support. This was proven in 1976 during his first campaign for the office, when he had garnered 48.6 percent of the vote for the CDU/CSU. Strauss was a good example of the rule that one cannot first polarize society and then expect to win its majority. Kohl knew that the "Bavarian lion" would get in his own way, and coolly factored Strauss' defeat into his timetable. Strauss outmaneuvered himself, and Kohl was not to be outdone in terms of either loyalty or self-deception. Whether the relationship between these unequal partners could really be termed a "friendship between men" is rather doubtful. Certain only is that many of yesterday's headlines are no longer valid today.

It is undeniable that Strauss was Kohl's toughest opponent, whom he did not merely avoid by "sitting out," but outmaneuvered in his own way. The first debacle for Strauss was his fierce attack at the Kreuth meeting on the Union alliance,[2] then his own failed candidacy for the office of chancellor, and, finally, the scheme that left him holding the bag for the billion-mark loan to East Germany.[3] With this, Strauss lost the image he had carefully cultivated within the CSU as the last of the steadfast "Cold Warriors," and for the first time Strauss, the CDU chairman, joined the chancellor on basic issues of all-German policy. To what extent Kohl was pulling the strings in all of this is open to question, but nothing was left to chance. When asked, during his tenure as opposition leader, what advantage he enjoyed over Strauss, his terse answer was: "Our age difference." One could choose, of course, to interpret Kohl's subsequent strategy in light of this answer, but the constellation of the political personalities has changed so fundamentally that any serious discussion of a successor fades as soon as it arises. In the early stage of the reunification process the author tried to come up with an analysis of Kohl's brand of power politics that would be easy to grasp and hard to refute. The title of the resulting work, *Helmut Kohl—wer sonst?* (Helmut Kohl—Who Else?)[4] has lost none of its (relative) force in the interim, and has even become a catchphrase of sorts, as evidenced by a cover story in *Spiegel*, for instance. In the early summer of 1993 the leading French daily *Le Monde* described the Bonn political scene in the following words:

■ Less than eighteen months away from the next *Bundestag* elections only the CDU, with its chancellor, can lay claim to an undisputed leader, not to mention a program that appeals to those disheartened voters disillusioned by reunification. Despite the recession, the bitterness felt by the new federal states, and the wear and tear of the power that he has held in his hands for eleven years, Kohl, for "lack" of an alternative, remains the favorite in the political battle to come. This situation—a bit paradoxical in Western Europe, where all of those in positions of power are facing voter dissatisfaction—is proof of the chancellor's extraordinarily political skills. ■

Those who understand how to plan with the element of time can get time to work for them, and Kohl is a great virtuoso of this art. What was wrongly termed "sitting it out" proved itself, in fact, to be the art of waiting. Quick decisions are almost always irreversible. But that the chancellor, in fact, is capable of reaching quick decisions was demonstrated impressively by the historical events of 1989 and 1990.

Kohl attained his first major goal in 1973, with his election as CDU chairman. Once again he represented not only youth but renewal and, renewed, he then took his greatest risk. Kohl gave up his safe post in Mainz and—without the security of a federal office—moved to Bonn, where he accepted the position of caucus leader in 1976, developing an opposition program that almost unobtrusively connected budgetary and social-political issues to foreign policy. He targeted the FDP (and its chairman, Hans-Dietrich Genscher) as future coalition partner, and patiently waited for October 1982—when the time would be ripe for the second major power shift in the Federal Republic's history.

Who brought Kohl to power? Arguably it was his opponents, the Social Democrats themselves. By refusing to support their own chancellor, Helmut Schmidt, on issues of social policy and rearmament, they forced Genscher—after long and torturous deliberations—to switch sides and end the socialist-liberal coalition. The constructive vote of no-confidence and resulting election in March 1983 earned the Union a clear majority and brought the FDP to the edge of ruin. It is dubious whether the issue of Schmidt's "intellectual leadership," raised by Kohl, had anything to do with the developments that followed. But what did follow was change. Financial and economic policy was rejuvenated, and for the remainder of the eighties the economic

Taking oath as federal chancellor, administered by Bundestag *president Richard Stücklen, October 1, 1982.*

Federal President Karl Carstens receives Kohl's first cabinet, October 4, 1982. Bottom row from left: Friedrich Zimmermann, Hans-Dietrich Genscher, Carstens, Kohl, Dorothee Wilms, Rainer Barzel, Norbert Blüm, Gerhard Stoltenberg. Top row from left: Hans A. Engelhard, Manfred Wörner, Jürgen Warnke, Werner Dollinger, Otto Lambsdorff, Heiner Geissler, Oscar Schneider, Josef Ertl, Heinz Riesenhuber, Christian Schwarz-Schilling.

situation continued to revive. Passage of the NATO double-track decision gave Gorbachev the decisive go-ahead for his sensational disarmament initiatives, for the reform measures that would usher in *perestroika*, unopposed by the West, and, finally, for the end to East-West confrontation. That this important phase has almost disappeared from public consciousness in no way diminished its significance to what then occurred at the end of the decade; it enabled what followed to become possible. Reunification came as a surprise; but it did not fall out of the sky. It was something for which Kohl was programmed and prepared.

Federal President Karl Carstens receives Kohl's second cabinet, March 30, 1983. From left: Friedrich Zimmermann, Heinrich Windelen, Hans A. Engelhard, Manfred Wörner, Otto Lambsdorff, Hans-Dietrich Genscher, Jürgen Warnke, Werner Dollinger, Norbert Blüm, Ignaz Kiechle, Carstens, Oscar Schneider, Heinz Riesenhuber, Kohl, Dorothee Wilms, Heiner Geissler, Christian Schwarz-Schilling, Gerhard Stoltenberg.

What is Kohl made of—a man who stands like a bronze statue dominating the German political scene as no other except Adenauer before him? Though it is clear that Kohl's image has gained in profile in recent years, he has yet to become a figure who is beloved or adored. Yet those who understand politics take him seriously, a fact even more appreciated abroad than in Germany. The familiar bromide of the born power broker comes to mind, of course, and is difficult to contradict. Kohl's feel for power is coupled with a sure instinct, and excellent memory, and a large dose of strong will held in check by an equanimity which keeps his emotions largely under control. His armory is the telephone, a direct line to the players, and a precise knowledge of people: "I study people like other people study books." He himself is not Janus-faced.

It would be shortsighted to dismiss Kohl as a pragmatist. He has a definite perspective, but also unshakable personal principles that guide his life. These principles are the source of the legendary self-confidence, which, during the turbulent periods of his life, has astounded and even shocked others. He is a long-range thinker, as few others. Those who want more, who would like to find the visionary or utopian in him, will, of necessity, be put off by Kohl's sense of reality. Kohl rarely gets caught up in the fractious side of daily political life, tempting the observer to conclude that he doesn't care about it. But this would be to ignore his ability to separate the essential

The federal chancellor during a plenary debate in the Bundestag, *September 1983.*

from the inessential, and to concentrate his energies on what is most important.

Kohl can be tough when the occasion calls for it, and inconsiderate, direct, and hurtful. He cannot be accused of sentimentality, and is in top form "under pressure" with his back to the wall. But he can also be congenial, pleasant in conversation, and sincere. Observers have noted that he has become more prudent, has begun to court understanding, admit mistakes, take issue with the country's general mood of despondency. His considerable self-assurance has grown, at any rate, his size filling the space around him. He knows how to make use of his heft, his profusely dominating physicality, to push aside his competition even visually. Others appear small next to him. There is a certain minister-president, Kohl once remarked ironically in a television interview, who almost has a heart attack every time he has to be photographed beside him. Kohl also knows how to play the game, how to skillfully maneuver himself into a scene, and can be equally as immodest as Adenauer, who was fully capable of coldly snubbing his adversaries. Kohl would prove a gold mine to a study of political gestures and mimicry.

The chancellor has also broken the unwritten law of this media age that only those who know how to use the media can attain power. He has left this prerogative to his predecessor, Helmut Schmidt. Kohl knows how to use television, and acknowledges its overpowering significance, but he rarely appears on it and does not avail himself of every possible photo opportunity. He is not a media favorite, as were Brandt and Schmidt. He lacks all the attributes of the actor—the art of dissimulation, the pose, the posturing. Many have wanted him to give more thought to the impression he makes, but to no avail. This may be a weakness, but at close range it appears to be a strength. Kohl has not conformed on this point; he has remained true to himself and refused to give in. He makes no attempt to pay tribute to the *zeitgeist*, nor is he dogmatic or ideological, but a realist to the core. His avoidance of certain mass media derives not only from his dislike of their style, but also from his opinion that the media use politicians to increase their own audience, only to drop them when convenient. This is one reason why Kohl is not more popular. There has always been incongruity between his political standing and his popularity. Nina Grunenberg once noted in *Die Zeit*: "Political aesthetes will never get their money's worth out of this chancellor," a fact that has led many to draw false conclusions, as if rhetoric were the sole measure of political power. In an interview on Swiss television Kohl himself once remarked: "I am certainly not the embodiment of elegance." But that does not change the fact that he possesses luck, the necessary amount of good fortune, without which no great politician can survive.

An important chapter in this brief psychograph must be devoted to Kohl's unbelievable regenerative capacity. He himself speaks of his "invincible nature of an ox." If the ability to put problems aside before bed each night is indeed a survival technique for the high-ranking politician, then Kohl will survive. "It is important, given the stress that comes with positions of leadership in our society, to possess robust health. That and the gift of being able to nap on the spot—whether in an automobile or a helicopter. Generally speaking, it is important to be able to turn things off." As part of his "survival training" Kohl, who unlike Adenauer is anything but an ascetic, is also able to give himself over to the joys of the table, which serves as a kind of sedative for his soul. A piece of cake in the afternoon can do wonders.

Reunification and Its Fathers

Is it possible that reunification already has faded from German consciousness? How else to explain the sober mood that followed the initial euphoria, and the fact that the historical significance of reunification scarcely rouses Germans anymore, while the "burdens" of the event are a constant topic of conversation? Or can the country's sullenness be read as a sign that everyday life has returned to normal?

Yet in recent history and politics no question is more exciting than that of how the "story of the century" came about. What forces were at work that were able to crush a world order in place since World War II? For the momentous collapse of the global status quo certainly cannot be ascribed to accident. But if not to accident, then to what? Perhaps to the law of history, possibly even to a *Weltgeist*. Or was it merely the far-sightedness of a few accessories to history?

The most curious and fascinating aspect of this is that no one saw the situation coming, though in retrospect everyone interprets events as moving in that direction. A few people—and their number continued to shrink over the years—considered reunification possible at best, while others considered it unrelinquishable. What no one foresaw was how feasible it had become by the end of the eighties. In retrospect, events take on a high degree of inevitability and certainty, above all in light of socialism's material and moral fragility. The bankruptcy of the socialist system implicit in its principles was unavoidable and had been coming for some time. But it was only when Mikhail Gorbachev became general secretary of the USSR in 1985 and attempted to reform socialism, thereby triggering the collapse of the Soviet Union, that the necessary conclusions were drawn. Gorbachev's role cannot be overestimated: The demise of socialism was foreseeable, but the speed at which events would take place, and above all the peaceful character of the reform attempts, based as they were on understanding and disarmament, were Gorbachev's doing alone. He is an example of how absurd it is to deny or downplay the role of the individual in the historical process—in a positive as well as a negative sense.

The same could be said of Helmut Kohl. It might be coincidence that reunification occurred during his watch. But the assertion that it fell into his lap, or that other politicians could have brought it about just as skillfully and prudently, is not supportable. There are a great many such embarrassing comments, like that of Social Democratic candidate for chancellor Oskar Lafontaine during the 1990 election, or the near-grotesque, wrong-headed opinions of several leading journalists, among them Theo Sommer of the weekly *Die Zeit*, who wrote of the "skeleton of German unification" that shouldn't be brought out of the closet. Add to this the belligerent voices of well-known writers such as Günter Grass, who spoke in favor of maintaining a divided Germany. To them, two German states were a reality, and a divided German citizenry the fulfillment of their political beliefs. They were convinced that East-West German relations should be conducted in the shelter of the superpowers, and that nuclear disarmament could be achieved through renewed pacifism. To quote one such voice, that of Green representative Antje Vollmer in 1984: "We are not utopians, but realists. That is precisely why we support the recognition of a reality as it arose in Germany: two German states and two German citizenries."

Such ideas may have sprung from honorable motives, but they totally misrepresented reality. They called for political "equidistance" between East and West, a third position, that is, between socialism and capitalism. They considered the Berlin Wall if not a useful, at least an inevitable edifice and fortification. They saw the NATO double-track decision as the devil's work, a slide into the nuclear inferno. From "change through reconciliation" to "change through ingratiation" (in the words of then–CDU general secretary Volker Rühe), they

conducted direct talks with the SED, bypassing federal authorities in
Bonn entirely. They tried to find a special path without knowing
where it would lead. The German brand of socialism was transformed or transfigured into a "niche society," a dependable, harm-
less idyll.

Hypothetical conjecture on what might have happened had politicians of their ilk been the ones to open the "window of opportunity"
are futile and, luckily, superfluous. But it can be said without qualifi-

*Federal President Richard von Weizsäcker receives Kohl's third cabinet,
March 12, 1987. First row, from left: Friedrich Zimmermann, Hans-Dietrich
Genscher, von Weizsäcker, Rita Süssmuth, Kohl, Dorothee Wilms, Gerhard
Stoltenberg. Second row, from left: Martin Bangemann, Hans Engelhard,
Manfred Wörner, Ignaz Kiechle, Oscar Schneider, Norbert Blüm, Hans Klein,
Wolfgang Schäuble, Christian Schwarz-Schilling. Third row, from left:
Jürgen Möllemann, Heinz Riesenhuber, Jürgen Warnke, Walter Wallmann.*

cation that there are those who would not even have *comprehended* the opportunity for reunification; and certainly not everyone would have *seized* it as did Kohl and Genscher. There is such a thing as the "right moment" in history, never to be repeated. It requires the right partners, those who are up to the task.

Historians have a great deal of work to do before the singular process that led to reunification can be illuminated in all its aspects and details, and researched with complete documentation. It is too soon to know the aftereffects and long-term changes. History never reveals all its cards, and a deterministic interpretation would miss its mark. But neither is history a succession of intangibles. With the collapse of socialism history, as emphasized above, took its revenge for all the unresolved problems, all the inconsistencies and injustices of Stalinist despotism. "History is always nemesis," Ralph Dahrendorf has noted succinctly.

In 1987, a few years before the final dissolution of the Warsaw Pact, American historian Paul Kennedy wrote a sensational analysis, *The Rise and Fall of the Great Powers*,[5] on the almost unavoidable demise of all great powers throughout history. Kennedy does not reduce everything to casual relations, but he does develop criteria which allow us to gauge the risks run by all imperial powers. Excessive military spending, and the geo-strategic "over-extensions" that go with it, are among the decisive factors leading to the almost certain ruin of a superpower.

Kennedy described it precisely. The Soviet Union's structural problems already had assumed such massive form that its fall was pre-programmed. This thesis does not contend that history is calculable or even predictable. It only offers evidence that certain mistakes are fatal, leading inevitably to an end sometime in the future. The socialist empire cracked at exactly the point where it appeared strongest—in its military complex. And it failed precisely where it imagined itself to be victorious: in the destruction of fascism, with its attendant superpower delusions. The *pax sovietica* in Eastern Europe was concluded on the bayonets of the Red Army, and this peace of terror was stable for only as long as military power could be maintained. Soviet Russia lost the Cold War above all because it lost the arms race it had waged for over forty years. Because the growing military budget made the development of consumer society impossible. In short, because the Red Army was no longer affordable. At the nuclear level war as a means to power had become ineffectual. One of the great lessons of this century is that military superiority is no longer worthwhile, only economic superiority is. It is a lesson that recent local and regional conflicts do not refute, but confirm.

Kennedy's analysis also throws a critical light on the situation of the American superpower, and his conclusion is by no means rosy. In his judgment, the Cold War was a costly venture for the United States as well. The financial strains it created (above all during Ronald Reagan's administration) came close to their limit, and perhaps surpassed it. Excessive armament tore big holes in the national budget, and was perhaps the primary cause for the end of the economic boom and the paralysis of innovative energies in the United States. Not to mention the diminished U.S. military presence all over the world.

In retrospect there is much that can be explained point by point. It is only when a house collapses that one can see the extent of the rot within. Gorbachev himself could not have seen to what degree the Soviet Union was incapable of reform, even then. Otherwise he would not have undertaken the experiment of *perestroika* and *glasnost* so optimistically. Gorbachev increasingly fell victim to his own rhetoric—a great irony that did not, however, justify Kohl's gaffe, in which he compared Gorbachev to Goebbels. Gorbachev was in almost total possession of what it takes to become a great politician—charisma, a willingness to take risks, decision-making ability, and a thoroughly appealing eloquence. But what he manifestly lacked was economic competence, a firm knowledge of people, and perseverance. Gorbachev's standing in history will vacillate, and always be of a dual nature. The more rapidly the situation developed, the less he had it under control.

And from a German point of view, that was obvious in the final outcome. It was a good thing—for all those involved and for the thing itself—that no one fully comprehended all its consequences. The far-reaching and peaceful reshaping of Europe succeeded not least due to the breathtaking speed with which this avalanche overwhelmed the historical process of collapse. Some things are easier to cope with when they are unforeseen. The force of historical events literally swept everyone along with it, one of the many paradoxes of this fascinating period.

And that also explains why the majority of Germans did not consider reunification possible, and for the most part had already written it off. Having witnessed the Red Army's various forms of military repression, which time and again were used as an instrument of political subjugation, any change in the power structure appeared hopeless. Expert testimony of this is provided by historian Golo Mann's 1959 work, *Deutsche Geschichte des 19. und 20. Jahrhunderts* (German History of the 19th and 20th Centuries).[6] Mann wrote:

> ■ If by reunification is meant that Germany should and could return to conditions comparable to those of 1920, that Germany should again become a Weimar Republic, with Berlin as its capital, but a much smaller, more crowded and fragmented republic than Weimar, its capital backed right up against the eastern border of the "Reich," if Germany is to become a republic again, one which moves freely between the powers of the East and of the West, taking its advantage now here, now there, then reunification is mere twaddle. It cannot and should not be, it would be a terrible thing. ■

Mann's quote is notable, above all, because it exposes the essential differences to actual events as they happened, and succinctly describes the danger (banished by Kohl) of Germany's "unique" position in the no man's land between East and West. "There should be less talk of reunification, which is a flimsy goal that does not conform to the new conditions of a profoundly altered world. One should more seriously pursue the detoxification of the relationship between East and West, in its immediate as well as its broader sphere." This additional remark by Golo Mann precisely indicates the goal that then indeed was attained in 1989, and which both preserved peace and protected the republic.

It should not be forgotten that the Cold War had definite rules of the game, which no one broke despite many temptations. Even the Brezhnev Doctrine,[7] which rested on the "integrity" of the Warsaw Pact, that is to say, on the Kremlin's indisputable claim to power, was respected—though with certain verbal reservations. No one seriously considered employing force to dispute it. The two sides accepted reality for the sake of peace, and tried to make it more tolerable, more "human," through collective agreements, though never at the price of abandoning cardinal legal positions.

For over forty years the Western Allies, repeatedly reminded of their obligations by the successive administrations in Bonn, never made any agreement or accepted any regulations which would have passed over the German question. It was always written into treaties, and included all kinds of complex protections and reassurances, some of which—so some people believed—were not worth the paper they were printed on. They were mere formalities and ritual affirmations of unity. Who among the Allies truly believed that one day these affirmations would be honored?

Which is precisely why this mutually imposed discipline by treaties functioned to such an amazing degree, both domestically and in foreign policy. It doomed all domestic sorties from the beginning. Neither revanchism from the right nor the left's tendency to abandon the idea of unification had a chance of success with the majority. The Brandt-Scheel government's policy of rapprochement toward the East offers as much proof of this as do the discussions on rearmament, with their attendant pacifism.

It can be said that none of the various Bonn governments committed any fundamental error, or was guilty of any fundamental oversight. From the standpoint of the end result nothing occurred that could have blocked unification. In this particular point German policy found itself under an unusually lucky star. This was due, above all, to a well-functioning parliamentary control, but also to the fact that the national consensus held, despite all opposition. For now this general statement leaves open the question of just how much political credit is due each of the parties and the individuals involved in the final outcome. A verdict must be left to a more detailed investigation, for this point is one on which considerable difference of opinion and partisan debate persist. It deserves careful historical analysis. This author is of the opinion that a basic national consensus, one that bridged all differences and endured beyond them, was both starting point and guideline for the divergent policies put forward.

Helmut Kohl belongs to that small group of politicians who never lost sight of the idea of reunification, nor put it out of their hearts. He never ceased to believe in it, he desired it and believed it possible, not necessarily in the here and now, but over the course of history. And history, in the end, followed its own rules. There is ample proof of Kohl's commitment. In July 1989, speaking of Germany's legal situation, he declared: "The German question remains open, legally and politically." He then went on pointedly at length to articulate the specific points in support of his assertion:

> ■ Our policy on Germany, as well as our policy concerning
> the countries of Central and Eastern Europe, continues to
> be determined by the Basic Law, the General Treaty, the
> Moscow and Warsaw Treaties of 1970, the Quadripartite
> Agreement of 1971, the Basic Treaty with the GDR of

1972, the letters on German unity, the joint resolution of
the German *Bundestag*, which was agreed to by all factions—CDU/CSU, SPD, and FDP—and the relevant rulings
of the Federal Constitutional Court. ∎

He then added that it was not enough to merely mouth these
claims, and that anyone satisfied with doing nothing more was
betraying the cause.

One month later, in an interview with the *Süddeutsche Zeitung*,
he stated: "I have not the slightest doubt that history is working for,
and not against, us. . . . I shall not yield any principle position. . . .
Time is working not against, but for us." When asked: "Are you convinced that in the next few years, or at any rate during your lifetime,
the Berlin Wall will come down?" he answered, "I consider it to be
more than likely."

At the time, such statements could be misinterpreted as naive, or
even dangerous. In retrospect, they suggest that Chancellor Kohl
knew more in mid-1989 than he could say openly. His personal
breakthrough with Gorbachev had occurred, according to Gorbachev,
in June 1989, during the general secretary's state visit to Bonn. One
warm summer evening the two men, who are almost the same age,
had a private talk in the garden of the chancellor's office. Both had
experienced the war as adolescents, and concurred that such a thing
should never be permitted to happen again. They agreed it was time
to make a clean break with the past and find a new path to "overcoming the blocks." It was on that evening that Gorbachev and Kohl
achieved an understanding of each other; it was in that place that the
idea of mutual cooperation on a radically different basis took shape.
This was the beginning of a political friendship between these two
men that was to survive Gorbachev's fall from power. In unsentimen-
tal terms, it was a deal of global-political proportions agreed upon on
the basis of reciprocity. It was also the first time that Kohl had
offered Gorbachev concrete assistance.

Thanks to his intense contacts with the Soviet general secretary,
Kohl at that time presumably had a six- to nine-month jump on
intelligence information. He could not, of course, have known exactly
what would be possible within that time frame. But he must have
realized by the time of his conversation with Gorbachev that the
foundations were beginning to crumble, and this realization derived
significance above all from the fact that he never lost sight of the goal
of reunification.

Kohl's policy objectives on Germany over the years essentially never needed revision. In his first statement of government policy he outlined the future with the words: "The nation-state of the Germans has been shattered. The German nation remains, and shall continue to exist. We all know that overcoming the division of Germany is imaginable only in terms of historical time." He then expressed it more precisely:

> ■ For us, German policy, *beyond German-German relations*, shall always remain a question of the unity of the country. . . . We Germans are not resigned to the division of our fatherland. We shall purposefully and steadfastly pursue the mandate of the Basic Law, "to achieve the unity and freedom of Germany in free self-determination." We are not resigned, for we know that history is on our side. The present situation is not inalterable. We know from historical experience that the restoration of German unity can only be realized within the framework of total peace in Europe. The division of Germany is always simultaneously the division of Europe, and for that reason policy on Germany must always be defined as contributing to the unification of Europe, and therefore as a European policy of peace. To overcome the division of Germany we need the support of the Atlantic Alliance and the European Community. We need the alliance and a united Europe more than others do. ■

This is a programmatic and conclusive statement, the reality of which was to prove itself at the end of the eighties. Point for point it spells out the concept that was to serve him as a guideline for reunification. To repeat: Kohl was internally programmed for reunification and prepared for it conceptually down to the last detail. He always thought in terms of both Europe and the nation, and that has not changed. One year after the policy statement, he again made his point clearly when, in his Report on the State of the Nation (a tradition the chancellor of the conservative-liberal coalition had revived), he said:

> ■ We know that the national concept of the Germans and the idea of Europe presuppose one another. For us, policy on Europe and policy on Germany are two sides of the same coin. To be the motor for the unification of Europe is one part of our national mission, the Federal Republic's

reason of state from the beginning. Our free political
culture requires a European horizon of common basic
values. ■

As a politician Kohl has always rejected the idea of two German
states. From the very first day of his political career his eyes were
always fixed on unity. And his apprenticeship as historian sharpened
his sense for this eventuality.

The key event was Erich Honecker's state visit to Bonn in September 1987, which had been previously arranged by Helmut Schmidt.
Drawing himself up to his full height next to the chairman of the
German Democratic Republic's Council of State, the German federal
chancellor declared:

> ■ The people of Germany are suffering from the division
> [of their country]. They are suffering from the Wall, which
> literally stands in their way and repels them. . . . This visit
> cannot and will not change our different opinions or the
> fundamental questions, among them that of the German
> nation. Speaking for the Federal Republic I repeat: The
> preamble of our Basic Law is unequivocal, because it corre-
> sponds to our convictions. It calls for a united Europe,
> it calls for the entire German people to achieve unity and
> for freedom of Germany by self-determination. That is
> our goal. ■

What could be clearer?

A discussion of Kohl's role in German unification inevitably
arrives at the question of how he became chancellor in the first place.
He certainly had no popular advantage over Schmidt, a man many
saw as a kind of storybook chancellor competent in a number of
fields, supposedly a superman when it came to decision making,
articulate in any given situation, authoritarian to the point of arrogance, a master of self-presentation to the media, his indestructible
charisma enhanced by his years of wielding power in office, his
"hanseatic" coolness, and submissive to no one, except to his own
party. Kohl did not primarily have himself to thank for the political
shift that brought him to power, but rather the constellation of political parties at the beginning of the eighties. But his obvious competence in addressing concrete questions in the life of the nation did
play a role. In strategically important fields—those of domestic and
foreign policy—the SPD withdrew its support from its own chancellor.

That Kohl's government soon steered the economy onto a successful course was due to a certain degree to the international economic recovery. But the legendary upswing can also be credited to the successful budget-cutting policies of Finance Minister Gerhard Stoltenberg, which proved to be both appropriate and adequate. Kohl's long tenure in office has been marked by economic prosperity, with only occasional clouds appearing on the horizon.

Postwar German foreign policy could be characterized as "change through continuity." Almost silently, Kohl directed the Union parties toward the path of détente with the East, which the Union for years had approached with nothing but mistrust, uncertainty, and a great deal of reservation. Concretely, Kohl and Genscher joined the Conference on Security and Cooperation in Europe (CSCE), which derived from a Kremlin initiative, and above all was meant to serve the established status quo of power politics in Europe by confirming the European borders as defined in the treaties with the Eastern bloc. Or, more precisely, by securing the Soviet sphere of influence. In the iron-clad words of the Eastern bloc treaties this meant the renunciation of all border revisions. It was this basis of trust, never to be breached, which allowed the initial conditions for the free flow of information in Europe and for the recognition of human rights—at the price of unconditional *non-intervention* in the internal affairs of other countries. This breakthrough was to have unimagined consequences. Above all, it made the increasingly fragile Iron Curtain much more porous for ideas and ideologies.

As often in life—and in history—things turned out differently than expected. The CSCE process opened up a broad basis for discussing East-West relations, and created an unanticipated opportunity for resistance pockets to develop in Czechoslovakia, Poland, and the GDR. In the lee of continuing "détente" the Solidarity movement developed under the leadership of Lech Walesa. German politicians and the German intelligentsia initially viewed the movement with reservations and distrust. Perhaps this was unavoidable, given their belief that things would progress more quickly on the level of governmental contacts than by forming alliances with opposition or marginal groups. But the political and the intellectual communities never managed to pull together as a team. German intellectuals failed utterly, notably in the way they received *The Gulag Archipelago*. Alexander Solzhenitsyn's disclosure of the brutality of the Stalinist regime was barely acknowledged, and altered practically nothing in the political consciousness toward "socialism." This was in contrast to France, whose leftist intellectuals, with the help of Solzhenitsyn, began to see through and to reject socialism's totalitarian system. Germany's left, on the other hand, succumbed—and many still succumb—to the mechanisms of suppression, dismissal, and blindness that seemed to be compensated, nourished, and justified by a militant "anti-fascism."

The significance of the process set in motion by the Conference on Security and Cooperation in Europe, the softening up, indeed the internal ideological destabilization, of the Warsaw Pact cannot be overestimated. Honecker and his East Berlin confederates were among the first to realize this, but they were unable to stop it. The realities of the collapsing socialist system forced the SED leadership into a substantial compromise of interests with Bonn. In the mid-seventies, at any rate, the mechanisms of "convergence" brought about in the socialist satellite states a burgeoning of democratic, freedom-oriented thinking with a subversive effect, especially in Poland, Czechoslovakia, and Hungary. Just as socialist ideas began to seep into the West, democratic ideas began to seep into the East. But while socialism remained marginal in the West, in the East the idea of democracy assumed irresistible force. In the Soviet Union itself, these democratic ideas were allied in the Gorbachev era with a basic and irrefutable demand for reform. Indeed, *glasnost* worked. Consciousness changed rapidly, while the social-political restructuring of the system limped along behind to this day.

But Gorbachev would never have risked putting *perestroika*—conceived as internal reform—into practice had he not been totally sure of the backing of the West provided by the Helsinki agreement. This is a profound, inestimable, yet seldom perceived aspect of the abrupt and radical changes in Europe which were to lead to the end of the Cold War, the implosion of the Soviet empire, and the volcanic development of a totally new situation in global politics. Gorbachev needed flank protection, and he found it in Bonn. He needed an intermediary with Washington, and he found that in Bonn, too.

The collapse of the socialist system had various intertwined causes, each with a mutually compounding effect. No doubt this collapse was a consequence of the USSR's own unresolved contradictions, of systematic economic inefficiency, of a planned economy that crippled all private initiative, and of unrelenting mind control. These self-created problems doubtless were multiplied greatly by the ideological, economic, socio-political, and military-technological competition with the West during the Cold War. The interplay between the rivals, the checks they placed on each other, and the "respect" created by the threat of nuclear self-destruction, represent a chapter in themselves of postwar history, and demand a detailed analysis. Their roots can be traced back to the Adenauer era.

That there is direct continuity between the era of the first federal chancellor and the person of Helmut Kohl is evident in the events of Kohl's career. It is evident as well in the analysis of his foreign policy doctrines, whether concerning Germany's tie to the West, defense, the concept of Europe, the Franco-German alliance, or the commitment to a free and democratic order. That these doctrines were not empty abstractions is obvious on close examination of the reunification process. The epithet "Adenauer's grandson," which Kohl himself accepted for a long time, was slow to fade. It must now give way to an evaluation based on Kohl's own achievements.

Kohl, due to the circumstances, could not simply restrict himself to continuing Adenauer's course. Instead, he expanded the "policy of strength" through a cautious adaptation of Eastern policy and détente, and in doing so firmly established it on the basis of a policy toward the East and a policy toward the West. And that is why the pre-history of reunification was of such significance.

Immediately after assuming office Kohl set about repairing damaged relations with the U.S., something he achieved quickly. This was quite important at that time, because a stubborn, latent anti-Americanism, expressed by the pacifist *zeitgeist* of the Federal Republic and the Social Democrats' military stance, which consisted of ousting the Americans, had taken on dangerous proportions. This situation had been fostered above all by the socialist left wing of the SPD, and Helmut Schmidt, certainly no leftist himself, had been unable to contain this trend. In addition, more out of personality reasons of his surly arrogance, Schmidt had never enjoyed relaxed relations with either President Carter or President Reagan. Surely it was an exaggerated sense of caution that led the U.S. leaders at that time to fear the danger of a "Finlandization" of German foreign policy. But Schmidt also refused to play the role of bridge builder, or even of mediator, between East and West, though it might be objected that during Schmidt's time in office conditions were not ripe for this. But there can be no question that, particularly during Jimmy Carter's administration, relations between the two countries had become difficult, and were taking on a traumatic character on both sides.

Nor did this change when Ronald Reagan came to office. Helmut

Close contacts with U.S. alliance partners. With Vice President George Bush in Bonn, 1983.

With President Ronald Reagan in the White House garden, 1986.

With President Bill Clinton in the Oval Office, 1993.

Schmidt—and this is understandable to a certain extent—saw the dangers of the arms race, which in his view entailed incalculable risks. But his reservations led to a faulty understanding of Reagan's arms policy, which strove to re-establish American military strength and restore American self-confidence, which had been lost in Vietnam. Schmidt, as many other of Reagan's European critics, failed to realize that when Reagan spoke of the "evil empire," he was setting the stage for an agreement on disarmament. This possibility was widely overlooked during Reagan's first term, but he was quick to make it reality in Reykjavik, to the dismay of his own defense experts and to the astonishment of the whole world.

When Kohl became chancellor he did not have to face this psychological obstacle. Under his leadership the Atlantic Alliance soon became again Europe's safety anchor. Kohl was the first postwar German chancellor to achieve a balanced policy between East and West. This was accomplished on the basis of unquestioned loyalty to the West, coupled with a readiness for reconciliation and mutual peace arrangements with the East. Kohl was able to banish the latent, and in no way unfounded, distrust in Western capitals that Germany once again might lean toward its old *Drang nach dem Osten* (thrust to the East). Specifically in terms of the American administration he established a new relationship of trust that, at the crucial point, was also to secure him the leadership role in Europe.

The overwhelming value of partnership in leadership has, meanwhile, been proved in resolving the most pressing of all European issues—support for the economic and political recovery of Russia. This show of solidarity, in which Germany assumed the chief burden with a contribution of almost eighty billion Deutsche Marks and unceasing political effort, has yet to bear any visible fruit. While critics might be skeptical, it is all too easy to forget what was at stake and what a miracle it was the that Soviet Union dissolved into the Commonwealth of Independent States (CIS) with no incidents of widespread bloodshed or, with the recent exception of Chechnya, reactionary violence. As of this writing, the understanding between the U.S. and Russia has brought far-reaching and positive results in the regulation of global conflicts. The first demonstration of this was the Gulf War of George Bush, which could not have been waged had the Soviet Union (still under the leadership of Gorbachev at the time) not remained on the sidelines. And cooperation between these former adversaries, with the USSR now replaced by Russia and Boris Yeltsin, has fundamentally contributed to a reevaluation of the United Nations. In practical terms this means the resolution of conflicts within the U.N. Security Council. Even in the case of the civil war in the former Yugoslavia these attempts at communication were not wholly unproductive.

Any attempt at an historical evaluation unavoidably interweaves the outlook for the future with a look back at the past, the only way in which complex events can be illuminated. In the light of the past Kohl's foreign policy clearly appears as a synthesis of Adenauer's policy of strength and Schmidt's policy of détente. It was precisely where these two met that Kohl took the decisive step beyond Adenauer, under different foreign-policy conditions, of course. He did so with such unerring determination that resistance and opposition within the Union to the policy of détente, which was not insignificant, quickly and smoothly vanished. This included the opposition of spokesman Franz Josef Strauss and of caucus leader Alfred Dregger, a man deemed rather militant who was won over to the chancellor's side.

Historical scholarship agrees that Adenauer failed at precisely the moment at which his policy of strength could not adjust or reconcile itself to the needs for relaxing European tensions—when he failed to acknowledge apparently irreversible realities. This view is supported by, among others, Hans-Peter Schwarz in the second volume of his Adenauer biography. In the end, Adenauer's persistent "claim to sole representation," entailing the nonrecognition of the "existence" of the GDR, proved an obstacle to a development that clamored for détente to secure the peace and freeze the Cold War in the status quo. The situation demanded it, and young U.S. President John F. Kennedy was pushing in this direction as well. Willy Brandt was also beginning to think in these terms, and with the construction of the Berlin Wall, at the latest, Brandt realized that behind the curtain the stage was empty. No one was prepared to go to war for Berlin, or over the Berlin Wall, and it was during this period that Brandt had his "Damascus experience" and was transformed from a Cold Warrior into a politician of détente.

Brandt's policy (not to speak of euphoria) concerning détente failed because the Kremlin saw the growing yearning for peace and the rise in pacifist sentiments in the Federal Republic as a unique opportunity to gain superiority in the arms race. Militarily speaking, the Soviet Union was never stronger than after its SS-20 missiles were deployed at the height of the Brezhnev era. The immense range of these weapons represented for the first time a true threat to the entire European continent, for the West at that time had nothing to equal them. These Soviet medium-range missiles were the thorn in the side of European defense.

Helmut Schmidt, without any doubt a true expert on defense, recognized the problem and made such a hue and cry about it in Washington—to the great displeasure of Jimmy Carter—that the Americans finally had to react, though it took some time for the Pentagon to begin to address this problem. For the SPD, which in the meantime had evolved into a party of pacifists and peace demonstrators, the call for rearmament represented a severe test, and the longer it persisted, the less the SPD held its ground. Even Willy Brandt, who well recognized the danger that the Soviets would seize the advantage in armaments as a reflex against détente, opposed the chancellor of the socialist-liberal coalition in the end, though less out of conviction than out of opportunistic desperation, because it was the only way to hold together the disparate wings of the Social Democrats. Schmidt had to fall in order for the SPD to survive and to (vainly) pursue a new defense-policy path toward peace via the GDR.

Only the detour of the NATO double-track decision brought the Soviet willingness for détente. The series of offers, one coming on top of another, with which Mikhail Gorbachev had the world holding its breath for years, made him a wildly popular figure in the West, and rightfully so. Nevertheless, it would be naive to attribute the success of détente to Gorbachev alone. He knew only too well that in order to dare proceed with the experiment of basic reform he had to jettison all ballast, radically reduce the costs of the strongest army in world history, and dismantle an overextended foreign policy step by step.

It is impossible to describe in brief the drama surrounding this development. It is sufficient in this context to point to the significance of the policy of détente, the establishment of the Conference on Security and Cooperation in Europe, and the effect of the NATO double-track decision. To put it succinctly, Ronald Reagan armed the Soviet Union to its death. The decisive blow to the senseless arms race was cast at the moment Gorbachev knew that the Soviet Union could no longer compete, financially or technologically. Whether or not the much-debated SDI, or "Star Wars" program, within which Reagan pledged to develop an interstellar missile defense system, was a bluff or an impossible (and financially prohibitive) *fata morgana* remains open to debate. What is certain is that Reagan reasserted his country's military superiority, and of the many factors in the battle between the superpowers, this was a decisive one, having a precipitous effect: It signaled the West's absolute technological superiority in the sphere of electronic control systems.

Valentin Falin, an expert on Germany who had advised several Central Committees—the last under Gorbachev—acknowledged in *Die Zeit* in March 1992: "The economic and social situation in our country was of crucial importance. At the beginning of the eighties the economy was in catastrophic shape. We had armed ourselves out of existence, or, if you will, both we and the Americans had each armed ourselves against ourselves in the last fifteen to twenty years. Which also explains the present problems in the American economy."

This Soviet view of things offers support for the effectiveness of Reagan's strategy, the "pay-off" being the end of the Cold War. The meeting at Reykjavik, which even shocked the Pentagon, signaled what was to come. It was followed by the more or less parallel moves toward American-Soviet and German-Soviet rapprochement, which would later facilitate Kohl's spectacular dual strategy as intermediary between East and West.

But it bears repeating that this was possible only because the Germans were sure of the Americans and the Americans were sure of the Germans. This was even more important because it gave Soviet "reformers" Gorbachev and Shevardnadze the assurance that neither Washington nor emerging Europe's predominant power in Bonn would stab them in the back as they attempted to bring about peaceful change. Whether or not Gorbachev correctly assessed his own opportunities is left open to question. But he did not err in his judgment of Western "loyalty" in terms of the reform process. Without Germany—and this is part and parcel of the Russian political tradition—the Soviet Union's break with its self-imposed isolation, and its turn toward a democratic society and market economy, would have been unthinkable. As Gorbachev's problems increased, he became more dependent upon coming to an agreement with Kohl, and therein lies the true secret of what Kohl was able to accomplish. Gorbachev, who discreetly buried the "Brezhnev Doctrine," needed the safety net of Western assistance, nor did this change for his successor, Boris Yeltsin. Helmut Kohl recognized this at an early date—and made use of it. Gorbachev, for better or for worse, accepted this flank protection, coming to rely on it more and more as events progressed. This created the basis of trust between the German chancellor and the Russian general secretary that was to have increasingly far-reaching effects.

Many politicians, both past and present, are due good grades in the paternity process of German unity. This goes for Gorbachev without a doubt; for Ronald Reagan, and George Bush after him; and certainly for Kohl and Genscher. But these stars did not perform unassisted—others set the stage for their achievements. Although it is difficult to assess Helmut Schmidt's contribution, justice plainly demands that Willy Brandt receive ample credit for taking a creative part in bringing about détente, for encouraging the two blocs to greater flexibility, and for bringing the hostile parties closer to one another in perceived possibilities and interests. No matter what false conclusions some parts of the SPD drew from this, Brandt himself must receive high marks. It is no coincidence that at the end of 1989 he was the first among the SPD to perceive the historical importance of what was taking place and to welcome it, promptly to find himself under fire from his own party and almost shunted aside at the party's

Berlin convention. Attempts within the Union parties to deny or downplay Brandt's role are small-minded and do not correspond to the facts, even if justified to some extent by the deviant course some sections of the SPD pursued during the second opposition period. These aberrations do not reflect the essential views of the Social Democrats as revealed when they were in power.

In recapitulating the process of unification itself, it is helpful to call on the diary kept by Horst Teltschik, foreign-policy advisor and member of Kohl's "kitchen cabinet." Published as *329 Tage* (329 Days),[8] its matter-of-fact prose gives it the air of a thriller. Teltschik begins with the fall of the Berlin Wall. Despite his proximity to the chancellor he admits that "it is always difficult to decipher Helmut Kohl's emotions. Only the way in which he briskly issues orders and his increasingly quick movements betray disquiet and tension—the Berlin Wall has fallen." Gorbachev, in yet another sensational move, orders the heads of the SED to make sure the "transition" of the GDR is peaceful. Unification is within reach, for Soviet troops will not move against it, a fact that Kohl is aware of from his talks with the general secretary. There is no fear of a "Chinese solution" like Tiananmen Square. Gorbachev's sole concern is that things proceed peacefully in an orderly fashion. Kohl can guarantee this. The sensational "ten-point program,"[9] by this time long superseded, nevertheless remains the cornerstone for everything that follows. Within a few weeks East Germans accomplish a peaceful "revolution" that provides the dynamic thrust for a breathtaking year.

In the West, at first, only George Bush in Washington unconditionally supports the course Kohl is taking toward unification. Kohl pursues this course with no disagreement on the part of Foreign Minister Hans-Dietrich Genscher, who plays his part no less masterfully than the chancellor. Genscher, a dyed-in-the-wool Free Democrat, never once attempts to challenge Kohl's primacy on this crucial issue. Cooperation between the two proceeds so smoothly and efficiently that Kohl is moved to comment, "Genscher simply has done this very well." Kohl and George Bush are in agreement that "a way must be found not to push Gorbachev to the wall, and yet hold the West together." Kohl has one major reservation: "The President must not fail to realize that the German question is developing 'like a groundswell in the ocean.'"

Indeed, the groundswell gains momentum: "All timetables are being scrapped." Bonn realizes that the window to unification could quickly close again; time is of the essence. French president Mitterand's attempts to effect the decision-making process one way or another with sudden trips to the GDR and to Kiev quickly fade into the background without affecting Franco-German relations. Equally insignificant is the irritation caused by British prime minister Margaret Thatcher in her obscure Germany seminar.[10] Kohl, with consummate tact, holds to his course, seemingly unmoved.

But by January 1990 it becomes clear that "large sacrifices" might be called for that could effect a change in the mood of the country and relegate the "euphoria" of unification to distant memory. This perception proves correct, though it is ignored at the time. "Polls confirm growing concern among West Germans that they might become the special victims of reunification." Was this at the root of the greatest of all errors committed, the all-too-facile promise not to increase taxes—a promise that could not be honored in the face of growing needs? There is the dawning recognition that real troubles would occur only with the introduction of the monetary union, but it fails to prompt the right conclusions.

The SPD's "campaign of fear," vigorously stoked by Oskar Lafontaine, helps to rob unification of its momentum, and a general feeling of disillusionment sets in. Concrete issues take on their own weight. In negotiations with the Soviet Union there is the question of united Germany's membership in NATO. "Legitimate Soviet security interests" are met with a considerable reduction in troops, and with political and practical reforms of NATO. The concept of a European "defense partnership" begins to take shape. And there is the issue of financial aid, which has to be renewed several times. Voices from both West and East continually urge conclusive recognition of the Oder-Neisse line, which, however—as any informed person must know—only within the framework of the Two-plus-Four agreement can have the validity of international law. On the domestic front there are disputes with the transitional government in East Berlin, led by Egon Krenz and Hans Modrow, and constitutional debates concerning Article 23,[11] which is derided by critics as "colonization." In rapid succession Germany experiences the March elections in the GDR, the implementation of the German economic and monetary union, the formulation of the unification treaty by Interior Ministers Wolfgang Schäuble and Günther Krause, and the first all-German "plebiscite," held at the beginning of December 1990. The political situation holds everyone in its grip, including Chancellor Helmut Kohl, who finds himself rushing from one pinnacle to the next.

With British prime minister Margaret Thatcher in Frankfurt am Main, February 1989.

With French president François Mitterand in Bonn, November 1988.

*At an election campaign event organized by the Saxony CDU for the first
all-German elections, Dresden, September 1990.*

Never has the primacy of Bonn's policies been so little questioned,
not even in light of then *Bundesbank* president Karl Otto Pöhl's economically founded objections to the immediate introduction of the
economic and monetary union. Germany's politicians all find themselves standing in Kohl's shadow. Helmut Schmidt retires to the Canary
Islands to write a book, Brandt speaks in support of unification—the
lone voice in the SPD. Federal President Richard von Weizsäcker
appears to be waiting it out. Though his role in unification is noticeably reserved, he is soon accepted by the new federal states, whereas
Helmut Kohl is held responsible for everything that goes wrong.

The end of one history and the beginning of another: Germany divided is reunited as a sovereign state, its membership in the Western alliance unquestioned, a bitter pill the Kremlin has to swallow. Germany—according to a moving declaration by Gorbachev—can begin to go its own way in freedom. The country is no longer riven by borders where blood is spilled. Germany regains its territorial integrity with the definitive recognition of its borders and the categorical renunciation of territorial claims of any kind. Kohl did not do things by half measures; according to Teltschik, his motto was: "Everything that can be gathered into the barn now is secure. Now is the time to take advantage of all opportunities and to overlook none." The decisive breakthrough in the eyes of the public is Kohl's visit to Gorbachev in the Caucasus. But in truth, this meeting is only to finalize the substantive agreements negotiated several days earlier in Moscow. The journey to Stavropol is the crowning touch. The public needs symbolic gestures and they get them—not least in the colorful depictions provided by Hans "Johnny" Klein, who in his book, *Es geschah im Kaukasus* (It Happened in the Caucasus),[12] documents in detail the background, and course, of events. The happy news is announced during Kohl's return trip: "It is done."

During the Two-plus-Four talks that follow, intended to be the last joint appearance of the former occupying powers, Kohl—as he often did during this period—insists with "almost ferocious vehemence" on the absolute equality of the two German negotiation partners. He categorically rejects any negotiations that would take place over the Germans' heads, saying, "We don't need four midwives."

The two first-hand accounts authored by the co-pilots of policy at the Caucasus meeting, Horst Teltschik and Hans Klein, provide important clues to the dynamics of the events. For it is necessary to reinhabit this shining hour of the Kohl chancellorship to comprehend the intensity, the adroitness, and the singlemindedness with which Kohl followed his course. He strove at every stage of the process to attain the unconditional sovereignty of a united Germany. This meant, above all, the unconditional freedom of alliance and the inclusion of all of Germany in the Western system of defense. With this the Soviet Union once and for all renounced all hope of neutralizing Germany in the center of Europe in order to use it, as it had been used in the nineteenth century, as a pawn in international conflicts. Many, even in the government, considered the demands that Kohl made successfully during this period to be exaggerated and illusory. But one of the most important of them was barely noticed. Kohl refused to sign anything that resembled a conventional peace treaty, and yet what he achieved had the quality of precisely that. This was a double victory for Kohl, for it also signified the end of the European totalitarianism, in which the Germans had played such an indelible part.

The quick tempo and almost harmonious handling of such high-caliber tasks can be explained by the fact that the group of decision makers and advisors was quite small. This was the administration's finest hour, and the legislature had simply to look on. But as is often the case with such successes, it was consumed, celebrated, and then rapidly supplanted by new tensions.

Federal President Richard von Weizsäcker receives the fourth (and first united German) cabinet of Chancellor Helmut Kohl, January 18, 1991. First row, from left: Angela Merkel, Theodor Waigel, Kohl, von Weizsäcker, Hans-Dietrich Genscher, Jürgen Möllemann. Second row, from left: Rudolf Seiters, Norbert Blüm, Ignaz Kiechle, Hannelore Rönsch, Irmgard Adam-Schwaetzer, Gerhard Stoltenberg. Third row, from left: Günther Krause, Rainer Ortleb, Klaus Töpfer, Christian Schwarz-Schilling, Gerda Hasselfeldt, Klaus Kinkel, Wolfgang Schäuble, Heinz Riesenhuber, Carl-Dieter Spranger.

In the Beginning Was Adenauer was the title of a paperback by Arnulf Baring,[13] published over twenty years ago. Well-respected historian Thomas Nipperdey later adapted this succinct phrase for the first and second volumes of his great *Deutsche Geschichte* (German History),[14] in order to stress, contrary to prevailing popular and academic views, the dominant roles played by two key figures of the first and second halves of the nineteenth century: *In the Beginning Was Napoleon*, and *In the Beginning Was Bismarck*. But for postwar Germany and the Federal Republic, the account of creation must indeed open with "In the beginning was Adenauer."

This lapidary phrase makes sufficiently clear the significance of the first German chancellor to German and European postwar history, a towering significance that provides history with a rare example. Adenauer demonstrated that even total defeat can be turned into victory. And total defeat was the point from which Adenauer set off on an unparalleled ascent. West Germany became the number one economic power in Europe, the most important partner of all European alliances, and an anchor of the Atlantic Alliance. Adenauer's guiding role in the Federal Republic's political development and direction has long since ceased to be a topic of debate. He well knew how to use the global-political constellation at the beginning of the Cold War— the growing confrontation between the victorious powers—not only to create an historic realignment of German policy, but to rapidly overcome material deprivations and the great hardship experienced by German refugees from the East. At some point all of his adversaries, this author included, acknowledged the propriety and inevitability of his policy of integration. History had taught us that the Federal Republic had to cast its lot, one way or the other, in order not to be used as the pawn of the superpowers. Contemporary historians, in as far as they dealt with Adenauer at all, could only confirm his unique position, occasionally transfiguring his thoroughly impervious and certainly not infallible personality. And yet his fame grew in proportion to the degree to which the inner logic of his ideas was revealed. Former U.S. president Richard Nixon, in his own inimitable fashion, painted a "statesman's" portrait of Adenauer: "He was our own Iron Curtain. A man of iron, but also of infinite patience. He towered over the ruins of postwar Germany like a great cathedral."[15]

But the question of whether even the miracle of "reunification" owes its existence to his much-debated "policy of strength" remains an open one, and is once again the object of partisan debate. Did "*Der Alte*," castigated as the "Rhenish separatist," truly desire the unification of Germany? Did he believe in it? Was it a solid policy goal, or merely an empty formula used to pacify the nation in its dreams and illusions? These questions took on new importance after 1990, and have forced a revision of Adenauer's image. The SPD once dubbed him the "gravedigger of unification"—today he is seen as its first and major birth attendant. The frequent claim by skeptical critics that incalculably fortunate conditions led to unification, in spite of and not because of Adenauer's policy of strength, is refutable. The first chancellor saw the division of Germany as a European tragedy that should not and would not be allowed to endure.

Adenauer's policies have been blamed for the fact that unification was long thought unlikely by most Germans, and eventually no longer desirable by many, and for the fact that the longer the two Germanys were divided the more they drifted apart. Many believed, or maintained, that Adenauer considered unification "counterproductive" and would sacrifice it to pay for the Federal Republic's prosperity and its acceptance into the community of Western nations. They believed Adenauer deliberately intended a future "without Prussia." Security at the cost of unification—for many Germans this was the lie of the Adenauer era. But none of these constantly repeated assertions stand up under informed scrutiny.

The most typical stock phrase was the criticism that Adenauer didn't even explore the various offers made by the Kremlin concerning unification. It is said that he knowingly sabotaged the "opportunities" he was given; that unification was not dear to his heart; that he sacrificed it on the altar of his policy of integration, well knowing that none of his declarations on unification were realizable. Each of these assertions is equally false. In light of the historical documents, and also in reviewing Adenauer's concepts, it can be established that he did indeed desire Germany's unification (precisely for the sake of defense), and that, moreover, he considered his to be the only correct strategy. It was well known that he "took up the cudgels" against anyone who dared as much as suggest a softer policy on unification. The decisive difference between Adenauer and Kurt Schumacher, the first chairman of the SPD, was that Adenauer's point of departure as a partner in the Atlantic Alliance was the "inevitability of the detours," the necessity of indirect methods, and the reassurance of German interests. The heart of his strategy was that if he held fast to this course and practiced the necessary patience he could not fail to reach his goal. And that, as history has demonstrated since, was correct.

But this does not contradict the crucial fact that, in its end phase, Adenauer's position on Germany was too rigid, too intractable, too doctrinaire to evolve an aggressive policy on détente. He took the first major step to set the switches of history's track, but not the second; that was to be reserved for the socialist-liberal coalition's "policy of détente" under Brandt. It remains for historians to explore just what were the limits of Adenauer's opportunities and his abilities to exploit them.

And yet there is evidence that Helmut Kohl might not have been given his great historical opportunity were it not for the consistent implementation of the "policy of strength" as a foundation for all later developments. Adenauer's Euro-Atlantic bond was, and is, the fundamental law of existence for the Federal Republic both in foreign and domestic policy. All the major parties accommodated themselves to it and, despite conflicts, submitted to it in principle. From an objective point of view and judging by the end result, there can be no doubt that the first chancellor's strategy, his grasp of power politics, his far-sightedness, and the firmness of his actions all make him the "super-father" of unification.

Those who do not comprehend this fail to comprehend German postwar history, for only in this light does that history become a coherent whole, a consistent and conclusive political pattern with an implicit agenda with a relevance for the future. To fathom the fundamental historical reorientation associated with Adenauer's name in history, and to grasp its trend-setting relevance one must seriously consider this assessment. "Superfather of unification" is a large claim to make, yet one may be sure that it passes historical muster. This is not to heap belated praise on Adenauer, but to invite an accurate analysis that takes the historical context into account. Nor does this in any way detract from the extraordinary accomplishments of Helmut Kohl, who, after all, did more than merely draw the lucky number in the lottery for a one-time chance at a fateful moment to revise the most recent chapter in Germany's ominous history. The achievement of Adenauer's "grandson" can be appreciated only by recognizing it as continuation and culmination of Adenauer's agenda, which Helmut Kohl himself always viewed as principle and guidepost, and applied as practical policy.

In the meantime, much scorn and ridicule has gone into the discussion of Adenauer as "superfather of unification." Unjustly so, as closer examination shows. With astonishing—even fascinating—precision Adenauer's strategy contained all the preconditions that eventually led to the end of the Cold War—from the dissolution of the

Warsaw Treaty Organization to the downfall of the Soviet Union and the extensive disarmament process between East and West.

The old man who first became chancellor at age seventy-two took his direction from a simple basic concept of overpowering consequence and efficacy: If the Federal Republic joined the West and never again submitted to the temptation of a treacherous seesaw policy; if Germany unerringly pursued the process of integration into the political, economic, and military defense systems of the West, then the day must come when the West's solidarity, and the superiority of its democratic order and social potential would force the Soviet Union, in the interest of its own survival, to open itself to talks on the basic issues, from disarmament to the reunification of Germany.

Among the wealth of evidence supporting these thoughts is the following statement, quoted in its entirety:

> ■ Soviet Russia cannot tolerate the unification of Europe, because it knows this would stop its drive to the West, and because it knows that the day would come when Soviet Russia would have to realize that a Cold War, which was also costing Soviet Russia a great sum of money, no longer had any purpose, and it therefore would have to sit down with the others at the negotiating table as an equal. It is not as if Soviet Russia could continue ad infinitum to shoulder the burden of armament it has take upon itself. ■

Adenauer occasionally said that the Soviet Union had "gorged" itself with its gigantic expansion of power following the Second World War. In essence, his ideas already contained Paul Kennedy's aforementioned theory of the "rise and fall of the great powers," which delineates why it was inevitable that the West would "win" the Cold War.

If there is renewed appreciation of Adenauer's policy in light of present events, one must still marvel at its extraordinary logic. From a defense perspective it could be described as follows: As long as the West stands together the Cold War cannot heat up. Soviet appetite for expansion will be nipped in the bud because of the risk of nuclear war, and the Cold War will then turn into an arms race, which only the West—thanks to its technological and material superiority— will withstand. But as soon as the Kremlin recognizes that it cannot win the Cold War it will be willing to enter into disarmament talks and accept a new order in Europe. And that is exactly how it happened. Socialism drew the short straw in the competition between the two superpowers, something *"Der Alte"* was clear about from the beginning.

Crucial criteria for an evaluation flow from this. Adenauer's strategy, prompted above all by deep skepticism, even distrust, of his own people's psychological stability, required farsightedness and an incalculable amount of time and patience. Indeed, it included the resolute rejection of all reunification offers originating in Moscow, for the Soviets at the time always attached to such offers the condition of Germany's withdrawal from the Western alliance and declaration of neutrality. And for Adenauer that meant that unification could come only at the price of the "Sovietization" of Europe. With this, the list of political priorities was clearly programmed: Freedom and peace ranked above unification, without the idea of unification ever being surrendered. "Germany cannot be permitted to be caught between the grindstones, otherwise it will be lost," Adenauer said in 1953.

In his mammoth biography of Adenauer, historian Hans-Peter Schwarz has furnished evidence that, his critics notwithstanding, the first chancellor never lost sight of reunification. Adenauer's policy of strength was never an end in itself, but rather the instrument of a long-term strategy of visionary power. "When the West is stronger than the Soviet Union," his constantly repeated assessment of the situation went, "then the day of negotiation with Soviet Russia has arrived." That has proved correct (even, in a sense, the slip of the tongue coupling of the Soviet Union with Russia).

In the long run—and this was something Adenauer repeated not once, but hundreds of times—the Soviet Union would lose the battle between the two superpowers, both economically *and* morally. Indeed, he always kept in sight the competition of the systems, the internal superiority of the West and the system-driven inferiority of the East in all decisive aspects. That is why he never considered possible—on the national level and in the shadow of the superpowers—a so-called *lesser solution* to the issue of unification. According to his primary political doctrine, the resolution of the German question depends fundamentally on the international "weather situation." It can be arrived at only within the global framework of an agreement between East and West, that is to say, only under the European roof. The internal logic of this was such that Helmut Kohl returned to it again and again, even in his choice of words, and used it to create the framework within which unification was then indeed realized. Even if *"Der Alte"* never imagined it, Kohl was his eager "pupil."

Neutrality was anathema to the first postwar chancellor. One could probably speak of a (historically well-founded) "neutrality trauma," which he cultivated, and not only as election propaganda to be used against the Social Democrats. He knew only too well that "the left" was susceptible to the allure of neutrality, even if he didn't live to experience the great and dangerous effect this tendency would have on the "freedom marchers" in the later debate on rearmament. The Kremlin, which Adenauer greatly distrusted, would do anything to break the Federal Republic's ties to the Atlantic Alliance. And for a long time he feared that the SPD would succeed in cutting those bonds and creating a de-militarized vacuum in the center of Europe. To avoid misunderstanding it must be emphasized that Adenauer's "policy of strength" never assumed a militant character, but rather a politically operative one. His main concern was maintaining the peace and securing German interests as best he could in a polarized world.

No one today would contend that Adenauer actually foresaw events as they would happen. With trepidation one might ask what could have occurred differently, or gone wrong, for the imagination knows no bounds. All the more astonishing, therefore, is the logic with which history ultimately moved toward overcoming the division of Europe. Adenauer's position looked forward, it was oriented to the future, which is to say it did not rely on coincidence. It was grounded in a realistic and sober assessment of the possibilities—and impossibilities—of power politics, including the underlying assumption that the German question could be resolved only within the context of "collective disarmament," and could not be "isolated." It presumed that the superpowers would come to an understanding and firmly repudiate the temptation for Germany to go it alone. There was constant concern that one day the victors of the Second World War would come to an agreement over the Germans' heads. Adenauer even distrusted his friend Dulles, and he totally distrusted the American administration under young President John F. Kennedy.

To appreciate Adenauer's concerns ("What is to become of the Germans?"), and his desperate struggle to keep developments from going off track, it should be remembered that the Cold War did not progress in linear fashion, and that the West was also constantly considering "flexible" responses and thinking about détente and ways to end the Cold War. Adenauer was under pressure not only at home from an opposition that was growing stronger, he was also under pressure from the West. And without a doubt the Kremlin as well was thinking about easing East-West tensions, and at the same time about a way to drive the United States out of Europe. The mood in postwar history underwent constant change. (Even the Kremlin must have questioned the sense of the arms race early on, for soon after Stalin's death in 1953 Khrushchev attempted to steer the two world powers into a contest of social and economic systems, prophesying that America would reach the limit of its prosperity in twenty years and then be surpassed.)

Adenauer doubtless wished to sabotage any hint of détente, and for that reason alone preferred to deal directly with Moscow (as in 1955). Adenauer the pragmatist was close to unscrupulous, though ingenious, in his means, and for his every evasive maneuver there is now a plausible explanation. An example of his response to the "neutrality trauma" was his distrust of the U.S., which was already evident in the Eisenhower/Dulles era, and full-blown in the climate of appeasement during Kennedy's administration. He searched desperately for a counterbalance in Europe, which resulted in reconciliation with France and his own bonding with de Gaulle. Adenauer would not have hesitated to forge Germany's defense in alliance with France, as is evidenced by the negotiations on the EDC (European Defense Community). They were unsuccessful only because the French parliament failed to approve.

The contradictions of Adenauer's policy, which became increasingly evident toward the end of his tenure, were nothing more than a reflex of the developing view that his "policy of strength" could not, in the long run, preclude an arrangement with the Soviets. Adenauer saw this problem but was no longer able to resolve it. In an illuminating dissertation entitled *Gezeitenwechsel—Aufbruch zur Entspannungspolitik* (Turn of the Tide—The Emergence of the Policy of Détente),[16] published in 1990, though written earlier, Peter Siebenmorgen furnishes proof that Chancellor Adenauer recognized the risks in the absence of détente early on without being able to do anything about it. At the beginning of the fifties it was Adenauer himself who had first mentioned the issue of détente. But he stuck to his belief that relations with the East would normalize only once talks on the German question progressed. He therefore did everything in his power to avoid an upgrading of the GDR, whereas the SPD accepted this risk. This was the phase in which Egon Bahr, hoping to achieve progress precisely by acknowledging the status quo of power in Europe, came up with his strategy of "change through rapprochement." The fact that this gave the GDR more legitimacy—clashing with the SPD's doctrine, sacrosanct since Schumacher's time, of absolute priority for unification over everything else—thus was one of its paradoxes. The Adenauer government, in any event, resisted it fiercely, not least because it feared the Federal Republic would be uncoupled from the Western defense system, and that the West would betray German interests.

None of the parties wanted unification at any price. There was always agreement about that. Their political differences lay in the methods each used to move within the magic triangle of freedom-unity-defense. But the terms of this discussion were set during the immediate postwar period by the Union camp, and then further developed by the Social Democrats. But in politics, the most important changes, as a rule, are made in response to reality. With their Godesberg Program the Social Democrats took the decisive step toward domestic "equality of status," therewith avowing their loyalty to the Federal Republic, recognizing the treaties with the Western powers, and accepting the free market economy. It was Herbert Wehner who in 1960 sought to align himself with Adenauer, declaring before the *Bundestag*: "The SPD proceeds from the assumption that the system of treaties with Europe and the Atlantic Alliance, to which the Federal Republic belongs, provides the basis and framework for all efforts being expended in German foreign and reunification policy."

The SPD wanted to come to power at last. But it was only during the Great Coalition, with Schiller in charge of economic policy and Brandt in charge of foreign policy, that it succeeded in taking a more progressive position, thereby creating more room in which foreign policy could maneuver. The opening moves of détente proved to be a tightrope walk, but in the end it led to a breakthrough of internationally recognized proportions. Nevertheless, differences were not as fundamental as they appeared. Adenauer was anything but a committed opponent of détente; he merely judged those risks involved to be much higher than did the SPD. That is why, during his time in office, he remained a prisoner of the claim that the Federal Republic was the sole representative of Germany. This increasingly tied his hands in foreign policy. One constitutional basis for the idea of "sole representation" is the unification mandate written into the preamble to the Basic Law—it furnished a convincing reason for Adenauer not to abandon this claim. He and the Union doubted that the willingness to enter détente was compatible with the advancement of national unity.

The resolution of this doubt became, in a sense, the true achievement of Helmut Kohl, in his own "turning point" at the beginning of his first term in office. This author is unaware of any systematic treatment of this thesis, and for this reason I stress it here. Kohl established contact with both lines of German postwar policy, with the vigorous support of Hans-Dietrich Genscher as foreign minister in both successive coalitions. Genscher's role in the continued development of the CSCE cannot be overestimated. He introduced to the conservative-liberal camp the concept of his foreign policy, and with it the reasoning behind the beginning East-West rapprochement, which was now reaching into such vital areas as human rights and information exchange.

To fully explore the complex interactions between the at first divergent foreign-policy views of the Union and the liberals would need a lengthier discussion than this chapter permits. But any inquiry into the specifics leading up to reunification will certainly confirm that the process can only be understood as the dialectical interplay between national and international forces as well as between opposing and alternative concepts. One might well cite Hegel's "cunning of history," which on occasion works without the knowledge and against the will of the players. In a similar vein, one could also speak of an unarticulated "national consensus," forged and produced by constitutional law and democratic interactions, which continues to exist despite all differences. In addition to this underlying societal consensus, which, regardless of individual merits, prevents anyone from claiming reunification as a partisan achievement, there is yet another cunning of reason, which might be called the political cunning of reason. Each of the coalition governments in Bonn addressed itself to the very same problems the previous coalition government had been unable to resolve, because it had run out of ideas. The Social Democrats, for instance, soon ran out of ideas for détente. From a national perspective this interplay between antagonistic democratic forces could be represented as a spiral turning on a stable axis, as consensus in divergence.

During his time as chancellor, Adenauer was unable to respond to the imperative of détente, though after his "retirement" he attracted attention with mysterious-sounding statements to the effect that "the Soviet Union has joined those nations who want peace." Heinrich Krone, chairman of the CDU, and a man who knew Adenauer better than most, noted in his diary (as quoted by H. P. Schwarz) "that Adenauer views the international political situation under the sign of détente, and we Germans should take note of that." But in his final years Adenauer became noticeably entangled in the "contradictions and inconsistencies" (Schwarz) of the consequences of his "policy of strength," something no one active in politics has ever been spared. It was Willy Brandt, seconded by Egon Bahr, who, in an extremely risky but ultimately successful act, positioned his socialist-liberal coalition at the forefront of the détente movement. But then, in the midst of the euphoria surrounding détente, the Soviet Union came up with its "prearmament."[17] The socialist-liberal coalition under Schmidt and Genscher was faced with a much greater security risk, which the administration recognized but was unable to resolve, due to boisterous leftist peace marchers and pressure from the street. It was Helmut Kohl's hour.

What is to become of Germany? Adenauer devoted his life's work to this central question, and it has lost none of its validity. Reunification has not relieved anyone from worrying about his country; if anything, the concerns have increased. They are not of a temporary nature, but are long-term. The material problems of budgetary and of financial policy are one thing, but the more difficult question is that of the search for a national self-image in a radically changing world. One need only contemplate the re-emerging "curse of geo-politics" (which comes with the position in the middle of Europe) the rise of anti-German sentiment (not least in the West), or the difficulties in achieving political consensus while defining Germany's role in future military missions as a member of the international community. Is Germany a mature nation ready to assume its new responsibilities, or does the crisis in which it now finds itself touch the very core of its inner insecurity? Underlying all these concerns is the search for the identity of the new Federal Republic, which cannot simply take up where German history left off, nor can it deny the past.

These reflections can be viewed in the light of a near-bizarre realization. It can be said with astonishment of the old and departed "Bonn Republic" that it was loved more than we ever dared hope. It was loved not least of all by its untiring foes and critics. But this was a love that declared itself too late. At any rate, West Germany was never crowned with such laurel wreaths nor was it sung such hymns of praise—by all its parties left to right—as it has been since its demise. It was only postmortem that the former Federal Republic was truly appreciated and loudly lamented, a fact that psychologically is altogether understandable and not to be ignored politically, though opinions on the issue are mixed.

The new federal states of former East Germany are manifesting similar symptoms. Tears are being shed for what has been transformed in nostalgic memory into social security and sheltered existence. The "blessings" of an open and consumer-oriented society are by no means universally perceived as such. Though the Germans continue to grow together in spite of these doubts, it would be an exaggeration to speak of a general "identification" with the Federal Republic as it exists. The antagonism of the two systems, with their opposing economic, social, and intellectual structures, was greatly underestimated. Therefore no one can foresee each and every problem unification will yet create. Unification has given Germany an identity "kink" if not an identity crisis. This makes even more important and interesting the question of which concept of identity Chancellor Kohl adopts as the leading actor in this still unresolved situation.

The answer is plain. Kohl's idea of identity embraces all of German history, from its heights to its depths, in a universal formula he has often expressed. During the 1989 *Bundestag* debate about the construction of a house of history he said: "We must—and we shall—accept our history as a whole, with its good as well as its terrible side." But that is also to say that for Kohl a specific insoluble problem of identity does not exist, as it does for so many other Germans. As a historian, Kohl's point of departure is that Germans must "accept" the whole of their history, without letting the past place them in damnation. Confronting preceding generations the way the student movement of 1968/69 confronted its fathers arouses little sympathy in him, for Kohl had no traumatic fixation on the Third Reich, cultivating no guilt complex as did many leftist intellectuals, who remained as blind to the censurable elements of socialism as they did to the historical transformation of the West. Anyone aware of the misconceptions of many pseudo-socialists and socialists in the last few years knows that their selectively cultivated guilt is related to a particular chapter of Germany's repressed reality and to a disdain for politics. Taken to its logical conclusion, this mindset almost always leads to the abandonment of politics and to an incessant focus on *Vergangenheitsbewältigung* (coming to grips with the past)—a stance of moral sterility, for in effect it stands in the way of any politics that has the future as its objective. It is obvious that this is not Helmut Kohl's choice.

At the same time, he has never denied that all Germans must share in the responsibility for Germany's past, even those who were not personally involved. "It cannot be disputed that Germans bear responsibility for the Second World War, for Nazi atrocities, for Auschwitz, Treblinka, and the Holocaust," he stated in the aforementioned interview in *Süddeutsche Zeitung*. But using "anti-fascism" as a politically transparent stratagem, as the GDR did (with the active support of the Federal Republic's left)—to draw attention away from the totalitarian character of its own system—to Kohl would appear as implausible as it would grotesque.

Again in the Adenauer tradition, Kohl always considered European integration to be the only response equal to the issues of past and future. If you have acted wrongly in the past, then you must try to do better in the future: so simple and straightforward is his rule of life in politics. It answers the attempt to define German identity solely in terms of the unique event of the Holocaust, which politically incapacitates with the burden of indelible guilt. That such a view of German identity relates to a deep-seated rancor toward those who died in the war, or fell in battle, was revealed by the violent reactions to President Ronald Reagan's and Chancellor Kohl's visit to the Bitburg military cemetery.

In an article for the monthly *Merkur* (issue 526), Gustav Seibt, a young historian, wrote:

> ■ In a different fashion the "historians' debate"[18] also resulted in the entrenchment of a special West German identity. The meta-historical anomaly of the mass crimes committed by the National Socialists sanctioned the unique role of the divided nation, which was to be denied naive access to the time preceding the epoch-making year of 1945. Viewed in this light, West Germany's "lack of a history" was the inevitable answer to Auschwitz, the dimension of which had exploded all previous historical experience. ■

Several passages later Seibt continues: "On the eve of the events of 1989, the Federal Republic—there can be no doubt of this in retrospect—was on the verge of becoming a country with its own history and tradition." This revealing closing remark once again underscores that many Germans had long since come to terms with the division of the country and the separate existence of a German rump state left to its own "dearth of history." And this explains the immense obstacles in the parliamentary political spectrum that must yet be overcome in order for Germany to meet its new responsibilities. Many Germans believe it would be more moral and more humane to remain in a state of historical "non-responsibility." Nor did it seriously disturb these people that this turning away from historical responsibility gave vent to militant acts of violence.

By the same token, there is a connection between the most egregious forms of terrorist violence from the right, including that against foreigners, and the search for a German identity. Surprising confirmation of this can be found in a *Spiegel* essay (issue 26, 1993) by author Martin Walser, who—reacting to a massive attack from the "left"—writes compellingly of the entire complex surrounding the disastrous dismissal of all national feelings. "But the forty-year exclusion of the word 'nation' from the vocabulary of those in responsible positions, the opinion makers, the politicians, the intellectuals, has not changed the fact that the word 'nation' has survived apart from public opinion." And just as the concept of "nation" was to be excluded, so, too, was its object. Hence the division of Germany. "It [the division of Germany] was to appear reasonable and enduring. And toward this end was introduced the self-bridled leftist intellectual just as he was ridding himself of his own harness." In this context Walser leaves no doubt that the restoration of the "nation" is not at issue. "Nation—that is nobody's main problem. Not for a long time now. And never again." Which lends credence to his following statement:

■ I believe the growth of right-wing extremist groups is a response to the fact that we have all neglected the concept of nation. And we have all always denied these keepers of the national flame any sort of legitimacy. . . . Only through demonization are demons produced. . . . One must accept one's own children, even if they have developed into something monstrous. We must change the climate in which these deeds become possible. Through further and pointed exclusion, condemnation, demonization, and criminalization we only contribute to their next egregious act. ■

This neither denies nor diminishes the danger of right-wing extremism, but it does make clear that the repression and the condemnation of what is considered "national" is one cause of the right's radicalization and leads directly to the social isolation of those damned to remain alone and uncounseled with their disturbing beliefs. Here, again, is evidence of the interplay between essentially totalitarian ideologies on the left and the right.

Helmut Kohl, incidentally, was not at all surprised by Germany's right-wing extremism. He recognized it early on, long before its sharp escalation: "The danger of right-wing extremism is always present—even in a free and open society." The answer of how to effectively respond to this danger has yet to be found, which Walser's critical remarks only serve to confirm. Nor can the judicial system alone—or the police—supply it. The solution, rather, is closely connected to the internal well-being of society, to overcoming the structural problems at almost all levels of society, from the economy to the educational system, from the practical management of the asylum issue to the containment of the growing rate of crime and violence. No doubt we are dealing with a collision of crises that were to some extent unleashed, or brought to the surface, by unification. There will be no quick solution. The new situation in global politics, combined with economic recession and the outbreak of regional conflicts in Europe, has burdened Germans with problems they evidently are learning to cope with only gradually.

This might, in fact, have its positive side, for the return of German "nationalism," feared both inside and outside of Germany in the aftermath of unification, has failed to materialize. The fact is that "the state" is having trouble enough just coming to terms with itself and its new responsibilities. The prophesies of the return of Germany's demons proved false, and, at a deeper level, wishful thinking. The issue of the national state has not been an acute one; it is discussed by the experts and practically ignored by the rest of German society. Unification—and this is one of the surprises of recent events—has not unleashed a glut of nationalism. Its stigma is the sober mood in the country, a turning away from the issue of national identity and toward the material problems of dealing with integration. Seen from this point of view, the increasing disillusionment with politics, particularly with party politics, is a clear sign of a national "lack of connection." Germany is more a society than a state. And when the state is invoked, it is the social-welfare state.

This is not to say that the issue of the national state has been resolved once and for all. This becomes quite apparent in the debate surrounding Germany's capital city, in which parliament has expressed a postmodern identification with "Bonn" across the board. This split-identity syndrome has been articulated best by Kurt Biedenkopf,[19] in an interview in *Transit 3:* "The fact that this is a search for something new, and not for the old certainties, is exemplified by the vehement debate on whether Berlin or Bonn is to be the capital of Germany. If there were such a thing as a securely anchored national consciousness, as there appeared to be in the wish for unification, there would be no question of the choice of Berlin—for the nation's capital is at the same time a symbol of national identity."[20]

Biedenkopf then adds a memorable remark concerning European identity: "The projection of our identity onto Europe, which up until now has served as a major component of West Germany's self-image, no longer applies. The time for such improvisation is past. Europeans are saying now that we are a nation again, irrefutably, and demanding of us that we recognize this."

There is a great deal of evidence that this recognition, urged by those outside Germany, has yet to be acknowledged on a broad basis within Germany. Thus the issue of a new national identity, urgent since reunification, cannot be resolved for the present, nor can it even be articulated precisely. Identity is something the state cannot simply ordain. But if it is true that Germany can neither return to nor negate its past, then one thing becomes clear—a new and updated "enlightened national consciousness" must develop, incorporating tradition at the same time that it allows for Germany's future self-image gradually to unfold.

Where is Germany's connection to its past to be found? In its culture, its humanistic tradition, in the autonomy and productivity of its individual regions? There are many answers to this question, but no single one. The political case is more easily stated, though to no greater satisfaction. The nation-state of Bismarck, the Reich, at any rate, is dead, and Prussia is gone, though it remains a fond memory, and even an ideal, to many. These models cannot, nor should they, be permitted to be revived. The integration of German history dictates the integration of its transgressions. The past cannot simply be smoothed over and transformed into a success story.

But the fact that the conventional nation-state is dead does not mean that united Europe "lives" or even has taken its place. The integration of western Europe was a fitting response to the division of the continent, which also divided Germany. It served, primarily from the French point of view, to bind the German Federal Republic to the West, even to domesticate it. Great progress has been made toward integration, but the shortcomings are also great. The damage done to the European idea by the recent tremors in Europe itself is unmistakable. The agreements on the economic and monetary union, incorporated into the Maastricht Treaty after reunification, repeatedly came close to failure. Every reservation and objection expressed by economists, monetary experts, and specialists has left its mark. The momentum has been checked. The hope for political union—in light of the seemingly intractable conflict in the former Yugoslavia—has become ever more tenuous. The bureaucracy and centralism of the European

Helmut Kohl and Russian president Boris Yeltsin at a ceremony on August 31, 1994, receiving official report of completed Russian military departure from Germany. In his short address Kohl said: "This is the final end of the postwar era in Europe."

Celebrating the withdrawal of the Western Allies from Berlin, September 8, 1994. Helmut Kohl with, from left, U.S. secretary of state Warren Christopher, French president François Mitterand, British prime minister John Major, and Berlin mayor Eberhard Diepgen.

A triumphant Helmut Kohl facing the cameras after his re-election for another four-year term on November 15, 1994, after his coalition government of the CDU/CSU and the FDP had been returned by a narrow margin.

Community in Brussels have been cast into the role of scapegoat, making it clear that the European idea still lacks political and parliamentary legitimacy, and revealing the skepticism that still attaches to giving up national rights of sovereignty one after another.

Separate from the critical mood, the decisive question, in general, is: "How can European identity be balanced and reconciled with national identity, and at the same time become stabilized?" Any "harmonious" response to this question would be premature, the only certainty being that this dual identity must assume some shape or other. As Kurt Biedenkopf well understood, the European concept is less able now than ever to substitute for a lack of national identity. But that is not to say that it is "extinct" or obsolete. Helmut Kohl expressed it succinctly when he said: "Germany is our fatherland, Europe our future."

Admittedly, nothing about shape and content will have been decided by joining national to European identity. The hurdles to a European future that Kohl must overcome have become more perilous, and that makes even more astounding the fact that he, as a

Federal President Roman Herzog receiving the fifth Kohl cabinet on November 17, 1994. First row, from left: Helmut Kohl, Herzog, Theodor Waigel, Claudia Nolte; second row, from left: Norbert Blüm, Horst Seehofer, Günter Rexrodt, Sabine Leutheusser-Schnarrenberger, Manfred Kanther, Angela Merkel, Klaus Kinkel, Matthias Wissmann, Volker Rühe, Jürgen Rüttgers. Third row, from left: Klaus Töpfer, Jochen Borchert, Wolfgang Bötsch, Carl-Dieter Spranger, Friedrich Bohl.

German European, has steered a European course, and now an all-European course, with such unfailing self-assurance. That Kohl's outlook is in no way limited to the West is indicative of Germany's growing responsibility. There has been no new architecture created for the house of Europe, nor is there even a common foundation, but one thing is certain—no one will be excluded. In this context Kohl in February 1989 once again specifically summoned up the memory of Adenauer: "The hand we extend to the East, the offer of cooperation in the interest of humankind, has been a constant in our foreign policy since Adenauer first set the course during his visit to Moscow in 1955."

Even a cursory examination reveals that the German national identity has more than its share of ruptures and catastrophes, which cannot simply be patched up or denied or glued back together. Germans lack a coherent and self-contained national identity such as that of the French; it is something they have yet to find. But never in their history have they had the opportunity they have now, at the end of the twentieth century. For the first time, Germans can live *in peace with their past*, because reunification, viewed from a historical perspective, brought about a closure binding on all. This does not signify an end to German history, but a new beginning, a unique, single opportunity and challenge. In terms of the future the entire political scope of, and ambivalence, surrounding this challenge can be summarized thus: External unification has been achieved, internal unification is still to come.

Conclusion

This portrait of Helmut Kohl is incomplete for two reasons. First, the end of the story has yet to be written by the chancellor himself. And second, a brief essay can offer only an outline of the dominant precepts of Helmut Kohl's political thought. This necessitated a concentration on his outlook for the future, for Kohl expressly intends to make the path to Europe irreversible. In addition, unification must be reinforced, budgetary policies consolidated, and expectations concerning prosperity readjusted—he will not have an easy time of it. Also, inevitably, a second central theme was that of the personal caliber of the man, the issue, that is, of what enabled him to fully exploit the historic opportunity for unification to the advantage of his country.

One personal motive for the attempt this essay represents is the odd fact that Helmut Kohl is only seldom granted a just and unbiased assessment, an evaluation based not on externals, but on the substance of his policies and his requisite ability to accomplish them tenaciously and with diligence in the face of adversity. Those familiar with Max Weber will understand what is meant when it is said that Kohl willingly tackles the most onerous of tasks. At a time when the stage of political action keeps getting smaller and smaller, a chancellor

Cabinet meeting in Bonn, November 1994. From lower left, Claudia Nolte, Horst Seehofer, Jürgen Rüttgers, Carl-Dieter Spranger, Klaus Kinkel, Helmut Kohl, Friedrich Bohl, state ministers in the chancellery Anton Pfeiffer and Bernd Schmidbauer, state secretary Dieter Vogel, state minister in the

Foreign Office Werner Hoyer. From upper right, Klaus Töpfer, Wolfgang Bötsch, Angela Merkel, Matthias Wissmann, Manfred Kanther, Theodor Waigel, Günter Rexrodt, Sabine Leutheusser-Schnarrenberger, Jochen Borchert, Norbert Blüm, and Volker Rühe.

of Kohl's caliber is necessary to deal with a more critical situation. The future will confirm this.

But time and again the man keeps on being underestimated. He himself has said, "It has served me well that for years people have chronically underestimated me." Indeed, this has brought him political profit, for each time his opponents believe him finished, Kohl has seized the reins of action anew, a fact confirmed by any detailed examination.

The *Solidarpakt* (solidarity pact)[21] came into being after much effort and a lengthy tug-of-war. And after agonizing anticipation of the SPD's appraisal, the compromise on asylum was passed into law.[22] Arduously working its way past a veto by the SPD, and with the express help of the Constitutional Court, the federal government fulfilled its obligations concerning the deployment of German troops for United Nations missions, and will meet the goals it set for itself in this regard. Despite great trepidation following Denmark's rejection of the Maastricht Treaty, the pact was then ratified even by Great Britain, so that the timetable set for Europe may be maintained. Though mired in the market's downward trend, budgetary austerity measures and the redesign of the welfare state have been belatedly implemented. Despite weaknesses and signs of wear in the government camp, and despite its own majority in the *Bundesrat*, the Social Democratic opposition has been unable to gain a foothold.

The *costs* of unification were greatly underestimated in every respect, whether on the ideological or the material side. Could a more accurate assessment at the beginning essentially have altered or eased the situation? Has anyone developed a convincing model for how things could have proceeded in a better, quicker, less contentious fashion? What would an accurate report on the state of this society—west and east—look like? And who, in the midst of the storm of events, would be the one to unite it, in all of its facets, taking proper account of the shift in the balance of international relations and the obvious difficulties the United States is having in coming to terms with its new leadership role. But also considering the shift in the balance of European politics, which has thrown Germany back into the arena of mid-European tensions, surrounded by more neighbors than any other country—"encircled by friends," as Defense Minister Volker Rühe allegedly said—a "mid-sized major power" on a continent where almost everyone's expectations are focused on Germany.

Foreign policy alone demands a careful examination of the shifts in power, hidden rivalries, the historically determined conflicts of interest, the undercurrents of animosity coupled with barely concealed hints for ambitions of hegemony. The downward economic trend may have assuaged these ambitions somewhat, or transformed them in part to *schadenfreude* or anxiety, but they continue to exist, if only latently. And they could assume new characteristics as soon as the recession recedes and the final books on German unification show a positive balance.

An analysis of foreign policy would have to be complemented by a look at the domestic state of the Federal Republic, which is not in the best of shape. The crisis could be given many names, whether it is disaffection with politics or with government. Any report on the state of the country would have to talk about the end of "fair-weather democracy" and the "tearful self-pity" of the Germans, the need to renew the structure of both the economy and society, to dismantle subsidies and encourage more innovative action, and for a review of purpose now due in all social institutions. In short, there has been a plethora of changes in consciousness and climate, generally dismissed as "identity crisis," if only to call this hard-to-define phenomenon by a different name.

But any single analysis can only result in a snapshot devoid of any conclusive judgment about how the ever-changing problems will play out, so that a final assessment of the successes or omissions of the Kohl era is still premature. But it may be cautiously stated that what this chancellor wants, and what he was able to accomplish, is evident. What he will yet accomplish is written in the stars.

Notes

1. Arnulf Baring, *Deutschland, was nun?* (Germany, What Now?) (Berlin: Siedler Verlag, 1991).

2. Led by Franz Josef Strauss, the Bavarian CSU, predominantly Catholic and conservative, threatened at a meeting at Kreuth to compete for right-wing votes outside its Bavarian domain, thus breaking their parliamentary alliance with the CDU, which is predicated on both parties respecting each others' territorial exclusivity. The threat fizzled when in return the CDU threatened to invade Bavaria to compete for the conservative electorate, which would have cut into the CSU's dominant position there.

3. In July 1983, the Federal Republic of Germany guarenteed a loan of one billion Deutsche Mark to East Germany. The credit was provided by a Bavarian bank, and Franz Josef Strauss is widely regarded as the initiator of the agreement.

4. Oskar Fehrenbach, *Helmut Kohl—wer sonst?* (Helmut Kohl—Who Else?) (Munich: Verlag Bonn Aktuell, 1990).

5. Paul Kennedy, *The Rise and Fall of the Great Powers* (New York: Random House, 1987).

6. Golo Mann, *Deutsche Geschichte des 19. und 20. Jahrhunderts* (German History of the 19th and 20th Centuries) (Frankfurt am Main: S. Fischer Verlag, 1960).

7. Brezhnev doctrine. The proposition that Soviet intervention in the affairs of any other communist state is justified when communism is threatened, first published in *Pravda* on September 26, 1968, was applied to the invasion of Czechoslovakia the same year.

8. Horst Teltschik, *329 Tage. Innenansicht der Einigung* (329 Days: Inside View of Unification) (Berlin: Siedler Verlag, 1991).

9. On November 28, 1989, barely three weeks after the Wall came down, Kohl presented a ten-point program to the *Bundestag* proposing as the first step toward unification a federation of both German states. But this plan was soon dropped when events moved so fast that a currency union, established in June 1990, and actual unification became inevitable.

10. At the end of January 1990, then British prime minister Margaret Thatcher called together a number of politicians and historians, Gordon Craig and Hugh Trevor-Roper among them, at a secret meeting at Chequers to discuss the dangers of a united Germany, such as aggressiveness, arrogance, intimidation, and fear among its neighbors. For a while these considerations ruled British policy on German unification. When the transcript of the meeting became public it caused a public furor in Britain.

11. Article 23 of the Federal Republic's constitution allows Germans not residing within its jurisdictional territory to decide in free self-determination whether to join that territory. The *Volkskammer* (People's Chamber) of the GDR voted in the spring of 1990 to join in accordance with this provision, leading to the final negotiations for the unification treaty, which was signed on August 30, 1990. After unification this article was dropped from the constitution.

12. Hans Klein, *Es geschah im Kaukasus. Der entscheidende Schritt in die Einheit Deutschlands* (It Happened in the Caucasus: The Decisive Step in Germany's Unification) (Berlin: Ullstein, 1991).

13. Arnulf Baring, *Am Anfang war Adenauer* (In the Beginning Was Adenauer) (Munich/Vienna: Oldenbourg Verlag, 1969).

14. Thomas Nipperdey, *Deutsche Geschichte* (German History) (Munich: Beck, 1986).

15. Richard Nixon, *The Memoirs of Richard Nixon* (New York: Grosset & Dunlap, 1978).

16. Peter Siebenmorgen, *Gezeitenwechsel: Aufbruch zur Entspannungspolitik* (Turn of Tide: The Emergence of the Policy of Détente) (Bonn: Bouvier-Verlag, 1990).

17. While negotiating with the U.S. to bring deployment of missiles in Europe under the arms control agreement, the Soviets increased and modernized their conventional forces, which had not been subject to these discussions.

18. In the eighties, Ernst Nolte, a right-wing conservative historian, became the spokesman for the view that the Nazi period was merely one of many episodes in Germany's history, whether good or bad, and that the time had come to regard it with greater detachment, rather than single it out for its atrocities. This was disputed by other historians who argued that the Nazis had committed crimes of a dimension unknown before in the history of mankind, and that the time of Nazi rule required especially intensive study to make sure future generations of Germans are made aware of it. This clash, known as the "historians' debate," flared up again in 1995 with the fiftieth anniversary of the end of World War II, raising the question whether the end of the war was a defeat, liberation, or a catastrophe.

19. Kurt Biedenkopf, CDU, minister-president of the state of Saxony.

20. *Transit 3*, published by Verlag Neue Kritik, Frankfurt am Main, 1991.

21. *Solidarpakt*, see Note 8 in Chapter 5.

22. In a compromise vote in the *Bundestag* in 1993, the CDU/CSU and the SPD agreed to tighten the Federal Republic's liberal immigration laws, under which a flood of "asylum seekers" — most of them economic refugees from depressed parts of the world — had poured into the country.

About the Contributors

Reinhard Appel was born in Königshütte, Upper Silesia, in 1927. Drafted into the army in 1945, he was taken prisoner of war in Russia. In 1946 he joined the newspaper *Stuttgarter Zeitung*, advancing eventually to political reporter assigned to Bonn. From 1971 to 1973 he headed the Bonn bureau of *Süddeutsche Zeitung*, and from 1973 to 1976 he served as director of *Deutschlandfunk* radio station in Cologne. He was also editor in chief of *Zweites Deutsches Fernsehen* (ZDF), Second German Television. In 1992 he was appointed representative of the radio broadcast section of ZDF for German Cultural Radio in Berlin. He has received numerous journalistic awards, including the Theodore Wolff Prize, the Adolf Grimme Prize, and the Golden Camera award.

Günther Diehl was born in Cologne in 1916. During the war he served as research assistant in the Foreign Office in Berlin, later becoming secretary to German embassies in Brussels and Vichy. In 1945 he began working as a journalist, and he joined government service in 1950 as departmental chief of the Press and Information Office of the Federal Republic and, from 1952 to 1956, as Foreign Office spokesman, after which he was posted to Santiago, Chile, as embassy counselor and head of the foreign bureau of the Press and Information Office. In 1966 he became head of the Foreign Office planning staff and two years later chief of the Federal Republic's Press and Information Office. He was appointed West Germany's ambassador to India in 1970 and, in 1977, ambassador to Japan. From 1981 to 1987 he served as President of the German Society for Foreign Policy. He now lives in Remagen. Among his many publications are the books *Denken und Handeln: Planung in der Aussenpolitik* (Thought and Action: Planning in Foreign Policy) and *Ferne Gefährten: Erinnerungen an eine Botschaft in Japan* (Distant Companions: Memoirs of an Embassy in Japan).

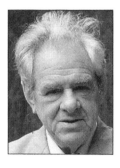

Oskar Fehrenbach was born in Karlsruhe in 1923. He entered journalism in 1953, first with the *Südwestpresse* in Tübingen, and then at the Tübingen studio of *Südwestfunk* radio. He joined the *Stuttgarter Zeitung* in 1962, serving first as Bonn correspondent and eventually advancing, in 1971, to the position of editor in chief. Now living in the Black Forest near Freiburg, he writes a regular column for *Sonntag Aktuell*. Among his many published works is *Helmut Kohl—wer sonst?* (Helmut Kohl—Who Else?).

Hans Klein, born in Mährisch-Schönberg in 1931, worked as a journalist in Bonn before joining the foreign service, which brought him to West German embassies in Jordan, Syria, Iraq, and Indonesia. In 1963 he became Chancellor Ludwig Erhard's political press and publications officer. In 1972 he was named press secretary of the 1972 Olympic Games in Munich. Since 1976 he has served as CSU representative to the *Bundestag*. He was named Federal Minister for Economic Cooperation and German Governor of the World Bank in 1987, and Federal Minister for Special Tasks and Federal Republic spokesman in 1989. He is vice president of the 12th German *Bundestag* and the author of a number of biographies and political studies, among them *Ludwig Erhard* and *Es begann im Kaukasus* (It Began in the Caucasus).

Horst Osterheld was born in Ludwigshafen in 1919. In 1951 he joined the foreign service and was posted to embassies in France and the U.S. From 1960 to 1969 he directed the foreign-policy bureau of the chancellor's office under Chancellors Adenauer, Erhard, and Kiesinger, becoming undersecretary in 1966. He was West German ambassador to Chile from 1970 to 1973, director of the central office of the World Church in the German Bishop's Conference from 1974 to 1979, and section head in the office of the president of the Federal Republic in 1984. He lives in Bonn. His publications include *Konrad Adenauer, Ein Charakterbild* (Konrad Adenauer, A Character Study), *Ich gehe nicht leichten Herzens: Adenauers letzte Kanzlerjahre* (I Don't Go With a Light Heart: Adenauer's Last Years as Chancellor).

Peter Zudeick was born in Haan in 1946. His career in journalism began in 1977, first with the Cologne *Stadt-Anzeiger*, then, in 1980, the Baden-Baden radio station *Südwestfunk*. He became the station's Bonn correspondent in 1982, and has been freelance correspondent in Bonn since 1985. His book publications include *Alternative Schulen* (Alternative Schools), *Der Hintern des Teufels: Ernst Bloch—Leben und Werk* (The Devil's Hindmost: Ernst Bloch, His Life and Work), and *SABA—Bilanz einer Aufgabe* (The Black Forest Instrument Construction Office—Survey of a Project), co-authored with H. Brunner-Schwer.

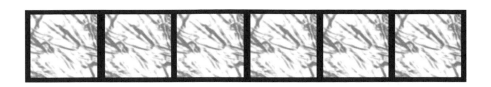

Abbreviations

APO	Ausserparlamentarische Opposition (extraparliamentary opposition)
Benelux	Belgium, Netherlands, Luxembourg
BfV	Bundesamt für Verfassungsschutz (Internal Security Agency)
BHE	Bund der Heimatvertriebenen und Entrechteten (League of Expellees and Disenfranchised)
CDU	Christlich Demokratische Union (Christian Democratic Union)
CEEC	Committee for European Economic Cooperation
CFM	Council of Foreign Ministers
CIA	Central Intelligence Agency
CSCE	Conference on Security and Cooperation in Europe
CSU	Christlich Soziale Union (Christian Social Union)
DDP	Deutsche Demokratische Partei (German Democratic Party)
DGB	Deutscher Gewerkschaftsbund (German Trade Union Federation)
DKP	Deutsche Kommunistische Partei (German Communist Party)
DP	Deutsche Partei (German Party)
DVP	Deutsche Volkspartei (German People's Party)
EC	European Community

ECSC	European Coal and Steel Community
ECU	European Currency Unit
EEC	European Economic Community
EPU	European Payments Union
ERP	European Recovery Program (Marshall Plan)
FDP	Freie Demokratische Partei (Free Democratic Party)
FRG	Federal Republic of Germany
GDR	German Democratic Republic
KPD	Kommunistische Partei Deutschlands (Communist Party of Germany)
MLF	Multilateral force
NATO	North Atlantic Treaty Organization
NPD	Nationaldemokratische Partei Deutschlands (National Democratic Party of Germany)
NSDAP	Nationalsozialistische Deutsche Arbeiterpartei (National Socialist German Workers' Party)
OECD	Organization for Economic Cooperation and Development
OMGUS	Office of Military Government for Germany, United States
RAF	Rote Armee Fraktion (Red Army Faction)
SA	Sturmabteilung (Storm Troopers)
SALT	Strategic Arms Limitation Talks
SAP	Sozialistische Arbeiterpartei Deutschlands (Socialist Workers' Party of Germany)
SBZ	Sowjetische Besatzungszone (Soviet Occupied Zone)
SDI	Strategic Defense Initiative
SED	Sozialistische Einheitspartei Deutschlands (Socialist Unity Pary of Germany)
SJV	Sozialistischer Jugendverband (SAP youth organization)
SPD	Sozialdemokratische Partei Deutschlands (Social Democratic Party of Germany)
SRP	Sozialistische Reichspartei (Socialist Reich Party)
SS	Schutzstaffel (Nazi Elite Squad)
UN	United Nations
WEU	West European Union

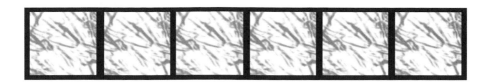

Index